Local White Slave Officer Badge of William T. Jackson, Jr., Jackson Family Papers, WH1017, Western History Collection, The Denver Public Library, Denver, Colorado.

POLICING SEXUALITY

POLICING SEXUALITY

The Mann Act and the Making of the FBI

Jessica R. Pliley

 Harvard University Press

Cambridge, Massachusetts, and London, England ◆ 2014

First Printing

Library of Congress Cataloging-in-Publication Data

Pliley, Jessica R., 1977–
    Policing sexuality : the Mann Act and the making of the FBI / Jessica R. Pliley.
        page cm
    Includes bibliographical references and index.
    ISBN 978-0-674-36811-8 (alk. paper)
  1. Prostitution—United States—History—20th century.   2. Human trafficking—
United States—History—20th century.   3. United States. Federal Bureau of
Investigation—History.   4. Vice control—United States—History—20th century.
5. United States—Moral conditions—History—20th century.   I. Title.
    HQ125.U6P62 2014
    364.15'3409730904—dc23   2014007800

For my mother, Toni Lynn Staffieri, 1953–2013

Contents

POLICING SEXUALITY

Introduction

The Mann Act and Federal Sexual Surveillance

In October 1920, an Oklahoma City federal judge sent Hewitt Ratcliffe to jail for the crime of white slavery. Earlier that summer, police arrested Hewitt's wife Janie when bellboys at the Lee-Huckins Hotel informed them that she was practicing prostitution in the hotel. The bellboys had been approached by Hewitt, who offered them a generous tip if they would arrange "dates" for his wife. When the city police discovered that Hewitt and Janie had come to Oklahoma from Little Rock, Arkansas, they immediately contacted the Bureau of Investigation because they suspected a violation of the White Slave Traffic Act, also known as the Mann Act. Passed in 1910 to protect women and girls from forced prostitution and sex trafficking, the federal statute made it illegal to transport, or cause the transport of, women over state lines for the purposes of prostitution, debauchery, or "any other immoral purpose." The Bureau of Investigation, as it was called until 1935 when the agency would be renamed the Federal Bureau of Investigation (FBI), enforced this antitrafficking law.

The Bureau built a strong case against Hewitt Ratcliffe. Janie stated that she had started dating Hewitt in 1914 and by 1918 they had married in Atlanta. Hewitt claimed to be a travelling salesman, but made most of his money by gambling. He travelled throughout the country looking for poker games, and Janie always accompanied him on the road. About a year after their wedding, after a particularly brutal losing streak in Kansas City, Hewitt recommended that Janie should "hustle," or prostitute herself, to earn some extra cash for the couple. When she balked at his suggestion, he gave her what she called "an unmerciful beating." From this point onward, she hustled for him everywhere they went. Using bellboys, Hewitt arranged all of her customers, ensuring that she usually brought in fifty dollars a night, which he used to stake his gambling habit.[1] With a bevy of witnesses prepared to testify against him, Hewitt chose to plead guilty with the promise that he would not serve more than two years in jail; instead he served only eight months. For the Bureau, Hewitt represented a professional pimp "of the worst type," and was exactly the type of scoundrel that the Mann Act was aimed at stopping.[2]

The ranks of prostitutes had been growing steadily in the late nineteenth and early twentieth centuries, becoming spectacularly visible in red-light districts throughout the country.[3] Fears about the prevalence of prostitution led to the rise of the white slavery narrative that asserted—in various forms— that vicious procurers seduced, coerced, lured, tricked, or forced girls and young white women into brothels far from their homes and the protections those homes offered. Antivice activists thought of white slavery as an international and transnational crime, and they were particularly fearful that a young girl would be stolen from one country and placed in a brothel in another country where she would not speak the language and have no friends. Fear of sex trafficking prompted the United States to amend its immigration laws, to join the 1904 International Agreement for the Suppression of the "White Slave Traffic," and to create state-level antitrafficking laws. Such fears culminated in the passage of the federal White Slave Traffic Act, which was intended to address domestic trafficking. Much of the public discussion of white slavery characterized it as a crime that was connected to immigration and immigrants. Some reformers argued that young women who migrated alone to the United States remained especially vulnerable to exploitation, whereas others suggested that white slavery, itself, was a crime brought to the United States by deviant immigrants. Woven throughout discussions of prostitution and white slavery, and the enforcement of anti–white slavery provisions, a tension developed between punishing and expelling foreign-born prostitutes and protecting native-born white women from prostitution. Thus, *white slavery* was a term that evoked racialized understandings of female vulnerability, prompted vigorous debates about prostitution, rampant sexuality, and urban life, and conjured a particular set of conceptions that rendered women as both victims and as subjects of sexual surveillance.

Sex trafficking, the problem at which the Mann Act was aimed, challenged law enforcement officials due to its inherent extrajurisdictional nature; traffickers and those trafficked moved in and out, and frequently beyond single jurisdictions. It was this very characteristic that prompted the U.S. Congress to pass the White Slave Traffic Act because local and state law enforcement could not easily reach sex traffickers and prostitutes who fled to other areas of the country. The national and international scope of sex trafficking necessitated national laws like the White Slave Traffic Act. After Congress passed the Mann Act, the Bureau of Investigation took up enforcement of this new national law, and just as the Mann Act expanded the jurisdiction of the federal government to police sex, so too did the law significantly expand the presence of the Bureau throughout the country.

The Mann Act was the product of the Progressive Era's faith that thorough investigation could lead to solutions for any social ill. As more and more observers fretted about the growing visibility of prostitution in American cities, the profitability of sex trafficking, and the dangers of white slavery, they couched these concerns into calls for investigations by journalists, social scientists, and government officials. From 1910 to 1917, vice commissions were established in 43 different cities to examine the prevalence, causes, and remedies of prostitution.[4] But these investigations did not occur just at the municipal level: the federal government, concerned as it was with the national borders and migration, launched several white slavery investigations. Taken together, these investigations prompted calls for legislation, resulting in the passage of a flurry of local antivice laws, state-level antitrafficking laws, and the Mann Act. Though the investigations that led to the Mann Act helped to establish the fact of white slavery, the Bureau still had to puzzle out exactly what white slavery was and was not, and, more problematically, it had to contend with that vague and expansive category of "any other immoral purpose." Did the law only cover sexual slavery characterized by violence and bondage, or did it also apply to voluntary prostitution? Could "any other immoral purpose" apply to consensual, noncommercial interstate sex like adultery and fornication? In addressing these questions, the Bureau had to grapple with the vexing problem of female consent. The enforcement of the Mann Act yielded strange outcomes that were shaped by the Bureau's understanding of the "any other immoral purpose" clause at any given moment. This is a story about how addressing these challenging questions helped to build the bureaucratic culture of the Bureau of Investigation, and also reflected the pervasive sexually conservative values of the agency.

This is also a story of traversing, maintaining, and negotiating boundaries. For the White Slave Traffic Act to be invoked a geographic border had to be crossed. The law applied to travel over state borders, territorial borders, and borders that hemmed in Native American reservations. But it also applied to areas under federal jurisdiction—such as Washington, DC, and colonial possessions. National borders came into play as well because U.S. white slavery policy was preoccupied with halting international sex trafficking; the distinctions between the international and national, the external and the domestic, and the foreign and native-born emerged with particular salience. Other borders were more figurative. As a federal antiprostitution law enforced by an agency without the ability to arrest or detain Americans, the lines between state and federal jurisdiction and authority had to be constantly mediated by the Bureau of Investigation. The object of protection (or policing)—prostitutes—revealed the permeability of the boundaries between public and private sexual behavior. Janie Ratcliffe was a public prostitute who had been trafficked to Oklahoma by her pimp Hewitt Ratcliffe. But she was also a wife and in pursuing Hewitt the Bureau denied the legitimacy of their marriage because it did not conform to standards of a monogamous marriage and respectability. As the Bureau enforced the "any other immoral purpose" clause, the lines between prostitutes and wives, bad women and good women, and the brothel bedroom and the marital bedroom became increasingly blurred. The Bureau used the law to police what they considered inappropriate sexuality and those bodies that deviated from respectability.

Implementing the law, the Bureau revealed a peculiar logic in the state's conception of female citizenship. From the early-twentieth-century perspective, women's citizenship was defined through her sexual contract with her husband (the marriage contract), and U.S. policy towards women generally emphasized women's reproductive service to the nation. Between 1855 and 1922, the most common way for immigrant women to achieve citizenship was through marriage to a U.S. citizen (native born or naturalized). More importantly any and all women could become mothers of the next generation of U.S. citizens. Her private domestic service—wifely labor—serviced a public goal, though contained in domesticity, under a male head of household. During the Progressive Era, public women, a euphemism for prostitute, and women in public spaces—like the growing numbers of wage-earning women, the feminists taking to the streets demanding the vote, and migrating women moving from countryside to city—upset these conventional understandings of women's roles. In the case of migrating sex workers, they were perceived as a threat to the health of the body politic because they could spread vene-real disease to customers, who in turn could introduce it to the marital bed. But she was also a threat because she might mother future citizens. With all of these anxieties—about women in public, about racial decline, about the spread of venereal disease—U.S. anti–white slavery policy tended towards criminalizing sex work primarily through the use of state power. The Mann Act helped construct this punitive state by closely monitoring the mobility of sex workers. By casting a wider net to police women's illicit sexuality more broadly, it managed to bring a wide variety of women under the gaze of the state.

The Bureau's enforcement of the Mann Act before World War II exhibited an uncanny vision of women as either moral wives and mothers or immoral and vulnerable loose women. The governing gender system configured wives and prostitutes as opposites, connected, if at all, where a man occupied the role of anonymous "John" in the space of the brothel, while also acting as hus-band when he returned to the domestic space of his home. Moving between spaces, in and out of disreputable sites and the sentimentalized home, the individual man could traverse respectability and vice with little risk to per-sonal reputation, class standing, or status as a citizen. This was in stark contrast to the gendered world that women negotiated, which cleaved to standards of sexual behavior and an idealization of sexual purity in the unmarried, and sexual fidelity in the married. For women, there was no risk-free traversing of space. Because marriage prospects depended on notions of sexual virgin-ity, whispers that cast doubt on a single woman's behavior could undermine her economic future. A failed wife-to-be, either a woman who violated sexual norms and was rejected from the marriage market, or an abandoned wife, deserted by her husband, or a widowed wife, left without resources by a dead husband could all cross into prostitution. In a labor market defined rigidly by sex, women's ability to support themselves and any children could be se-verely compromised.

The double standard of sexuality, which allowed men's promiscuity while severely restricting women's sexual behavior to marriage, shaped early-twentieth-century conceptions of victimhood, protection, and moral-ity as well. The Bureau's Mann Act investigations reflected this double stan-dard. In choosing some victims to protect, while ignoring the fate of other women seeking aid, the Bureau reinforced this double standard. The Bureau

consistently advocated on behalf of women who shared the same constellation of characteristics: they were white, young, and had reputations for being
previously chaste. Sex workers who did not fit this narrow mold frequently
found themselves subjected to state surveillance and punitive intervention.
In the early twentieth-century, racialized conceptions of morality excluded
nonwhite women from the category of the sexually virtuous. When African
American women turned to the Bureau for help, they rarely received it.

The FBI's enforcement of the Mann Act acted as a bulwark in defense of
traditional gender roles at a time when American women were experiencing
incredible social and political change. By federalizing the fight against prostitution, the Bureau sought to protect American daughters from being lured
into brothels, thus retaining their chastity for marriage. Sex workers were
seen as victims of others' greed. Yet, in its fight against trafficking, the Bureau
did not challenge prostitution's exploitative characteristics nor the right of
male customers to purchase sex. After the Supreme Court empowered the "any
other immoral purpose" clause of the law, the agency used its investigations to
uphold ideals of chaste daughters, faithful wives, and women as dependent domestic beings.

The White Slave Traffic Act fell well within the Progressive Era's legal reform agenda dedicated to protecting innocent young women from sexual
exploitation, but it had the added effect of federalizing this "protection." The
laws passed in this larger effort often had the consequence of closely policing young women's sexuality, frequently criminalizing their sexual activity,
and punishing young women under the guise of protecting them. As the Bureau considered how best to enforce the Mann Act and protect America's
young women from sexual slavery, it had to puzzle out whether the Congress
intended the law to protect innocent young women or to police professional
prostitutes. The lines between these two categories of women often collapsed,
as investigations hinged on special agents' ideas of female innocence and reputation, as well as young women's own volition. In Mann Act investigations,
protection could easily slip into paternalism and prosecution. The central
question confronting special agents was this: were victims of the Mann Act
really victims? Or were they criminals complicit in the violation of the law?
The tension between protecting and policing was ever present.

This tension spoke directly to the challenges posed by recognizing female
sexual activity in the early twentieth century. Narratives of white slavery

minimized female sexual assertion by arguing that no woman would sell sex in the marketplace unless she was under duress, whether that duress was the result of economics, fraud, deceit, or enslavement. In these tales, the conditions of women's lives produced a situation where consent to sex work was rendered meaningless. But as the Bureau began to enforce a law that had been passed to "protect" young women, it encountered a dynamic social world where female sexual desires and consent could not be so easily swept aside. In October 1921, only free from jail for a few months, Hewitt Ratcliffe was arrested again in Dallas, Texas, when city detectives swept up his new wife—Grace Ratcliffe—in a vice sting at the Adolphus Hotel. Hewitt had divorced Janie immediately after he was released from the Comanche County Jail and married Grace, with whom he had grown up and who had been his girl friend on the side for several years. At age twenty-seven and fully aware of Hewitt's work as a gambler, Grace Ratcliffe refused to cooperate with the Bureau's special agents as they tried to build a second case against him for violating the White Slave Traffic Act. She argued that she had chosen to prostitute herself and that Hewitt was unaware of her actions, and she adamantly refused to testify against her husband. Grace's defense of Hewitt confounded the logic of the White Slave Traffic Act, which assumed all prostitutes to be victims. Instead it prompted the Bureau to look at her as a co-conspirator and criminal.[5] Realizing that they were unlikely to get a Mann Act conviction with such an unwilling witness, the Bureau handed Hewitt over to Mississippi state authorities, who had a warrant out for his arrest. He was sentenced to serve five years in the Mississippi State Penitentiary for fraud and forgery.

When Congress passed the Mann Act in June 1910, the Bureau had only sixty-one special agents on its payroll. Though its jurisdiction was national, in practice those agents were based in Washington, DC, and their sphere of activity centered on the mid-Atlantic states on the Eastern seaboard. Based on the vast mandate within the Mann Act the Bureau expanded rapidly. Not only did it have a new jurisdiction—Americans' sexual behavior—but to enforce the law it also had to establish itself throughout the country, setting up field offices and local representatives in each state. When it could, the Bureau yielded prosecution of Mann Act offenders to local authorities, as it did with Hewitt Ratcliffe, a practice that in itself represents an extension of state authority. When the Bureau took on the broad and undefined authorization of the Mann Act, it stimulated federal law enforcement, but it also fortified the power of law enforcement on the local and state levels.

Historians of the FBI typically emphasize the Bureau's role in domestic political policing of ideological and racial minorities. This preoccupation with the Bureau's sins is certainly appropriate considering the FBI's activities against organized labor, leftist, and civil rights organizers, but it overlooks how central policing of sexuality was to the development of the FBI as a national agency with the capacity to conduct such political surveillance.[6] The FBI's policing of sexuality sheds light on the conservative culture within the FBI. Gender conservatism permeated the Bureau's Mann Act investigations, which were routinely among the largest category of cases pursued by the Bureau during the years before World War II.[7] Though American society went through a revolution in ideas and values about women's roles, marriage, and sex during the years between 1900 and 1941, the Bureau consistently served as a defense against these cultural shifts. Instead it celebrated the male-headed household and the dependent wife, just as it policed prostitutes' mobility and fought the sexual exploitation of young white women. The FBI spread nationally in order to enforce the Mann Act. The law became central to the day-to-day operations of the Bureau. Indeed, policing sexuality shaped the early history of the FBI.

1

The American Myth of White Slavery

In 1888 Dr. Kate C. Bushnell launched an investigation to discover if there was any truth to rumors that the lumber camps of northern Wisconsin were rife with white slavery, or the forced prostitution of white women. She found the moral conditions of the camps alarming. In her report she told of a woman fleeing a brothel, her eyes alight "with horror." According to Bushnell, the woman wore a garment "that was flowing loosely around her, and spread out with the wind. Her dress was all up on one side, and she was holding in her hands a ball that was fastened around her ankle by the chain that I heard rattling." Just as it seemed that this nameless specter of a white slave might escape, the brothel owner scooped her up, and dragged her back to his den.[1] Stories like this haunted Bushnell as she completed her inquiry on behalf of the Women's Christian Temperance Union (WCTU). Her investigation took her to fifty-nine brothels where she interviewed 575 sex workers. Bushnell's report painted a torrid picture of a degraded moral environment where city officials, judges, and police colluded with brothel owners to keep a steady supply of vulnerable sex workers available for the pleasure of northern lumberjacks and for the profit of northern towns and cities. In her telling, brothel owners kept prostitutes in slave-like conditions, where they were forced to service a large number of customers to work off bogus debts owed to the brothel owner. City officials conspired to maintain this slavery by medically registering sex workers and pocketing the licensing fees. Prostitutes had no legal recourse against exploitative conditions because Wisconsin state law allowed for the third-party profit of sex work as long as the individual prostitute had not had a "previous chaste character."[2]

While Bushnell consulted a wide variety of interested experts when conducting her investigation, her final report privileged the voices and experiences of sex workers themselves. She focused on how women's migration for work left them vulnerable to entrapment, unfair working conditions, and exploitation. Bushnell argued that the loophole in a Wisconsin law allowing the prostituting of a woman who lacked a "previous chaste character" resulted in the protection of those who made money from the business of prostitution at the expense of the prostitutes who actually conducted the labor. Brothel owners and pimps could confiscate the wages of a prostitute, and she would have no legal recourse because she could not turn to the courts. If the courts investigated charges of exploitation, brothel owners and pimps merely painted their sex workers as previously *un*chaste. Bushnell claimed that many of the women she interviewed had been hired to work in hotels, suggesting that fraud and coercion stood at the center of brothel owners' recruitment strategies.

Bushnell's studies of Wisconsin brothels in 1888 uncovered the fact that brothel owners frequently kept prostitutes entrapped through elaborate debt relationships: girls were forced to pay the cost of their transport, at least 50 percent of their earnings, fees associated with regular medical exams, room and board, and other living expenses. Bushnell argued that the women working in Wisconsin brothels became a new kind of slave "in that they are compelled to acquire property for others and not for themselves."[3] Yet, because of the irretrievable loss of reputation and the stain of shame associated with sex work, she believed the debt bondage of the Wisconsin dens to be worse than forms of chattel slavery that, in her formulation, merely resulted in the loss of profit from one's own labor.[4]

Bushnell excoriated members of her own profession—physicians—for the profit they earned from brothels. Most of the towns she visited had local "Contagious Disease Acts . . . patterned after the English acts" that required all "degraded" women to be examined for venereal disease infection. By segregating vice into brothels, allowing municipal authorities to profit through medical fees, certifying the venereal health of prostitutes, and turning a blind eye to the coercive labor conditions, Bushnell insisted that virtuous members of the communities were as implicated in vice found in northern Wisconsin as direct profiteers. Bushnell's sensational report spurred the Madison branch of the WCTU to lobby Wisconsin state legislators, who in turn significantly tightened state laws to address the most coercive employment practices and to empower private citizens to initiate investigations into alleged brothels.[5]

That the issue of prostitution should be a concern of the women's rights movement in the late nineteenth century should come as no surprise. As the United States emerged as an industrial capitalist nation, the primacy of cash and the value it put on the body and the body's labor seemed to some to threaten the very foundation of decency. Throughout the nineteenth century the visibility of prostitution in urban locales grew steadily as sex became as commercialized as other goods and services.[6] During the 1840s, various observers claimed that New York City had between ten thousand and fifty thousand prostitutes who lived in the city's brothels; sold their services on the street; solicited customers in the city's many theaters, saloons, and cafes; and spread venereal disease to unsuspecting clients and innocent wives. The growing presence and visibility of commercial prostitution was not limited to the largest cities like New York and Chicago. Prostitutes could be found in cities throughout the nation. For example, New Orleans's Storyville garnered an international reputation by the 1890s as the premier sex tourism destination with bordellos of every type that catered to the desire for interracial sex. And, of course, the image of the prostitutes formed a staple of Anglo society on the frontier that lived in the imagination and in settlements of the American West, especially in the rough and rowdy world of Gold Rush San Francisco. Women's limited economic opportunities and low wages made prostitution an important survival strategy for those caught in the vicissitudes of nineteenth-century life that was characterized by extreme economic fluctuations. Between 5 and 10 percent of all women between the ages of fifteen and thirty years old in nineteenth-century New York are estimated to have been engaged in prostitution at one point or another.[7]

As the commercialization of sexuality was woven into American's urban fabric, women's rights activists and purity reformers protested the ubiquity of prostitution, criticizing its immorality and the vulnerability of girls and women to sexual exploitation. As early as the 1830s, church-affiliated groups like the New York Female Moral Reform Society sought to rescue prostitutes while also reforming the sexual misbehavior of men. Later in the century, others suggested that the primary threat of prostitution was the spread of venereal disease. To combat that threat, reformers like renowned New York physician William Sanger suggested that prostitution should be regulated as it was in many European cities to include compulsory medical examinations.

St. Louis famously attempted to legislate regulation in 1870, passing a law that required prostitutes to be confined to one area of the city, register with local authorities, undergo regular medical examinations, and face quarantine if found infected. Outrage over the city's role in supporting prostitution grew to such a degree that the state legislature nullified the law, and the city was forced to abandon its experiment in 1874, though other U.S. cities like El Paso, Texas, would quietly introduce similar measures. Rather than developing plans of explicit regulation, most American cities adopted informal policies of segregation—confining prostitution, brothels, and other forms of vice into recognizable red-light districts that remained under the surveillance of the city police. These neighborhoods grew to be very profitable for real estate owners who were able to charge high rents due to the disreputable clientele they attracted. Red-light districts, called segregated districts by city officials and reformers to reflect the moral geography of the city, typically overlapped with racially segregated districts in most American cities. The increased visibility of prostitution in the nineteenth century was not only an American phenomenon, but reflected a world that was increasingly economically interconnected, accompanied by international migration and the ever increasing sophistication of bureaucracy, industry, and urban modernity. Associated trends such as the revolution in transportation and militarization produced large populations of men that could support larger populations of prostitutes, meaning that prostitution could be found side by side with colonial projects and the mobilization of a large number of male laborers and soldiers.[8]

State efforts at the regulation of prostitution first emerged in Napoleonic France in 1802 as an attempt to control the spread of syphilis among French troops. States that regulated prostitution typically identified putative prostitutes, registered them (usually in some type of licensing procedure), placed them into a licensed brothel, required that they undergo regular medical examinations, and severely curtailed their mobility. Regulation spread throughout most of Europe and then beyond to European colonies during the nineteenth and twentieth centuries. Regulation served many purposes: to fight the spread of venereal disease, to protect morally clean women by providing an acceptable sexual outlet for male desire, to control disorder, and to segregate vice to a closed environment thus moralizing the city.[9]

By segregating vice and separating "bad" from "good" women, the system of regulation formed the foundation of governmental support for the sexual double standard. The sexual double standard, articulated in Victorian terms, allowed men sexual access to women of their own class and to classes (and races) below them on the social hierarchy yet insisted on absolute chastity in women. Women who violated the norms of chastity fell outside of the bounds of respectability and often forfeited legal and, possibly, familial protection. Discourses and laws regulating prostitution remained central to the control of *all* women, especially those of the working classes. Additionally, discourses about, and the actual experiences of, "good" women were buttressed by the presence of "bad" women. Policy makers premised the regulation of prostitutes on their belief, attributed to St. Augustine, that the availability of prostitution was necessary and contributed to the stability of society because it operated as a safety valve to release men's "capricious lusts."[10]

As the regulation of prostitution spread throughout the European and colonized world, it began to attract opponents who argued that regulation constituted state-sponsored vice. British women's rights activist Josephine Butler gave birth to the movement against white slavery when she established the Ladies National Association (LNA) in the winter of 1869–1870 to fight the regulation of prostitution in England—specifically the Contagious Disease Acts of 1864, 1866, and 1869. This organization soon sought to address regulation beyond the British Empire and in 1875 established the British, Continental and General Federation for the Abolition of the Government Regulation of Vice, renaming itself the International Abolitionist Federation in 1898. After relocating its headquarters from London to Geneva in 1898, the International Abolitionist Federation quickly sought to establish branches throughout the globe.[11]

Butler and her allies in the LNA developed a feminist critique of regulation that focused on how regulated prostitution served to exploit women's sexuality for the gain of men and the state. They sought not only to abolish medical regulation of prostitution but also to eradicate the brothel system that ensured that numerous others—madams, pimps, doctors, police— profited from the sexual labor of women. Importantly, the LNA did not advocate criminalizing individual acts of prostitution, and they resisted any laws that treated prostitutes as a group or applied the legal label of "prostitute" onto a woman. Butler and her allies situated the problem of prostitution into a broader framework of women's employment, often arguing that women's low wages contributed to the rise in prostitution. They rejected the gendered mores of the time that asserted that men could not reasonably be expected to be chaste and therefore a population of primarily poor women had to be maintained who could serve them sexually, which in turn resulted in the state-sanctioned commercialization of poor women's bodies and sexual labor. Butler protested the way that this system of the state-sanctioned sexual double standard devalued the role of respectable women in marriage while protecting the state's power over the rights of individual women. She challenged the hypocrisy of the sexual double standard. She noted that under the double standard, nominally respectable men (who secretly visited brothels) permanently condemned prostitutes, placing them into a category of shame from which they could never escape. Most radically, Butler countered this characterization and advocated for what she called the reclaimability of all prostitutes, whom she considered to be the victims of sexist circumstances and male abuse.[12]

As Butler and the LNA agitated for the repeal of the Contagious Diseases Acts in England, other British reformers, motivated by Christian purity and the desire to protect female innocence but with little shared interest in the LNA's feminist politics, entered the anti–white slavery movement in the 1880's.[13] The English journalist W. T. Stead published a series of sensational articles that claimed to expose the thriving presence of child prostitution in London and the "international slave trade in girls." "The Maiden Tribute of Modern London," as the series was titled, first appeared in July 1885 on the pages of the *Pall Mall Gazette,* but soon newspapers throughout Europe and North America reprinted the exposé. Stead boasted that his findings appeared in newspapers in every major city in Europe, as well as in the "purest journals in the great American republic."[14] With his lurid tale of debauchery and corrupted innocence, Stead effectively launched a white slavery discourse that titillated readers with tales of corrupted innocence, dreadful loss, and dangerous cities. From 1885 to the mid-1910s, stories abounded within the Western world's popular media of the sexual dangers posed to innocent young women by strangers, cities, and modern life. Stead's story galvanized purity activists in London who gathered to form the National Vigilance Association in 1885 under the leadership of William Alexander Coote, who expanded the organization internationally in 1899 when he established the International Bureau for the Suppression of the White Slave Traffic.[15]

The term *white slavery* first appeared in conjunction with prostitution in the 1830s when a London doctor wrote about Jewish pimps as "white-slave dealers" who "trepan [ensnare] young girls in their dens of iniquity."[16] Yet this use of the term was ahead of its time. Most authors, both in Britain and the United States, who utilized the phrase *white slavery* in the early to mid-nineteenth century were referring to underpaid wage laborers. In this context, the term was intended to distinguish white (presumably male) wage slaves from race-based chattel slavery practiced in the American South.[17] The term *white slavery* and its French counterpart—*traite des blanches*—became more firmly associated with prostitution (forced or voluntary) in the 1870s. Victor Hugo, corresponding with Josephine Butler in 1870, wrote, "the slavery of black women is abolished in America, but the slavery of white women continues in Europe and laws are still made by men in order to tyrannize over women."[18] Anti–white slavery activists frequently built upon this comparison of prostitution to trans-Atlantic slavery. Writing in 1880, British activist Alfred Dyer declared, "English speaking girls . . . are systematically sought after, entrapped, and sold into a condition of slavery infinitely more cruel and revolting than negro servitude, because it is slavery not for labour but for lust; and more cowardly than negro slavery, because it falls on the young and the helpless of one sex only."[19] Of course, in comparing regulated prostitution with American slavery none of these European activists acknowledged the central and constitutive role the sexual domination of African American women had in maintaining American slavery. Yet, as Dyer's quote suggests, utilizing the comparison to African American slavery served to bolster the claims that white slavery was about *white* women. In the British context *white* women frequently meant *English* women. In the late nineteenth and early twentieth centuries, the term *white slavery* reflected and reinforced prevalent ideas of nationalist paternalism. For Dyer and his allies in the LNA and the National Vigilance Association, what was at stake was England's ability to protect English women placed in foreign and colonial brothels. European anti–white slavery campaigns occurred in the context of empire and frequently focused on ending regulated prostitution both in the metropolises but also in colonial lands, something that activists were considerably less successful at achieving. When framing white slavery as comparable to American race-based chattel slavery, British anti–white slavery activists drew on the moral power of the British and American abolitionist movements—certainly two of the most dynamic and successful social movements of the late eighteenth and nineteenth centuries—and then utilized that moral authority for their own nationalist, imperial, and reformatory ends.[20] This rhetoric of enslavement resonated at a different frequency in the United States, a country that still had a vivid memory of the war to end slavery—the Civil War.

While British activists worried about the fate of white slaves in London and European brothels, some American purity activists fretted over the fate of "yellow slaves" entrapped in San Francisco and other Western-city brothels and cribs, tiny shacks that offered little protection or comfort from the elements. Discourses of slavery strongly figured in discussions of Chinese prostitution and arguments for Chinese exclusion, and they would continually re-appear in social purity publications and newspapers from the 1870s through the early 1900s.

Chinese immigrants first came to the United States in significant numbers after the discovery of gold in California in 1848, though men composed the vast majority of these sojourners. In 1849, 325 Chinese men joined the flock of forty-niners, and by 1870 that number had grown to 63,000. Almost immediately the presence of so many Chinese workers in the American West stoked nativist fears among the white working class, as Chinese migrants quickly made up 25 percent of the workforce in California. The arrival of Chinese immigrants on American shores coincided with the development of the pseudo-scientific rationale of modern racism. Consequently, American attitudes towards the Chinese during the late nineteenth century were punctuated with "progressive" arguments that purported to demonstrate the inferiority of Chinese culture, religion, social structures, and morality. For some, these arguments rested on new ideas about the relationship between dirt and disease; others focused on the scarcity of women among the Chinese sojourners for proof of sexual and social deviancy; and still other arguments presented the prevalence of Chinese prostitution in Western cities as evidence of Chinese immorality and debauchery. All of these arguments and their variations articulated a case that Chinese immigrants were unfit for American citizenship and posed a threat to American culture. Additionally, the first wave of Chinese immigration coincided with the increasingly sectional slavery crisis, and some anti-Chinese commentators feared that the labor systems the Chinese brought to the United States constituted new or alternative forms of slavery. Many of these anti-Chinese concerns centered on the body of the Chinese prostitute, whom Anglo commentators perceived to be a vector of disease, the embodiment of immorality through their natural lasciviousness, and also a powerless slave controlled by others.[21]

The immigration of Chinese men seeking riches and employment in the American West produced one of the most glaring sex imbalances among any immigrant group in the nineteenth century. The few Chinese women in the American West worked primarily as prostitutes. In 1860, some 85 percent of the Chinese female population, a population of only 654 women, served as sex workers; in 1870, that number had dropped to 71 percent of the 2,018 women living in San Francisco. The prevalence of Chinese prostitution confirmed earlier ideas of Chinese licentiousness disseminated in American missionary publications. In contrast to Stead's narrative of enslaved white girls in London's brothels, Anglo commentators saw Chinese prostitutes as enslaved, but enslaved by their own dissolution, greed, and cultural backwardness.[22] For Anglo commentators, the image of the Chinese woman and the Chinese prostitute became one and the same.

In the 1870s the anti-Chinese movement in California contended that Chinese labor systems—either the "coolie" system of contract labor or the selling of daughters to brothels—threatened American institutions and freedoms and ultimately reintroduced slavery onto American soil. Additionally, the trafficking of Chinese women for prostitution created a female sexual slavery that, according to a California state senate committee, "made African slavery appear as a 'beneficent captivity.'"[23] In the post–Civil War political climate of the 1870s, the language of slavery grew especially salient. The free labor ideal that emerged before the war—an ideal that enshrined the notion that each man (and woman) could consent without coercion to his (or her) own labor contract and marriage contract—provided the foundation for the postwar worldview and political economy. After emancipation and the Thirteenth Amendment's declaration that the United States would be a society free of slavery, broad-based understandings of contract replaced bondage in governing societal and labor relations. Since contracts require freedom, the rhetoric of slavery resonated deeply.[24] In debates about Chinese immigration, congressmen outside of California quickly adopted the narratives of slavery to support excluding Chinese workers from entering the United States. One Massachusetts congressman declared that Chinese immigration constituted a "modern slave trade system."[25]

To fight this new form of "slavery" Congress passed the Page Act in 1875. The legislation constituted the first federal attempt to limit Chinese immigration as well as the first law designed to prohibit the entry of "immoral" women. The Page Act forbade the "importation into the United States of women for the purposes of prostitution" and essentially halted female immigration from China seven years prior to the passage of the 1882 Chinese Exclusion Act that limited Chinese immigration to narrow categories of students, merchants, and diplomats. Yet the Page Act did not address the problem of existing Chinese prostitutes in the United States that anti-slavery activists believed to be trapped in Western brothels. According to a California state committee: "These women are compelled to live as prostitutes for the pecuniary profit of their owners; they are under constant and unceasing surveillance; they are cruelly beaten if they fail to make money for their owners; and they are left to starve and die uncared for when they become sick or unprofitable." The committee declared these conditions to be "a peculiar, but revolting, kind of slavery."[26] Even in their practice of slavery, Anglo commentators saw evidence of Chinese depravity that could not be assimilated in the American polity.

Stories of the harsh working and living conditions found in Chinese brothels prompted some members of the missionary community in San Francisco to "rescue" Chinese prostitutes. In 1870 the Reverend Otis Gibson, the head of the Chinese mission for the Methodist Episcopal Church in San Francisco, established a "Female Department" intended to convert Chinese women to Christianity. Within a year, Gibson's project turned into an asylum for Chinese prostitutes seeking to escape from exploitive sex work. Missionaries' activities rescuing "enslaved" Chinese prostitutes constituted an important antecedent to anti–white slavery reform work. They established both a narrative of rescue and a precedent of direct action that would be prevalent in later Progressive Era anti–white slavery activism. From 1874 to 1880 a group of Protestant women in San Francisco used the rescue work of Chinese prostitutes to establish their own moral authority, inculcate Chinese women with Anglo-Victorian gender values, and promote Christian marriage within the Chinese-American community.[27]

Yet, even the rescue work and the declining numbers of Chinese prostitutes could not erase fears of "yellow slavery." An 1892 *San Francisco Chronicle* article entitled "Chinese Slavery" asserted, "With the abolition of slavery through the terrible medium of the war of rebellion there came into the minds of progressive American citizens a feeling of complacency akin to one who has laid aside disreputable garments and donned a new suit of clothes. It is not pleasant, therefore, for Americans to be told that . . . human beings are to-day bought and sold into a worse slavery than ever Uncle Tom knew of, and that the laws of our country are powerless to crush out the curse."[28] Though the Page Act and the Chinese Exclusion Act halted the majority of Chinese migration into the United States, fears of "yellow slavery" still animated discussion of the Chinese community and of Chinese women. The focus on "yellow slavery" reified the notion that immigrants imported social problems like prostitution and sex trafficking from foreign lands. It also introduced a gendered use of the term *slavery,* which increased the word's association with prostitution and sexual exploitation. The idea that these problems did not have American origins remained common in San Francisco newspapers into the 1920s.[29]

American fears of Chinese prostitution and "yellow slavery" provided a foundation for the development of an American anti–white slavery movement at the end of the century. In the 1870s, women's rights activists joined in the moral reform movement to fight prostitution. By the 1880s, American moral reformers and women in organizations like the WCTU shared the common critique of the sexual double standard that was foundational to Butler's British anti–white slavery movement. One reason that the American movement and the British movement shared this critique is because the American and British antiprostitution campaigners reached out to one another to establish a tentative network that traversed the Atlantic. For example, an 1876 visit of two British social purity reformers—the Rev. J. P. Gledstone and Henry J. Wilson—resulted in the establishment of the New York Committee for the Prevention of the State Regulation of Vice, renamed the American Purity Alliance in 1895. The two British activists met with former abolitionists where they found a receptive audience for their antiregulation politics. Gledstone and Wilson converted many of the former abolitionists to the "new abolitionism"—the fight against white slavery. A survey of the 106 American purity leaders in 1895 revealed that twenty-eight of the thirty-five leaders over the age of fifty-five (that is, old enough to have participated in the first abolitionist movement) were confirmed abolitionists, including seven women. Aaron Macy Powell, the president of the New York Committee, had been the former editor of New York's *Anti-Slavery Standard*. As Gledstone and Wilson toured the Northeast, they utilized older abolitionist networks and established antiregulation societies in each place they visited. From the 1880s to the 1900s, British anti–white slavery activists routinely visited the United States to help regalvanize the ties between the two countries' movements.[30]

American activists eagerly embraced the language of abolitionism and the analogy of slavery in their publications. In the first issue of *The Philanthropist*, the official organ of the New York Committee, Powell described W. T. Stead as the "John Brown" of white slaves. While invoking images of African American slavery and appropriating the language of abolitionism, social purity activists applied it exclusively to white women, revealing that race frequently determined the boundaries of protection. In 1899 one writer connected white prostitutes' experiences with debt bondage in brothels with African American slavery when she declared: "There is a slave trade in this country, and it is not black folks this time, but little white girls—thirteen, fourteen, fifteen, sixteen, seventeen years of age—and they are snatched out of our arms, and from our Sabbath-schools and from our communion tables."[31] Authors of white slavery narratives consistently contrasted white sex slaves' bondage with the bondage of African Americans to underscore the grotesque nature of the white women's entrapment by implicitly drawing on the rhetorical power of the most successful social justice movement in Western history while simultaneously highlighting the perversity of the race reversal that left black men and women free and white girls enslaved.[32] These narrative strategies remained frequent from the 1880s through the 1910s, which is remarkable since this period corresponds with rise of the share cropping system in the Jim Crow South that similarly kept many African Americans in a form of debt bondage.[33] Yet the contemporary discussions of the economics of white slavery did not make this connection.[34] American discourses of white slavery created a new body of knowledge—a new mythology—about African American slavery: first, that it did not contain a sexual and reproductive component; second, that it was only a labor system, not a racial caste system; and third, that because African American slavery was only a labor system where laborers did not enjoy the profit from their labor, it did not infringe upon the dignity of the laborers in the same ways that coercive prostitution permanently marked prostitutes with the loss of virtue. In nineteenth-century racial discourses of sexuality and morality, African American women had no such virtue to lose, so they were cast outside of the category of sexual victim. This expulsion is a remarkable development given that the sexual exploitation of enslaved black women had formed one of the staples of abolitionist imagery prior to the Civil War. But by the 1880s, white slavery reconfigured victims of sexual exploitation as fundamentally white, and white slavery narratives consistently celebrated the racialized victim as *white*.[35] White slavery narratives that invoked African American slavery buttressed white supremacy in the late nineteenth and early twentieth centuries by minimizing the brutality and sexual and reproductive violence that supported African American slavery, while also putatively uniting a country that had been torn apart by slavery over the fate of a new form of slave that every moral citizen would want to protect. She was invariably white, young, and innocent.[36]

The WCTU emerged as the most powerful and widespread ally of the fledgling social purity movement in the late nineteenth century. The founding of the WCTU resulted from middle-class women's temperance activism in 1874 when the organization was formed to fight the scourge of alcohol and for "protection of the home." Under the astute leadership of Frances Willard, the organization broadened its agenda beyond temperance to a wide variety of social reforms. At the helm of the women's club movement and a key exemplar of the domestication of politics by women's groups during this period, the WCTU signaled its support of the social purity movement when it launched its rescue work campaign in 1876. The organization's commitment hardened when it established a separate division devoted to social purity work in 1883. The WCTU's social purity work spread rapidly throughout the organization, with thirty-four state-level departments, and just under two hundred local divisions established by 1886. The purity movement and the women's movements coalesced to reform the sexual expectations of the white middle-class gender system.[37]

At the root of this social purity activism lay the shared belief in a single standard of morality. Like the British feminists in the LNA, women and purity activists in the United States articulated a pointed critique of the double standard of sexuality. In their eyes, the double standard threatened familial health by introducing venereal disease into the marriage bed, degraded some women into sexual objects of purchase, made hypocrites of men, and perpetuated inequality between men and women.[38] Most importantly to the ideology of universal sisterhood celebrated by the WCTU, temperance women deplored the way the double standard divided women from one another. "Consider the great underlying fact in this whole dreadful business, the fact that womanhood is divided into two distinct and hostile bands," lamented one letter writer to the WCTU's organ, the *Union Signal*. She continued, "One, inside the walled fortress of home, is protected, is respected, is beloved and honored. The other, having passed the gateway by a single sin, . . . is thrust without the wall. . . . And between these women and those within home's fortress, pass and repass, welcome both ways, men, the most respectable in reputation and position, the most blessed in powers and opportunities, the most blessed in legitimate domestic relations."[39] In addition to dividing women into artificially and opposing camps of "good" and "bad" women, the double standard of morality enshrined male privilege to traverse the borders of morality, the boundaries of fidelity, and the threshold of the urban vice world and then return to the protected fortress of respectability and middle-class domesticity with impunity.

Men in the purity movement shared these ideas with women and actively searched for ways to implement their ideals of a single shared moral standard—meaning that men and women would be held to the same chaste moral and sexual standards. The WCTU promoted the importation of the British organization, the White Cross Society. Local White Cross Societies required men to sign a card pledging that they would live their life according to a specific standard of morality. Conversely, White Shield Societies asked women to pledge that they would not tolerate men who deviated from the single standard. These societies proved very popular, forming a mass movement. One White Cross Society meeting held by the New York City Young Men's Christian Association drew over 1,000 men, and purity reformers boasted that White Cross Societies could be found in every state and territory. The single standard of morality offered a new ideal of gender relations that posited that women, as the moral protectors of family and home, could offer valuable and necessary assistance in purifying society. In this equation, respectable middle-class white women prevailed as inherently moral, and it was men's behavior that needed reform. Furthermore, prostitutes, who had been the most immediate victims of the double standard of morality, could be and should be redeemed and returned to their proper roles within the home as daughters, wives, and mothers.[40]

The social purity movement's interest in cleansing society by remaking gender relations soon inspired it to pursue a wide variety of reforms under a growing number of local associations. The establishment of Magdalene Societies spoke to its interest in redeeming prostitutes. Women developed ideas of moral education to teach the next generation a single standard and disseminated these ideas via mothers' meetings. They sought to protect working women from the dangers of the city by establishing organizations like Boston's Women's Educational and Industrial Union (established in 1881), which quickly grew to be regional in scope and strongly aligned with social purity reform. And most significantly, social purity reformers sought to change the law to protect young women by waging campaigns to raise the age of consent above its typical placement at ten years of age. Age of consent laws covered a wide range of sex crimes, including seduction, abduction for an immoral purpose, statutory rape, sexual assault, and procurement for the purposes of prostitution. The WCTU, the New York Committee for the Prevention of the State Regulation of Vice, and other social purity groups led the campaign to raise the age of consent laws across the country. The celebration of a single standard of morality united these disparate activities and contributed to the creation of a uniquely American narrative of white slavery.[41]

Dr. Kate C. Bushnell's 1888 investigation into vice conditions in the lumber camps of northern Wisconsin produced the first American narrative of white slavery and signaled that the American social purity movement was moving from its dependence on British narratives. British activists primarily expressed concern over the fates of English women working in foreign brothels. Reformers conceived of these women as white slaves who had been tricked into migration and whose safety needed to be maintained and honor defended from nonwhite and foreign men. Thus, the hysteria over white slavery had, at its foundation, a concern with European countries protecting their female nationals' sexual and racial integrity. Prior to Bushnell's revelations, *The Philanthropist* occasionally adopted this narrative for American uses. In 1887 it reported that the WCTU had received word that American women were being trafficked from San Francisco to Hong Kong, Shanghai, and other Chinese cities.[42]

The American narrative of white slavery that Bushnell produced for the WCTU in 1888 inverted the British narrative. American women were not in danger of being trafficked to foreign bordellos, but rather they were in danger of being trafficked into American bordellos run by foreigners. Essentially Bushnell's narrative asserted that immigrants, unfamiliar with American values and with inferior moral bearings, brought foreign bordellos (and their presumed moral deviancy) into the United States. Immigrants imported white slavery and the dangers it posed, infecting the nation with degraded morals, deviant practices, and dangerous venereal diseases. In her report on the conditions discovered in Wisconsin, Bushnell wrote, "The men who run these dens are all either foreigners or of foreign extraction," while she described the sex workers as "largely young American girls who, if in times previous guilty [of immorality], are of a higher grade of civilization" than the brothel owners who profited from their labor and exploitation or the men who pleasured themselves from their bodies.[43] *The Philanthropist* went further than Bushnell by directly blaming European regulation for the Wisconsin vice situation. An editorial, probably written by Powell, declared, "These foreign brothel keepers come to our shores to do here, without law and in defiance of law, what they have been accustomed to do with its sanction, under the regulation system at home."[44] The ways that European regulation posed a threat to American values emerged again and again. From the late 1880s to the 1910s, nativist fears of moral contagion and European decadence would form the foundation of the white slavery stories spread in the purity press.[45]

Within this American white slavery narrative and key to this process of moral (and possibly racial) degeneration or degradation stood the nonwhite man—immigrant or African American—who, depending on the telling, was either the seducer who lured the girl into a life of shame or who, by gaining sexual access to white innocence, embodied, through his sexuality, the moment of her full moral and physical subjection. The heyday of the white slave narrative, roughly 1890 to 1917, coincides with the Great Migration, a period when half a million black southerners rejected Jim Crow segregation and headed north looking for a better life.[46] Anxieties produced by the increasing number of African American men in northern cities appeared in white slavery tracts and newspaper articles, in papers such as the *New York World, New York Evening Post,* and the *Evening Sun.* In one 1906 white slave scandal, an alleged African American trafficker named Robert H. Spriggs captured white women, some as young as fourteen years old, and placed them in "negro dens" where they would service a nonwhite clientele. Some of the women claimed to have been held captive, behind "barred windows and doors," for as many as five years.[47] In white slave exposés, journalists routinely described white slavers as swarthy, having a "dark face," intending to associate them in the mind of readers with recent immigrants from southern and eastern Europe.[48] Similarly, George Kibbe Turner's 1909 best-selling exposé into the international trafficking of white slaves, entitled "The Daughters of the Poor," asserted that white slavery in New York was essentially a Jewish enterprise.[49] Anti–white slavery activist Ernest A. Bell widened the scope of blame when he asked: "Shall we defend our American civilization [from the threat posed by white slavery], or lower our glorious flag to the most despicable foreigners—French, Irish, Italians, Jews and Mongolians?"[50] Reports like these served to associate white slavers with nonwhite men while simultaneously transforming all white slaves into "white daughters of America" (regardless of their potential immigrant background). According to U.S. immigration law, the easiest way that a female immigrant could become naturalized citizens was through marriage to an American citizen.[51] Consequently, immigrant daughters all held potential to become American citizens through marriage to an American citizen. White slave narratives seemed to scrub immigrant "white" slaves white in acknowledgement that they could enter the citadel of citizenship and mother the next generation of citizens.

Bushnell's discovery that Wisconsin doctors examined the inmates in brothels for venereal disease and then offered certificates of physical cleanliness convinced her that state-regulated prostitution—or "contagious diseases acts," as she called them in a clear reference to the British Contagious Diseases Acts—had crept into the United States.[52] Her study demonstrated that, in fact, regulation did exist on municipal levels. Bushnell's investigations generated much publicity about white slavery in Wisconsin lumber towns and suggested that social purity activists needed to be vigilant against plans to introduce regulation to other American cities. Although women's rights activists had defeated attempts to introduce regulation in New York in 1867, arguments for some type of licensing and medical procedures remained strong throughout the 1880s and 1890s, and activists fought attempts to introduce regulation in a wide array of cities, including Cincinnati, Los Angeles, and New York City.[53] Fears of covert regulation animated social purity activists. *The Philanthropist* confessed, "What we do fear is a form of *secret* regulation of vice in our cities, a form in which there is a collusion between the keepers of evil resorts, the police, the politicians and city officials, for mutual advantage; and in which young girls are ruined, sold and hired, and kept in hopelessness and hideous slavery."[54] The importation and implementation of foreign regulation for the benefit of foreign brothel owners positioned white slavery as a problem coming *in* to the country. Yet the profitability of vice could lure commercially-minded Anglo citizens and politicians into collusion with foreign vice.

America's forays into colonialism demonstrated that the problem of regulation could move in multiple directions. As American soldiers left American shores, they became vulnerable to the moral and physical contamination found within foreign brothels, presumably foreign venereal diseases, and the country as a whole ran the danger of adopting foreign policies of regulation to protect soldiers' health. America's entry into the clique of colonial powers in 1898 raised the stakes for anti–white slavery activists in a number of ways. Anti-imperialists utilized fears of foreign brothels to articulate their opposition to the Spanish-American and Philippine-American Wars as America's colonial mission introduced the idea of federal regulation of prostitution through the military. In their fight against regulation and the colonial mission, anti–white slavery activists used the dangers of colonial brothels to express fears of interracial sexual contact.

The debates over America's colonial mission highlighted the idea that brothel-based immorality was a foreign product that could subvert American values. One anti-imperialist doctor reported that in Manila the military had set up "a system of nasty weekly medical inspection of hundreds of women by our army surgeon . . . [so that] our officers and soldiers and sailors, and men and boys generally, might safely commit fornication and adultery, saving their bodies and destroying their souls."[55] Anti-imperialists painted Filipino brothels as sources of moral and medical decay that would threaten the purity and vigor of American manhood. The WCTU joined the tradition of seeing danger in foreign brothels yet added a maternalist twist when a *Union Signal* editorial proclaimed: "Our boys are being debauched.

Mothers tell us that they go away from them in the very flush of ripe manhood and they come back to them disgraced, dishonored, diseased, and this American nation is to blame for it."[56] The various ways in which anti-imperialists used fears of vice and prostitution demonstrated how the politics of prostitution could easily be utilized for other political goals.

The complicity of the federal government in spreading regulation in colonial settings enraged social purity activists. From the Spanish-American War to World War I, American military leaders implemented different plans to regulate prostitution near military installations. During this twenty-year period, regulation was put into effect in Puerto Rico, the Philippines, the Panama Canal Zone, Cuba, Santo Domingo, Haiti, Nicaragua, Hawaii, and in sites near military bases along the Mexican-American border.[57] These plans generated protest among social purity activists who throughout the period became more and more successful at challenging U.S. military policy toward prostitution. In 1899 when Major Owen Sweet was stationed in Jolo, in the southern Philippines, he found vice conditions that left him appalled. He immediately launched a moral clean up to "limit, restrict, control, and finally if possible, eliminate the unbriddled [sic] status of drunkenness, gambling, smuggling and prostitution that prevailed."[58] Sex workers came under immediate military surveillance, and they were forced to register with military authorities for licenses, undergo medical examinations by army surgeons, and face deportation if found infected with "so-called Asiatic diseases"—a system that on the surface resembled state-regulated prostitution found in British colonial settings. When news of Sweet's system of regulation reached mainland American in June 1900, social purity forces reacted with outrage. Even more troubling than the initial reports of state regulation and the prevalence of prostitution in the Philippines was the revelation that white women were among their numbers. A November 1901 report about the inmates of a hospital for prostitutes in Manila found two "Europeans," two Italians, one Hungarian, one Australian, one Spaniard, twelve Russians, and fourteen Americans.[59]

Social purity activists in the American Purity Alliance (APA) feared that regulated prostitution in the Philippines would lead their country down the path paved by Britain. APA President O. Edward Janney wrote, "We may be reasonably sure that the same problems as to the morality of the soldiers and the degradation of womanhood will stare us in the face as disturb English people in reference to their army in India."[60] American social purity activists suggested that by embarking upon the imperial mission America risked her exceptional moral purity because regulation was a natural consequence of empire. British voices bolstered the association of regulation with empire when *The Shield,* the primary publication of the International Abolitionist Federation, noted that the American "New Imperialism" spread regulation from the Philippines to Hawaii. Social purity activists sounded the alarms, reaching out to their allies in the women's rights movement. The annual meeting of the National American Woman Suffrage Association passed a resolution condemning regulated prostitution in Manila on the grounds that such a policy was morally repugnant, upheld a double standard of morality, and was medically ineffective in curbing the spread of venereal disease.[61]

When pressed for a response to the official protest and a WCTU letter-writing campaign, the War Department first denied any knowledge of regulated prostitution in the Philippines. It claimed to have no knowledge of Sweet's way of approaching vice. Then, throughout 1901, it slowly admitted to regulating prostitution, but claimed regulation was a necessary step to maintaining military readiness. Faced with little action, WCTU lobbyist Mary Dye Ellis circulated a book that she claimed to be the "official registration book issued by the U.S. authorities" to a prostitute who seemed to be no older than seventeen years of age. Ellis distributed the book to members of Congress, their wives, and social purity and women's rights groups, effectively re-igniting the fight against the War Department and regulated vice by providing a victim and giving her a face and a name—Maria de la Cruz. Additionally, by 1901, purity activists had an ally in the White House. President Theodore Roosevelt rejected the medical rationale for state-regulated prostitution and offered an alternative model of civilized masculinity that emphasized physical activity outside the home and contained sexuality within the home. Consequently, Roosevelt ordered the War Department to cease regulating prostitution. Social purity activists emerged as the victors in the Philippines case, but the War Department learned a valuable lesson—only by making regulation invisible could the War Department avoid criticism. In spite of Roosevelt's orders, the military would continue regulating prostitution in varying degrees of formality until World War I, while eliminating the most obvious accoutrements of registration, such as the licensing books.

As a result, no such outcry would emerge over the regulation of prostitution in other colonial sites such as Puerto Rico.[62]

According to social purity activists, America's regulation of colonial market places of sex had the potential to encourage miscegenation abroad and contagion at home. In the late nineteenth century, germ theory and eugenics emerged as important components of modern racial thinking.[63] An 1882 *Popular Science Monthly* article asserted that social characteristics were as "fundamental and as immutable as are the physical characteristics of the races."[64] According to this logic, co-mingling of the races had the potential to threaten American culture and institutions, and nonwhite peoples could not be expected to assimilate. Discussions of Filipino prostitution painted the nonwhite prostitute as a vector of foreign disease that by infecting American soldiers also threatened American values, institutions, and homes. Senator Richard F. Pettigrew (R-SD) declared, "The vigorous blood, the best blood, the young men of our land, will be drawn away to mix with inferior races."[65] Speaking of the Filipina women available to American soldiers, one WCTU investigator reported, "The women who consent to live with Americans are, as a rule, ignorant, lazy, and filthy in their habits, generally afflicted with some loathsome cutaneous disease, and it is hard to comprehend that an educated American, decently brought up, can live among dirty, frowzy natives, who have not one redeeming quality."[66] Ellis, for her part, focused on the ways that American soldiers dragged "down hundreds of pure Filipina women into lives of shame and degradation."[67] Animating many of these fears was the idea that the habits formed and diseases acquired by soldiers serving in the Philippines would inevitably be brought back to American shores when those same soldiers returned home. *The Philanthropist* despaired that soldiers who availed themselves of Filipino sex markets "will return to the states, those that survive, and help to poison American society and send a stream of entailed vice though the lives of their posterity in the home land."[68] Thus, like regulation and white slavery, immorality and venereal diseases emerged from foreign sources and would pollute an imagined pure homeland. Furthermore, critics charged that Manila's brothels introduced soldiers, white and black alike, to the pleasures of sex across the color line. African American journalist T. Thomas Fortune observed, "Marriages between white American men and Filipino women are regarded with as much horror as marriages between blacks and whites in Tennessee." But while marriage between American men and Filipina women violated Jim Crow norms, he noted that interracial sex was a common feature of daily life in America-occupied Manila and that many servicemen established common-law relationships with Filipina women. Fortune worried that these relationships would upset the racial norms in the United States, asserting, "American wrong and outrage existing and tolerated in our colonies and dependencies are bound sooner or later to color our thinking and conduct at home."[69] In his view, the sexual license encouraged by American regulation of sexuality in colonies encouraged miscegenation, brought disease to American boys and shame to Filipina women, and institutionalized the sexual double standard.

◆ ◆ ◆

The British anti–white slavery movement initially inspired the U.S. anti–white slavery movement by providing a narrative of white slavery, exchanging correspondence and visitors, and by building on American worries that slavery could be re-introduced to American shores. Consequently, the American movement shared the British movement's feminist critique of the double standard of sexuality as a source of prostitution. The WCTU formed the most important element of the American social purity movement, and it educated thousands of its members about the plight of white slaves in Wisconsin lumber towns when it commissioned and publicized Kate Bushnell's landmark study.

Bushnell's study marked the emergence of a distinctly American narrative of white slavery. Nativism and racism shaped the American narrative, which focused on the threat foreign and nonwhite men posed to the sexual purity of native Anglo women. By invoking African American slavery when discussing Chinese prostitution or white slavery, social purity activists created their own reconciliation myth that lessened the horrors of African American slavery and ignored the centrality of sexual domination to the institution on the one hand, while positing that sexual labor resulted in the loss of more than the fruits of one's labor on the other hand. At its foundation, the American myth of white slavery asserted three intertwined ideals: that the equal standard of morality and sexuality was the key to eliminating prostitution and promoting the foundation for healthy and productive American marriages; that miscegenation, whether in the brothel or elsewhere could stand as a threat to American values, institutions, and vigor; and, that white slavery was a foreign, or at least nonwhite, threat to the innocence of girls who through their purity were rendered racially white.

At the turn of the century, the American social purity movement stood united with a burgeoning social hygiene movement, and both represented an important strand of progressive activism. Committed to a broad social plan that spanned from fighting white slavery to protecting American families from venereal disease, these reformers sought pragmatic solutions to complicated social problems. Their interest in social efficiency led them to establish voluntary associations committed to fighting vice and educating the public. Organizations begat organizations: some branches of the American Purity Alliance dedicated to the social hygiene movement formed the National Vigilance Committee in 1906, which in 1912 became the American Vigilance Association. Similarly, the American Society of Sanitary and Moral Prophylaxis became the American Federation for Sex Hygiene in 1910, which in turn merged with the American Vigilance Association to form the American Social Hygiene Association in 1913. All of these organizations, and the many like them, were dedicated to publicizing the dangers of vice and exploring governmental and bureaucratic solutions—state solutions. Yet these activists could seldom foresee how different bureaucratic cultures shaped the implementation of anti-white slavery policies.

2

A National White Slavery Squad

As an immigrant-receiving country, the American narrative of white slavery emphasized the supposed foreign origins of white slavery: it told of swarthy foreigners who imported the practice of trafficking when they preyed upon young immigrant girls who had migrated and labored outside the protections traditionally offered by patriarchal families. Without familial protection, these young girls, rendered white via their innocence, would fall into depravity. These white slaves were women and girls, "who," as one congressman put it, "if given a fair chance, would, in all human probability, have been good wives and mothers and [and through marriage made into] useful citizens."[1] Anti-white slavery activists in the WCTU and the social purity movement claimed that white slavery formed a scourge threatening the purity of American bedrooms and undermining the liberal labor and marital contract. Yet in spite of their proclamations, outside of the purity movement circles, white slavery languished as a galvanizing public issue until the early 1900s. Due to the way that it dovetailed with growing panic about the number and quality of immigrants flowing into the country, white slavery emerged as a visible mainstream concern in 1907. If states must puzzle before they power, then it fell to the Bureau of Immigration and Naturalization to make sense of white slavery. From 1907 through 1909 the Immigration Bureau sought to make white slavery legible to itself and to the broader public by conducting a series of investigations into the dimensions of the problem.[2]

Pressure mounted on the Immigration Bureau to investigate white slavery when newspaper reports circulated throughout the country suggested that Chicago's vast transportation and migration network had a dark underside. Ministers, judges, and civic reformers, like Chicago U.S. Attorney Edwin Sims and the Assistant State's Attorney Clifford Roe, argued that Chicago sat at a grand intersection of the international and interstate white-slave traffic and the city constituted a "headquarters for distribution of girls to all large [U.S.] cities."[3] In June 1908, these community leaders launched a campaign against the trade in women as part of an ongoing campaign to clean up Chicago's Levee, considered by many to be one of the most debauched red-light districts in the country. Their campaign led to the arrests of French brothel owners, including Eva and Alphonse Dufour. Rumors of the immense wealth gained by importing French prostitutes circulated widely. Newspapers reported that the Dufours purchased girls for as little as fifteen dollars and later sold them to other brothels for between one hundred fifty and five hundred dollars. The proceeds from their trafficking and brothel earned the Dufours as much as $200,000 in 1907. As a result of the raids, newspapers speculated that over two thousand French prostitutes faced deportation, a gross exaggeration. Secret Service agents reported that the raid caused an "exodus" of French women from Chicago. The judge in the case set the bond for each of the accused brothel owners at an astonishing twenty-five thousand dollars. While the Dufours spent six weeks in jail before their bond was granted in the summer of 1908, President Theodore Roosevelt increased the pressure on traffickers like the Dufours by announcing that the United States would adhere to the 1904 International Agreement for the Suppression of the "White Slave Traffic." The agreement formed the basis of international cooperation in the battle against white slavery and had been signed by Germany, Belgium, Denmark, Spain, France, Great Britain, Italy, the Netherlands, Portugal, Russia, Sweden, Norway, and others. As the case against them developed, the Dufours fled the country forfeiting their extraordinary bond. Meanwhile, the Immigration Bureau deported the five French prostitutes who had been found working in their brothel on Dearborn Street. The Dufours's case illustrates the growing role of the federal government's Immigration Bureau in taking up the fight against white slavery. The sensational case would contribute to internal pressures to uncover the extent of white slavery to the United States and within the United States.[4]

At the turn of the century, reformers primarily framed white slavery in the United States as a foreign problem—a problem related to immigration. As a result, the Immigration Bureau needed to formulate a response to the crisis posed by sex trafficking. Immediately, it agitated for and aggressively enforced the Immigration Act of February 20, 1907. The new immigration law specifically outlawed any non-naturalized women from practicing prostitution within three years of her entry into the country, providing for the deportation of foreign-born sex workers discovered in brothels.

Congress had first attempted to police the moral borders of the country when it passed the Page Act of 1875, which outlawed the importation of immoral women into the United State and was conceived as an anti-Chinese immigration restriction. Congress strengthened the moral borders of the country again in 1882 when it included convicts and people deemed "likely to become public charges" in the excludable classes. Members of Congress and the Immigration Bureau viewed poverty as a moral failing and believed it bred potential sexual immorality in women because they assumed poor women would turn to prostitution to survive. The list of excludable classes expanded again when Congress passed the Immigration Act of 1903 which excluded procurers of prostitutes and the Immigration Act of 1907 that excluded "persons who admitted the commission of a crime involving moral turpitude, and women coming to the United States for immoral purposes."[5]

Congress established the Immigration Bureau in 1891 to supervise immigration to the United States, and by 1907 the Immigration Bureau was seeking ways to protect the country from the "morally, mentally and physically deficient" as it enforced the immigration provisions passed by Congress.[6] Built to enforce the ever-increasing number of immigration restrictions and rules, by the turn of the century the Immigration Bureau had become one of the largest migration-control bureaucracies in the world.[7] The leadership and the administrative personnel of the agency embraced a generally anti-immigrant/restrictionist position in spite of the fact that many of the immigration inspectors came from recent immigrant stock. The commissioner-generals of immigration during this era (Frank P. Sargent, 1902–1908, and Daniel J. Keefe, 1908–1913) were drawn from the labor movement—typically an anti-immigrant constituency—and tirelessly advocated for more restrictionist legislation and procedures in newspaper articles and before Congress.[8] One former nativist civil servant who worked at Ellis Island contended, "As commissioner-general, Hon. Frank P. Sargent did more than had ever been done to recruit new blood of the needed type [i.e. restrictionist] and to put an esprit de corps into the Service."[9] Consequently, the average immigrant inspector shared the same restrictionist world view touted in the upper echelons of the Immigration Bureau and they would bring this ideology to their inquiries into white slavery.

To test whether white slavery constituted a legitimate threat to U.S. immigration laws, in the fall of 1907, the Immigration Bureau appointed several inspectors to a white slave division that investigated and enforced the prostitution provision of the new immigration law in Philadelphia and New York City.[10] At the time, the lead New York City investigator Helen Bullis put together a list of over one hundred brothels in the red-light neighborhood of the Tenderloin in an effort to determine the role of immigrants in the business of prostitution. Before taking a position with the Immigration Bureau, she had served for many years as a representative of the Traveler's Aid Society. Bullis encountered considerable difficulty gathering enough evidence to deport male sex traffickers because as a middle-class respectable woman she could not loiter inconspicuously in cafes collecting evidence against traffickers without risking her reputation. As a result she requested that the Bureau provide her with a male counterpart, Andrew Tedesco, who could conduct investigations within the gendered and sexualized sites that were off limits to her.[11] Frank Garbarino faced no such obstacles in his investigation of alien vice in Philadelphia. Bullis' New York City and Garbarino's Philadelphia investigations convinced the Immigration Bureau that white slavery was a problem that demanded the agency's full attention.

With that goal in mind, the Immigration Bureau ordered special investigator Marcus Braun to unearth white slavery conditions in fifteen cities throughout the United States during the summer of 1908. His report and recommendations led the bureau to launch a widespread dragnet against white slavery in the spring of 1909, which dramatically increased the number of foreign prostitutes barred from entering the United States or deported from it. At the same time, the bureau sent Braun to Europe to "ferret out" the methods and manner of importation utilized by European procurers of white slaves.[12] While the Immigration Bureau researched the scope of the white slavery problem, the congressionally-empowered Immigration Commission devoted one volume of its forty-one-volume investigation of all aspects of immigration to the issue of white slavery. These investigations formed the first steps the U.S. federal government took toward building an understanding and working definition of *white slavery*. If white slavery was a problem of immigration, as anti-white slavery activists had contended, then the Immigration Bureau was seeking to assess the extent of the threat through thorough investigation.

The Immigration Bureau commissioned Marcus Braun to investigate the conditions surrounding white slavery in the United States. He embodied a larger-than-life character; the type of man who, when covering the 1893's World's Fair in Chicago for the *New York Herald,* reportedly took a wager to eat his lunch in a cage full of lions.[13] Braun had come to New York in 1892 from his homeland of Hungary. In New York, he gained success as a news-paperman and later served as a spokesperson for "Little Hungary" by founding the *Austro-Hungarian Gazette* and serving as president of the Hungarian Republican Club in New York City. As leader of the Hungarian Republican Club, Braun mobilized support for Theodore Roosevelt in his gubernatorial and presidential campaigns. After winning the White House, Roosevelt praised Braun as one of his "staunchest political supporters," and rewarded him with an appointment as a special investigator for the Immigration Bureau in 1903. In his new role, Braun made an annual trip to Europe to investigate various aspects of immigration to the United States, including the emigration of anarchists and the role of steamship companies in the immigration process. Rumored to be worth $5,000 a year, the post allowed Braun to return home to visit friends and family once a year on the U.S. government's dime. As a Hungarian Jew who had embraced a nationalistic Americanism, Braun marshaled his language skills—fluency in English, Yiddish, Hungarian, French, and German—to serve as a cosmopolitan middleman who could translate European conditions for American purposes.[14]

After a scandalous run-in with Hungarian secret police during a 1905 investigation, the Immigration Bureau kept Braun stateside and in July 1908 it ordered him to travel throughout the United States to make a "thorough investigation" of white slavery and assess the extent of the traffic in foreign-born women. The Immigration Bureau assigned Andrew Tedesco to serve as Braun's assistant. Tedesco, a remarkably able immigrant investigator based at Ellis Island, had been tracking white slavers in New York City with Helen Bullis in the fall of 1907. He was also a Hungarian immigrant who spoke several languages. Whereas Braun had experience investigating *for* the Immigration Bureau, Tedesco actually worked *as* an immigration agent, negotiating the procedures of exclusion and deportation and conducting investigations into particular immigration violations.[15]

Although many investigative models existed, the Immigration Bureau left the methods of investigation up to Braun and Tedesco to invent. Typically, in his New York City investigations, Inspector Tedesco would lounge in cafes and bars "undercover" and observe. Receipts turned in to the bureau by other male white slave investigators reveal that investigations consisted of sitting in saloons and cafes and fitting in with the locals. One investigator in Philadelphia submitted receipts totaling $38.50 for fourteen days' worth of "entertaining."[16] Braun sought a more proactive and less time-intensive method for conducting his undercover investigation. He found that he could protect his identity if he called a brothel and hired a girl whom he suspected of violating the three-year ban on practicing prostitution for an automobile ride—thus avoiding "commotion in the street." Once the girl joined him in the car, Braun would simply drive her to the immigration office and, according to Braun, "up to the time she arrived at that office she did not know she was under arrest."[17] He argued that his method avoided any publicity in the newspapers that would undermine ongoing investigations. Although their greatest allies were naturally immigration officers assigned to the individual cities, both Tedesco and Braun tried to cooperate with local police departments when they would arrive at a new city. Still, local police frequently sought to obstruct federal interference in their jurisdiction, especially if they were actively profiting from the earnings of prostitutes.[18]

Braun's investigation discovered that white slavery within the United States did constitute an immigration problem. Further, he claimed to "know of an international band of scoundrels engaged in" it. Braun conservatively estimated that over fifty thousand foreign prostitutes and ten thousand procurers and pimps, most of whom were French, Belgian, and Jewish, worked in the United States. Japanese prostitution, Braun suggested, remained a particular problem in the West with Japanese women entering illegally as picture brides, women who married husbands by proxy in Japan (and Korea) and then joined their husbands who lived and worked abroad. American immigration officials remained very suspicious of marriage by proxy and insisted that the practice allowed Japanese prostitutes to enter the country. From 1908 to 1920 it is estimated that over ten thousand picture brides entered the United States from Japan.[19]

In his search for white slaves, Braun found few women that he could describe as "weak, frail, thoughtless women fallen from the pathway of honor," the type of victim at the center of white slavery stories. Instead, he discovered professional prostitutes, "hardened" women in the language of the day, in the brothels he toured.[20] These women tended to enter the United States via Canada, and they often traveled with men posing as their husbands. Chicago stood as a major "distribution place" for the traffic.[21] To his outrage, Braun discovered that local police officers would inform brothels to hide any foreign-born inmates before he could investigate. He noted, "whenever I applied to the Police Departments of the various cities for aid and assistance, I could have just left the town immediately without making any further investigations, because I was sure to find nothing, owing to the fact that the keepers of the houses, pimps and procurers, and the alien prostitutes themselves were 'tipped off,' that there was somebody from the Bureau of Immigration in town making an inquiry."[22] This process of tipping-off undermined Braun's surveys of several cities including Seattle, Butte, and San Francisco.[23] Regardless of this challenge Braun and Tedesco combed through the cities they visited looking for women to deport.

Yet foreign-born women who sought protection from deportation found it by simply marrying a man who had U.S. citizenship. In the United States a woman's citizenship was intertwined with her marital status because the Immigration Bureau prioritized the conjugal heterosexual family as a source of social stability. The Immigration Law of 1855 ruled that a married woman adopted the citizenship status of her husband; the primary way for foreign-born women to gain U.S. citizenship was through marriage to a native-born or naturalized citizen. Indeed, U.S. policy makers privileged the male right to marry to such a degree that even through periods of racialized immigration exclusion, the right of all male citizens to have access to wives (even foreign-born excludable women) has been held sacrosanct.[24]

For Braun this situation was maddening. Throughout his report he noted that well-known prostitutes would pose as wives of their pimps in order to enter the country. "Of course, girls who have followed the vocation of prostitutes in the old country," he wrote, "usually also come as the 'wife,' and the other girls who come along are 'sisters.'"[25] Women who faced deportation hearings for practicing prostitution could evade that fate merely by marrying an American citizen. Braun told of François Perinet, a French immigrant who had applied for and received naturalization. Perinet married Marie Ruhlmann at the insistence of the border inspector when they entered the United

States at Mission Junction, Canada. Several months later immigration agents arrested Ruhlmann when they raided a brothel in Seattle and launched deportation proceedings against her. Perinet appeared at the bureau's office, admitted the first marriage had been a farce, and then begged to be allowed to marry Ruhlmann "in order to save her from deportation." According to Braun, his subsequent investigation into the matter revealed that Perinet had been married to multiple prostitutes in Denver and Seattle. Cases like this caused him to advise the Immigration Bureau to "throw as serious obstacles as possible in the way of marriages of alien girls" to native-born or naturalized citizens. In advocating for obstacles to marriage at national borders, Braun articulated a position that contradicted the policies pursued at ports of entry that frequently required dock-side weddings of unaccompanied women and their supposed mates. One Immigration Bureau boarding matron bragged of overseeing "scores" of weddings as she worked to ensure that young women's moral safety was secure upon entry to the country.[26] Nonetheless, for Braun, convenient marriages between pimps and prostitutes formed a way for hardened sex workers to make a joke of U.S. immigration laws. He even suggested amending the law so that any naturalized citizen, like Braun himself, who married a foreign-born prostitute would forfeit his citizenship. "I would be so jealous of our American Citizenship—that right or wrong—the moment an American Citizen stoops to be willing to marry a Prostitute as in the case of Marie Ruhlmann and others," he wrote, "I would declare him to be unworthy of his American citizenship, and if possible deprive him of it."[27] Contrary to the legal tradition of femme coverture that dictated that a woman's citizenship status derived from her father or husband, Braun's suggestion that a man should lose his citizenship status by marriage to a prostitute inverted this notion. In tying women's citizenship status to marriage, U.S. immigration policy reified the idea that women were fundamentally dependent upon male breadwinners.[28] But Braun upended this understanding of gendered dependency noting that in contrast to traditional arrangements, pimps perversely gained their livelihood from the public sexual labor of their 'wives,' sexual labor that U.S. legal traditions and social norms embedded within the private sphere of wifely duties. Thus, for Braun, the total inversion of U.S. policy became justified, one perversion begat another.

Braun had one final recommendation for fighting what he saw as illegitimate marriages. He thought that the 1907 Immigration law, which read "that the importation of any alien woman or girl is forbidden," would be improved by striking out the word "alien" thereby opening up the opportunity to prosecute any man who was an American citizen for trafficking regardless of whether or not he had married the woman and transformed her into a citizen.[29] Though calls for legislation to fight domestic white slavery circulated in 1908, Braun's proposal was narrowly focused on the threats posed by immoral immigrants whose vice trafficking he saw as "a downright shame to humanity in general and a disgrace to the free institutions of the United States in particular."[30] No doubt he also worried about how white slavery reflected on recent immigrants, of which he was one, and more particularly on the Jewish community, again a community of which he was a member. Braun's attacks on the institution of marriage and its place in immigration policy must be contextualized in his larger experience as an immigrant deeply devoted to his identity as an American citizen.

Andrew Tedesco issued his own supplement to Braun's report, in which he outlined a series of issues that he had noticed in the course of the investigation, most of which drew upon his experiences working as an immigrant inspector. He specifically emphasized that special boards of inquiry, the administrative apparatus that heard exclusion and deportation hearings, posed a particular problem in deporting immoral women. The citizens who sat on the boards, according to Tedesco, would deport or debar women from entering only when they were convinced beyond a doubt that a woman really worked as a prostitute. This formed an unnaturally high burden of proof for immigrant inspectors, for how do you really prove that someone is a prostitute without being present at the exact moment of exchange? He claimed that the board members' "misplaced chivalry" undermined the inspectors' work. Even when identified through the hard work of immigration inspectors, foreign prostitutes used "cunning methods to mislead" the boards of inquiry.[31] Because of this administrative hurdle, inspectors at ports of entry tended to label morally suspicious women as "likely to become public charges" (LPCs), a status that effectively and more easily barred them from entry because it required a much lower burden of proof. The problem with this solution for Tedesco was that inspectors did not photograph the women excluded as LPCs; therefore, if a woman succeeded in entering the United States at a later date and the bureau began deportation proceedings against her, agents had no way to confirm or deny that it was the same woman who had been previously barred from entry. As Braun would later observe, "these people change their names oftener than they do change, perhaps, their shirts."[32] Immigration statistics from the period confirm Tedesco's observation that most immigration inspectors working at ports of entry barred women as LPCs rather than as prostitutes.

Braun included a series of recommendations for action to be taken by the bureau in its efforts to combat white slavery. His report revealed which immigration inspectors aided him, and more importantly, who had failed to properly comply with the anti–white slavery sections of the 1907 immigration law. Swift recriminations to several head agents in various cities followed Braun's report. He also included many suggestions that could be, and were, easily taken up by the bureau. He proposed that greater vigilance be demonstrated at the ports when examining the papers of current and prospective husbands. He advised that the addresses of all known houses of prostitution be gathered and then be distributed to the ports of entry so that passenger manifests could be compared to the list. And throughout the report he called for the bureau to establish a white slave squad of sixty or so agents who could coordinate their actions against foreign prostitution throughout the country. He urged simultaneous action, noting that a moral clean-up campaign like the one that had been ongoing while he visited Portland functioned to scatter prostitutes to surrounding cities and that only by taking simultaneous action could the networks established by foreign pimps and their prostitutes be eradicated.[33]

The Immigration Bureau took up Braun's suggestion for a national white slavery squad, assigning immigration agents in nineteen cities throughout the United States to the special duty of enforcing the immigration law related to immoral women and their procurers from March to July 1909. The purpose of such an extraordinary plan was to "secure active, concentrated and simultaneous action all over the country in an effort to make the importation of alien women for immoral purposes so dangerous and costly as to deal the 'white slave traffic' a severe blow, or to completely break it up so far as the United States is concerned."[34] The bureau instructed its agents to: try to avoid publicity in their investigations; focus on pimps and procurers rather than individual prostitutes; and to be "zealous" and "unflagging," but to avoid resorting to "persecutory methods," meaning no employment of "intimidating or sweating measures." It also advised agents to forward all material gathered in investigations to Washington, DC, where relevant information could then be sent to individual European countries in compliance with the 1904 international agreement, and to gather the addresses of all brothels and the names of their inhabitants and send them to the ports of entry, compiling the list of known brothels that Braun had suggested.[35] With these instructions the Immigration Bureau launched its coordinated dragnet against white slavery.

Beyond these basic directions, the Immigration Bureau gave agents no guidance about how to approach their assignment. Most agents favored the undercover methods that Braun and Tedesco utilized. Others worked with local police officers or posed as census takers. Leaving the individual methods to the discretion of agents bred confusion about how white slavery investigations related to the day-to-day fieldwork in immigration offices within many of the cities slated for white slavery round-ups. Boston Commissioner George Billings, who publically denied the existence of white slavery in interviews published in local newspapers, complained that his office had been forced to hold a group of Bulgarian immigrants for eleven days after they landed because the only agent who could speak Bulgarian was away from the office searching for white slavers and their victims.[36] In spite of these types of complaints, the bureau ordered each of the commissioners of immigration or inspectors in charge to allow the agents assigned to the white slave detail to focus on their white slave work over other duties they might have. Additionally, all agents for the bureau were reminded that they should keep their eyes open for cases that fell under the sections of the immigration act concerning immoral women.[37]

Some heads of immigration field offices argued that the resources given to white slave inspectors were not extensive enough to make a dent in the traffic. According to the inspector in charge in Montana, Alfred Hampton, the bureau was passing to its special agents a "big juicy lemon," because it did not provide sufficient resources, especially in the form of money to pay interpreters and informers, for the dragnet to produce "startling results." More to the point, he argued that a dragnet of this type ignored the ongoing anti-white slavery work that the Helena office and the U.S. Attorney had been completing. He wrote, "This is no virgin territory where a man can walk in and make a number of sensational arrests, gather a lot of statistics and write the bureau a glowing report to help swell the annual report of things accomplished."[38]

Other agents saw assignment to the white slave detail as an opportunity to do exactly that—make a number of sensational arrests and write glowing reports. One such man was Frank Stone, assigned to the San Antonio office. Stone savored traveling to the different cities in Texas—Dallas, Fort Worth, Waco, Austin, and Laredo—and uncovering the unique vice conditions in each city. He excelled at undercover work, easily conversing with pimps who would start telling tall tales and end up divulging life histories. In addition, police commissioners and chiefs seemed to like him just as well. In each city, Stone explored the unique moral and racial geography. In Austin, he noted that the madams luxuriously furnished the brothels and that members of the state legislature and government composed their main clientele. As a result, these elite customers preferred American-born Anglo prostitutes. In Waco, the corrupt police officers ensured that Mexican pimps and procurers operated beyond city limits so that Anglo sex workers could dominate. Stone found this to be "paradoxical" considering the large Hispanic population that lived in Waco. In Fort Worth, he uncovered the "rottonist" [sic] city he had ever seen. It was a city in which the Anglo commercial property owners of the red-light district, called "The Acre," encouraged foreign prostitution (mainly French and Jewish), protected vice interests, and battled reformers within the political arena. One Fort Worth judge told Stone that for him it was a question of "dollars and cents" and that he needed the graft money that the vice interests gave him to cover his expenses. The same judge tried to bribe Stone, promising him a "good, hot time." And in Laredo, one of the most significant entry points into the United States from Mexico, Stone found that almost every prostitute working in a brothel was in violation of immigration laws, all having visited Mexico within the past three years. The city hosted only one brothel that contained Anglo women, appropriately named Casa Blanca. Ironically it occupied the former offices of the immigration service. He detected a large-scale system of procuring Mexican women to provide the sexual and care labor within the city. Young Mexican girls came to Laredo to work as domestics, private concubines, and public prostitutes. Alerted to the white-slave dragnet as Stone conducted his investigation, the same system of procurers that brought Mexican sex workers to Laredo worked in reverse sending the women back to Mexico where they would be safe from deportation proceedings; one brothel that had had twenty-three Mexican girls working when he arrived in town, had only two remaining when he left. He celebrated the system of expulsion "by other means" noting that it saved the government significant money and time associated with formal deportation proceedings.[39]

Like Braun's investigation, individual immigration agents encountered uncooperative and complicit police departments. In upstate New York, where houses of prostitution had been outlawed, some local police refused to help the investigators because they did not want to be held liable for knowing that such houses continued to thrive. However, this legacy of police corruption was not always present. Unlike Braun, many of the immigrant bureau agents lived in parts of the communities they investigated and approached the police with more respect and in return gained greater cooperation. Agent Frank Stone's campaign against Mexican prostitution in San Antonio and surrounding cities was possible because of the support of local police. And even in upstate New York, the investigating agent, David Lehrhaupt, who hated the white slavery assignment because he objected to having to entertain "the low and unscrupulous class of people with whom I have to come in contact," found that generally the commissioners of public safety and chiefs of police extended "every possible courtesy" in using local laws to arrest those pimps and prostitutes who could not be deported under federal law.[40]

While the investigations were ongoing, Commissioner-General of Immigration Daniel J. Keefe declared that the Supreme Court "severely handicapped" the bureau's dragnet against foreign prostitution when it issued the *Keller v. United States* decision in early April 1909. The case looked at the Immigration Act of 1907 and found the section that outlawed harboring a foreign prostitute within three years of her entry to be unconstitutional because it represented the federal government infringing on states' powers to exercise police functions.[41] The 1907 law had made brothel operators criminally liable for employing foreign-born women to practice prostitution within the three-year window. The Immigration Bureau had hoped that the dragnet would result in brothel owners refusing to employ foreign sex workers because of the risk of housing foreign prostitutes would be too great. But the *Keller* decision took away this weapon, and the bureau now could focus only on deporting individual foreign-born prostitutes—not pimps, procurers, brothel operators, or any other third-party profiteers.

The Immigration Bureau's white slavery dragnet echoed many of Braun's conclusions as the reports of the individual agents confirmed his assertions that foreign prostitution was a national problem, that prostitutes entered the country via Canada, and that corrupt local police supported prostitution. Although the white slave dragnet confirmed Braun's findings, it differed from Braun's report in its immediate consequences. Deportations of foreign prostitutes increased dramatically during the dragnet and for many years would stay higher than they had been before the dragnet. The bureau concluded, "The most alarming feature of this traffic from the bureau's point of view consists . . . in the vastly increasing numbers of alien prostitutes flooding the country, finding in the existing immigration laws, with their present means of enforcement, only slight impediment to their passage back and forth, and in the great and callous indifference displayed to the existence of these leprous sores upon the body politic in the various cities which throw the cloak of protection over the districts wherein are gathered the brothels, dives, and houses of assignation."[42] As a result of Braun's U.S. report and the Immigration Bureau's coordinated drive against white slavery, the bureau recommended that the 1907 immigration law be amended to be more severe against foreign-born women found practicing prostitution within the borders of the United States.[43]

While the individual immigration agents of the white slave detail toiled against foreign prostitutes during the summer of 1909, the Immigration Bureau dispatched Marcus Braun to investigate white slave conditions in Europe. He was ordered to visit England, France, Belgium and Germany—Poland and Russia were added to the list after he departed. This was the first (and last) trans-Atlantic assignment Braun had received since his scandalous confrontation with Hungarian secret police in 1905, and the State Department forbade Braun from visiting his homeland.[44] But even with this precaution, Braun's brash personal style soon caused him and the State Department difficulties—this time in France.

The problem Braun encountered stemmed from two sources. The U.S. Immigration Bureau had an expansive definition of white slavery that covered the innocent, deceived woman or girl, but focused primarily on the professional prostitute. In Europe, from the state's perspective, the term *white slavery* applied only to the innocent, deceived woman or girl. European officials found U.S. immigration laws, passed under the guise of protection for women against white slavery, to be overly restrictive by actually denying entry to immigrant sex workers. Further complicating Braun's investigation was the fact that he never considered that the undercover methods he favored would be repugnant to the officials of countries he visited. Indeed, Braun seemed to believe that American immigration officials' sovereignty was unrestrained and that as a representative of the American government he had a right to investigate anywhere without any official sanction.

When Braun first arrived in France he met with the undersecretary of the minister of the interior, M. Hennequin, to inquire about the state of white slavery, prostitution, and emigration in France. In investigations within the United States, investigators repeatedly identified France as one of the main sources of prostitutes. Indeed, prior to leaving for Europe, Braun had planned to get the French government to extradite Alphonse and Eva Dufour, the French couple who had forfeited the $50,000 bond when they were arrested in the summer of 1908 for harboring foreign prostitutes in the United States. They had since been convicted in France for trafficking an American girl to Paris and the French court system sentenced Alphose Dufour to five years in prison and gave his wife, Eva, a two-year sentence. When Braun first met with Hennequin it is more than likely that he had a list of specific complaints and demands that Hennequin found obnoxious. Hennequin, a well-known figure in the international anti-white slavery movement, represented France at international anti-white slavery conferences and later would serve on the League of Nation's Committee on the Trafficking of Women and Children. Although he was an anti-white slavery activist, Hennequin was first and foremost a protector of the French Republic and its international reputation. According to Braun, Hennequin admitted that he thought the U.S. laws against entry of "immoral" women to be "outrageous" and that he was not in sympathy with the enforcement of any such laws. Hennequin argued that U.S. immigration laws that treated women who had been lured to the United States and put into a life of prostitution were inhumane and that the United States had "no right to treat them as prostitutes."[45] At their meeting, Hennequin argued that an American official had neither jurisdiction nor the right to make any investigations in France. According to Hennequin, all investigations needed to be conducted by French officials and if Braun needed anything, he should go through Hennequin's office (of course Hennequin denied all of Braun's requests for aid).

Not to be thwarted, Braun decided that he would play the part of the tourist while in Paris and find out all he could about vice in France. He argued that he did this in "an absolute inoffensive" way, but of course he was found out when he offended a suspected white slaver who complained to the police, who alerted the minister of foreign affairs, who in turn, lodged a complaint with the American ambassador.[46] Luckily for Braun, he had left Paris for Berlin just as these accusations began to circulate; and he avoided any formal charges, while the State Department and American ambassador smoothed the ruffled feathers of the French government. From this point on, the methods Braun employed in his investigations changed considerably. He no longer went undercover, instead limiting his investigations to discussions with police and governmental officials, anti–white slavery activists, Jewish prostitutes, and the people to whom they introduced him.

Braun found the opinions of government officials in Europe to be vastly different from those held by American officials. He discovered that the United States could not rely on European countries to aid in cracking down on the emigration of prostitutes to the United States. According to the representatives of the various signatories of the 1904 international anti-white slavery treaty, the treaty was strictly limited to cases in which an innocent woman or girl was transported due to fraud or force from one country to another. No European government was willing to obstruct the freedom of movement of women, whether or not they worked as professional prostitutes. More infuriating to Braun was the fact that "in all countries I was plainly told by officials with whom I had to deal, that 'You better keep those women, once they are there.' "[47] Even more confusing to Braun was the fact that many of the European officials with whom he met considered prostitution to be a legitimate vocation, and more troubling, that prostitutes could claim certain rights. While in Belgium, Braun met with a man who supplied prostitutes to the legal brothels within the country. In the course of their conversation, the man, Philippet, responded to Braun's line of questioning in anger, "The Belgian Government, and in fact every other European Government, with the exception of England, tolerates the existence of Houses of Prostitution. How dare you to make any reproaches to me that I am not in a legitimate business when I supply these houses with women? If it is legitimate for the Government to tolerate the existence of these Houses, why should it not be legitimate for me to supply the women?"[48] The legitimacy that most European governments gave to houses of prostitution through regulation extended to sex workers themselves. That prostitutes were not believed to be "white slaves" in Europe puzzled Braun, and he could not fathom how European officials thought that an adult prostitute should be allowed to do with "her body whatever she pleases" and go wherever she pleased.[49] European officials seemed to see prostitution more as a job than a state of immorality, as Braun and most American anti–white slavery activists perceived it. Numerous European officials thought it "cruel" to exclude a woman who may in the past have worked as a prostitute, but who could be on the path to becoming a "good woman."[50] But, according to the Immigration Bureau's policy, application of the label of "prostitute" was permanent. Any woman who at any time in her past had practiced prostitution would be excluded as a prostitute, and any woman who after arriving in the United States became a prostitute was assumed to have been a prostitute in the past. In this way, the Immigration Bureau applied the label of prostitute to indicate an immoral identity or evidence of moral turpitude, rather than a temporary type of work. As a result of this mindset, Braun found that many European officials were not in sympathy with a policy that seemed to deny even the potential for reformation.

While in Europe, Braun discovered the dark side to the "land of opportunity" narrative. Among the prostitutes he interviewed many of them mentioned that it was well known that vast amounts of money could be made in the United States. His research confirmed that the average sex worker made significantly more money for the same sex acts in the United States than in Europe, especially in Eastern Europe. A Jewish brothel madam in Warsaw reported that her sex workers received twenty kopecks, or ten cents, for each sex act performed, but after giving the madam her portion and paying room and board, most girls earned a mere seven kopecks per act. Braun was astonished to learn that the workers in this brothel serviced from forty to fifty clients a night, and significantly more on holidays.[51] Employment in a U.S. brothel represented a more profitable and leisurely venture. Four years later, vice investigator George J. Kneeland found that the typical New York City brothel charged customers one dollar per sex act and the worker usually retained about half of the profits. Furthermore, the average workers served between five and thirty clients a night.[52] Additionally, because many cities in the United States rejected the invasive medical licensing of prostitutes that was common throughout much of Europe, European prostitutes found the United States to be an attractive destination. More troubling to Braun was that of all the sex workers he interviewed, he never encountered one who was not well and accurately informed about U.S. immigration laws. All claimed that if they wanted to get into the United States, then they could. Braun repeatedly noted that it felt as though these lewd women were laughing at him and the Immigration Bureau. One reportedly called him a "chump" when he mentioned that U.S. law excluded sporting women from entering the United States. Another group also laughed, saying they each knew colleagues who went back and forth across the Atlantic at will. He was baffled that none of these women had heard of any prostitute being deported, nor any stories of prostitutes being mistreated by clients or pimps, or dying in hospitals, or having "gone down in the gutter."[53]

The sex workers' testimony that immigration laws did little to impinge on their mobility underscored the monumental task the Immigration Bureau faced in screening each of the thousands and thousands of immigrants that traveled to American shores each year. Historians have emphasized the ways in which the Immigration Bureau's policies towards immoral women served to construct a gendered state apparatus that perceived morality through stereotypically Anglo, middle-class, and Christian values. Certainly, research on deportations and who was barred from entry bears this observation out, as properly contained (meaning conjugal) heterosexuality seemed to have been aggressively policed at the border. Yet, far more immigrants entered the United States than were halted. Given the vast number of immigrants entering the United States in the early 1900s—1,285,349 in 1907 alone—it is entirely likely that sex workers who educated themselves about U.S. immigration policy easily evaded detection. Resisters to exclusionary policies, like the sex workers Braun interviewed, easily responded to changes in policy, thereby producing a dance of action and reaction between policy makers and those classed as illegal or immoral immigrants. Like the Chinese Exclusion Act, which allowed for Chinese who occupied certain statuses to be admitted to the United States, policing of prostitutes at the border generally failed to accurately determine the status of applicants. These statuses, whether they be "student," "merchant," or "prostitute," were not automatically self-evident and prospective immigrants enthusiastically exploited the expectations of immigration officers to gain entry. Immigrants' intimate understanding of border-control policies and procedures was characterized by a shared ritual, with elements mutually understood by examiner and examinee, and resulted in, paradoxically, inclusion; since, if an immigrant knew the right steps, he or she proved his or her acceptability. Sex workers seeking access to American market places eagerly engaged in "formalized deception" to gain entry.[54] Commissioner-General of Immigration Daniel J. Keefe complained about sex workers' intimate awareness of the Immigration Bureau's procedures saying that "familiarity with the mode of inspection often enables them to easily pass the necessarily hurried inspection given at border ports and on the trains."[55] This familiarity and ability to react to new border controls was especially true for women free of racial associations of exclusion and immorality—unlike Chinese and Japanese women whom immigration officials assumed to be prostitutes-in-hiding—and constituted an important privilege of whiteness for European sex workers.[56]

By far the most important finding that Braun made was that the international traffic in women, although it did exist, was not organized. He discovered that the recruitment of existing prostitutes was common, and even more sex workers found ways to come to the United States without a procurer. But there was no organization having a headquarters on both continents that existed for the purpose of "bringing innocent and virtuous women into this country for such purposes of prostitution."[57] There did exist, however, a certain "esprit de corps"—kindred spirits who gathered at the same locales, traded the same gossip, and loosely coordinated their activities.

As a result of his investigation, Braun called on the United States to amend its immigration laws so that foreign-born prostitutes, procurers, pimps, brothel-house owners, and even homosexual prostitutes would be barred from entry and deported upon discovery. He advocated that the three-year buffer be abolished in favor of a lifetime prohibition against sex work for all foreign-born women (and men). He suggested that every incoming immigrant be morally cleared by the U.S. consul in his or her country of origin before being admitted to the United States. He argued that medical examinations for venereal disease at ports of entry would exclude many sex workers and should be conducted more vigorously; the Immigration Act of 1903 did provide for exclusion of people infected with syphilis and gonorrhea, though the Public Health Service did not conduct invasive genital examinations on women and even if it had, both diseases can be asymptomatic and frequently do not visibly manifest in female carriers. Braun issued a stunning indictment of the 1904 international treaty, declaring that it did not compel

European countries to aid the United States in barring foreign prostitutes from entry, and concluding it was of little use to the United States.[58]

While Braun and Tedesco had been infiltrating the city of Chicago, their work overlapped with the intensive white-slave investigation of the Immigration Commission. Immigration to the U.S. peaked in 1907, the same year that the U.S. Congress amended immigration eligibility and established a nine-member commission tasked with investigating the many aspects of the subject of immigration, including white slavery and the trafficking of women. The commission, known as the Dillingham Commission, was comprised of nine members, including two avid restrictionists, one antirestrictionist, and five moderates who supported some level of immigration restriction. All of the members shared a "steadfast commitment to the concept of the 'American standard of living,'" which celebrated the male breadwinner model of family structure and suggested any variation from this model to be threatening to American institutions.[59] The Commission's shared suspicion of women who worked and migrated outside of patriarchal family structures shaped its investigation into white slavery which began in November 1907 and was presented to Congress in December 1909. Favoring the undercover methods developed by Braun, its investigators had visited twelve cities, uncovering foreign-born prostitutes, police collusion, and a general "esprit de corps" among pimps and brothel owners throughout the country—echoing the Immigration Bureau's findings.[60]

These echoes resonated because both of the reports that Braun had written (the U.S. and European) had been forwarded to the Dillingham Commission. The Commission's report on white slavery for the most part repeated many of the claims of Braun's investigations and confirmed the experiences of the immigration inspectors working on the white slave dragnet. Yet in explaining white slavery and foreign prostitution, the Commission favored an economic analysis, noting that any international trade existed only for profit. It pointed to the case of the Dufours to demonstrate how lucrative the trade in women could be. In the gendered imagination of the Commission, every prostitute was subjected to a male pimp who confiscated a majority of her earnings. It suggested that women's choice to participate in prostitution could never be freely given due to the social context in which the decision was made (low wages, coercion, lack of paternal protection). No woman would reasonably consent to sell sex, or what one congressman later called, "that which to her and every female on this earth is worth more than life itself."[61] The Commission repeated the common thinking that prostitution resulted in early death for the prostitute, a wanton waste of reproductive potential.[62]

Where the Commission differed from previous Immigration Bureau investigations was that it identified white slavery as a primarily Jewish phenomenon, specifically pointing to the cases where Jewish men were found to be pimps or procurers. Braun, for his part, tended to de-emphasize the Jewish connection to prostitution, while at the same time he stressed the important role of Jewish charities in fighting white slavery. In condemning Jewish criminality, the Commission cited the example of the New York Independent Benevolent Association, a Jewish organization devoted to providing for the health care and burial needs for its members, most of whom were pimps, brothel owners, or prostitutes. The existence of such a benevolent society for Jewish "white slavers" convinced many that although an international syndicate may not exist, Jewish pimps and procurers were still very well organized, even if the organization "was no more than the scaffolding for Jewish commercial vice."[63] Beneath it lay a myriad of petty jealousies and rivalries that obstructed the development of an organized trade. Yet, the Commission's declaration that Jewish criminality formed the foundation of underworld sex trafficking would permanently cast white slavery as a Jewish criminal enterprise and would mark sex traffickers as non-Anglo others. The report on white slavery issued by the Dillingham Commission echoed anti-Semitic assumptions that white slavery was an organized trade dominated by Jewish pimps who trafficked young Jewish women from eastern Europe to commercial sex centers in Buenos Aires, Constantinople, New York, and Chicago (as well as reflecting the anti-Semitism, especially towards Russian Jews, present in the Commission's wider study of immigration).[64] In repeating these claims, the study legitimized anti-Semitic discourses that had been circulating within the popular media. Numerous anti-Semitic white slavery tracts featured Jewish white slavers profiting from the sale of prostitutes. George Kibbe Turner declared in the pages of *McClure's Magazine* that "largely Russian Jews" headed the trade in 1907, and just one month before the publication of the Immigration Commission's report in 1909 he repeated these claims that Jewish traffickers dominated prostitution in New York City. Meanwhile, in 1908 New York City police commissioner Theodore Bingham added fuel to the anti-

Semitic fire when he proclaimed that half of the criminals in the city were Jewish.[65] The claims that Jewish organized crime reflected two intertwined trends: the ever-present anti-Semitism of the Progressive Era that often reflected a "paranoia about conspiracy" that exaggerated Jewish participation in vice, and the reality of Jewish participation in vice.[66]

Beyond the hysteria of anti-Semitic white slavery tracts, considerable evidence has emerged that eastern European Jews did engage in international sex trafficking. For example, the Zwi Migdal Society, a benevolent society for prostitutes and pimps, operated in such far-flung cities such as Buenos Aires, São Paolo, and New York City.[67] The existence of Jewish trafficking caused Jewish reform organizations throughout the world to spearhead the fight against white slavery as a strategy to fight the inherent anti-Semitism of white slavery narratives. American activist from the National Council of Jewish Women, Sadie American, reported that at the 1910 International Congress for the Suppression of the White Slave Traffic held in Madrid, "There were representatives there from every European country, and underneath it all, like powder ready for the match, was the fear that the whole Conference would be turned into detestation and denunciation of the Jews because of the Jewish traffickers."[68] Ever sensitive to the ways white slavery narratives could be marshaled into attacks on the Jewish community, Louis Marshall, the chairman of the New York State Immigration Commission and a respected Jewish leader, was prompted to write Congressmen William S. Bennet of the Dillingham Commission. He argued, "to hold Jews, as such, responsible for the white slave traffic throughout the world has never occurred to any right-thinking man." He went on to proclaim that prostitution and sex trafficking "has been held in especial abhorrence by those of the Jewish faith."[69] The Dillingham Commission's characterization of the white slavery trade as a particularly Jewish phenomenon generated protest on the floor of Congress as Illinois Congressman Adolph J. Sabath (D-IL) called the report a "malicious and cowardly libel upon the Jewish people."[70]

In summarizing its own work and the work of Braun, the Dillingham Commission found that one of the most basic characteristics of pimps, prostitutes, and all others connected to sex work was their basic mobility. Like so many before it, the Commission noted that when a city relaxed an ongoing moral clean-up campaign, "the news spreads with wonderful rapidity, and the statement that the city is 'wide open' means the flocking back of this element from other States, and an increased tendency toward the violation of the laws of importations."[71] In seeking to counter this mobility, the Commission called for stricter immigration laws by abolishing the three-year period in the 1907 Immigration Act and further empowering the Immigration Bureau to investigate and deport all violators of the law.

The Commission's investigators believed its report to be so groundbreaking that it published it before other reports of the Commission, and Senator Dillingham received congressional approval to print four thousand copies for distribution to the general public in early December 1909.[72] Newspapers across the country covered the report's publication, repeating its most salient points.[73] The *Chicago Tribune* declared the report to be "revolting," "shocking," and consequently "a large part of it unsuitable for publication."[74] In addition to adding more publicity to the issue of white slavery, the Commission's investigation into sex trafficking offered anti–white slavery activists the mantle of government authority as they raised the alarm that white slavery posed a danger to American morality. Its findings were somberly reiterated in numerous publications about the topic. For example, the National Vigilance Association's O. Edward Janney more or less reprinted the findings of the Commission in his 1911 book, *The White Slave Traffic in America,* though he couched it in more lurid and sensational prose. By conferring governmental legitimacy to the claims of anti–white slavery activists, the Dillingham Commission reiterated the ideas that white slavery was a danger, it was foreign in nature, and reform legislation was required to address the complicated problem of international sex trafficking.

◆ ◆ ◆

Amid declarations that insinuated that white slavery posed a foreign threat to American values and institutions, the Immigration Bureau launched a series of investigations to render this vague and contested idea of sexual slavery legible to itself and the public. It sought to assess the extent of the white slavery threat and in doing so puzzled over and struggled to define *white slavery.* The collective puzzlement about white slavery did not occur in a sterile environment, but amid a cacophony of voices, including those of reformers, police officers, pimps and prostitutes, U.S. Attorneys, and civil servants like Marcus Braun. Each of these voices offered opinions, past insights and future anxieties. The Immigration Bureau's investigations and dragnet combined with the Dillingham Commission's study demonstrated that "the power to investigate, inherent in the modern state, furnishes the sensorium of the public."[75] These investigations were inspired by the outcry against white slavery that emerged in places like Chicago, and they pulled together the various facets of the emerging public discourse on white slavery. In publishing the findings of the Dillingham Commission, which combined the insights of the other Immigration Bureau investigations, Congress legitimized the growing notion that white slavery was a modern problem of migration and that Congress must act to protect the moral borders of the country. The investigations also reflected one of the most basic characteristics of the Progressive Era—the almost religious belief that scientific and thorough investigation could uncover the roots of social problems and provide solutions in the form of government intervention. But investigations by government agencies spoke to their own interests, including the restrictionist impulses of the leaders of the Immigration Bureau and the Dillingham Commission. The Immigration Bureau's investigations into the extent of the white slavery problem in the United States and Europe were always conducted with the view that independent foreign women posed a moral threat to the United States. Its investigators' reports confirmed that informal trafficking of women from Europe and throughout the United States did indeed occur, even if there was no organized syndicate. It noted that the vast majority of foreign-born sex workers coming to the United States "are prostitutes by choice, and a great many of them are women of maturity."[76] Furthermore, the studies revealed that the United States could not rely on European aid in combating white slavery, in spite of its participation in the 1904 treaty, due to the different understandings of what constituted white slavery and who comprised a victim and who did not. Commissioner-General of the Immigration Bureau Daniel Keefe pronounced "that practically no steps could be expected [from European signatories of the 1904 treaty] to prevent the free passage from their country to this of the professional prostitute or procurer, who constitute the bulk of the 'white-slave traffic' in this country."[77] Additionally, the studies publicized that immigration agents were deeply hampered by the 1907 immigration law that made prostitution within three years of entry a deportable offense. The Immigration Bureau's 1909 coordinated dragnet on white slavery confirmed this point when agent after agent complained that any arrest of foreign prostitutes devolved into an argument about when the women entered the country. Keefe bemoaned the fact that most foreign-born sex workers and their pimps were "intimately aware" of U.S. immigration law, policy, and procedure, and were frequently armed with a story and false embarkation papers that dated their entry to the United States as prior to the three year period. He affirmed that "[a] removal of the time bar to deportation in the cases of alien prostitutes and procurers would be by far the most effective method that could be adopted to break up the 'white slave traffic.'"[78] The inquiries into white slavery provided a forum for the Immigration Bureau to articulate what its role could be in the fight against white slavery and the tools needed for it to successfully take up that role—appropriations, expanded jurisdiction, legislative reform, and abandonment of international protocols that subjected U.S. policy to foreign conceptions of morality.

As a result of these studies, the bureau developed an understanding of gendered immorality that had little use for the narratives of innocence common in the media and activists' discourses of white slavery. Instead the term *white slave*, in the bureau's parlance, always meant *prostitute*, and it was these foreign prostitutes who according to the bureau threatened to "flood" the country and needed to be stopped. Remembering his investigations in 1910 Braun noted, "I failed to find any organized traffic in women, and I do not believe now, that such an organized traffic exists, nor do I believe, that with the exception of sporadic cases, innocent girls are sold or driven into this life, but nevertheless I regard every prostitute in this country more or less a white slave."[79] Taken together, the Immigration Bureau inquiries and the Dillingham Commission produced new kinds of knowledge that seemed to demand a legislative response. The Immigration Bureau turned to Congress to amend the immigration law to more firmly ban the entry of any foreign-born prostitutes. Seeking to protect the shores of American morality, while also addressing the white slavery problem, the Immigration Bureau pursued a policy that repeatedly envisioned sex workers as criminal, and single female immigrants as potential deviant prostitutes.

Immigration to the United States peaked in 1907, with 1,285,349 immigrants flowing into the country, the same year that the white slave scare broke in Chicago. As a topic of public concern, or indeed, hysteria, the issue of white slavery spoke to a range of intermingled anxieties. On the one hand, some reformers saw white slavery as the product of a job market that was segregated by sex and paid women significantly less than men ensuring their poverty. The critique of women's poor wages accompanied calls for a minimum wage and swirling anxieties about how the increasing numbers of women in the industrial wage labor market might undermine the nation's reproductive capacity. Indeed, low wages seemed to be a chronic cause of immigrant women's entry into commercial prostitution. A majority of the thirty-four Jewish sex workers who violated probation in 1905 had first worked as garment workers in New York City. As Mollie Kessler admitted, "I cannot exist on $4 to $5 per week."[80] Jane Addams suggested that entry into sex work was a rational decision, considering that young women could make significantly more in commercial sex than in industrial or service economy, though she noted that the short shelf life of a sex worker and attending health risks undermined a sex worker's life-long earning potential.[81] On the other hand, others like anarchist Emma Goldman argued that it wasn't just the way wage work was segregated by sex, but also the way young women were socialized to sexually service husbands, yet were kept in ignorance about their own sexuality, which condemned them to sexual exploitation, whether foreign-born or native.[82]

But as much as women's increased labor participation—accompanied as it was with less paternal supervision—could be a factor in women's entrance into sex work, many anti–white slavery reformers feared it was the breakdown of families that set young women on the path to prostitution. As Maude Miner argued, "Her home has failed not only to protect her, but to develop in her that strength in character by which she might protect herself."[83] Still, others saw the prevalence of foreign-born prostitutes as the result of the vulnerabilities of immigrant girls, unfamiliar with American language, customs, and morality. Women like Grace Abbott contended that these friendless girls formed fertile fields for exploitative traffickers. Here it wasn't only low wages that caused prostitution, but also the breakdown of familial structures in new environments that could lead to debasement. Abbott wrote, "It is the same story of the desire for affection, together with loneliness, lack of knowledge of herself, and long hours of hard, monotonous work. The difference between the temptations which meet the American country girl who comes to the city and those of the immigrant girl, is in the main, one of degree and not of kind."[84] In this structural analysis it was the new environment, always urban, combined with less stable family structures and exploitative labor conditions that posed the great danger.

But the most common assertion within white slavery narratives was that foreign-born men, strangers from afar, had brought the practice of white slavery to the United States, and exploited vulnerable young women for profit. This narrative, put forth by muckrakers like George Kibbe Turner and repeated by public officials like New York City Police Commissioner Theodore Bingham tapped into the widespread anxiety about immigration during the Progressive Era. The publicity surrounding the publication of the Dillingham Commission's white slavery study added fuel to growing nativist concerns that immigration posed a danger to the United States. It seemed to suggest a basic immorality of immigrants, while also hinting that women who migrated without their family were vulnerable to immorality at best, and were prostitutes in hiding at worst. White slavery narratives and the investigations generated from the Immigration Bureau consolidated these anxieties about women's entry into the paid labor force, rapid urbanization, and immigration. The investigations into white slavery of the Immigration Bureau and the Immigration Commission reflected the swirling anxieties surrounding white slavery while simultaneously grounding them by giving them legitimacy and establishing the "fact" of white slavery.

Ever since 1875's Page Act, Congress had responded to fears about the threat of foreign prostitution by amending immigration laws to be more restrictive, a move widely supported by the Immigration Bureau and the Immigration Commission. Yet as Congress constructed a moral fence around the country to keep white slaves and white slavers out, the gaze of the state fell disproportionately on women migrants. In 1917 Grace Abbott noted this disparity when she commented, "These laws applied the double standard of morality in the tests for exclusions and deportation. The man who profits by the social evil or who brings a girl into the country for immoral purposes is subject to punishment, but the man who is himself immoral is not regarded as an 'undesirable' immigrant."[85] Yet, women thought to be immoral were easily excluded as prostitutes or LPCs. Furthermore, laws passed to "protect" immigrant girls seemed to equate protection with punitive exclusion or deportation. Abbott worried that this type of "protections" functioned to deny some immigrant girls a pathway to redemption. Enforcement of white slave provisions of the immigration laws meant that "we deny girls who have made some serious mistake at home the chance which they need to begin a new life here in United States."[86] For the Immigration Bureau, protection was conceived around national interest, specifically the interest in keeping foreign-born prostitutes out, excluding pimps and procurers who might prey on American girls, and building a stronger, more effective bureaucratic apparatus to police the moral boundaries of the country. Tightening immigration laws might combat the international trafficking and mobility of sex workers, but it would do little to address domestic trafficking of women and girls—a concern that more and more Americans worried over. "Through the care of the Immigration Department, it is hoped that foreign girls will soon be well protected until they are able to take their place as citizens," argued O. Edward Janney. "But so long as the white slave traffic exists in America, it will continue to menace both them and native girls."[87]

3

Endangered Daughters

Anti–white slavery purity and social hygiene activists defined *white slavery* as a problem of immigration, a "European business," and characterized the victim of sex trafficking as the "unprotected immigrant girl."[1] The Immigration Bureau also saw white slavery as a problem related to immigration, but in contrast to social reformers, the agency understood it as a problem of foreign-born prostitutes bringing their immoral trade to the United States. By focusing narrowly on foreign-born prostitutes, the Immigration Bureau cast suspicion upon the morality of any immigrant girl or woman traveling outside of conventional family structures. Although these two perceptions existed in tension with one another, prior to 1907 most public discussion about white slavery remained limited to social purity journals and audiences. But as city officials, states' attorneys, and the Immigration Bureau coordinated the cleanup of Chicago's Levee, the popular press began to draw attention to the issue of white slavery, and as it did so, it effectively produced a third perception of white slavery: that white slavers preyed on young, native-born, white American girls. White slavery emerged as a popular public issue in the last years of the first decade of the twentieth century, and it quickly became a political issue. Americans demanded that Congress act to limit sex trafficking within the nation's borders.

The anti–white slave campaigns conducted by the Immigration Bureau, the Dillingham Commission, and the U.S. Attorney in Chicago in 1908, which swept up the Dufours, confirmed that Chicago, in the words of the *Chicago Daily Tribune,* was "becoming the greatest 'white slave' center of the world";[2] but more problematically the vice raids revealed that "Chicago is a producing center as well as a market in the 'white slave' traffic."[3] At the turn of the century, Chicago's many railroads channeled the nation's commerce through the city, leading it to dominate in the trade of grain, lumber, meatpacking, food processing, and wholesale and retail commerce. The city claimed a large and diversified industrial base.[4] In 1890, the city boasted the third-largest number of industrial workers, and as a result, Chicago was an attractive destination for migrants from all over the world, with 2.5 million immigrants coming to the city between 1880 and 1920.[5] Observers worried that in addition to its rising prominence as the country's second-most-prosperous and populated city, Chicago was also earning a reputation as a city of sin where girls were seduced, bought and sold, and trafficked to other U.S. cities. One newspaper reporter asked, "White slavery? In how many guises it is one of the giant 'industries' of the second city of the United States?"[6] Newspaper story after newspaper story reported that native-born, white Midwestern girls faced the same dangers of entrapment that immigrant girls encountered. Many of these cases came across the desk of Clifford G. Roe in the state's attorney's office.

Roe, an Indiana native who attended the University of Michigan law school, was only thirty-three years old in 1908 when he helped lead the city's campaign against vice. In fighting white slavery, Roe discovered a mission that would shape much of his adult life. He became so inspired by his work against sex traffickers that he joined the Illinois Vigilance Association and helped draft the Illinois White Slave Bill, the nation's strictest white slave law, which was enacted on July 1, 1908.

It was the discovery that native-born white girls could be ensnared in the city's brothels that particularly outraged Roe. He declared, "Every home in the country is threatened by the menace, and it is time that the entire public took a hand in the fight that has been spreading from one branch of officialdom to another."[7] Throughout his many anti–white slavery speeches and publications, Roe highlighted the vulnerability of white American girls. He started his 1911 exposé, *The Great War on White Slavery or Fighting for the Protection of Our Girls,* with a retelling of the trials and tribulations of Mildred Clark, whose real name was Mary La Salle. In his narrative, sixteen-year-old Mildred had been staying with friends in Nashville, Tennessee, while working as a laundress when she met the charming Clarence Gentry. Clarence courted Mildred and after only three days persuaded her to marry him. He arranged for his new fiancée's transport to Chicago, and once there he got her a room at what she thought was a boarding house, but was really one of Chicago's 350 bordellos. Clarence revealed himself to be a villain who kept Mildred prisoner by confiscating all of her clothing and threatening to beat and maim her. The madam of the brothel told Mildred that she would have to prostitute herself because not only was she already in debt for her room and board, but she would need money to purchase new clothes and a train ticket back home. According to Mildred's court testimony, as recounted by Roe, "I wanted to get out of there, but I was afraid they would kill me because Clarence told me if I ever tried to get out of there he would."[8] Beaten, tormented, raped, and exploited, Mildred found relief when during an anti-vice parade conducted by renowned evangelical minister Rodney "Gypsy" Smith she yelled out the window: "For God's sake come and get me!"[9] Smith and several police officers breached the door of the brothel and took Mildred to safety, later getting her a job as a domestic, and informing her parents of her whereabouts. Roe celebrated his successful prosecution of Clarence Gentry, who was sentenced to six months in prison and fined $300, by calling for nationwide anti–sex trafficking laws that would ensure that "men like Gentry can be put away where they never can wreck the lives of our daughters."[10]

For Roe and many of his allies in the Chicago antivice movement, the threat of white slavery seemed particularly dangerous to American daughters, many of whom were leaving home for the first time, entering the paid workforce, and enjoying the burgeoning leisure sites offered by urban centers. According to prevailing opinion, white slavery was a danger that thrived in the city.[11] Even Jeremiah Jenks, one of the primary authors of the Dillingham Commission's white slavery study, emphasized the threat white slavery posed to native-born girls when he stated, "This traffic has been carried on for a good many years with immigrant girls, and, to a much greater extent, with American girls, especially those found in country villages and the smaller cities who are brought to the great cities."[12] As the campaign against foreign-born prostitutes gained momentum, the dominant white slavery narrative put forth by anti–white slavery activists and the popular press emphasized the dangers that white slavery posed not to immigrant girls, but to white, native-born young women—the daughters of the countryside—and this danger became intertwined with the massive internal migration to large urban centers like Chicago and New York.

No longer just the purview of the purity press, by 1908 white slavery was the subject of sensational stories published by big city newspapers and national periodicals.[13] In Chicago's newspapers, it was from 1908 to 1910 that the narrative of white slavery as a threat to white, innocent American girls emerged with the most force; smaller cities' newspaper coverage of white slavery peaked in 1913. Readers of the *Chicago Daily Tribune* encountered at least 117 articles about white slavery from 1906 to 1911, most of those appearing in 1908 and 1909. These articles included exposés of specific cases, editorials, reports of the federal cleanup of the Levee, accounts of social reformers' activities, and sordid stories of sex trafficking. Within the numerous articles, there were mentions of ninety-six unique victims of white slavery. Of the girls and women whose ages the newspaper noted, the average age was seventeen years old, but the age range stretched from eleven to thirty years old. Story after story told of girls from the countryside or from out of state becoming ensnared in a brothel for the profit of a third party—a trafficker and brothel owner.

Clarence Gentry's cynical tactic of promising marriage to Mildred Clark as a way to gain her trust was typical of procurers' methods of entrapping girls. Antiprostitution activist Maude Miner argued in 1916 that "the most frequent method is to win the affection of a girl and promise to marry her."[14] Newspaper reports echoed this assertion. Abe Weinstein hired Jacob "Whitey" Jacobson and Louis Brodsky to get some new girls to work in his South Side brothel, The Silver Dollar. While walking in Lincoln Park, Whitey struck up a conversation with sixteen-year-old May McConnell. He kindly walked May home, met her mother, and asked if he might court her. The couple met several times, attending the theater and going for walks. One day Whitey appeared with his friend Louis and asked if May had a friend who might be interested in being Louis's date. May invited her friend, sixteen-year-old Adele Schubert. While on the double date, May later testified that the young men "told us they were rich and wanted to marry us and take us to New York. They said they would give us lots of money and fine clothes and that we would never have to work any more. We thought it would be nice to get married and have pretty clothes and money, so we agreed to go with them."[15] But before the couples could go to New York, they headed to The Silver Dollar where Abe Weinstein plied the girls with beer and confiscated their clothing. Weinstein paid Louis and Whitey for procuring the girls, and, in all likelihood, that money was then charged as a debt that the girls would need to work off through prostitution. Describing a typical brothel's acquisition of new talent, muckraker George Kibbe Turner noted that these relationships of debt bondage ensured that each coerced or forced sex worker essentially "pays . . . for her own sale."[16] Roe and several city detectives raided The Silver Dollar rescuing May McConnell and Adele Schubert. A Chicago court convicted Weinstein of pandering, the crime of encouraging a woman to enter prostitution.[17] In the increasingly popular tale of white slavery as a danger to native-born white girls, newspaper accounts, vice reports, and magazine exposés generally featured tales of false promises of love and marriage.

But romance was second to the primary way that traffickers entrapped unwilling women into sex work—the promise of a job. Again, Miner noted that procurers found young girls to place into brothels "by advertising for servants, waitresses, companions, chorus girls, or workers in massage or manicure parlors."[18] Eighteen-year-old Ida Parker and her roommate and friend sixteen-year-old Evelyn Krause were working together at a Chicago department store when a "fashionably dressed women" approached them and asked Evelyn, "How much lining does it take to line an actress' dress?" When Evelyn admitted that she did not know, the women expressed surprise, flattering the young woman, pretending she assumed Evelyn had stage experience. She then told Evelyn that if she wanted to get into the theatrical world the man to see was William Henderson on LaSalle Street. "He will put you on the stage and your fortune will be made."[19] The next day, Evelyn and Ida met with Henderson who promised not only to get them positions in a musical comedy troupe performing in Springfield, but also to purchase their railroad tickets for the journey. That evening, after he had purchased the train tickets he took the pair to dinner and then up to his hotel room where they were "measured" for their costumes. The "measuring" quickly merged into molestation, causing the girls to grab the train tickets and the letter of introduction, and flee. The following day they arrived in Springfield and presented themselves at the theater where they were told that rehearsals would not begin until later in the week, but that they could start selling beer right away. One of the girls testified, "That evening a lot of girls were sitting around in the balcony with the men. . . . After we had been there a little while we saw some of them get up and sit on the men's laps."[20] What the girls thought was a respectable theater was in fact a dancehall.

Although brothels like The Silver Dollar remained the most visible sites of sexual commerce, in fact they comprised but a small percentage of diverse places of prostitution. More common in Chicago were the disreputable hotels, saloons, and dancehalls; in 1906 the city had 292 separate hotels with a capacity for 10,000 rooms, 7300 licensed saloons and about half as many unlicensed speakeasies, bars and pubs, and just fewer than 300 dancehalls.[21] Dance hall theaters, like the one where Ida Parker and Evelyn Krause arrived, made most of their profits from the sale of alcohol. Managers hired young women to sell beer to the customers. The waitress got paid for every pint of beer she sold. If there was any entertainment on stage, it usually consisted of bawdy skits, songs, and dances like the cancan.[22] Many of the women who worked in these places also sold sex or the promise of sex. In 1910 the Chicago Vice Commission described one of the largest Chicago dance halls: "Every girl who frequents this place is a professional prostitute, groomed and trained to coax money out of the pockets of visitors for the benefit of the managers and then to persuade them to go to a hotel or to their own flats. One of the rules of this place is that a girl is supposed to make each man spend at least 40 cents for every round of drinks. . . . The girls are very aggressive, and do not wait for an invitation, but sit down at the tables, and as pointed out above, order a round of drinks that cost no less than 40 cents."[23] The Commission discovered that girls at this establishment charged five dollars for their sexual services. In the eyes of antiprostitution activists like the citizens who sat on the Commission, dance halls were disreputable sites of sexual commerce and key suppliers of the city's population of prostitutes. When Roe prosecuted the case against Henderson, he declared, "Ten dollars a head for white slaves"—the amount paid to Henderson for Ida Parker and Evelyn Krause. He believed that the girls had narrowly escaped a ruinous fate as white slaves.[24]

Stories of false job opportunities and fraudulent marriage offers leading to brothel enslavement filled Chicago's newspapers and reflected a reality of sexual exploitation as well as a means to titillate readers and sell papers. Although many in the Progressive Era saw in these stories the reflection of their middle-class anxieties about class, ethnic, gender, and political upheaval, they also uncovered the sexual marketplace young women wittingly or unwittingly encountered as they negotiated urban environments. In a period of only nine months spanning from 1907 into 1908, Chicago police arrested 157 women for luring young women into working in brothels, and they claimed to have rescued 329 girls from bordellos.[25] Though the immigration law "protected" immigrant women (by forcibly repatriating them) and discouraged trafficking, there was no similar national law to protect native-born white girls like Mildred Clark, May McConnell, Adele Schubert, Ida Parker, and Evelyn Krause.

Chicago's U.S. Attorney Edwin W. Sims joined Roe in his crusade against white slavery. By 1907, Sims had gained an enviable reputation for being an honest and dedicated lawyer and reformer, especially from his successful prosecution of the Standard Oil Company, which led to a $29 million ruling against the industrial giant. As a U.S. Attorney, he found the Immigration Act of 1907 to be exciting because it gave him a weapon for attacking foreign prostitution in the Windy City. Sims reported that he was "determined to break up this traffic in foreign women" and thus protect the American people from "contamination."[26] Sims used his connections in Washington to get a cadre of Secret Service agents and twenty-five U.S. marshals to aid in his quest. In June 1908, Sims led the attack on the Levee, targeting French-owned brothels like the ones owned by the Dufours and other French émigrés. Sims's raids resulted in twenty-seven indictments, seventeen convictions and guilty pleas, and the collection of $125,000 in fines. Sims adeptly handled the press interest in the raids, drawing on his experience working as a journalist during college.[27]

As much as he was determined to fight the traffic in foreign prostitution, Sims worried that there existed no legal weapon to wage against the dealers in white American-born white slaves. He saw American "country girls" headed to large cities as especially vulnerable. A father of four, he wrote, "In view of what I have learned in the course of the recent investigation and prosecution of the 'white slave' traffic, I can say, in all sincerity, that if I lived in the country and had a young daughter I would go any length of hardship and privation myself rather than allow her to go into the city to work or to study."[28] Sims saw an opportunity to protect native-born white women and girls in the Constitution's Commerce Clause. Conveniently he had a working relationship with Illinois Congressman James R. Mann, who sat as chairman of the House Committee on Interstate and Foreign Commerce. Mann was a native of Illinois, attending the University of Illinois and the Union College of Law, later Northwestern University Law School, in Chicago, before launching his own law practice in 1881. He was first elected to the House of Representatives as a Republican in 1897 and he served continuously until his death in 1922. Not known as a radical progressive, he nonetheless shepherded many of the era's most important regulatory laws through Congress, including the Pure Food and Drug Act of 1906 and the Mann-Elkins Act of 1910, which increased regulations of the railroad industry. With a reputation as an effective legislator who could effectively steer proposed statues through Congress, Mann was the ideal sponsor for Sims and Roe's anti–white slavery law.[29]

Sims and Roe wrote the law that would become the White Slave Traffic Act and took it to Mann. The law Roe and Sims drafted made it illegal to transport or facilitate the transport of any woman or girl over state lines, or within a territory and the District of Columbia "for the purpose of prostitution or debauchery, or for any other immoral purpose"; induce or cause any woman or girl to cross state lines, again, for the purposes of prostitution, debauchery, or any other immoral purposes; and, fail to report to the Bureau of Immigration any foreign-born sex workers practicing prostitution within a brothel within three years of their entry into the United States. With only minor changes, Mann presented the drafted bill to President William H. Taft on November 24, 1909. Taft signaled his support for the bill, and Mann introduced it to Congress on December 6, 1909, referring it to his own committee. The next day, Taft lent his public support to Mann's act in his annual address to Congress, saying that he believed it was "constitutional to forbid, under penalty, the transportation of persons for purposes of prostitution across national *and* state lines." Taft buttressed his support for anti–white slavery legislation when he called for a larger budget for the Immigration Bureau.[30]

As head of the House Committee on Interstate and Foreign Commerce, Mann drew upon Congress's power to police interstate commerce to justify the creation of a national anti–white slavery law. He proclaimed, "The legislation is needed to put a stop to a villainous interstate and international traffic in women and girls."[31] Mann worried that his law could be framed as stretching the Interstate Commerce Clause beyond its traditional, and constitutional, limits. The *Keller* decision, which had declared portions of the

1907 Immigration Act unconstitutional because they infringed on the states' police powers, loomed large in his justification of relying on the powers embedded in the Commerce Clause. So, to justify the constitutionality of his proposed law, Mann carefully laid out a series of arguments to convince other members of Congress that his law would withstand the scrutiny of the Supreme Court. He proclaimed that the courts had affirmed that the transit of individuals from state to state indeed constituted commerce, a principle all agreed upon.

Mann noted that Congress had already passed federal morality legislation based on the power of the Commerce Clause. He pointed to the federal ban on lotteries that had also been justified via the Commerce Clause and upheld by the Supreme Court. The 1890s had witnessed a national campaign against lotteries, especially the Louisiana State Lottery Company, which sold tickets nationwide and delivered prizes through the nation's mail system. Christian activists opposed the lottery because it promoted gambling and the idea that wealth could be won rather than earned through one's own labor. Consequently, Southern Methodists aligned with Southern Baptists, Presbyterians, Episcopalians, and the small Jewish community to form the Anti-Lottery League, which quickly built relationships with Northern social purity activists. In the lottery campaign, Southern support for a "single national standard of morality" could be seen despite some dissenting Southern voices expressing suspicion about empowering the federal government at the expense of the states' sovereignty.[32] This same coalition of Southern moralists who willingly turned to the federal government for aid in policing personal behavior in playing the lottery argued for the passage of Mann's anti–white slavery law. The lottery cases formed an important precedent for Mann's law because the interstate transportation in both instances was incidental to the object that Congress pursued by passing federal legislation. In the case of the lottery, the piece of paper that crossed state lines had no inherent moral value; it was not in itself rotten. It only gained its injurious nature because of how it was connected to gambling. Mann saw a direct parallel to his proposed law: "It is true the act of prostitution is not committed in connection with the interstate transportation nor was the drawing in connection with the lottery a part of interstate commerce."[33] Yet the Supreme Court in 1903 upheld the lottery law, declaring: "As a State may, for the purpose of guarding the morals of its own people, forbid all sales of lottery tickets within its limits, so Congress, for the purpose of guarding the people of the United States against the 'widespread pestilence of lotteries' . . . may prohibit the carrying of lottery tickets from one State to another."[34] The federal anti-lottery law was the first time that Congress used the Interstate Commerce Clause to police morality, and the Supreme Court's support of the law signaled to Mann that the his anti–white slavery law could also withstand judicial review.

Mann firmly believed that Congress had the authority to legislate against white slavery because no other legislative body could really combat the reach of the trade. In his view, white slavers traversed boundaries by establishing both international and national trafficking networks, the broad scope of which required congressional intervention. He objected to those who worried that passing a national anti–white slavery law would infringe on states' police powers by contending, "The simple test [as to the constitutionality of a law] . . . is whether or not the State, in the exercise of its police power, could have prohibited the things at which the act is aimed."[35] State anti–white slavery laws could not reach white slavers once they crossed out of a state's jurisdiction. Mann argued that his anti–white slavery law was intended not to replace states' power to police immorality within their own borders, but to supplement existing laws while "comprehensively and effectively" targeting procurers and panderers to keep them "from compelling thousands of women and girls against their will and desire to enter and continue in a life of prostitution."[36] Mann contended that his law addressed the international aspects of the trade in women by requiring brothel owners and managers to report the presence of any foreign-born prostitutes to the Immigration Bureau. This part of his proposed law drew on the authority of the president's treaty-making powers rather than the Commerce Clause and explicitly called upon the 1904 international agreement that Braun and the Immigration Bureau had found so useless. Mann saw potential in the agreement and invoked the treaty-making powers and the international agreement as a way to dodge the legacy of the *Keller* decision, while also replacing the section of the 1907 Immigration Act that the Supreme Court had struck down.[37]

Mann's anti–white slavery bill targeted traffickers by capturing them at the moment of trafficking—in passage—and in doing so it differed significantly from the existing Immigration Law because it did not seek to criminalize or punish the female white slave. Mann's law offered white slaves salvation rather than deportation. But, conceptions of what constituted a white slave varied widely. Mann offered a very broad definition, coupled with an exclusive racial conception, of white slavery. He claimed that "careful investigation" into why the vast majority of prostitutes had entered sex work revealed that most had entered the profession for the profit of "some men who are in the business" of profiting from women's sexual labor. "The term 'white slave,'" he declared, "includes only those women and girls who are literally slaves— those women who are owned and held as property and chattels—whose lives are lives of involuntary servitude."[38] This conception of white slavery seemed to suggest that only the most extreme cases of sexual slavery would be touched by the law; cases that could be characterized as maximum coercion.[39] After examining the testimony of thousands of prostitutes interviewed about why they entered sex work, cases with maximum coercion accounted for less than 10 percent of the population of prostitutes during the Progressive Era.[40] Thus, Mann's formulation of white slavery seems rather narrow, until one reads his secondary definition of what the term *white slave* includes: "those who practice prostitution as a result of the activities of the procurer, and who, for a considerable period at least, continue to lead their degraded lives because of the power exercised over them by their owners." Here he broadened the umbrella of *white slave* to cover almost all women who worked in America's red-light districts, most of whom participated in complicated debt relationships with their pimps and madams who thereby exercised power over them. By including any sex worker who entered the profession at the suggestion of another and who might owe a debt, Mann included most of America's brothel-based sex workers. He then racially restricted his broad understanding of white slavery by summarizing: "In short, the white-slave trade may be said to be the business of securing *white* women and girls and selling them outright, or of exploiting them for immoral purposes."[41] His racialized conception of sex trafficking is remarkable because it ignored the well-documented trade in Asian women like the Japanese picture brides Marcus Braun fretted over, and it was noticeably silent on the sexual exploitation of African American women and girls.[42] For Mann, white slavery victims constituted a "whites only" class.

White slavery became one of those public concerns that was easy for public officials to oppose. After all, who would want to be seen as supporting white slavery? Indeed, while representatives debated Mann's anti–white slavery bill in the House, several opponents of the law suggested that congressmen flocked to signal their support for the law because of its political popularity rather than any entrenched interest in fighting sex trafficking or prostitution. A wide variety of progressive reformers—from suffragists to social hygienists eagerly supported the law, sending in thousands of letters to Congress.[43] Organizations leading and allied with the anti–white slavery movement showed their support in force. These included the Women's Christian Temperance Union, the National Council of Jewish Women, the Jewish Society of B'nai B'rith, the American Purity Alliance, the National Florence Crittenden Mission, the National Federation of Women's Clubs, the American Societies of Social Hygiene, the Young Women's Christian Association, and the National Vigilance Association, as well as numerous other civic and religious organizations. With ongoing agitation by reformers, the *New York Times* reported that the passage of the bill by Congress was "pretty much admitted."[44] Yet vigorous debate about the constitutionality of the measure still erupted on the floor of the House.

The primary opposition to Mann's White Slave Traffic Act centered on the arguments that it exceeded the powers of Congress, centralized federal authority, and infringed on the states' right to police their own populations. Not surprisingly, the voices asserting these points the loudest were Southern Democrats who repeated familiar states'-rights arguments. William N. Richardson (D-AL) declared: "I am just as much in favor as any gentleman on the floor of this House to upholding any theory, policy, or principle of morals, but I am not willing to see the rights of the State in so important a matter as the police rights of the State invaded by the Federal Government under the pretense of aiding and improving morality."[45] The ideas that the White Slave Traffic Act was a charade, enacted to encroach upon states' rights and a fraud as dangerous as white slavery itself were repeated frequently during the debates. Charles Bartlett (D-AL) and William C. Adamson (D-GA) joined Richardson in writing the "Views of the Minority" in which they insisted that the proposed law was "drastic" and its results would be "revolutionary."[46] Adamson further maintained that not only should the federal government not police white slavery, but also that it could not because it lacked the basic bureaucratic infrastructure. "As a member of the Federal Government," he stated, "I protest against the reckless injustice of piling up work here impossible for this Government to perform, never intended for it to perform, and which it is never called upon to perform except through ignorance or improper motive."[47] He suggested that the legal reasoning edifice that Mann used to construct the constitutionality of the White Slave Traffic Act by way of the Commerce Clause—the lottery cases—did not relate to the trafficking of women at all. He argued that "in order to parallel the case of the lottery ticket, [they must show] the horrible falsehood that women are creatures per se vile and immoral, designed and intended in nature for no other than immoral purposes."[48] This objection suggested that Mann's bill reduced women to objects, a complaint shared by Edwin Yates Webb (D-NC) who recognized that the laws governing interstate commerce "all apply to chattels, something that has no volition in the transaction at all."[49]

In addition to the improper use of the Commerce Clause and co-opting states' rights to police morality within their borders, the opponents of the White Slave Traffic Act raised concerns about the inherent vagueness of the law that required purposes to be discerned. Adamson noted that with the new legislation, a man could be convicted for purchasing a railroad ticket for a woman unless the purpose of the act was proven, and the "only way you can prove the purpose is to follow the woman and prove the prostitution."[50] That being the case, why not just defer to state-level prostitution laws? But Edgar D. Crumpacker (D-IN) pondered if Congress had the right to police morality at all when he asked, "The question is upon the subjective purpose she might have, innocent though she may be. Is that sufficient to justify Congress in excluding her from the right to interstate transport? . . . So that the subjective purpose of the bill would be that, if the female undertook to go to another State, and at the end of her journey enters a house of ill fame, you make her a criminal, although she has never engaged in the practice before."[51] Gordon J. Russell (D-TX), a supporter of the White Slave Traffic Act, assured Crumpacker that the law would not criminalize women, but instead would target only pimps, panderers, and procurers. But his assurances that women would not be punished bothered some opponents who again raised the question of volition. William N. Richardson pointed out the gendered assumptions of innocence and guilt embedded in the Mann Act when he observed, "Yet you punish the man who aids the woman. You punish him for aiding a crime that you do not punish her for committing."[52] Webb echoed this point, noting that if the purpose of the law is to break up the trafficking of prostitutes, then the law should be amended to ensure that female sex workers "come under the condemnation of the law as well."[53] Opponents to the Mann Act, most of whom were Southerners, found themselves arguing that Congress needed to respect the women's agency and participation in the vice economy and that the Mann Act rendered them figuratively innocent in inappropriate ways. They rejected the economic rationality that explained prostitution and sex trafficking asserted by the Dillingham Commission's report on trafficking and shared by Mann, and instead insisted that prostitution fit into the realm of morality. Then, as a crime of morality, it should be firmly in the states' purview, and states should exercise their right to punish women who chose to step down from the pedestal and into the muck.

The broad scope of the law, which outlawed the crossing of state lines for the purpose of prostitution, debauchery, or any other immoral purpose, worried some members of Congress because character would emerge as a key feature in determining morality and immorality. Adamson argued, "The only professed and possible purpose of this legislation is to purify interstate commerce, making character the test. Of course, carried to the last analysis, that proposition would endeavor to exclude all vile and impure people from the use of interstate facilities for commerce. Then there would be a wide field of different opinion as to who was vile and impure and what practices constituted immorality."[54] The question of how to determine immorality prompted Richardson to ask: "Immoral purpose? There are a great many good and benevolent people in this country that think that horse racing is immoral and that chicken fighting is immoral. There are a great many people that believe that. How are you going to define immoral purposes under this bill? They are vague and indefinite. There is nothing tangible in such a declaration."[55] Would the law be intended to break up professional interstate prostitution networks or could it be applied to other cases of immorality like seduction and adultery? Questions about how far the "any other immoral purpose" clause stretched lingered.

Texas Democrat Gordon J. Russell dismissed the points put forth by opponents to white slave legislation calling their arguments "'the visions of the minority,' because they see visions of state autonomy destroyed, of state rights roughly ridden over, a consolidation of government, and the police powers of the States absolutely set at naught."[56] Southern states'-rights advocates faced a challenge in articulating their opposition to the Mann Act because they ran

head-on against the other great pillar of Southern political rhetoric—
protecting white womanhood.[57] Russell insisted that states'-rights arguments
be set aside because pure *white* womanhood needed congressional protection. Russell got to the heart of the matter when he read an article written by
Georgia populist and well-known white supremacist Tom Watson. In the
excerpt, Watson wrote, "Some weeks ago a negro who signed himself 'John
Frankling' wrote me from Tifton, Ga, a letter in which he stated that he had
a white wife whom he had bought out of a group of twenty-five that were offered for sale in Chicago, and that she was the third white 'wife' that he had
purchased. Upon making inquiry of prominent men in Chicago, I was told
that there was reason to believe that the negro has told the truth."[58] This
strange and suspect story struck at the core of many Southern Democrats'
arguments against the bill. Surely, protecting white women from black men,
and the South from miscegenation, was worth setting aside some of the
states'-rights doctrine. Russell's use of Watson's article demonstrates that for
the rising Jim Crow South Chicago's sinfulness and reputation as a place of
unruly race relations had great discursive importance. Russell went on to proclaim to great applause that "no nation can rise higher than the estimate
which it places upon the virtue and purity of its womanhood." He challenged
Congress to act with courage reminding them that "more than forty years
ago this country was drenched in fraternal blood and offered up the lives of
nearly a million of the very pick and flower of its citizenship in the struggle
to abolish the slavery of the black man. In God's name, can we do less now
than pass this bill, which will be a step toward abolishing the slavery of
white women?"[59] Again, we see the rhetorical linking of African American
chattel slavery to argue for the protection of some "blue-eyed girl."[60] This
protection seemed so pressing that the House passed the bill by voice vote
on January 26, 1910.

Mann's bill, now in the hands of the Senate, first went to the Senate Committee on Interstate and Foreign Commerce, then to the Committee on Immigration. The only opposition to the bill emerged from the Immigration
Committee, which, though in favor of the White Slave Traffic Act, registered
two concerns. The committee worried that grounding the law in the purposes
of the person who facilitates transportation formed a "very flimsy basis upon
which to rest a criminal statute." The minority on the committee also worried
that in casting such a wide net with the "any other immoral purpose" clause

the law did not recognize "that there are degrees in chastity and morality."[61] Even with these reservations, the minority on the committee noted that the white slave traffic was of paramount legislative importance, and they suggested the Senate should act accordingly.[62] After clearing these committees relatively unscathed, it was presented to the floor of the Senate on June 25, 1910 by Senator Henry Cabot Lodge (R-MA) on behalf of Senator William Paul Dillingham (R-VT), where the bill passed by voice vote the same day with minimal debate. President Taft briskly signed the bill into law the very same day.

While Mann and his allies had proposed the White Slave Traffic Act, defended it in the House, and kept a close watch over its progress through the Senate, the Immigration Bureau was busy on another front. Building on the momentum generated by the Dillingham Commission's report, it argued throughout January 1910 that any non-naturalized prostitute should be deportable regardless of how long she had been in the country. Congress granted the bureau's wish when on March 26, 1910, it amended the immigration law and dispensed with the three-year limitation. Now, immigration inspectors no longer had to quibble with prostitutes about entry dates. Almost immediately the new power the bureau had against prostitutes of foreign birth showed results. Taken together, the Immigration Act of March 26, 1910, and the Mann Act ensured that the country's external and internal borders were protected against the threat of white slavery. Now, any sex trafficker crossing colonial, territorial, state, or national boundaries with his or her "wares" faced significant legal obstacles.[63] This was a full-fledged national war on visible prostitution, and the White Slave Traffic Act formed the federal front of that war—a front that was manned by the special agents of the young Bureau of Investigation.

The Bureau of Investigation was born out of a fight between President Theodore Roosevelt and Capitol Hill. At the turn of the century, the Department of Justice relied on the Secret Service to conduct its investigations because an 1892 federal law had banned the Department of Justice's use of private detective agencies like the Pinkerton Detective Agency. Congress launched an investigation into the Secret Service to show that the executive branch had overstepped its bounds when, in 1904, the Department of Justice, borrowing Secret Service investigators, oversaw an investigation of a western land fraud case that threw suspicion on a U.S. senator. Angry about the investigation of one of their own, Roosevelt's foes on Capitol Hill created

significant political leverage out of their investigation into his use of the Secret Service, which, they maintained, showed his intent to establish an illegal "spy system." The investigation into the presidential use of the Secret
Service revealed two surprising and forgotten facts. The Secret Service itself
had been created by the Treasury Department without congressional authorization. And, ever since it was founded in 1870, the Department of Justice had always had the right to develop its own detective force; it merely
needed to account for it in its annual appropriations. Nonetheless, Congress
passed a law prohibiting the Treasury Department from loaning the Secret
Service to any other federal department, thus leaving the Department of
Justice with no means to investigate violations of federal laws.[64]

Irritated with Congress's presumption and invigorated by the revelation
that a simple executive order would allow the Department of Justice to have
its own detective force, Roosevelt and Attorney General Charles J. Bonaparte
immediately created the Bureau of Investigation, and set about hiring former Secret Service and Immigration Bureau agents under the leadership of
Chief Examiner Stanley W. Finch. By July 1, 1908, thirty-five investigators,
or special agents, reported to the Department of Justice. On July 26, 1908,
Bonaparte instructed that all investigations, except naturalization and bank
examinations, be designated to Finch. The new agency was purely investigative, meaning its special agents had no authority to arrest alleged criminals or carry weapons. A conflict between the executive and congressional
branches of government, in which the legislative branch sought to limit executive power, resulted in a tremendous expansion of federal power in the
body of the Bureau of Investigation.[65]

In the two years prior to the passage of the White Slave Traffic Act, the
Bureau investigated violations of antitrust laws, the bucket-shop (phony
stock brokerages) law, national banking laws, peonage laws, and impersonation of government officials. Additionally, agents investigated offences for
which there was no other designated investigative agency, such as customs
fraud, internal revenue fraud, "Chinese" smuggling, land fraud, and some
immigration cases. The bureau's work on immigration cases had already
brought white slavery to its attention. When President Taft signed the Mann
Act, Bureau agents were several months into an investigation of a network of
French procurers of prostitutes that spanned from Canada to Chicago to
New Orleans.[66]

Although white slavery was on the Bureau's radar, the ambiguities surrounding the new law and the competing and contradictory definitions of white slavery did not disappear. In the initial years of enforcement, the young agency and the U.S. Attorneys in the Department of Justice struggled to develop their own understanding of white slavery, the scope of the new law, and the implications of policing trafficking. The unexpected ramifications of enforcing the White Slave Traffic Act can be seen when the following two 1911 cases from Tampa, Florida, are set side-by-side. Both of these cases echo the narratives of the sexual danger posed by women's public employment put forth in the media.

In early October 1911, the U.S. Attorney in Tampa requested that the Bureau launch an investigation into an alleged violation of the Mann Act and in doing so handed the Department of Justice what seemed to be the perfect case of white slavery because it shared many of the features that characterized white slavery stories in newspapers and magazine exposés. The September 6 edition of the *Atlanta Journal* included an employment advertisement listing a job opening for "bright girls between 16 and 22 years of age."[67] The employment agency offering the jobs claimed it was looking for ten chorus girls to work at the Imperial Theater in Tampa, a theater that was reputed to be like an Atlanta theater, well known for serving non-alcoholic beverages to its middle-class clientele—in other words, a respectable theater.[68] Three women went to the employment bureau and signed an employee contract that specified that they would be required to live at the theater and that their behavior would be closely monitored by management. When seventeen-year-old Agnes Couch arrived at the Imperial Theater—tired, nervous and alone—she grew dismayed at the general conditions of filth. The other two women were nowhere in sight, and not knowing anybody in Tampa she felt she had no choice but to stay.

That night the owner and operator of the Imperial, Louis Athanasaw, instructed Agnes in the duties of her new job. He dressed her in a costume that was "a very brief affair, very short and very low neck" and told her that she needed to sell beer and wine to the men in the theater's boxes by flirting with the customers. He complimented her saying that she was very "good looking" and that "He wanted me to be his girl; to talk to the boys and make a hit, and get all the money I could out of them."[69] The customers with whom Agnes was instructed to flirt were boisterous and "indecent," and several of the men "insisted on her drinking" beer. She later said that they "put their arms around her and put their hands on her" and would "blow some kind of little rubber things in the face of the girls."[70] Overwhelmed by such vulgar teasing, Agnes began to cry. At this point, Arthur Schleman, one of the young men visiting the box Agnes worked, suspected that Agnes was different from the other young women, and he insisted on escorting her out of the theater. As the couple tried to leave, Louis stopped them and told Agnes she had to stay and to get back to work. Arthur went to the police who returned and secured Agnes's freedom and placed her in the hands of the matron of Tampa's Women's Hospital and Home.

The Bureau investigation quickly revealed that the Imperial Theater was a well-known brothel or, as the police chief called it, "nothing but a whore house."[71] Louis Athanasaw technically hired the girls who worked at the theater to sell drinks, and they received a cut of the liquor profits, like the dance halls of Chicago. However, if a girl sold a bottle of wine or champagne to a customer, then the theater's management allowed her to take that customer into her own room, presumably to engage in any type of arrangement with the customer that she negotiated.[72]

This case seemed to confirm several tropes of the white slavery narrative asserted by the journalists, moral reformers, and activists who had lobbied for the Mann Act. It featured elements of the dangers posed to dutiful daughters leaving home to enter the labor market, the tactics of deceitful employment agencies who cared only for profit, the attempt to use fraud and force to sexually compromise an innocent girl, a gallant young man who rescued the white slave, and a shameless villain who preyed on a young girl's naïveté while seeking to profit from her sexuality. To demonstrate the depravity of the Imperial Theater, the prosecuting attorney took the jury on a surprise visit to the theater during the trial so that each member could personally witness its filth and moral decay. The jury had no difficulties returning a verdict of guilty after only fifteen minutes of deliberation, and the judge sentenced Louis Athanasaw and his business partner to two and half years in a federal penitentiary for violating the Mann Act.[73]

Although the Athanasaw case seemed to confirm the suspicions of anti–white slavery activists that innocence needed to be protected and the Mann Act was the tool to provide that protection, the case was actually atypical precisely because it did fit the public narrative so well. Slightly more typical was the case of Pearl Snyder that Bureau agents pursued while they investigated the Athanasaw case. Pearl, a twenty-year-old girl from Harned, Kentucky, visited Louisville to look for work. When trying to get a job at a movie theater, the manager told her that while there were no jobs available that she knew of in Kentucky, she did have a friend who ran a boarding home in Tampa who was hiring. The manager offered to pay the cost of Pearl's train ticket south because it would help out her friend. Pearl eagerly accepted the offer. Late at night she arrived at the address she had been given and was immediately taken in by Ethel Evans and Marian Lawrence, the two women who owned and operated the house. After getting settled in a room, Ethel invited Pearl down to the parlor, and it was there that Pearl began to suspect that she might be in a brothel. According to her statement to the Bureau, she told Ethel that she intended to leave the next morning. Ethel consoled her and offered her a drink that would "make her feel better." According to Pearl, after drinking the beverage she began to feel dizzy, and she "started for her room, and before she got there she seemed to lose control of herself and did not know what was going on." Ethel led Pearl to a room where she insisted that Pearl have sexual intercourse with a man. When Pearl refused, Ethel stripped her of her clothing, "forced her on the bed and held her while the man had intercourse with her."[74]

For Pearl, this first night of rape would be the beginning of several weeks of terror. The following night Ethel again drugged Pearl and arranged for her rape, and this continued nightly until Pearl had "become so torn and so swollen and weak and sick that she thought she could not live and they [Ethel and Marian] sent for a doctor for her."[75] The doctor who examined Pearl believed her to be a common prostitute, perhaps a little "green," who did not know how properly to take care of her vaginal health. A week later, the morning of the day after the nurse stopped coming to the brothel because Pearl was deemed healthy enough, Pearl woke up early and snuck out of the house. Stumbling down the street, dressed only in her undershirt, and clinging to fences "to keep from falling" she kept walking until she ran into a police officer who immediately took her to the Women's Hospital and Home where she shared a room with Agnes Couch, with whom she became close friends.[76]

The case of Pearl Snyder posed more problems for Bureau investigators as well as for the U.S. Attorney who would bring the case to trial—the very same attorney (and Bureau special agent and judge) who investigated and prosecuted the Athansaw case. The brothel run by Marian Lawrence and Ethel Evans was one of Tampa's more high-class brothels, which meant that it had considerable connections to the local power structure. The fact that the two defendants in this case were women concerned the judge who wondered about the ramifications of sending women to serve time in a penitentiary not designed for female prisoners. Judge James W. Locke noted that before he sentenced any female defendants, "he desired to learn from the [Justice] Department what penitentiary was designated for the women prisoners."[77] Interviews with Ethel Evans quickly revealed that the defendants planned to argue that Pearl had been fully aware that the house was a brothel and that she had previous experience as a prostitute in Kentucky, as proven by the fact that she was infected by a sexually transmitted disease. In her defense, Pearl argued she had been infected during the numerous sexual assaults she suffered at the hands of the defendants.[78] This meant that the Bureau would need to spend considerable resources proving the sexual innocence, or conversely the sexual promiscuity, of a twenty-year-old girl several states away. Finally, to take the case to trial would require Pearl to testify about her repeated sexual assaults, something she was understandably reluctant to do while suffering, as she most certainly must have been, after the trauma of her ordeal.[79] In the end, the U.S. Attorney dropped the case against Ethel Evans, and Marian Lawrence pleaded guilty rather than face trial. Judge Locke fined Lawrence $500 for violation of the Mann Act and, due to her poor health, suspended any prison sentence after she promised to leave Tampa.[80] Courts found the woman who had initially provided Pearl with the train ticket in Louisville guilty of violating the Mann Act, and she was similarly fined $200 and did not serve any time in prison.[81]

Setting the cases of Agnes Couch and Pearl Snyder side-by-side suggests a few characteristics of early enforcement of the Mann Act as the Bureau attempted to develop its own understanding of white slavery and the purpose and intent of the new law. First, when Congress passed the Mann Act on June 25, 1910, it made it illegal to take a woman or girl over state lines "for the purpose of prostitution or debauchery, or for any other immoral purpose," but the scope of the law remained unclear to the Department of Justice and the Bureau. Was the law intended to protect chastity as some congressmen had claimed, or was it intended to interrupt the profitability of vice within the United States? Defense attorneys for Louis Athanasaw wondered, "how can a purpose be illegal?" And how can intent be proven?[82]

In the face of such broad and important judicial ramifications, the Bureau struggled to maintain an objective, yet practical, view of its role in enforcement, and it favored cases that had demonstrable vice elements as well as cases with similarly demonstrable elements of innocence (and youth) among the victims.[83] Thus, the case of Agnes Couch was always more attractive than the case of Pearl Snyder, because it was easier for the Bureau to point to Agnes's continuing and rescued innocence—virginity—than it was to confirm Pearl's innocence prior to her rape or to contend with the possibility that Pearl had willingly entered a brothel. Virginity (and stolen or lost virginity) emerged as an important marker of proper victimhood.

The Bureau was unprepared, as was the entire Department of Justice, for the gendered implications of enforcing the White Slave Traffic Act. Policing prostitution meant that many of the owners and managers of houses of prostitution came under the gaze of the Bureau. The Dillingham Commission and the Immigration Bureau's reports had almost always described white slavers as male, but many of the people who owned property in vice districts and encouraged prostitutes to move from state to state, brothel to brothel, were women like Ethel Evans and Marian Lawrence. Although Congressman Russell had assured other congressmen and the American public that the law would not target women but would target "the person who furnishes transportation to a woman or girl," a category assumed to be filled largely with men, Bureau investigations uncovered women acting as brothel managers, talent scouts, sex work recruiters, and so on. It was not an aberration that the first person indicted under the newly passed Mann Act was brothel-owner Nettie Jenkins, who was charged with inducing five sex workers in Chicago to come and work at her house in Houghton, Michigan. Indeed, the passage of the Mann Act precipitated a minor crisis at the Bureau of Prisons, which did not have facilities to house the women who were being sentenced to the federal penitentiary system due to Mann Act convictions.[84] For the first time, the U.S. federal government was investigating and convicting a notable number of women.

The cases of Agnes Couch and Pearl Snyder reinforced the notion that the White Slave Traffic Act protected *white* women and girls from exploitation. The rhetoric surrounding white slavery focused on the threat strange men posed to white native-born girls.[85] The very title of the act seemed to pre-clude it from protecting women of color. As one African American newspa-per declared, "If under the term 'White Slave Traffic' the same protection is given to women of other races, then the law is a blessing, if not, then it is bias."[86] Yet, women of color rarely benefited from the protection of the act. The Bureau's enforcement of the Mann Act revealed that the racialized rhet-oric surrounding white slavery shaped the implementation of the act. Bu-reau agents tended to pursue only cases with white victims during the early years of enforcement. The *Cleveland Gazette,* an African American newspa-per, proudly reported in 1912 that they were "pleased" to announce that the Mann Act was used to convict a man who had trafficked a black woman to Cleveland from Detroit via Canada.[87] But cases like this were remarkably rare, and the Bureau probably only pursued this case due to the interna-tional border involved. Most Bureau agents applied the White Slave Traffic Act to protect white women only. In spite of the assumption that foreign men most often trafficked white women, a common feature in the white slavery narrative, a 1917 study of 229 men serving time for violating the Mann Act in federal prisons in Atlanta and Leavenworth revealed that 72 percent of the men were native-born whites.[88]

◆ ◆ ◆

Stories of the sexual dangers cities posed to immigrant young women who could be vulnerable to white slavers quickly gave way in 1909 to a growing concern over the fate of native-born, white women who were migrating to the cities in large numbers. Chicago's newspapers regularly announced that the city was laden with traps to lure and ensnare young women into the city's brothels and sexual marketplaces. As journalists, prosecuting attorneys, and activists spread awareness of this reality of sexual exploitation, some like Clifford Roe and Edwin Sims turned towards legislative solutions, like the White Slave Traffic Act of 1910 to combat sex trafficking. Although con-gressional opposition to the Mann Act was limited to Southern states'-rights advocates, the questions they raised about the vagueness of the law, espe-cially the "any other immoral purposes" clause, and the dangers of policing such a slippery and subjective concept like morality would linger, permeat-ing enforcement of this new national morals statute.

With the passage of the White Slave Traffic Act in 1910, the Department of Justice took over as the main federal agency pursuing white slavery within the United States. To be sure, the Immigration Bureau in the Department of Labor and Commerce continued to police prostitutes at the country's borders and among its immigrant population, but it often did so in cooperation with the Department of Justice. Within the Department of Justice, investigation into alleged violations of the White Slave Traffic Act fell to the barely two-year-old Bureau of Investigation.

Ambiguous and competing understandings of *white slavery* persisted in spite of the passage of the Mann Act, as the Bureau quickly learned. This uncertainty was underscored by perplexing and persistent questions about the constitutionality of the law. Into this conflicted landscape charged the Bureau.

4

Creating a Moral Quarantine

As early as April 1911, William H. Armbrecht, an enthusiastic U.S. Attorney in Mobile, Alabama, decided against waiting for violations of the White Slave Traffic Act to be reported to him and instead chose to launch an investigation into how prostitutes came to his city. He asked Bureau of Investigation Special Agent James L. Bruff and the postmaster to order all letter carriers to confirm the residents in each house in the red-light district, thereby composing a registry of the city's prostitutes. Then, he issued subpoenas for the sixty to seventy residents of the district to appear before a grand jury. Even with no indictments, probably because the vast majority of prostitutes in Mobile were from Alabama or came to Mobile of their own choice, Armbrecht judged the experiment a success. "[S]till the investigation had been of great value," he proclaimed, "in that it had frightened the proprietors and inmates of local sporting houses and had increased their respect for the federal courts to such an extent that they would probably be careful not to violate the law in the future."[1] This legal-judicial surveillance of Mobile's red-light district formed the genesis of the Bureau's initial scheme to enforce the White Slave Traffic Act. The Mann Act formed a powerful weapon for the Department of Justice's fight against white slavery, although exactly how to wield such a weapon remained open to considerable debate within the Bureau of Investigation and the Department of Justice, among anti–white slavery activists, and between private citizens.

When Congress handed the Bureau of Investigation the mandate to enforce the 1910 White Slave Traffic Act it also implicitly tasked the agency with puzzling out the mystery of what exactly constituted white slavery. Some activists, like Jane Addams, allowed for economic coercion, whereas others, like Clifford Roe, used more traditional narratives of deceit, kidnapping, and imprisonment. Activists and journalists frequently argued about the scope of the "white slavery" problem. Antiprostitution reformers rarely agreed on a common definition of white slave, while many law enforcement officials suggested that white slavery was a much-hyped myth. The Immigration Bureau took a decidedly conservative perspective when it argued that white slavery referred to the problem of foreign-born prostitution. Meanwhile, Congress envisioned white slaves to be the deceived, native-born, white daughters of America who would have otherwise been the mothers of productive citizens. With so many competing understandings circulating, the Bureau faced the challenge of deciding how to enforce the White Slave Traffic Act, and in doing so it would construct a logic of enforcement that stemmed from its conception of the congressional intent within the law. At issue was whether Congress intended the law to protect innocence or to police deviance.

The Bureau internally debated about the scope of the law, who constituted a white slave, and the best course of enforcement; yet this process did not happen in a vacuum. As the Bureau constructed the category of the white slave, it responded to the institutional legacy it shared with the Immigration Bureau, while also fending off demands for an expansive definition of white slavery proposed by private citizens. From 1910 to 1917, this process of defining occurred within an atmosphere of doubt concerning the constitutionality of the White Slave Traffic Act, doubts that had first been proposed by congressional opponents of the law. Operating under a cloud of uncertainty, the Bureau initially offered a narrow reading of the law, limiting its investigations to the world of commercial vice, yet throughout the period citizens would demand that the "any other immoral purposes" clause of the law empowered the Bureau to police general immorality. The tensions between these competing understandings of white slavery and the potential offered in the White Slave Traffic Act for enforcement of the federal law, would initiate the dramatic expansion of the Bureau's presence throughout the United States.

White slave investigations like the ones into the activities of Louis Athanasaw, Ethel Evans, and Marian Lawrence required more investigative man hours than the Bureau could easily provide with its relatively small force of detectives. As of the day Congress passed the Mann Act the Bureau had only sixty-one active agents. Yet, building individual white slave cases entailed countless hours spent confirming prostitutes' precise travel arrangements, as well as interviewing often hostile witnesses. Bureau Chief Stanley W. Finch believed that preventing violations by taking a census of brothels and teaching madams about the nuances of the new law would be a more efficient use of the Bureau's limited resources. He was convinced that a very large number of men were engaged "in the business of procuring women and girls for houses of ill-fame, the number amounting to the thousands, in all parts of the country," and that such numbers made it "necessary to adopt a special system."[2] Enumerating, interviewing, and educating brothel-based prostitutes and their madams emerged as key features of the Bureau's White Slave Division as it moved from investigating alleged violations of the Mann Act to attempting to prevent any future violations. The preventative approach focused on controlling the movement of morally suspicious women, while looking for those girls who could be reformed.

Stanley W. Finch, born July 20, 1873 in Ellenville, New York, joined the Department of Justice in 1892 as a librarian. Taking night classes at National University Law School, he earned his law degree in three years, and he quickly began working as a chief examiner for the department. In this capacity, he travelled the country as he promoted systemization of procedures and policies throughout the federal court system while also cracking down on graft and fraud.[3] Described as "a young man, incisive, alert, effective," at the age of thirty-five Finch was tapped by Attorney General Charles J. Bonaparte to lead the newly minted Bureau of Investigation.[4] In April 1912 he stepped down as Chief of the Bureau of Investigation to take a position as Special Commissioner for the Suppression of the White Slave Traffic within the Bureau. Although this move might appear to have been a demotion, the new job was accompanied by a significant pay raise to $6,000 a year. As head of the White Slave Division, Finch would develop his own particular understanding of white slavery, which at times clashed with the conception of white slavery held by the special agents who worked under him.

From the purity reformist circles of the anti–white slavery movement, Finch adopted the belief that prostitution resulted from men's greed and women's vulnerability. He rejected the idea that women's lack of economic opportunities or moral failings led them into sex work. Rather he proclaimed that the cause of women's entry into brothels was "ninety percent the fault of the man."[5] He argued that dissolute men seduced young girls, promised marriage, and actually entered marriages to gain emotional control over young women.[6] He suggested that these men targeted younger girls because they could earn as much as twenty-five dollars from a brothel for bringing in a "broiler," a girl between the ages of thirteen and sixteen, and slightly less for a "chicken," a girl between sixteen and eighteen. After installing her in the brothel, the pimp retained access to half her earnings, while the brothel operator profited from the other half.[7] For Finch, this system of debt bondage was not only akin to slavery, it was slavery. "It will perhaps be somewhat surprising to learn," he growled in frustration to purity audiences, "that there is no federal law which makes it a crime for one person to hold another in slavery or involuntary servitude, unless such person has been, in the first instance, kidnapped or carried away or bought or sold."[8] He even suggested that the Mann Act should have been grounded in the authority of the Thirteenth Amendment that outlawed race-based chattel slavery because the "white slave traffic is a species of involuntary servitude."[9] Suspecting that conservatively there were over 250,000 brothel-based prostitutes in the United States, Finch looked for a way to target the men that profited from their sexual labor by going after procurers and traffickers, while also reaching sex workers through one-on-one contact and offering them opportunities for reform.[10]

Finch was rare, though not alone, among Progressive-Era reformers in his belief that young sex workers could be redeemed. Most juvenile justice reformers considered girls who had violated social rules of chastity to be permanently "morally tainted."[11] But in his conception of young prostitutes as innocent victims, Finch advocated a very gendered understanding of prostitution. He suggested that young women who had been properly shielded from sin were vulnerable to exploitation by greedy and deceitful men. He characterized the victims of white slavery as "honorable and virtuous" yet, "inclined to be somewhat careless" if left to their own devices. Due to their innocence, their ignorance, and their femaleness, young women were easy prey, or a "fertile field," for traffickers.[12] The question of how to target men while rehabilitating young women was up to Finch to formulate.

Faced with the overwhelming, if unclear, task of policing immorality within the United States, the Bureau's initial challenge was to overcome its limited resources. Attorney General George Wickersham reported that the Bureau ran out of funds allotted to investigate white slave cases in October

1911, causing the Bureau to shut down investigations several months before the end of its fiscal year. In response to this situation, Finch reached out to moral reform and social hygiene activists, asking them to pressure Congress to increase appropriations for white slave work. To support this publicity campaign, the Attorney General's office prepared a list of cases showing the success and necessity of the Bureau's white slave work to circulate among Congress. These cases, including the Athansaw case were far from typical; they consisted of cases that conformed to preconceived notions of white slavery that highlighted the dangers of female employment, Jewish vice rings, and foreign men. The moral reform magazine *Vigilance* published detailed accounts of these cases in its April 1912 issue as part of its attempt to raise awareness of the funding shortfall the Bureau faced. The campaign worked as letters poured into Congress and the Department of Justice, resulting in Congress allocating $50,000 more for the specific use of fighting white slavery (this amount was increased by an additional $200,000 in 1913).[13] With this money, Finch implemented his plan of prevention.

Finch began in Baltimore, Maryland, and Washington, DC, where in November and December 1911 he required every person living in the red light districts to fill out a form that gave his or her personal history. This command extended to maids, musicians, bartenders, and any other people peripherally employed in vice; however, female sex workers and madams bore the brunt of the census. If a woman moved from one brothel to another, the Bureau expected her to update her status. As the Baltimore and Washington registries moved forward, Finch established a separate division within the Bureau dedicated to the brothel census, with its own offices, staff, and records in Baltimore. It was while he was establishing the Baltimore office that he stepped down as Chief of the Bureau and took the position of Special Commissioner of the White Slave Division.[14]

Finch's eyes soon wandered beyond the red-light districts of Baltimore and Washington to the rest of the country. He launched a system where his Bureau agents established local white slave officers in 310 cities in 26 states, mostly east of the Mississippi. Finch's goal was to set up a local representative of the Bureau—deputized volunteers—in all towns that had a vice district and a population larger than five thousand people. The Bureau tasked these local white slave officers with coordinating with local police to maintain accurate addresses and census information for all of the prostitutes housed within brothels. Local white slave officers reported any violations of the White Slave Traffic Act to the head office in Baltimore, and a special agent would be dispatched to investigate. Finch hoped that with enough appropriations, he could establish as many as one thousand local white slave officers.[15]

The special agents selected middle-class, respectable, white men who had some standing within the community to be local white slave officers. Almost all of the officers were attorneys, since the Bureau gave preference to lawyers because their legal education, in the words of Finch, made them "best qualified to judge as to the evidence necessary to sustain prosecution for violation of the various laws involved by our work."[16] Most importantly, the Bureau intended the position of local white slave officer to be part-time, and any white slave officer had to have "other regular employment."[17] The Bureau did compensate the officers for their time and labor, offering up to twenty dollars a month. But it did not want local white slave officers who were motivated by monetary gain. The maximum annual amount a local officer could earn was $250 (about a tenth of what Bureau special agents earned annually). Finch wanted officers who were "in this work because they believe it is of benefit to the community and to humanity generally."[18] In establishing a local white slave officer corps, Finch mobilized a voluntary army of respectable, professional, white men in his fight against commercial vice.

Most of the volunteers were in the prime of their lives, married with young children at home, when the Bureau issued them their local white slave officer badge. They attended church and frequently were members of numerous fraternal and community organizations and involved in local politics. The separate records of the Bureau's White Slave Division appear to have been destroyed between 1917 and 1921. As a result, identifying who composed the white slave officer corps is especially challenging. From the Bureau records and the 1910 or 1920 census, forty-three local white slave officers who served from 1911 to 1913, and an additional fifty-eight local white slave officers who served in 1916 can be identified. Not surprisingly, all of the local white slave officers were white. Their average age was thirty-eight and a half years, and by 1916 the average age had dropped to just under thirty-five years old. The vast majority worked as lawyers or had a background in criminal justice. Linzy Otto Thompson was thirty years old in 1913 when the Bureau appointed him to be white slave officer in Lexington, Kentucky.

Born and educated on a farm, Thompson served as an itinerant high school teacher throughout the South for several years before he attended the University of Kentucky to earn his law degree. He started his law practice the same year he joined the White Slave Division. He solidified his connections to the community by joining the Independent Order of Odd Fellows and registering as a Democrat. Similarly, William Luxon Wallace was the privileged son of a prominent Richmond, Kentucky, family who sent him to Phelps Academy, a prep school in Massachusetts, and then on to Yale University's Law School. After graduating in 1911, twenty-two-year-old Wallace returned to Richmond to set up his law practice. Two years later he signed on to the White Slave Division. He, too, joined the Odd Fellows, although unlike Thompson, Wallace was a life-long Republican. He quit the White Slave Division to enlist in the military during World War I, and upon returning after the war he would serve in the Kentucky State Senate and several distinguished judgeships. While Thompson and Wallace came from different class backgrounds and political traditions, they shared the benefit of their racial privilege, their respectability through life-long dedication to public service, and the expectations of their shared legal profession. Most of the white slave officers were lawyers, and they were expected to be guided by their reason rather than their lustful desire or fantasy. As representatives of the Department of Justice, they embodied values of restraint, moderation, and order.[19]

The FBI's corps of local white slave officers represents a particular type of masculinity approved of and sustained by the state. Individual men's ability to embody the ideals of sexual restraint was intimately tied to notions of self-government in the Progressive Era. In the case of the local white slave officers, their respectable masculinity was a novel performance in that it embraced restraint in a place designed for and devoted to the performance of male sexual release. These men could enter such liminal and seductive spaces as brothels because they were cloaked in their respectability, shielded by their legal authority, and ultimately shored up by federal authority represented by their White Slavery Division badge.[20]

Occasionally, the Bureau had difficulty filling local positions. The nature of the work, with its emphasis on close contact with prostitutes, alienated the very type of respectable men the Bureau desired. In Tulsa, one young lawyer expressed interest in the position, but turned it down "on account of his wife's feelings in the matter."[21] In Muskogee, Oklahoma, the special agent charged with finding local white slave officers reported failure after failure, with one attorney echoing the others' thoughts that the "office did not appeal to him."[22] Men might have had a variety of reasons for rejecting the post, ranging from a lack of interest in the project, to concerns about damage to one's reputation, to simply being too busy with their own law practices, or even to supporting brothel-based prostitution. Maintaining the ideal of a respectable community-minded man combined with the tawdriness of spending time with police officers, counting prostitutes, and interviewing madams continued to create a paradox that the Bureau struggled to solve.

The Bureau's local white slavery officers were embedded within the communities they monitored, yet their jobs as representatives of the Bureau spread federal policing power throughout much of the country. When the Mann Act passed in 1910, the Bureau had sixty-one agents. By February 1913, the Bureau had well over three hundred representatives, including the local white slave officers, and was still growing.[23] These men were not employees of the state, but they did the work of the state. These deputized volunteers were "subnational bureaucratic actors" who nationalized the enforcement of the White Slave Traffic Act and the reach of the Bureau. In this case, by using a volunteer corps of deputized professional men, the Bureau (the state) infiltrated local communities and encouraged the policing of prostitutes and the enforcement of local and federal white slave laws. Although the operations of the local white slave officers was obscured by their being embedded within local contexts, their activities on behalf of the Bureau constituted an impressive expansion of (federal) state policing power.[24]

The basic task of local white slave officers was to register brothel-based prostitutes. When first visiting a brothel, a white slave officer like Wallace would meet with the madam and give her a printed copy of the White Slave Traffic Act, teaching her about what did and did not constitute a violation of the law. Then, he would ask for a list of inhabitants of the brothel and interview each prostitute in an attempt to ascertain her general background, any aliases she might have, how she had arrived in the specific brothel, and a general physical description of her for Bureau records. Upon leaving, he would distribute copies of the law and self-addressed envelopes and cards so that any change in address could be reported immediately to the Bureau. These cards read: "Dear Sir—I beg to inform you that _____ arrived in my house today from _____" or "Dear Sir—I beg to inform you that _____ left my house today bound for _____."[25]

Over the course of the twenty-month existence of the White Slave Division, local white slave officers entered into the registry 39,021 names. When the sociologist Howard B. Woolston examined the entries in 1917 he found a number of duplications and reduced the number of individual women listed in the Bureau's census to 31,689. He also discovered among these 31,689 women 90,000 changes of address were reported over the course of three years, demonstrating that prostitutes were, as Woolston termed it, "notoriously peripatetic," and, more importantly, that many prostitutes complied with Bureau orders to report changes in addresses.[26] The White Slave Division's ability, through the use of local white slave officers, to monitor over 30,000 prostitutes represented an impressive, if not chilling, achievement. This had much to do with technological advancements that benefited the development of the surveillance state: the typewriter, the telegram, and filing innovations like the Dewey decimal system.[27]

In the course of registering all the prostitutes in a given city, Bureau agents frequently encountered women whom they suspected of being in the country illegally. Because the Immigration Act of March 26, 1910, passed in tandem with the White Slave Traffic Act, forbade any non-naturalized woman of foreign birth from practicing prostitution within the country, this was a special concern for Bureau agents, many of whom had previously worked for the Immigration Bureau. Baltimore-based Special Agent John J. Grgurevich started his career with the federal government at the Immigration Bureau, and even as a white slave investigator he frequently served as a translator in immigration investigations. Similarly, Special Agent Frank L. Garbarino's first investigation into white slavery occurred in 1909 under the auspices of the Immigration Bureau's dragnet, and when he joined the Bureau in 1910, he brought with him the same investigative techniques.[28] The transfer of personnel from the Immigration Bureau to the Bureau of Investigation ensured that the Bureau and the Immigration Bureau would initially share, at the mid-administrative level, the conception of white slavery as primarily a problem of prostitution, even if this position was at odds with Finch's understanding of white slavery. The shared personnel also helped to facilitate close cooperation between the two agencies. When agents or local white slave officers interviewed women whom they suspected of being of foreign birth,

they quickly contacted the Immigration Bureau. When Special Agent Betjamin met Elizabeth Nichols, a Canadian, and Kitty Brown, a Russian in December 1911, he immediately reported them to the Immigration Bureau.[29]
Cities on the border fostered even closer cooperation between agents of the
Immigration Bureau and Bureau. In El Paso, a city that shared a reputation
for vice tourism with its Mexican sister-city Ciudad Juárez, the Immigration
Bureau agent and the Bureau agent passed tips and cases back and forth and
even toured brothels on both sides of the border together.[30]

The increased surveillance of red-light districts and brothels motivated
many brothel owners, concerned about their criminal liability, to purge non-
naturalized women from the ranks of their workers. Native-born sex workers were exempt from the threat of deportation. San Francisco bordello owner
Mike Mack told Special Agent Garbarino that brothel keepers had grown
"alarmed" by the Mann Act and any potential liability they faced by hiring
foreign-born women.[31] The close enumeration of brothel-based prostitutes
tightened the noose around the neck of foreign-born women practicing
prostitution in the United States and led to a steady increase in their deportation. During this decade, the close cooperation between the Bureau and
immigration agents illustrated how immigration policy spread from policing the borders of the country to also policing immigrants in the interior of
the country.[32]

The close supervision of brothels occasionally placed local white slave officers and special agents in odd positions where the agents of the White
Slave Division were pulled into the competitive vice world they monitored.
In July 1913 a newly appointed commanding officer of the Baltimore Police
Department issued a rule that prevented prostitutes within the vice district
from moving from one brothel to another and required any prostitute who
retired from a house to leave the district entirely. Several prostitutes complained about the new rule to Special Agent Grgurevich. They said that madams used the order to take advantage of them because the women could not
easily leave if they wished to continue working in the sex trade. The new rule
gave madams too much power and undermined sex workers' abilities to gov-
ern the conditions of their employment. Grgurevich went to the police department to complain on behalf of the prostitutes, in effect becoming their
advocate.[33] In another case, a man who lived off the earnings of a prostitute
named Anna Thomson arrived at the brothel she worked at in Baltimore

and demanded all of her money. When she told him that she had none, he attacked her, beating her viciously. When the madam of the brothel stepped in to intercede, he assaulted her too, as well as two other prostitutes before he dragged Anna out of the brothel, leaving behind all of her belongings. The madam contacted the special agent in charge of registering the inhabitants of the brothel. She affirmed that in his anger the man had said that "if he could not treat Anna as he wanted to in that house, he would take her to another house where he could." Then she included the most significant recollection claiming that he had stated: "That he brought [Anna to Baltimore] from Pittsburgh, Pa. and that he did not intend to be dictated to."[34] It is unclear whether the man actually did admit to violating the White Slave Traffic Act or the madam cynically added to his quote to get the Bureau involved; nonetheless, a case against him was initiated, and the Bureau found itself tracking an abusive pimp-boyfriend at the request of a brothel madam.

The Bureau's focus on commercialized vice cases had the unintended consequence of making women the subject of federal investigations. Women comprised 28 percent (sixteen) of the subjects of investigation of the cases conducted in the first six months after passage of the act. All sixteen women investigated were involved in commercial vice cases. Another way of understanding this development is that cases involving non-commercial sexual immorality always had male subjects, whereas cases that involved the business of prostitution could easily have both female and male subjects because both women and men participated in the vice trade. The Mann Act had been passed to protect women, yet women increasingly came under its purview.[35] As brothel madams learned about the new law, they quickly took steps to protect themselves and their businesses. One agent commented, in December 1911, that he was certain the suspected victim of trafficking, a sixteen-year-old prostitute, had been "wised up on the kind of story to tell if she is ever questioned about her past. Leona Reed [her madam] is familiar with the law and would hardly fail to post a new girl on what to say."[36] The same agent heard a rumor that another El Paso madam hired a lawyer for the extravagant fee of $500 for legal advice on how to bring in girls from out of state without being vulnerable to prosecution for violating the White Slave Traffic Act. As a result, after the initial six months, the number of women prosecuted in white slave cases dropped to 14 percent (74 out of a total of 530 cases) from June 1910 to October 1912.[37]

Even women who were deemed to be victims in white slave investigations faced incarceration. Often Bureau investigations and U.S. Attorney's prosecutions could not move forward without the testimony of the person alleged to be trafficked, and these women were typically sex workers, a population known to be highly mobile. Consequently, if a city had no rescue home willing to take in prostitutes, the Bureau agents placed the women in a local jail until the case moved forward. City jails could be dangerous places for women, and the policy of housing witnesses in such locations came under criticism. As a result, in May 1912 the attorney general changed the policy, deeming it "inadvisable to confine the witnesses in a jail where she is held under the same restrictions as the sentenced prisoners in the jail and where she is subject to the abuse of such sentenced prisoners."[38] Even with the new policy, the Bureau continued to confine female witness and victims in reformatories, women's homes, rescue homes, and other disciplinary institutions.

In the years when the White Slave Division was operating, moral reformers expanded their antivice campaigns, which frequently undermined the ability of the division to keep track of brothel-based prostitutes. In June 1912, just as the Bureau expanded the registration campaign, a special agent reported that "all the houses of prostitution have been closed in Milwaukee within the last two or three days" leaving some question as to what work could be conducted in that town. The closing of a vice district in one city served to efficiently scatter the previously contained (and enumerated) prostitutes, frustrating Bureau agents. When the Milwaukee brothels closed, the same agent tried to circulate a list of Milwaukee's prostitutes to other cities, particularly Grand Rapids, Detroit, and Minneapolis, which he thought would be the most likely destinations for them.[39] Finch responded to situations like the one in Milwaukee with frustration, saying:

> *The forces of reform are working against each other.* Here is one city closing down its district without notice and turning hundreds of women on the streets (the city of Chicago); here is another city which has gone to its State legislature and secured a State law legalizing its segregated quarter (the city of New Orleans); here is another city which has not only closed down its district on five days' notice, but notified disorderly women to leave the town under penalty of law (the city of Atlanta); here is another city which tries to segregate its

prostitutes, and insists that its Board of Health shall examine them
and give them certificates of freedom from Venereal Diseases (the city
of Cheyenne), and here are the reform organizations . . . fighting the
so-called reform elements in civic affairs which advocate
segregation.[40]

The lack of coordination among reform organizations compromised the coordinated campaign the White Slave Division was trying to wage. But what
to Finch, in January 1913, looked like a lack of coordination, by January the
following year had coalesced into a united movement capable of fighting
prostitution nationwide.

The year 1913 marked a turning point in both the purity reform movement and the social hygiene movement because the American Vigilance Association and the American Federation for Sex Hygiene merged to form the
American Social Hygiene Association (ASHA), which quickly became the
most prominent national reform organization capable of producing a har-
monized plan for fighting vice.[41] ASHA's rise was stimulated by the formation of the Bureau of Social Hygiene—funded by John D. Rockefeller, Jr.—
which provided much of the research and financing for ASHA's reform
agenda. ASHA's eminence led to the rise of a medico-legal philosophy of social and moral hygiene that tended to discard the overt Christian themes of
suasion and appeals to morality and women's rights that had characterized
the late nineteenth-century purity movement. During the first decades of
the twentieth century, the feminist rationale for social hygiene, one that emphasized a single standard of sexuality as a path for equality between the
sexes, gave way to a medical male rationale, one that focused only on limiting
the spread of venereal disease. Most ominously, the state apparatus that had
been harnessed initially to support a single standard of sexuality shifted to
support the double standard, and often its full weight fell on women who
violated gender and sexual expectations.[42] This is not to suggest that the tactics
and support of the women's movement disappeared from the social hygiene
movement, but rather that they were subordinated to tactics developed by
ASHA that gave priority to developing new local public health and property
laws to combat vice.[43]

The wide-ranging reforms pursued by antivice activists contributed to
the demolition of the White Slave Division. When the Bureau shut down the

division in January 1914, it offered several reasons. The division cost a lot. Plus, although it policed existing vice zones successfully, surveying prostitutes did not result in any sort of accomplishment that the Department of Justice could point to when facing Congress. And most notably, in the words of FBI Chief A. Bruce Bielaski, the "wave of sentiment going all over the country to do away with segregated districts" had hindered the work of the White Slave Division.[44] In other words, although the White Slave Division was expensive and labor intensive, it did not seem to achieve much, especially in a moral reform climate that was working to close down the context of municipal regulation upon which the Bureau relied. As Bielaski admitted to Congress about the registry of prostitutes, "We have never found any use for it."[45] Though Bielaski found little use for the White Slave Division, Stanley Finch argued that the system had resulted in some important achievements. He claimed that the debt bondage practices that had so characterized brothel-based prostitution had largely been eliminated. He also contended that "the practice of confining girls in rooms and holding them absolutely against their will as slaves has been largely stopped in those cities" that had a local white slave officer.[46] The White Slave Division represents an attempt of the Bureau to form a unified white slavery policy, one that was top down, with federal forces tracking the mobility of prostitutes. With Finch's departure from the Department of Justice, it fell to Bielaski to reconsider how the Bureau would enforce the White Slave Traffic Act. Yet, the closure of the White Slave Division did not mark a turning away from enforcing the Mann Act nor the dismantling of the local white slave officer corps.

Bielaski, the son of a minister, embraced enforcing the Mann Act, but he and his special agents were searching for a stable understanding of the purpose and scope of the law. Bielaski had earned his law degree from George Washington University in 1904 and joined the Department of Justice the following year.[47] He worked his way up from a clerk to an examiner to an assistant to Finch, and finally, to head of the Bureau—a position he would hold until his resignation in 1918. Described by a newspaper reporter as "a silent man with every mesh of the [crime] web in his sensitive fingers," Bielaski led the Bureau during the tumultuous World War I years, and he oversaw the Bureau's growth into the nation's largest and leading national investigative force. The same reporter declared, "These have been the years during which the newest and greatest of the government's detective agencies has been taking definite form. Bielaski has been molding it."[48] Addressing Mann Act violations was a key element of shaping the Bureau. Unlike Finch, Bielaski allowed for women's culpability in trafficking and argued that women should be "punished jointly with the man" in Mann Act cases.[49] According to Bielaski, it was problematic that there was no way that "the woman though she may be equally guilty, can be made to answer for her acts."[50] Here, Bielaski allowed for and perhaps even expected women to be at fault in Mann Act violations, as he rejected Finch's more simplistic formulation that women were *always* the victims of men. This shift in how to comprehend the role of women in alleged violations would become more troubling under Bielaski's leadership as he and his special agents debated the scope of the "any other immoral purpose" clause of the White Slave Traffic Act.

While the Bureau's White Slave Division was busy counting prostitutes, individual citizens demanded a broader reading of the statute. Citizens' demands for the wide scope of the law implied in the "any other immoral purpose" clause compromised the Bureau's attempts to develop a stable understanding of the White Slave Traffic Act as an antiprostitution law and prompted a reading of the Mann Act as a federal immorality statute that covered a wide range of behaviors. Although the Bureau responded to citizens' complaints, which inundated Bureau offices the moment President Taft signed the law, it did so with reservations about congressional intent and concerns about the constitutional questions posed by opponents to the law. Throughout the 1910s, civilian pressure for a broad reading of the act remained constant, while the White Slave Division attempted a narrow understanding of the law. Torn between these two poles, the Bureau gingerly negotiated with citizens, ignoring some, while pursuing those cases the Bureau deemed to have the most obvious immoral characteristics—cases involving the corruption of youth and sex between nonwhite men and white women. In contrast, private citizens often asserted a broader view of the law.

The Bureau ruthlessly pursued some seduction cases, especially those dealing with very young girls that to modern eyes look more like cases of sexual predation and pedophilia. One such case that the Bureau deemed "extremely vicious" involved two sisters, Adessa and Elsie Ferrier. In the late summer of 1910, Edward Nichols met sixteen-year-old Adessa at the candy store where she worked. One day, he followed her to a chop suey house where she ate lunch with her thirteen-year-old sister, Elsie. At the restaurant, he approached the girls and struck up a friendship with them. During this courtship, or grooming phase, he frequently met Elsie at her school giving her as much attention as he offered her older sister. By October, Nichols had convinced Adessa that he intended to marry her, and he persuaded the girls to join him on a trip to Hammond, Indiana, because he argued that Indiana had a lower age of consent law than their home state of Illinois. There he and Adessa could be married without the girls' parents' permission. Once ensconced in their hotel room in Indiana, he sent Adessa out on an errand and raped Elsie. His ruse was so successful that he sent Adessa out on another errand the next day and accosted Elsie again. When Adessa discovered Elsie in tears and learned what had happened, she refused to leave her alone with him. Frustrated, Nichols abandoned the sisters in their hotel room in Hammond.[51] The courtship of one sister only to ensure sexual access to the younger sister scandalized the investigating agents. But the fact that Nichols was married with a thirteen-year-old daughter at home outraged the judge in the case, who excoriated Nichols before sentencing him to the maximum sentence of ten years imprisonment at Fort Leavenworth penitentiary.[52]

In investigating alleged Mann Act violations that lacked a commercial vice element, the Bureau and courts reserved their energies for those cases that involved the very young.[53] This was a privilege of protection available to white youth only. When fifteen-year-old Mary Lee Bolden was seduced and taken from her home in Madison, Indiana, by William Sullivan, no investigation was launched, presumably because the victim and subject were both black.[54] Similarly, reports that a very young African American girl who had been raped on a San Francisco jitney bus after being kidnapped from Salt Lake City went uninvestigated in 1916.[55] Race, age and sexual innocence would be key determinants to whether noncommercial cases would be pursued by federal agents.

During the first few years of Mann Act enforcement, the Bureau avoided using the law to police general immorality among adults. A train agent reported to the Bureau that he had observed a couple travelling together in the same berth from El Paso to Los Angeles, and he suspected that they were not married and could be involved in vice. Further investigation in Los Angeles revealed that the couple, Leon H. Lempert and Ruby Halamuda, had respectable acquaintances and stayed in a respectable area of town.[56] An interview with the woman uncovered that though the couple was sexually intimate they were not presently married to one another. The agent concluded, "I could not see any particular benefit in prosecution, still it *was* a violation of the law."[57] In another case, a husband reported that his wife had been induced to leave him by another man. Further investigation discovered that the illicit couple, "while living in unlawful cohabitation and adultery," was not "violating the White Slave Traffic Act as construed by the Department."[58] In the early years of enforcement, adultery and consensual sexual relations between adults fell outside the Bureau's conception of the "any other immoral purpose" clause.

This policy of interpreting the White Slave Traffic Act narrowly came under attack by reformers and even some inside the attorney general's office. One such lawyer, Henry J. Dannenbaum, argued that Congress intentionally used vague language in the act because it recognized that "[p]rivate use or public exploitation are both immoral, both are denounced by the state laws and moral sentiment, and they differ only in the degree of immorality," and Congress intended the act to cover both public immorality (prostitution) and private immorality (adultery and seduction). For Dannenbaum, Congress's inclusion of the phrase "any other immoral purpose" truly meant *any other immoral purpose.* He also argued that the age or moral character of the victim "is of secondary importance" to the purpose of the law.[59] Dannenbaum represented a lone voice arguing for a broader interpretation of the law from within the Department of Justice. Official Bureau policy for the early years remained characterized by the thinking present in the advice given by the attorney general's office to a U.S. Attorney in New Orleans in 1913: "The Department has maintained that the White Slave Traffic Act does not apply to the ordinary case of illicit relations between a man and a woman, when interstate travel happens to be involved."[60]

Even while the Bureau maintained a narrowed purview, cases that involved interracial couples drew attention. When interracial couples travelled together, other passengers, train conductors, police, and government agents noticed them and often assumed that something immoral was unfolding. Observers frequently misinterpreted the nature of the relationship. For example, an Immigrant Bureau inspector who witnessed Walter Jones, an African American man, and Sadie Clayton, a white woman, riding the train together from Boise, Idaho, to Baker City, Oregon, assumed that Jones was a pimp violating the white slave law. Further investigation uncovered that he was travelling with his white wife. In the 1910s, Oregon had one of the most severe antimiscegenation laws in the country, and the immigration agent advocated handing the couple over to state authorities who would take legal action.[61] In another case, a Bureau Special Agent Leon Bone witnessed a Chinese man get into an argument with train conductors who refused to believe that he and his white wife were indeed married. The agent initially described the wife—Irene Lasswell—as a "little white girl" who needed protection and decided to investigate. Lasswell repeatedly asserted that she had married her husband in Granger, Wyoming, the previous month. Bone doubted everything she said, but once it was clear that there was no question that she had willingly entered into a sexual relationship with her Chinese husband, Ku Wu, then the agent became repelled by her, painting her as a hardened prostitute in his reports. After interrogating Lasswell, Bone concluded "She repeatedly refused to answer questions, and in many cases told falsehoods."[62]

Bureau agents felt compelled to investigate interracial relationships to ensure that men of color were not trafficking white women, but the moment when it became clear that the white women consented to these relationships, then, in the eyes of the Bureau, these women forfeited the protection that the Mann Act offered white women. Similarly, the Bureau instantly stopped investigating any cases of interstate trafficking once agents discovered that a white woman suspected of being a victim had had consensual sexual contact with a man of color at any point in her sexual history. One agent wrote of such a case that the victim had "had one or more Jap lovers, . . . [and] can hardly be classed as a White Slave."[63] Even a commercial prostitution case was dropped when agents found out that the white victim, Ethel Rutherford, had once in her past been the lover of an African American man, because they believed that no jury would convict.[64] The "white" part of "white slavery" had a double meaning. On the one hand it referred to the race of the victim. On the other hand, it signaled the presumed state of sexual purity of the victim. Typically, in noncommercial cases, and even some commercial cases, without the presence of both factors the Bureau would not investigate.

The refusal of the Bureau to investigate alleged violations of the White Slave Traffic Act involving a white victim who had a history of romantic and sexual attachments to men of color made the Department of Justice's prosecution of famed African American boxer Jack Johnson that much more exceptional. On July 4, 1910, Johnson successfully defended his heavyweight boxing title from former heavyweight white champion Jim Jeffries in what many considered to be the greatest match ever. The fight was infused with racial meaning. Jeffries only agreed to fight, in his own words, "for the sole purpose of proving that a white man is better than a negro." When Johnson emerged victorious, race riots erupted throughout the nation and Johnson became the most famous black athlete in the world.[65]

More controversial than his athletic prowess was Johnson's preference for white women as his sexual and romantic partners. Just after the October 1912 suicide of his first wife—a white woman named Etta Duryea—Johnson drew the ire of much of country when he embarked on an affair with nineteen-year-old Lucille Cameron. Lucille's mother and Illinois police attempted to charge Johnson with the abduction of Cameron under Illinois state law, but these charges became difficult to substantiate when the couple married in early December 1912. Frustrated, the Illinois U.S. Attorney and Bureau agents looked for another white woman in Johnson's past whom he had transported over state lines in violation of the Mann Act, and they found one in the person of the prostitute Belle Schreiber who had been Johnson's mistress for a few months in 1909. Johnson's case came to trial in May 1913 amongst voracious publicity. The jury quickly found him guilty, and Johnson was sentenced to serve a year in jail and pay a $1,000 fine, which he evaded for a time by fleeing the country. The persecution of Jack Johnson illustrates the Progressive Era's gender and sexual biases that re-inscribed the sexual prerogatives of white men, tacitly allowing their crossing of the sexual color line, while at the same time severely punishing black men's sexual contact with white women.[66]

In comparison to other Bureau investigations of interracial relationships, the Johnson case stands out as exception—a case of political targeting of a celebrity amid standard Jim Crow racial scapegoating. The Bureau typically acted as if white women who had sexual contact with men of color had forfeited the protection that the Mann Act offered white female citizens. Maintaining racial purity emerged as an important feature of Progressive-Era politics and notions of gendered citizenship. Up until the 1922 Cable Act, a native-born woman who married a nonwhite foreign-born man lost her citizenship, and women who married men who were ineligible for citizenship—men of Asian descent—lost their citizenship until the law changed in 1931.

White women faced harsh retribution when they selected nonwhite men as their marital (or bed) partners. Furthermore, Johnson's case was one of noncommercial immorality. Although Schreiber had been a prostitute, Johnson did not take her across state lines for any commercial reasons, but rather for personal and recreational reasons. When the attorney general's office claimed that "[t]he Department has maintained that the White Slave Traffic Act does not apply to the ordinary case of illicit relations between a man and a woman, when interstate travel happens to be involved,"[67] yet ruthlessly pursued Johnson, he signaled that the Johnson/Schreiber case was not an "ordinary case of illicit relations." Instead it was a case meant to punish a black man who repeatedly, publicly, successfully, and without shame, sought sexual access to white women. When sentencing Johnson, the judge commented: "The defendant is one of the best known men of his race, and his example has been far-reaching, and the Court is bound to consider the position he occupied among his people."[68] Disciplining a notorious black man for his unrepentant sexual pursuit of white women within a context of Jim Crow America constituted the primary foundation for the Bureau's action against Johnson and it sheds light onto the "sexual infrastructure of racism."[69]

◆ ◆ ◆

With the congressional mandate to enforce the White Slave Traffic Act, the Bureau of Investigation saw its caseload and jurisdiction expand broadly, although what behaviors and relationships that jurisdiction covered remained uncertain due to constitutional doubts about the new law. As a result, the Bureau attempted to narrow its implementation of the Mann Act to cases involving commercial prostitution and sought to prevent violation of the law by monitoring the mobility of female sex workers. Even with its short life span, the Bureau's White Slave Division is notable for a variety of reasons. It represented one of the largest coordinated attempts at regulation of prostitution in the early twentieth century. The regulation of prostitution was most closely associated with the French system of licensing brothels by medical and police forces to control the movement of women who were deemed to be morally or medically unclean, yet socially necessary. Consequently, American reformers were forever claiming that theirs was a country free of the sin and decadence of regulation. But until the closure of red-light districts, informal police regulation was common on the municipal level of government. The Bureau's White Slave Division marks the only attempt at reg-ulation of civilian brothels by federal forces.[70] For its monitoring of prostitutes, the Bureau depended upon the continuing existence of brothel-based prostitu-tion. Although controlling venereal disease was not its *raison d'être,* for both Bureau agents and U.S. Attorneys, the law was, in the words of one U.S. Attor-ney, "a quarantine act against the morally and physically unclean."[71]

For Finch, the greatest contribution of the White Slave Division was that it stimulated enforcement of state vice or white slave laws. The Bureau fur-nished local white slave officers with copies of state laws connected to vice and gave the instructions that if, in the course of their work they encoun-tered violations of state laws, then they should go to state authorities and "suggest that they are willing, as a private citizen, to help them in the en-forcement of the State laws."[72] The progressive push for moral reform that led to the passage of the Mann Act in 1910 continued on the state level and was accompanied by a host of antivice laws. It was within this nationwide state-level campaign against segregated vice districts that the Bureau con-ducted its investigations, and whenever possible the Bureau encouraged prosecution under local laws rather than federal laws. In this way, state leg-islation became more significant due to federal action, and Finch could push the use of state laws for federal goals.

The successful implementation of the White Slave Division transformed the Bureau into a truly national agency, with representatives in more than three hundred cities and towns. Even after the White Slave Division closed its Baltimore offices in early 1914, the network of local white slave officers established throughout the country continued to investigate crimes, including alleged Mann Act violations. Additionally, white slave investigations estab-lished a more aggressive model for federal law enforcement than had previ-ously existed—both seeking to prevent law breaking and investigating ordinary citizens, thereby setting important precedents for the Bureau.[73]

Although the Bureau intended on focusing its attention on policing com-mercial vice, individual citizens demanded state intervention in their lives. Reformers, concerned parents, and outraged local police all clamored for a broad conception of the "any other immoral purposes" clause of the White Slave Traffic Act. They argued that the law could and should be more than an antiprostitution law, that it should also fight more general and pervasive sexual immorality. Faced with these demands, the Bureau conceded that some noncommercial cases deserved the Bureau's attention, especially those with very young (meaning innocent) victims or cases where men of color sexually and romantically engaged with white women. The White Slave Division's project of containing prostitutes in recognized brothels and the Bureau's concession that the Mann Act could be used to police the seduction of young girls and some interracial relationships gave birth to the surveillance state that functioned due to the cooperation of local actors. Yet this surveillance project remained focused on sexual market places because until the Supreme Court weighed in on the White Slave Traffic Act, the Bureau preferred to focus on commercial vice.

5

Defining Immoral Purposes

In looking back over his twenty-five years at the helm of the fight against prostitution, American Social Hygiene Association (ASHA) President William F. Snow noted that the year 1917 constituted "the pivotal point" in the fight against commercial vice.[1] Certainly, 1917 was a turning point for ASHA. That year the military tapped the organization to develop a plan for ensuring the venereal and recreational health for all service men drafted into the armed forces, placing ASHA at the forefront of social engineering in World War I while also expanding its playing field by infusing its policy measures with the urgency of war-time mobilization. But 1917 was also a pivotal year for the Bureau of Investigation's fight against white slavery because it was then that the Supreme Court finally determined the scope of the White Slave Traffic Act and shaped the Bureau's enforcement for decades to come. Cultural concerns about girls' emerging sexuality and anxieties about the dangers girls encountered, and perhaps posed to society at large, shaped these two developments. When Congress passed the White Slave Traffic Act in 1910, reformers believed that it would ensure the protection of American girlhood, yet by 1919 a new generation of reformers suggested that it was American boyhood/manhood that needed protection.

By the dawn of the 1920s America had entered a new sexual era. Popular representations of white slavery contributed to this shift. As local white slave officers continued their surveillance of vice districts and promiscuous women, even after the White Slave Division had been dissolved, they joined a growing legion of progressive reformers who fretted over the fate of the romantically or sexually careless girl. With the dawning of the war, the worry about this girl's fate became more urgent, and she was identified not as a victim in need of protection, but instead as a potential contagion who could undermine America's military readiness by exposing young men to vene-real disease. The legal conflation of promiscuity with prostitution and its equation with criminality reconfirmed the idea that the only accepted sex-ual relations were those contained within the institution of marriage.[2]

In the immediate years after the law's passage, confusion about what con-stituted white slavery and about the scope of the White Slave Traffic Act re-mained, both within the Bureau and in American society at large. Some antivice activists believed that the "any other immoral purpose" clause of the act authorized an expansive policing of interstate immoral behavior. The Bureau, in contrast, maintained that the law was an antiprostitution statute and preferred to direct its attention to policing commercialized vice. Of course, gratuitous cases of immorality, as construed by the Bureau, broke down this artificial division as the Bureau investigated cases of pedophilia and some instances of interracial sex, thereby revealing its own confusion over the scope of the law. In 1913, a case emerged from California that would finally settle the vexing constitutional questions about the White Slave Traf-fic Act's scope.

In March 1913, twenty-year-old Marsha Warrington and nineteen-year-old Lola Norris embarked on an adventure that would lead to their national infamy and a final determination of the scope of the Mann Act. The girls—recently out of high school, both still living with their parents, and well known and well liked by the "best of Sacramento society"—had become en-gaged in disreputable affairs with two of the most well-known men about town, Maury Diggs and Drew Caminetti.[3] Over the course of autumn and winter of 1912, the couples—Marsha and Maury, Lola and Drew—had taken long drives in Maury's Cadillac, spent time in the evenings drinking and carousing at his office building, visited roadhouses on the outskirts of town, met up at his flat, attended dances together, and traveled on day trips to nearby San Francisco and San Jose.[4] As the affairs grew more intense, the men became considerably less discreet—discretion that was required be-cause both men were married and had children under the age of five at home. The men invited the girls to dances their wives attended, and at one point Maury invited Marsha to a dinner party his wife hosted.[5] By late Feb-ruary 1913, the wives and parents of all of the parties involved knew what had been occurring, and the pressure in Sacramento grew too intense for the illicit couples—the *Sacramento Bee* was threatening to publish an account of the entire affair.[6] Maury convinced the others to join him on a trip to Reno where, he argued, he and Drew could arrange quick divorces from their current wives and new weddings to the young women. The trip would help the men evade imminent arrest because at nineteen and twenty, the girls were technically minors under California state law. Quickly, the group purchased train tickets and fled town on March 9, 1913. As the couples relaxed in Reno, local police, alerted to the couples' flagrant flaunting of convention by the *Bee* article, arrested Maury Diggs and Drew Caminetti for violation of the White Slave Traffic Act, and catapulted the story of the affair into the national spotlight by raising questions about the meaning of the "any other immoral purpose" clause. Questions emerged because the Diggs-Caminetti case contained no connection to commercial vice. Was this case of pleasure escapading and adultery really white slavery?

In the summer of 1913, newspapers across the country eagerly covered the sensational white slave trial of Maury I. Diggs and Drew Caminetti.[7] Newspapers extensively covered the trial for two reasons: the U.S. Attorney pursued the case, though there was no demonstrable connection to commercial vice present; and more importantly, the defendants of the case came from two prominent political families, and the victims in the case also came from well-connected, respectable families. The case had political dimensions, and its trial, set for the summer, became the subject of intense national political infighting. That spring, President Woodrow Wilson had appointed Drew's father, Anthony Caminetti, to the top position in the Immigration Bureau, and he asked that his son's trial be delayed so that he could attend. When California Republicans charged that Drew Caminetti was benefiting from his family's close connections to the Democrats in power, the Wilson administration caved and withdrew its support for a postponement of the trial. Discussions about the political scandal and denunciations of cronyism and political influence erupted on the floor of the U.S. House of Representatives.[8] Before the case had even been heard, it generated an unusual amount of emotion, public furor, and congressional attention.[9]

Throughout the trial, the prosecuting attorney emphasized the girls' previously chaste state. Both Marsha Warrington and Lola Norris claimed that their first sexual encounters occurred with Maury Diggs and Drew Caminetti, respectively. Additionally, the young women's respectable middle-class white backgrounds mitigated any guilt assigned to them. When discussing the

Diggs-Caminetti case, Representative James Mann (R-IL), the author of the White Slave Traffic Act, declared, "I shed my tears for those who have been led astray, who have been debauched through fear and force. I shed my tears on behalf of the innocent, while you [Democrats] endeavor to protect the guilty."[10] According to the narrative asserted by Mann, the prosecuting attorney, and others, young women like Marsha Warrington and Lola Norris needed to be protected from predatory and selfish men, like Maury Diggs and Drew Caminetti, who set aside their respectable masculine roles as faithful husbands and fathers to adopt the disreputable roles of philanderers and debauchers of innocents.

As the trials commenced, the judge gave a broad reading of the White Slave Traffic Act. He charged that the fact the Maury Diggs and Drew Caminetti traveled to Reno to avoid arrest indicated a level of premeditation and awareness of their illegal actions and therefore subjected them to the "any other immoral purpose" clause of the act. The court found them both guilty.[11] As he waited for his bail to be arranged after sentencing, Maury Diggs told newspaper reporters, "If I am a white slaver, 90 percent of the men living are as guilty as I am."[12] By making men who engaged in sex outside of marriage subject to the White Slave Traffic Act, this judge threatened the male sexual privilege of numerous men, much to their consternation. Some newspapers celebrated the ruling, noting that it properly punished "the ghouls who seek to ruin young girls,"[13] but others warned that, although Diggs and Caminetti's actions were indefensible, they were but "minnows in the stream of vice," and that accepting the broader scope of the Mann Act could cause the Department of Justice to overlook the "sharks" of the vice world—those men and women who earned money from prostitution.[14]

The precedent set by the Diggs-Caminetti case opened a period of extreme judicial confusion about the scope of the Mann Act that lasted from August 1913 to February 1917. During this period, federal judges in different jurisdictions applied different readings about the scope of the law. For example, less than a month after Caminetti's trial concluded, a federal judge in Wichita, Kansas, asked the following question to a defendant who pleaded guilty to violation of the Mann Act: "Do you base this plea on the interpretation of the law in the Diggs-Caminetti cases?"[15] When the defendant admitted that he had, the judge allowed him to change his plea and then declared that in his interpretation of the law a commercial element must be present.

He stated: "It was not the aim of congress to prevent the personal escapades of any man."[16] An editorial published in the *Atlanta Constitution*, appropriately titled "The Chaotic Mann Law," bemoaned that lack of consistency and noted that as judicial conditions stood, Americans were witnessing the "undesirable spectacle of tribunals of equal jurisdiction all over the country reversing themselves, the one creating criminals and the other refusing to prosecute for the identical offense."[17]

The confusion about the scope of the law extended to the Bureau. After closing the White Slave Division in 1914, though retaining the services of local white slave officers, the Bureau reverted back to its policy of investigating individual cases of alleged violations of the Mann Act, and the number of convictions continued to rise.[18] Publicly, the bureau continued to claim that it pursued only commercial vice cases, but internally some individuals in the attorney general's office called for a broader understanding of the law.[19] After reviewing the conflicting judicial record of the Mann Act in October 1913, Blackburn Esterline, a special assistant to the attorney general, concluded that Congress intended the law to cover any interstate travel "in connection with, or as incidental to, any kind of sexual immorality."[20] He supported a broader and more aggressive reading of the scope of the statute. Others outside the attorney general's office urged for more action. Wilbur F. Crafts, of the International Reform Association, wrote a frustrated letter to the attorney general that criticized the Bureau's narrow vision of the law. He argued that it was the moral reform groups whose letter-writing campaign had gotten the Bureau its budget, yet many of them remained unsatisfied with the limited action of the Bureau. He wrote, "I positively know that somebody who is regarded as an authority in the Department of Justice has directed the agents of the Department in the field to proceed against white slave cases only when women have been rented out for immoral purposes, whereas the law, if I understand the English language, distinctly prohibits the transportation of women from one State to another for the purposes of debauchery, whether for their own carnal indulgence or to fill their pockets. Cases of greed and lust stand alike in the wording of the law."[21] The office of the attorney general responded to Crafts with a boiler-plate letter denying there was any such policy and stating that the department had avoided laying down any "hard and fast rule" about which cases to pursue. In the face of such contradictions, the Bureau failed to provide much guidance to reformers or much information about its activities to the public.[22] The emerging narrative in the press painted the White Slave Traffic Act as a "chaotic" law that could challenge men's right to engage in pleasure escapades.

Maury Diggs and Drew Caminetti appealed the ruling in their case, believing that that the judge had extended the scope of the Mann Act beyond constitutional limits and congressional intent when he decided that non-commercial interstate immorality fell under the purview of the "any other immoral purpose" clause of the statute. The Supreme Court accepted their case in late 1916 and offered its decision in 1917, thus defining the scope of the law—particularly if the "any other immoral purpose" clause truly meant *any* other immoral purpose, or if to violate the federal statue there needed to be some connection to commercialized vice, as Caminetti's lawyers argued. The Supreme Court declared, "Statutory words are uniformly presumed, unless the contrary appears, to be used in their ordinary and usual sense, and with the meaning commonly attributed to them. To cause a woman or girl to be transported for the purposes of debauchery, and for an immoral purpose, to-wit, becoming a concubine or mistress, for which Caminetti and Diggs were convicted . . . would seem by the very statement of the facts to embrace transportation for purposes denounced by the act, and therefore fairly within its meaning."[23] By endorsing the widest possible reading of the Mann Act, the Supreme Court struck a blow at interstate sexual immorality whether a commercial element existed or not, but some feared that it empowered a criminal class as dangerous as sex traffickers—blackmailers. Judge Joseph McKenna's dissent in the decision reinforced an emerging link between the Mann Act and blackmail when he wrote, "Blackmailers of both sexes have arisen, using the terrors of the construction now sanctioned by this court as a help—indeed, the means—for their brigandage."[24]

In the same year that gave birth to the Caminetti case, reports began to circulate that enterprising criminals were using the Mann Act to blackmail unsuspecting men. One of the earliest cases involved a young man, twenty-year-old Charles Johnson, who allegedly encouraged his wife to pick up strange men and take them to a hotel where she would exchange sex for money. Johnson would break into the hotel room at an inopportune moment and play the role of the angry cuckold, demanding money from the man "as a balm for his grief in finding his wife 'untrue' to him." The Bureau caught wind of the Johnsons' confidence games and built a successful Mann Act case against him because, in the course of conducting some of their scams he had taken his wife over state lines. The judge in the case ruled that the blackmail and sexual barter the couple engaged in constituted a violation of the "any other immoral purpose" clause, and he sentenced Johnson to five years in prison.[25] The Johnson case points to a vexing problem that the Department of Justice repeatedly encountered—what to do with women, like Johnson's wife, who had been trafficked, but who clearly were complicit in the violation of the law? "It is readily understandable," noted U.S. Attorney Guy D. Goff, "how practically in many of the so-called White Slave cases the man and the woman are equally depraved," and he suggested that punishment of the man while the woman went free constituted "an injustice."[26]

Issues of female culpability plagued the bureau and came to a head when a grand jury indicted forty-one-year-old Clara Holte for violating the Mann Act because she had "lured" twenty-one-year-old Chester C. Loudenschleger from Barrington, Illinois, to Milwaukee, Wisconsin, so that the couple could easily continue their "illicit sexual and libidinous relations."[27] The case hinged on the fact that although Chester provided for the transportation and technically violated the White Slave Traffic Act, the grand jury, looking at Clara's age, believed the couple to be equally guilty. Indeed, this case seemed to upset the entire gendered logic of the Mann Act, which presumed a female victim with the following characteristics: youth, innocence, and constrained or compromised capacity for consent. Clara Holte had none of these traits; instead she was older, sexually experienced, and aggressive, and perhaps the originator of the affair. The judge in the case agreed with the grand jury's assessment and sought to find Clara guilty of conspiring with Chester to violate the White Slave Traffic Act and liable for punishment under the Federal Conspiracy Statute.[28] But he was not sure if this reading of the law could hold up. In his words, "She cannot be both slave and slaver."[29] As a result of his uncertainty, he sustained a demurrer—a stay—to let the Supreme Court address the issue. The *New York Times* celebrated a reading of the law that opened up prosecution against the putative female victims of the white slave traffic. In an editorial provocatively titled "Uncle Sam, Blackmailer," the editors argued: "If two immoral persons pass a State line in the course of their immoral proceedings the man is guilty of a crime but the woman is not. The result has been that this law has acted as a direct inducement to blackmail. Women have waited until the partners of their guilt carelessly crossed a State line, and have then confronted them with a demand for money, with the alternative of a prison term. . . . The law is in itself an absurdity, but that is less serious than its direct inducement to crime. It breaks up no 'white slave' traffic, but it does make the Federal Government the accomplice and instrument of blackmailers and facilitates their operations."[30] The Supreme Court decision in the case, written by Justice Oliver Wendell Holmes, who urged people to "abandon the illusion that the woman always is the victim," agreed with the Wisconsin judge's ruling and found that women could indeed be found guilty of conspiring in their own illegal transportation over state lines.[31] Clearly, both the cultural and legal landscape that had led to the passage of the Mann Act was in the process of shifting as calls for gender equality proliferated to give cover for male sexual adventures.

Mann Act blackmail cases began to appear more frequently, peaking in 1916. Story after story of blackmail rings that used the Mann Act to rake thousands of dollars from prosperous yet foolish men appeared in American newspapers that year. One of the most sensational stories centered on a ring that operated out of Chicago, which police broke up in January 1916. The ring would find a mark, generally a well-to-do businessman, and observe his relations with any woman who was not his wife. Careful attention was paid to the details—what hotel the couple used for its assignations, how they registered, what time they arrived and departed—so that when a member of the blackmail ring confronted the mark, the businessman would be overwhelmed by the evidence against him. The member of the ring typically would falsely identify himself as a member of the Bureau and would suggest that between $500 and $20,000 would make the case disappear. This particular ring earned over $200,000.[32] Another well-publicized story, this time based in New York, featured many of the same elements, except that the women involved were members of the ring who intentionally set out to seduce the men from whom they intended to extort money. This *modus operandi* became almost a cliché as newspapers in Chicago and New York reported on the activities of blackmail rings, which replaced public anxieties about the white slave rings that had filled newspapers a few years earlier.

Cases like these posed a significant challenge to Bureau investigators because the victims of blackmail scams, fearing publicity, avoided reporting extortion. Indeed, the very dynamic of shame and secrecy that made blackmail possible thwarted the Bureau. For example, in May 1915, twenty-three-year-old Edith Crouch left her husband and young son at home in Saluda, South Carolina, to visit her friend, Nettie Reeder, for a few days in Augusta, Georgia. While strolling down the streets of Augusta one afternoon, Edith and Nettie ran into C. F. Smith, a mutual acquaintance and businessman from Saluda. Enjoying one another's company the threesome planned a day trip to Aiken, South Carolina, for the following day. While on the trolley car to Aiken, Nettie remembered that she had an appointment with her husband, and she disembarked, promising to catch up with the others later in the afternoon. Edith and C. F. arrived in Aiken and found a hotel, where C. F. registered them for a room. The friends wandered through Aiken, visiting a soda fountain and taking in the sights. Nettie met up with them in the early evening and the threesome enjoyed dinner at the hotel restaurant, and stayed up until 10 PM chatting in the lobby. After that, Nettie and Edith caught a trolley back to Augusta, and C. F. Smith stayed the evening, taking a train back to his home in Saluda the next day. Several days later, Edith returned home to Saluda and all seemed well.

But it quickly became clear the Nettie Reeder was no friend of Edith Crouch. Later that month, Nettie wrote to Edith demanding a $400 loan, and she hinted that Edith owed her because Nettie had covered up Edith's "act of indiscretion in making the trip to Aiken."[33] Though Edith's father was the head cashier at the Bank of Johnston, and her father-in-law served as Saluda's chief of police, she had no money of her own. She rebuffed Nettie, all the while becoming more and more anxious as Nettie told her that C. F. Smith had registered her as his wife under a fake name in the hotel's register—evidence enough to generate a Mann Act conviction. A few days later, two men appeared at Edith's door and identified themselves as detectives for the federal government. They told her that she had violated the Mann Act, could be prosecuted, and to avoid prosecution she would need to pay them $2,000, "but before leaving her, however, they agreed to take considerably less."[34] One of the "agents" wrote her a week later demanding $100 immediately. Frightened, Edith went to her father and borrowed $100 and gave it to the man representing himself as a federal agent—the lead blackmailer. This man had been seen around town in Augusta and Aiken, running up debts, and arousing suspicion, causing one of his creditors to complain to the police in

Aiken. The police searched his possessions, found a great deal of cash, and promptly arrested him. When the man was confronted with Edith, he confessed that he had been participating in a "frame up" that had been organized by Nettie. Local White Slave Officer Albert G. Ingram collected all of the evidence and took an affidavit. Throughout the investigation, Edith indicated that above all else she desired to "avoid publicity and notoriety" and refused to press charges against the man.[35] The following day, she met with Local White Slave Officer Ingram and "pleaded with him with tears in her eyes" that he drop any investigation into a Mann Act violation or blackmail.[36] According to Ingram, "She told me of being pregnant and that she believed if the thing was not dropped right where it was, she would give birth to a crazy child, unless she died of nervousness before it was born."[37] Swayed by her entreaties, Ingram promised that the investigation would be halted if Edith took twenty dollars of the money confiscated from the blackmailer and gave it to him—becoming a blackmailer in his own way. When the Bureau sent Special Agent George C. Calmes to investigate this strange case of blackmail, he agreed that though Edith may have acted with indiscretion, there was no evidence that she had improper relations with C. F. Smith, or ever was alone in a room with him. Throughout the investigation, Edith's father and father-in-law begged the Bureau to drop its case, arguing that they trusted that nothing improper had occurred, that Edith had only shown a lack of judgment, and that the notoriety from any prosecution would ruin their families' reputations. As a result, the U.S. Attorney decided, "If she should be forced into court as a witness in this case, I apprehend that it may result in a separation of her, and her husband, and probably destroying [*sic*] her health. Also both the Crouch and Watson families, who occupy high social positions, would be more or less affected."[38] The case was closed, though Bureau Chief A. Bruce Bielaski agreed with the assessment of Atlanta Special Agent in Charge Lewis J. Baley that Ingram was "not the proper man for a Local White Slave Officer,"[39] and Ingram was asked to hand in his Local White Slave Officer badge.

Some victims were so reticent to bring their cases of extortion to light that they empowered the blackmailers to act with impunity. Former Bureau Special Agent Dannenberg brought a case to the attention of the Chicago office. Dannenberg's friend Worth Hall was being shaken down by a former prostitute and lover, Florence Cooper, after Worth had married another woman. Over the course of several months, Worth had given Florence hundreds of dollars to keep her from accusing him of violating the Mann Act. Investigation revealed that Florence was attempting to blackmail several other men. One was a Mr. Snydecker, who was a "wealthy bachelor, residing at the Standard Club, Chicago, and frankly admitted having improper relations with Mrs. Cooper and numerous other prostitutes from time to time." He told her to go ahead and report him, saying he "did not care whether they filed a suit, sued him, threatened him, or anything else, as he was a bachelor, and most of his friends knew that he was a 'sport,' and that they could [not] hurt him anyway.'"[40] Others of her victims were not so flip. Florence was also trying to blackmail Henry M. Wallis, Jr., the son of the prominent Henry M. Wallis, president of the J.I. Case Threshing Machine Co. in Racine, Wisconsin. The Bureau's investigation revealed that Henry's family had already given her a thousand dollars. The Bureau decided to keep an eye on Florence Cooper, but they could not build a case against her because neither of the men she successfully blackmailed—Worth and Henry—would publicly testify. Worth Hall claimed, "If I had only myself to consider, I would not object to testifying as to these facts at any time, but my wife is in a highly nervous state on account of these things."[41]

In the summer of 1916 Attorney General Thomas Gregory convened a conference in Washington that included Bureau Chief Bielaski, Assistant Attorney General John C. Knox, and the special agents in charge in New York City, Philadelphia, and Chicago to coordinate the Department of Justice and Bureau investigations into cases of blackmail that originated from Mann Act cases.[42] Gregory placed Knox in charge of trying blackmail cases, and in September 1916 he went after several blackmail rings that operated between Atlantic City, Baltimore, Chicago, Philadelphia, and New York City.[43] In many of these cases, the lead investigating agent appeared as the complainant because, as Special Agent in Charge Frank Garbarino noted, "the interests of the people would be best served by concealing for the present the names of the actual complainants." Knox asserted that the victims in these cases were all "wealthy and eminently respectable men."[44] One blackmail victim, Edward R. West, the vice president of the C.D. Gregg Tea and Coffee Company of New York, decided to make his case public and expose himself to "public humiliation" so that others would not suffer as he had. According to his interview published in the (Baltimore) *Sun*, West met a woman in Chicago and after a few dates she proposed a trip to New York City. Once the couple was ensconced in their hotel room, three men broke in, showed West fake federal warrants and badges, and threatened a very public White Slave Traffic Act case. Over the course of the following week West paid the men fifteen thousand dollars to make the case disappear, and once the money had been delivered, the girl disappeared as well. Knox tried to calm public concerns about blackmail rings, arguing that there was no organized blackmail syndicate, but rather "it is just a case of confidence men working together from time to time. It is true these criminals always worked in groups, but these spasmodic alliances were more occasions of chance than systematized organizations."[45] The Mann Act provided fertile ground for blackmailers who targeted prominent men who sought to protect their reputations, while also enjoying sexual escapades that formed one dimension of their class privilege.

In 1916, the *New York Times* launched a war on the Mann Act believing it to be a law that "is chiefly a bid for blackmail and serves no other purpose worth mentioning."[46] One editorial excoriated the law, calling it the "Blackmail Act."[47] Another claimed that the white slave syndicate—fears of which led to the passage of the Mann Act—had proved to be nonexistent while a very real syndicate of blackmailers gained power every day due to the law.[48] One article, written by famed detective and future head of the Bureau William J. Burns, claimed that blackmail formed the number one large crime in the United States, stating that "more money is being extorted through blackmail than being lost through thievery." He identified it as a crime that disproportionately targeted the wealthy, claiming, "it is not safe for a man or a woman of wealth to make chance acquaintances in the City of New York, or in any other of our large cities."[49] Burns was right to draw attention to the class dimension of extortion, but he was disingenuous when he expressed concern about wealthy women. Of the individuals that historians have reported as victims of Mann Act extortion schemes, most were men; cases like Edith Crouch's appear to have been exceptional.[50] Indeed the vitriol that the *New York Times* directed towards the Mann Act reads like a defense of wealthy men's right to engage in sexual relations with women other than their wives without the fear of extortion.

In the narrative of blackmail asserted by the *New York Times,* the male criminal authored blackmail schemes, yet within these narratives, a beautiful

young woman baited the hook. As one article put it, the blackmail plot depended on "a kaleidoscopic conglomeration of bright lights, pretty girls, Atlantic City, the Mann act, fake detectives—and the victim's bankroll."[51] In
the story of the blackmail rings, women, especially young "pretty girls" became not only complicit in criminal acts, but often the entire plot hinged on
their duplicity. Concern about incidences of blackmail remained strong
enough that in January 1917 the Department of Justice instructed U.S. Attorneys to keep watch for cases that may involve blackmail and to avoid
those cases.[52] Some U.S. Attorneys believed that the press's focus on blackmail stories was overdrawn and that incidences of blackmail were "over-
estimated and exaggerated by those who are opposed to this law."[53] The stories of blackmail rings repositioned women in popular understandings of
the White Slave Traffic Act. No longer the victim, women became the extort-
ers, and the men they seduced assumed the position of victims. Promiscuous
young women were being reconfigured from victims of male lust into lures
baiting extortionists' traps and predators who could endanger America's
men and fighting forces.

In the 1910s, the reform movement dedicated to fighting vice underwent
a shift that can be best understood as moving its emphasis from social purity to social hygiene. In 1913 the social hygiene and moral reform movements came together under the umbrella of the American Social Hygiene
Association (ASHA). This group took a more scientific and professional approach to social problems than its predecessors had. It also preferred to
work quietly through governmental back channels. More importantly, medical and legal experts dominated the new organization. ASHA utilized the
existing network of local antivice organizations to spread its agenda, focusing on legal reform. Representatives from ASHA visited eighty cities in
twenty-five states from 1914 to 1916 to spread model laws on morality crimes.
The model law on prostitution eliminated the commercial element of the
transaction when it declared, "prostitution should be defined to include the
giving or receiving of the body, for hire, or the giving or receiving of the
body for indiscriminate sexual intercourse *without hire*." Most state legisla-
tures adopted this model law in part or in entirety.[54] ASHA's agenda and
reform activism emphasized the repression of prostitution, not regulation.
The organization's medical leadership and its focus on public health meant
that when diagnosing the problem of vice, which for them was really the

problem of venereal disease, ASHA leaders barely distinguished between the prostitute and the promiscuous woman because both could be equally venereal.

As America's entry into World War I seemed to grow more likely, the War Department choose ASHA to lead its social hygiene agenda, a task that ASHA was well situated to perform, considering that in addition to its municipal and state-level legal reform campaigns, it already had been studying the problems of military readiness, venereal disease, and prostitution policy. When in response to Francisco "Pancho" Villa's raid on the town of Columbus, New Mexico, in March 1916 the U.S. Army amassed 10,000 troops along the U.S.-Mexican border, ASHA decided to investigate the moral conditions of camp life in Texas, New Mexico, and Arizona. ASHA's investigator, physician M. J. Exner, spent seven weeks investigating, and he found that the areas around the camps "presented the severest temptations to immorality" with easy access to "extensive prostitution" in almost all of the camps along the border.[55] ASHA's complaints about camp conditions to Secretary of War Newton D. Baker resulted in Baker sending his trusted colleague, Raymond Fosdick of the Bureau of Social Hygiene, to the border to conduct his own inquiry.[56] Fosdick's confidential investigation also uncovered a miasma of vice in cities and towns near army camps along the border. As he recalled: "It was an almost unrelieved story of army camps surrounded by growing batteries of saloons and houses of prostitution. . . . As for prostitution, town after town was enlarging its facilities to meet the military demand."[57] Furthermore, the vice conditions Fosdick found along the U.S.-Mexican border led to high rates of venereal disease infection among soldiers stationed there. For example, in San Antonio almost 30 percent of the troops (288 per 1,000) reported infection.[58] ASHA decided to publicize the conditions along the border by publishing Exner's study in its journal, *Social Hygiene*. Exner summarized ASHA's desire to sever the link between the army and regulated prostitution when he wrote that "repressive measures well enforced have happy results and show that prostitution is not a necessity in connection with the army."[59] Fosdick agreed with Exner's assessment. He suggested composing a committee of "Army officers, physicians of modern training and scientific spirit, and perhaps civilians who have experience with the problem" who would be tasked to develop a program "applicable to the future as well as the present handling of the prostitute in relations to the Army."[60]

On April 17, 1917, just eleven days after the United States declared war, Baker created the Commission on Training Camp Activities (CTCA) and placed Raymond Fosdick at its head. Baker charged the CTCA with reaching out to civilian and military experts familiar with vice and developing a program that would keep American soldiers "fit to fight." Fosdick approached the Young Men's Christian Association, the Jewish Welfare Board, the Knights of Columbus, and ASHA to join the CTCA in its efforts to educate young soldiers about the dangers of venereal disease while also providing wholesome entertainment. Within the CTCA, ASHA's president, William F. Snow, accepted a position as head of the Social Hygiene section, and ASHA's Bascom Johnson led the Law Enforcement section. ASHA's agenda became the agenda of the CTCA and World War I provided, in Snow's words, the "laboratory for testing the social hygiene measures advocated."[61]

Pragmatic military concerns drove the CTCA's antiprostitution agenda as much as a concern about morality. Initial investigations discovered that venereal disease infection among soldiers at the beginning of 1917, before the draft had been instituted, were 240/1000 among white soldiers and 625/1000 among black troops. The primary goal of the CTCA's program was to bring down this infection rate, something it achieved, lowering it to 6 percent by 1919. Given the high rates of infection in 1917 among enlisted men, the Army viewed venereal disease infection as a civilian problem that could have a serious impact on America's fighting ability. It was rumored that the Austrian, British, and French armies had lost the manpower of millions of enlisted men due to venereal disease infections.[62] Fosdick explained, "Our argument has been not primarily one of morals, but of military necessity."[63]

To combat the invisible threat of venereal disease infections, Fosdick and CTCA proposed arming American soldiers with an "invisible armor" of social habits that protected their moral and physical health.[64] To accomplish this goal, the CTCA developed a program—called the American Plan—that combined "recreation programs, educational programs, law enforcement, and medical measures."[65] Additionally, the CTCA sought to cleanse the moral environs in communities surrounding the thirty-two training camps. Finally, as the war progressed and venereal disease remained a challenging problem, the CTCA developed an ambitious, far-reaching program to repress any form of "irregular" sexuality (meaning extramarital sexual relations). It was empowered to pursue this goal by Section 13 of the 1917 Selective Service Act that outlawed prostitution near any military installation.[66]

The physical prophylaxis program that formed the pragmatic element of the CTCA's activities had the troubling consequence of criminalizing sex for women, while medically excusing participation in the same act for men. When a soldier did have sexual contact, the army required him to report to a prophylaxis station as soon as possible, ideally within three hours, following the encounter so that he could be treated, thereby reducing chances that infection would take hold.[67] Failure to report to a station, as evidenced by contraction of a venereal disease, could in theory lead to harsh punishments. General Order No. 34 warned that the infected were "guilty of a serious offense under the 96th Article of War," and it promised that venereal disease infection would result in a court martial. However, instead of taking such drastic steps, most infected soldiers saw a "forfeiture of pay," which military leaders deemed as "more appropriate . . . than confinement."[68] Snow noted that the military's policy towards prostitution unfairly targeted women, while easily forgiving men for their involvement in the same transaction when he observed, "in practice this policy has been enforced more often against prostitutes than against male solicitors."[69]

By far the most successful element of the CTCA's program was its attack on the remaining red-light districts in the country. Antiprostitution reformers had been attacking segregated vice districts throughout the 1910s. Almost all of the forty-three cities that had published vice reports succeeded in eliminating their districts, but several other cities proudly maintained their sporting areas. To ensure that soldiers stayed free of temptation, the army included a provision in the Selective Service Act of 1917—Section 13— that empowered the secretary of army "to do everything by him deemed necessary to suppress and prevent the keeping or setting up of houses of ill fame, brothels, or bawdy houses within such distance as he may deem needful of any military camp, station, fort, post, cantonment, training or mobilization place."[70] Section 13 established "pure zones" that extended five miles, and later ten miles, around any military installation in the country. Some progressive reformers used the possibility of attracting military spending to justify closing their vice districts. Purity reformers in Houston took advantage of Section 13 to push their platform through city hall. In May 1917,

Texas Congressman-at-Large Daniel E. Garrett reported to the city that the War Department "does not look with favor upon the location of training camps near any city in which there is an established or recognized red light district."[71] Using this rationale, reformers, the city attorney's office, and city leaders succeeded in closing Houston's red-light district on June 15, 1917. Secretary Baker rewarded the city by establishing a National Guard training camp there.[72] Congress extended the "pure zone" policy to navy installations after the city of New Orleans refused to close its famed vice district, Storyville. On November 12, 1917, Secretary of the Navy Josephus Daniels told the mayor of the New Orleans, "You close the red light district, or the armed forces will."[73] As a result of these orders, the Law Enforcement Division of the CTCA closed 116 red-light districts over the course of the war, and numerous others closed due to local action—marking the end of the era of the public brothel in America.[74]

As the red-light districts closed for business, the CTCA turned its attention to other sources of contagion—clandestine prostitutes and promiscuous women. The line dividing the criminal prostitute and the promiscuous girl became increasingly blurred throughout the war. CTCA leaders were concerned that ordinary young women would fall for "the glamour of the uniform"[75] and that a source of venereal disease was not only the prostitute, but as Fosdick remarked, "the type known in the military as the flapper—that is, young girls who are diseased and promiscuous."[76] Fosdick explained that "we are confronted with the problem of hundreds of young girls, not yet prostitutes, who seem to have become hysterical at the sight of buttons and uniforms."[77] Contemplating the challenge that women infected with venereal disease posed to soldiers, one CTCA lawyer asked, "Why not make it a felony for a woman to commit fornication with a soldier or sailor anywhere?"[78] He was not alone in suggesting such an extreme course of action. In December 1917, a Mrs. Charles King wrote a letter to President Wilson entreating the government to arrange for the "internment . . . of all women of careless chastity."[79]

A coordinated wartime campaign against prostitution and promiscuity quickly drew upon Bureau resources. After all, the Bureau had been carefully monitoring prostitutes for over five years. Snow recalled that the Department of Justice was "recognized as the agency charged with enforcement of federal law" and it would stand as the intermediary between civilian and military law enforcement officials.[80] In practice, this meant Bureau special agents and local white slave officers would coordinate with military police and local law enforcement to ensure that America's soldiers remained "fit to fight." The experiences of Local White Slave Officer Charles B. Braun illustrates how this played out on the ground.

Although the Bureau eliminated the White Slave Division in early 1914, it still relied upon and extended its system of local white slave officers—those deputized volunteers—to do the work of the Department of Justice in localities throughout the country. The Bureau appointed thirty-seven new local white slave officers in new cities and towns in the West after the division had closed its doors. When current local white slave officers resigned, the Bureau searched for replacements. One local white slave officer who continued monitoring prostitutes after the closing of the White Slave Division was Charles B. Braun. Born in 1885 in Kentucky, in the 1910s he moved to Texas where, by 1913, he was officiating college football games and practicing law in Waco. In December 1913, Stanley Finch appointed Braun to be the local white slave officer in Waco, and directed him to work under the special agent in charge in San Antonio. Finch urged Braun not only to look for white slave cases in his vicinity, but to keep an eye out for violations of slavery and peonage statutes. Braun faithfully took up his work, making "one tour each week for the purpose of keeping in touch with the arrival and departure of prostitutes" in Waco.[81] His education into the seamy underside of Waco progressed. In June 1915, he wrote to Special Agent in Charge Robert L. Barnes: "In regard to the pimp situation . . . I stated that so far as we could ascertain there were no pimps or procurers in this vicinity."[82] Barnes doubted these findings and urged Braun to be more diligent in his surveillance of brothels. In response, Braun retoured the red-light district and resubmitted his report that offered detailed descriptions of eight pimps he had discovered who lived off the earnings of Waco sex workers.[83] By the end of 1915, Braun reported that he knew all of the inmates of Waco's brothels as well as the various individuals who populated the vice neighborhoods. But he did not limit his work to vice cases; he investigated eighteen cases of African American peonage, and violations of postal laws and interstate commerce rules. He also looked into individuals impersonating government officials, federal fugitives, and cases of bankruptcy.

World War I dramatically altered Charles Braun's day-to-day activities, as it did every other local white slave agent and Bureau special agent in the country. Even before U.S. entry into the war, Bureau Chief Bielaski advised Braun and other local white slave officers to consult librarians for lists of people checking out books on explosives since the outbreak of war in Europe. And in early 1917, he reminded local white slave officers to aggressively investigate violations of neutrality and any individuals who might be "connected with European interest" and to "keep such persons under surveillance as much as possible."[84] When President Wilson announced U.S. entry into the war in April 1917, and it looked likely that many local white slave officers would be drafted into the military. Bielaski sent his local white slave officers the following statement: "I wish to advise you that the Department considers that you can be of more service to the Government in your present position than in the Army, but if you feel it to be your patriotic duty to respond to the draft, no active opposition will be entered by this office."[85] Charles Braun chose to remain a local white slave officer for the Department of Justice.

Quickly, Braun found himself investigating a wide array of war-related issues, including conscription violations, rumors of German spies and sympathizers living among central Texas's many German towns and communities, theft of war materials, and still numerous white slavery cases. Clearly Braun's activities had spread well beyond white slavery, a fact he noted when he complained that his white slave office badge bred confusion when he investigated war-related issues. "The badge I am wearing is a white slave officer's badge No. 302," he began, "and on a number of occasions my authority to look into other matters has been questioned because of the limitations seemingly prescribed by this badge. . . . Isn't it possible for me to obtain and use a regulation badge as it would greatly help me in the handling of cases and not subject me to any embarrassment at the hands of others."[86] With the expanded scope of investigations, Braun, the Bureau, and the Department of Justice, were soon completely overwhelmed. According to Snow, "The war . . . found the national government without personnel, equipment or institutions with which to discharge the responsibilities incident to the enforcement of section 13 of the draft act."[87] For help, Braun, and local white slave officers and Bureau officials like him, turned to the American Protective League (APL).

In 1917, at the urging of Chicago's Special Agent in Charge Hinton G. Clabaugh, A. M. Briggs gathered together hundreds, and then thousands, of volunteers throughout the country under the umbrella of the APL to aid the Department of Justice and the War Department in all kinds of investigations. As one of the postwar hagiographers of the APL noted, the "APL is not and never was a part of any state or national arm, service, department, or bureau."[88] Yet, during the war, the APL functioned as a volunteer army of investigators for the local white slave officers, who were, in themselves, a quasi-volunteer army of investigators. When A. M. Briggs grew curious about the progress of APL branches in central Texas, he wrote to Braun. At his prompting, Braun established APL branches in the surrounding areas. Braun instructed local APL leaders to have members, unknown to one another, "look into everything as fully as possible, getting definite data, and then if, in your opinion the matter calls for more investigation or for more action notify me."[89] Department of Justice representatives like Braun functioned as intermediaries between the APL and the Department of Justice.

Local white slave officers also served as intermediaries between local police, military police, and the Department of Justice, particularly in investigations related to the violation of Section 13. Waco had closed its vice district in the summer of 1917 when the police chief ordered all residents of the red-light district to leave town by August 11 or face arrest, so working with military police to find clandestine brothels near Camp MacArthur, located just outside of Waco, emerged as Braun's primary antiprostitution activity during the war. On Christmas Eve of 1917, Braun accompanied military police when they entered the home of Maggie Foster and arrested her and Lillian Johnson for operating a bawdy house with the five-mile limit of Camp MacArthur. They had followed two white soldiers to Maggie's home, and discovered that the men had each paid two dollars to have sex with Maggie and Lillian, both of whom were African American. The military police charged Maggie Foster with violating Section 13, while Braun handed Lillian Johnson over to local authorities who charged her with vagrancy, a catch-all charge frequently used to police African Americans' public, and in this case private, behavior.[90]

White slave cases continued to be a priority for Braun during the war years because the Bureau's policing of brothels could contribute to the antipromiscuity agenda of the military. Braun's deep knowledge of the vice conditions of Waco proved to be invaluable to the War Department's efforts to enforce Section 13 around Camp MacArthur. In 1918, Braun gave Lieutenant

Darsie of Army Intelligence a tour of the vice neighborhoods in Waco, Texas, and Camp MacArthur, assuring him that the census and moral quarantine established by the Bureau of Investigation's White Slave Division in 1913 suited the military's purpose of keeping its soldiers "fit to fight." Over the course of their evening tour, Braun identified eighty-five women: forty-two had "questionable character" meaning they were likely prostitutes-in-hiding; twelve were former prostitutes in Waco's brothels before they had been closed by the military and were presumed to be continuing their work in the sex trade; eight were unknown to Braun, but he considered them to possibly be prostitutes; seven were designated as "not sure if all right," and sixteen were deemed "all right." Taken together, a majority of the women firmly fit in the immoral category, and Braun seemed to look at the rest with considerable suspicion. Most of Braun's white slave cases during the war dovetailed with war aims of eliminating soldier's access to promiscuous women by criminalizing those women.[91]

The tendency to treat all single women as potentially promiscuous threatened the freedom of mobility of all women and could lead to scandal as Braun learned when he attempted to build a case against Mattie H. Edwards. Mattie's mother had dispatched her to Waco in October 1917 to keep an eye on her seventeen-year-old brother, a private stationed in Camp MacArthur. Unable to find permanent lodging in Waco due to the wartime housing shortage, Mattie took up residence in the Hotel Raleigh. For two weeks her brother visited her frequently, spending time with her in her hotel room. Mattie's statement to Braun is worth quoting at length as it clearly illustrates how single women lived under a veil of suspicion during the war:

> He is only a kid and I, as his sister was here to look after him. I had been at the Raleigh two weeks, when he and a friend of his, a private in the same company, Fredolf Johnson, came to my room one Saturday night. While they were there I ordered up two bottles of beer, to be paid for by me on my bill. I did not think that there was any harm in this. The beer had not been touched, in fact the bottles had not been opened, when the house detective knocked at my door, and when I opened it, he said you will have to get out of here, because you are having beer and men in your rooms. Mr. Moore, the assistant manager, came in right behind him, Yes, you will have to get out right now,

for having a man in your rooms. I explained that the boy was my brother, and they said or intimated he was not and said I could not put anything like that by them. I offered to show a letter from my mother to prove that the boy was my brother and they said I could not put that by them. Mr. Fellow, the manager, came up and also said that I would have to get out because I had men in my room. I said he was my brother and he said I could not get by with that, and . . . Mr. Moore spoke up and . . . [intimated] that I was drunk. The beer had not been opened, no was never opened, and I had had absolutely nothing to drink.[92]

Mattie Edwards was so horrified at her treatment and the assumption that she engaged in immoral behavior that she later sued the manager and owner of the Hotel Raleigh for libel. But the operating logic that all single women could be covert prostitutes drove much of the moral campaign during World War I.

In fighting venereal disease, the Department of Justice and the CTCA established a policy of "quarantine and cure," which meant "quarantine, detention, and internment" for all women suspected of undermining military health by engaging in sexual contact with troops. The authority conferred on the Department of War through Section 13 paved the way for the arrest of women deemed to be a sexual threat to soldiers' health. Government documents from the period suggest that over 30,000 women were incarcerated in federal facilities. It is important to note that this figure of 30,000 does not include women arrested under local and state laws, women like Lillian Johnson whom Braun handed over to local police. All of these women essentially saw their writs of habeas corpus suspended.[93] Attorney General T. W. Gregory defended the practice as a necessary measure to ensure appropriate public health policy.[94] Women arrested under local laws faced a position just as challenging as those arrested under Section 13. One report from Augusta, Georgia, noted, "The sheriff of the county told me that on a recent raid on a country road he rounded up ten women with as many soldiers. He arrested the women but let the soldiers go free, one of the soldiers being a captain. Lewd women are dealt with severely in the police court and other courts in Augusta. Most generally they are given a work sentence without the alternative of a fine."[95] The number of women arrested and punished through local courts is unclear, but probably higher than those incarcerated under federal jurisdiction. Raymond B. Fosdick recalled, "a personal inspection of a women's prison in Newport News, Virginia where every single inch of floor space on three floors was covered with mattresses in an attempt to provide for the inmates."[96] Furthermore, all of these women were subjected to invasive, compulsory vaginal examinations and, if found to be infected with a sexually transmitted disease, underwent forced treatment.

For the most part, feminists in the United States did not comment on the repressive aspects of the CTCA's program, with the notable exception of Dr. Kate C. Bushnell, who wrote furious letters about the policy to friends at home and abroad in the United Kingdom. Bushnell, a long-time anti–white slavery activist with many allies in the social purity movement but none in the social hygiene movement, protested the compulsory medical exams arrested women were forced to endure.[97] Writing to the U.S. Public Health Service, she proclaimed, "You cannot appreciate how a woman feels to have her person exposed to the masturbating hand of a vile doctor."[98] She also criticized the way the policy collapsed all women into the one category of potential public health risk, and she protested that it was women who bore the brunt of any police action. As a strict supporter of the single standard of morality, Bushnell was deeply troubled by the CTCA's actions. She explained, "They are NOT bent on suppressing fornication in men by the same means, but in my opinion are coddling it. Their spy police run in girls, not the men associated, and it is girls only who are being given prison sentences, and that on the mere word of the policeman, without proper evidence. . . . On the other hand, I understand several 'clinics' have been established in San Francisco to give men prophylactic treatment after each act of sensual indulgence, at public expense."[99] Bushnell was disturbed by how this social hygiene policy set aside lightly, with little or no protest, women's civil rights. She noted that the actions of the CTCA "endanger the legal status and Constitutional rights of every woman in the land."[100] In an attempt to publicize the suspension of women's legal rights, Bushnell printed small cards to hand out to San Franciscan women. The cards warned that women incarcerated as vagrants lacked civil rights and warned that biased treatment of suspected prostitutes "tends to manufacture a slave class for libertines."[101] Furthermore she tried to interest editors of various publications in the story and lobbied local California politicians—all to no avail. In desperation, she wrote to the British feminists of the Association of Moral and Social Hygiene, the inheritors of Josephine Butler's Ladies National Association, for aid. Using their personal connections, these feminists focused the attention of the *International Suffrage News* on developing conditions in the United States and attempted to engage American feminists such as Carrie Chapman Catt in this question.[102] Yet, throughout the war, U.S. feminists like Kate Bushnell (and Lucy Stone Blackwell) were alone in the condemnation of the CTCA's increasingly repressive social hygiene program. According to the dominant logic, young American soldiers needed to be protected from women who were conceived of as vectors of venereal disease, and the preexisting Bureau network of local white slave officers was well positioned to help police these young women.

◆ ◆ ◆

During the 1910s, American sexual culture underwent significant change. Throughout this period, American law enforcement, public health officials, and reformers wrestled with the dilemma of whether to protect or police the sexuality of women and girls. Newspaper reports, antivice activists' speeches, and sensational magazine exposés emphasized the need to rescue girls with the federal government playing hero to thousands of exploited girls. Meanwhile, big city newspapers circulated another narrative of white slavery that focused on women's active participation in entrapping, luring, and seducing wealthy men for the purposes of blackmail. Additionally, as America mobilized for war, groups like the American Social Hygiene Association and the Department of War's CTCA positioned women as vectors of disease, which led to shifting the discourse from protecting white women from dissolute men to protecting young virile men from venal and venereal women.

The notion, common in the early 1910s, that sexually compromised young women, like Marsha Warrington and Lola Norris, could be deserving of rescue had disappeared by 1919. Instead, young sexually promiscuous young women like Marsha and Lola were more than likely to face incarceration. The Supreme Court's broad interpretation of the White Slave Traffic Act, which opened the door to pursuing noncommercial immorality, seemed out of step with this trend to see young women as dangerous to men. Yet the Supreme Court's *Caminetti* decision and the CTCA's repressive social hygiene program shared a condemnation of irregular sexual relations. In the reading by the federal government, "any other immoral purpose" constituted a broad call to action to protect intact marriages and police any form of sexuality that diverged from the ideal conjugal model. Mann Act investigation in the era after World War I reflected this ideology as the Bureau gave up protecting young women and girls and shifted to protecting patriarchal domesticity.

6

Policing Seduction and Adultery

Enforcement of the Mann Act in the 1910s focused on categories of illicit sex with the Bureau of Investigation looking into cases of pedophilia, sex between men of color and white women, and mostly, cases of interstate prostitution and sex trafficking. Yet, the twin developments of 1917—wartime conflation of prostitution and promiscuity, which criminalized female sexuality, and the *Caminetti* decision that empowered a broad reading of the "any other immoral purpose" clause of the statute—expanded the category of illicit sex that the Bureau pursued. Presumably, interstate cases of incest, same-sex intimacy, interracial sex, bigamy, adultery, fornication, rape, and seduction all fell under the Bureau's purview. Given the fact that marriage could legally cure cases of fornication, rape, and seduction, transforming these illicit acts into licit arrangements,[1] and that cases of bigamy and adultery constituted violations of marital unity, then marriage emerged as the primary institution that the Bureau policed in the 1920s as investigations into marital domestic discord quickly outpaced investigations into interstate prostitution in terms of special agents' case loads.[2] In the early twentieth century, marriage was the only locus for licit sex.

This shift in focus towards policing domestic arrangements can partly be explained by the fact that the wartime closing of vice districts and their brothels pushed prostitution underground, making invisible and clandestine what had been visible and public. But this shift to protecting marriage can also be explained by the fact that the *Caminetti* decision gave credence to the voices of disgruntled citizens who had, since Congress had passed the Mann Act in 1910, tried to turn to the Bureau for aid in their domestic crises. No longer did the Bureau ignore calls for help; rather during the 1920s, the Bureau enthusiastically responded to citizens' invitations for investigations into their own familial catastrophes and marital calamities. Private individuals initiated most of these cases—between 50 to 70 percent of them according to J Edgar Hoover—and from 1921 to 1936 the Bureau investigated around 47,500 Mann Act cases.[3] Yet during the same period of time, U.S. Attorneys achieved only 6,335 convictions.[4] In policing patriarchy and respectable domesticity, convictions were not necessarily the Bureau's goal, bringing order to disorderly homes was. Mann Act investigations had formed the cornerstone of Bureau investigations in the 1910s. Changing political and cultural forces would significantly alter the Bureau in the period between the World Wars, yet Mann Act cases continued to shore up the agency's authority. Bureau investigations into cases of interstate immorality, as distinguished from Mann Act cases characterized by commercial vice, brought average Americans under Bureau surveillance, frequently at their own invitation. Ordinary people sought out the Bureau's aid in their attempts to solve their interpersonal crises.

Bringing order to disorderly homes frequently meant monitoring women's mobility and regulating men's respectability all in the name of protecting the institution of marriage. The enforcement of the "any other immoral purpose" clause of the Mann Act to police extralegal sex was always defined in reference to the site of legal sex—marriage.[5] Throughout the 1920s, the Bureau found itself investigating violations of marriage, and woven through the investigative case files appears the key phrase "living as man and wife" to describe the fraudulent ways unmarried, heterosexual couples pretended to be married and thus did violence to those within a legitimate marriage. Operating as a euphemism for sexual relations, it emphasized the Bureau's position that existent marriages, particularly those with young children, must be upheld. In this understanding, legitimate children, and *real* wives had greater claims to protection. The Bureau defended the marriage contract that promised a man access to his wife's sexual and household labor, yet required him to financially support her and any children.[6] Merely "living as man and wife" was not enough; one actually had to *be* man and wife to enjoy the benefits of marriage. Marriage was a legal status (or a process of law) as much as an experience of companionship, and as such it had acquired its own legal history over time that shaped Bureau investigations into interstate immorality or illicit, nonconjugal, heterosexual sex.

Though the "any other immoral purpose" clause was broad, vague, and empowered by the Supreme Court, the Bureau did not use it to police same-sex sexuality—either commercial or recreational—prior to World War II. This glaring and perhaps surprising fact suggests that the federal government was still puzzling through homosexuality in the early twentieth century.[7] The fact that everyone, from purity reformers to critics of the Mann Act, agreed that Congress had always intended the law to police prostitution, first, and other forms of immorality, second, seemed to cast the entire affair in a heterosexual light. Though a thriving gay prostitution scene existed in places like New York City in the 1910s and 1920s, most conceptions of prostitution articulated it as a heterosexual script with gendered roles that were always cast the same: prostitute-female, customer-male.[8] In pursuing these cases of interstate immorality, the Bureau focused on heterosexual relationships, particularly cases of seduction, adultery, and bigamy.

Disgraced by its leading role in the Palmer Raids of 1919 and 1920 and implicated in the Teapot Dome and other Harding Administration scandals, the Bureau (and the Department of Justice in general) faced a serious public relations problem in the early 1920s. Harry M. Daugherty, attorney general in the Harding Administration, had been embroiled in numerous allegations of abusing his power in efforts to protect Harding's "Ohio Gang" and their illegal activities. The Bureau had been brought into the fray when newspaper reports and congressional investigations revealed that its director, William J. Burns, had employed his special agents to spy on congressmen who might expose the scandals. Consequently, when Calvin Coolidge assumed the presidency after Harding's death in August 1923, he immediately began to look for a new attorney general who could restore confidence in the Department of Justice. Coolidge ultimately ousted Daugherty from office in May 1924 and replaced him with Harlan Fiske Stone, the dean of Columbia University Law School. Upon becoming the nation's leading lawyer, Stone immediately fired Burns, whose misuse of the agency had come to light in congressional hearings, replacing him with Bureau Deputy Chief J. Edgar Hoover. Hoover had successfully insulated himself from the scandals of the 1920s, largely due to his youth. Most dismissed his participation in the Palmer raids as being inconsequential because it was inconceivable that a twenty-four-year-old man would have had much influence over the raids. Yet, even prior to his appointment as head of the Bureau, Hoover led much of the agency's day-to-day operations. In Hoover, Stone found a workaholic who was seemingly apolitical, morally conservative, and free of any scandalous association—just the type of man that was the antithesis of the gregarious and dramatic William J. Burns—and perfect for the job.[9]

Upon assuming the directorship of the Bureau in 1924, a position he would hold until his death in 1972, J. Edgar Hoover sought to establish the agency as the country's premier investigative force.[10] He immediately cut the Bureau's size, dismissing sixty-two employees, closing five of the fifty-three field offices, and returning $300,000 of its budget to the U.S. Treasury. Throughout the 1920s he continued to streamline the Bureau, reducing the number of agents in an effort to increase their supervision.[11] During the period from 1924 to 1938, Hoover and the Bureau concentrated their efforts on modernizing investigative techniques and professionalizing the agency. In this context, Hoover tightened standards about who could qualify to be an agent and established a special training school for agents.[12] The Bureau also launched a centralized Fingerprint Division, which by 1941 would hold the fingerprints of more than 23,500,000 individuals.[13] The agency began an intense process of working with local law enforcement bodies to standardize the collection of crime statistics—which in itself was nothing short of a modern miracle that redefined the field of criminology—publishing in 1930 two annual reports entitled *Uniform Crime Report* and *Fugitives Wanted By Police*.[14] During the 1920s, Bureau agents operated as a purely investigative force, with no authority to carry guns or make arrests, although this practice would change in 1934 after a series of highly publicized kidnapping cases.[15] In the realm of investigation, Hoover's Bureau focused on the traditional scope of the agency—Mann Act cases, peonage cases in the Jim Crow South, car theft, kidnapping and ransom cases, and bank fraud and robbery cases.[16]

In its role as a national crime-fighting agency enforcing the Mann Act, the Bureau fought the sexual exploitation of women. Yet histories of the Bureau focus almost exclusively on the Bureau's role in political policing, seeking to uncover the ways that the agency operated as a "secret intelligence system" that "trampled on civil liberties," while undermining democratic community organizing.[17] The day-to-day tasks of fighting crime have been de-emphasized in these accounts. But J. Edgar Hoover told the Wickersham Commission, or the National Commission on Law Observance and Enforcement, in 1930 that the majority of special agents' time was spent investigating the National Motor Vehicle Theft Act (30%), the White Slave Traffic Act (29%), and the National Bankruptcy Act (25.5%), with antitrust laws, impersonation of government officials, illegal possession of government property, and theft of interstate shipment investigations comprising the rest of their activities.[18] Though the sins of the Bureau are many, with its long tradition of targeting perceived symbols of subversion to the "American way of life," the agency also needs to be evaluated in its role as a law enforcement organization, revealing the growth of the criminal justice state. Examining the daily activities of the Bureau demonstrates the agency's long history in combating the sexual exploitation of young women. Hoover noted that Mann Act cases typically came from three sources: 70 percent came from private individuals connected to the case, especially in interstate immorality cases; 5 percent came directly from U.S. Attorneys; and 25 percent came from police or people connected to law enforcement or social services.[19]

Hoover's modernization of the Bureau was coupled with an attempt to use the agency to protect traditional morality and positioned the agency as a bulwark against the shifting gender, sexual, and cultural norms. In the 1920s, he launched an initiative to investigate violations of federal pornography laws, and in 1925 he created the separately maintained Obscene File, which would grow to be one of the largest collections of American pornography in existence.[20] Hoover used the politics of sex and morality to raise the Bureau's reputation, argue for federal law enforcement when criticized by state-rights champions, and highlight his own leadership.[21] Mann Act investigations fit nicely into Hoover's vision for the Bureau. Following the 1917 *Caminetti* decision, the Department of Justice advised district attorneys and Bureau agents that they should continue to investigate Mann Act cases that involved bigamy, "previously chaste, or very young women or girls," and "married women (with young children)."[22] With these guidelines, district attorneys and Bureau agents enthusiastically pursued these cases of "interstate immorality." Mann Act investigations constituted the largest part of Bureau agents' case loads during the 1920s.[23]

In pursuing cases of interstate immorality, Hoover positioned the Bureau as a defense against the rapidly changing American culture. A revolution in attitudes towards marriage and sexual behavior had begun in the early twentieth century but reached a full flowering in the 1920s.[24] This revolution, called sexual liberalism by some, was characterized by celebrating sexual development as key to personal development, emphasizing companionship and sexual compatibility as the foundation for happy marriages, and separating sex from its procreative functions.[25] For the purpose of Mann Act investigations, three cultural trends were particularly relevant: the rise of the companionate marriage ideal and the concomitant rise in divorce; the weakening of community surveillance of sexual relations; and the move of youth courting from "the front porch to the back seat" of automobiles.[26]

As companionate marriage—the idea that sexual expression for both men and women constituted an important facet of healthy living and that marriage should be defined by compatibility—emerged as the ideal, American couples felt new strains and stresses on their relationships.[27] Throughout the early decades of the twentieth century the divorce rate crept upward—one in every six marriages resulted in divorce by the 1920s.[28] Concerns about personal happiness emerged in divorce proceedings with far greater frequency than had occurred during the late nineteenth century.[29] But marriage rates continued to climb alongside divorce rates. Indeed, many Mann Act investigations revealed that Americans remained so enthusiastic about marriage that they often failed to terminate their previous marriage before launching into a new bigamous one. As a result, bigamy appeared frequently in interstate immorality cases.

Similarly disquieting to social traditionalists was the explosion of a youth consumer culture and sexual modernism in the era after World War I, which seemed to rock the very foundations of American morality and stability. At the center of much of this debate existed the reality that American youth, young women in particular, were operating from a different moral code from that of their parents' generation and that consumerism drove much of this code. The widespread panic over the shortening of hemlines reflected a stark change in American women's daily lives. In 1928, the *Journal of Commerce* reported that in fifteen years the quantity of material required for a woman's clothes had declined from nineteen yards to seven yards.[30] As women wore less cloth, they wore substantially more cosmetics. One study published in 1929 estimated that every year the average adult women purchased over a pound of face powder and eight rouge compacts. Sales of cosmetics rose from $17 million in 1914 to $141 million in 1925.[31] In Mann Act investigations, young women's clothing, length of hair, and use of cosmetics were noted when they seemed to denote a sexually liberal lifestyle—for Bureau agents, a woman's consumption of particular goods characterized her moral character and sexual behavior.

But nothing would exemplify the connections between consumer culture, youth culture, sex, and immorality more than that great emblem of American ingenuity, economic power, and consumerism—the automobile. Decried by social conservatives as a "house of prostitution on wheels"[32] and paired with the movie house and the dance hall to form "the triumvirate of hell"[33] for American youth, the car greatly expanded the mobility of the average American and often took individuals outside the purview of their community's watchful eyes. For example, by 1925, improvements in roads and cars meant that a motorist could cover about two hundred miles in an average day.[34] During the 1920s, the availability and affordability of cars put them within the reach of both rural and urban Americans, who rapidly purchased these new vehicles.[35] It seemed to many commentators that cars provided a uniquely private setting for immoral behavior. "One of the cornerstones of American morality," Frederick L. Allen wryly observed, "had been the difficulty of finding a suitable locale for misconduct," and during the 1920s the automobile quickly emerged as that locale.[36] The Lynds, in their famous 1929 study of life in Muncie, Indiana, found that teenagers frequently traveled twenty miles to attend dances "with no one's permission asked."[37] Furthermore the car grew into one of the preferred sites of courtship during this period. This combination of sexual discovery, mobility, and youth posed unique challenges to parents and law enforcement. Throughout the 1920s, the automobile replaced the train as the primary means of transport in Mann Act cases. Because of the privacy and independence afforded by cars, Bureau agents often had more difficulty tracking down suspects, retracing the journeys to interview witnesses, and determining exactly what had happened in the car.

On the whole, Bureau agents looked with horror at the culminating gender and sexual revolution that took women out of the home for work and pleasure. According to Courtney Ryley Cooper, a journalist and Bureau apologist, youth crime in the 1930s was wholly attributable to "sex in youth," and behind every boy committing a crime the cause "has to do with a girl."[38] Similarly, Melvin Purvis, a special agent throughout the country in the 1920s, saw women as "the protected rather than the protector."[39] Social conservatism dominated this masculinized, middle-class, Anglo-Saxon space. When agents investigated interstate immorality, they held at heart a gender ideology that celebrated female sexual innocence in the young, sexual fidelity in the married, and women in traditional sex roles such as mother and homemaker. In many of the cases investigated, the victims did not fit these somewhat narrow characteristics; such cases rarely went to a grand jury, denying to women who did not conform to gender norms protection that others received. Nonetheless, Hoover's Bureau used the Mann Act to pursue seducers of young women, to punish adulterers who had young children in their homes, to restore women and girls whose domestic labor was key to the family back in their homes, and to seek men who had abandoned their paternal responsibilities.

In 1921, Jacob Marcus called the Detroit field office of the Bureau of Investigation when his sixteen-year-old daughter Fay disappeared with her African American fiancée, Lloyd Lewis. The couple had been dating for over a year and wished to secure Marcus's permission to marry. Marcus had never met his daughter's boyfriend, and when he finally did meet Lloyd, it only took one look for him to refuse permission for the marriage. Moreover, he prohibited the couple from dating. Fay had told her father that Lloyd was Brazilian, but Marcus believed that Lloyd "was a negro although he was not very dark." When the young couple disappeared within the week, Marcus called on the power of the Mann Act to track down the couple, setting in motion agents in four cities—Detroit, Homestead, Pittsburgh, and Chicago—who used all their resources to track them down.[40] Parents in the 1920s saw the Bureau as another tool in their arsenal of ways to control their daughters' sexuality, especially when their daughters crossed state lines and evaded local jurisdiction.[41]

Since Congress had passed the Mann Act in 1910, parents had sought to use the law to either control their daughters who were experimenting with new sexual mores of the times or to gain some type of retribution when men callously seduced and discarded their daughters. State-level seduction laws emerged out of the social purity movement's campaigns to pass laws that regulated sexuality and protected vulnerable women. By 1921, thirty-seven states had adopted some kind of seduction legislation.[42] These laws all had the same basic features: some sort of sexual contact had to have occurred; the young woman needed to have been of "previously chaste character"; and, the man must have promised marriage in the process of persuading (or coercing) his partner into bed.[43] Most of these laws allowed criminal prosecution to be voided by a subsequent wedding between the victim and the defendant. The requirement of the "previously chaste character" of the victim, which typically meant a reputation as a previously chaste girl rather than proof of fact, demonstrates that one of the basic purposes of seduction legislation was to protect the reputation of respectable young women who might have been deceived.[44] Seduction laws criminalized the fraudulent and cynical use of promises of marriage to engage in the benefits of marriage—sex—without actually committing to marriage. By having stipulations like the "previous chaste character" and "promise of marriage" these laws carved out an implicit type of extramarital sex that could be condoned—sex with women of poor reputations with no promise of marriage.[45]

Another purpose of seduction legislation was to help ensure the economic survival of the victim. Purity reformers supported these laws because they believed that a single act of seduction could ruin a young woman's future by putting her on a path that inevitably led to prostitution, poverty, and death. Though this fate may have been overdrawn, due to the prominence of the sexual double standard, girls whose reputation had been tarnished by public whispers of sexual misbehavior certainly saw their outlook diminished. A girl's social ruin threatened her marriage prospects, which in turn would extend her economic dependency on her family, undermining the family's reputation and future solvency.[46] Marriage as a bar to criminal prosecution addressed many, but not all, of the harms associated with seduction—including providing for children and ensuring the economic survival of the woman (and child), while absolving the state of that responsibility. It essentially shifted the economic burden of the young woman and any children that might have been produced from the liaison from her family to the man who had "ruined" her.[47] The Mann Act operated as a federal seduction law, providing parents and victims a tool to use when the bounder who had promised marriage left for another jurisdiction. When victims turned to the Bureau, they often sought help in forcing men to take responsibility for fathering a child, or they desired that the men be punished for fraudulent promises of marriage. Like state-level seduction laws, Mann Act seduction cases privileged victims that had a constellation of the following attributes: whiteness, youth, previous chastity, and respectable reputations.

Parents like Jacob Marcus used the Mann Act to try to assert control over headstrong, runaway daughters. In 1927 Pearl Pomonis reported to the Denver office of the bureau that her fifteen-year-old daughter, Margaret, had run away from home with a twenty-two-year-old soda jerk she had met at the Princess Candy Shop named Gust Terzakis. The special agents tracked the couple from Denver, Colorado, to Raton, New Mexico, to Kansas City, Missouri, and, finally, to Chicago, Illinois, where local police arrested them. When interviewed, Margaret claimed that her "mother had not allowed her to go with any boys and had been rather strict with her at home,"[48] so when Gust suggested they run away and get married, Margaret eagerly agreed. The special agents and U.S. Attorneys in the case decided not to pursue prosecution because Margaret would be a terrible witness who would never testify willingly against Gust and in all likelihood would take the opportunity to rail against her mother. So they left her incarcerated at the Cook County Juvenile Detention Home, and alerted her parents to her location; thereby reuniting a recalcitrant daughter with her strict parents and upholding the principals and praxis of parental authority.

Parents turned to the Bureau when trying to track down runaway daughters who defied their parents' rules about who constituted an acceptable marriage partner. When they learned that their daughter had run off to Detroit, Michigan, with twenty-year-old Frank Palatrone, the parents of sixteen-year-old Theresa Antinacce of Cleveland, Ohio, contacted the Cleveland Police Department, the Detroit Police Department, and the Detroit office of the Bureau in their efforts to put a halt to any wedding. Theresa and Frank had met in late September 1929 and after a week of courting Frank proposed to Theresa. Knowing that her parents opposed the match, the couple took a bus to Detroit and immediately applied for a marriage license, which due to Michigan state law, required a five-day waiting period before a ceremony could occur. During this five-day period, Bureau special agents discovered the couple in a hotel, registered as man and wife, and with local police took them into custody. Theresa argued that she could not have been transported for an immoral purpose because, after all, she had been transported for the purpose of marriage, which was clearly a moral ambition and institution. She admitted that she and Frank had had sexual intercourse in the hotel— "had lived as man and wife"—but she suggested that if her parents had not opposed the match, then the couple would have married in Cleveland and they would have been a legitimate, respectable couple engaged in completely licit sexual activities. In Theresa's eyes, her parents' opposition to the relationship created the immoral context; but in the eyes of the law and Bureau, the immorality stemmed from Theresa's disobedience to her parents' will and her inability to wait five days until a marriage ceremony before entering into a sexual relationship. The investigating agents had little to say about Frank, other than to imply that they believed he had intended to marry Theresa, meaning his seduction of her was not a crass violation of good taste and did not even constitute a violation of state-level seduction laws that depended upon the combination of the previously chaste character of the girl and the *false* promise of marriage. Frank's apparent willingness to marry Theresa abrogated any criminal charges against him, so the assistant U.S. Attorney and the special agents closed the case and turned Theresa over to her parents, who had arrived in Detroit to ensure no marriage would take place.[49] Indeed, marriage records from Cuyahoga County reveal that within the following month, Theresa married Mike DeOreo, while in 1934, Frank married Caroline Russo.[50] In this case, the Bureau working with local police departments shored up parental authority over their daughters' romantic, sexual, and marital choices.

Many seduction cases emerged from parents outraged that their daughters had been deceived, impregnated, and abandoned by some cad. The Bureau helped locate these villains in an effort to gain justice, ensure punishment, and sometimes demand recognition of paternity. Pregnancy exacerbated the ruinous effects of seduction. Illegitimate children inherited their mother's loss of respectability, carrying a social stigma throughout their lives.[51] The restoration of family honor seemed to be an important goal of turning to the Bureau. In 1927 the father of Ethel Margaret Kennedy complained to local authorities that H. L. "Buster" Frierson—a man described as "exceedingly good looking"—had viciously deceived and assaulted his daughter. He had infected her with venereal disease, abused her, stolen her money, and left her pregnant. The couple had met in Hartsville, South Carolina, in February 1926. They had courted for a year, speaking frequently of marriage with Buster promising that when they tied the knot he would happily give up drinking and settle down. When rumors reached Hartsville that Buster might already be married, according to Ethel, "he told me that he had been [married] but was divorced. He swore to me that he was [divorced]."[52] With her parents' consent and support, Buster and Ethel decided to leave home on December 4, 1926, and head to Florence, South Carolina, where they would get married. Instead, he took her to Winston-Salem, North Carolina, where he snatched all of her money from her purse after finding a room in a boarding house. When she asked him when they were going to be married, he replied that the hour had grown too late for a wedding that day and that they would apply for a marriage certificate the next day. She replied that she could not spend the night in the same room with him without being married and started to gather her things to leave. According to Ethel, "He followed me upstairs, shut the door and said, 'What kind of a damn fool do you think I am to bring you here and then let you go[?]' He wouldn't let me out, holding me there by force. He made me undress and go to bed with him. That night he forced me to have sexual intercourse with him."[53] Ethel pleaded with him to legitimate the relationship via marriage, but over the course of the next few days a pattern emerged where Buster would promise to get a marriage license, but instead would buy a bottle of whiskey, or go carousing with some friends. After several weeks of this routine, Ethel got a job clerking at a local five and ten cent store, where she hoped she could save up enough funds to pay for a trip back home. She reported that Christmas came and went, and the relationship continued to deteriorate. Now, in addition to controlling her every move, Buster had started flaunting his relationships with other women in front of Ethel, even taking her jewelry and giving it to one of his "girlfriends." She remembered, "All this time I was trying to get enough money to leave him but he always managed to take all the money I could get."[54] Ethel's father arrived in Winston-Salem and had Buster arrested for violation of the White Slave Traffic Act and bigamy on January 13, 1927. He took Ethel and sent her to her aunt in Chicago where she could get treatment for the venereal disease that Buster had given her. Her family admitted that the most important reason they had sent Ethel to Chicago was "in order to avoid the embarrassment to the family through undue publicity in this case."[55] When interviewed in late April 1927 in Chicago, Ethel assured the special agents that she had never had sex prior to her relationship with Buster. She noted that he forced her to engage in sexual relations every night and that due to this she had become pregnant and contracted syphilis, though she was no longer pregnant by April. Special agents carefully noted that Ethel's doctor had testified that she lost the baby due to a natural miscarriage rather than an abortion, but given the availability of therapeutic abortions in Chicago in 1927 combined with the way that this pregnancy had been conceived and the trauma surrounding Ethel's experience, it is exceedingly likely that she had decided to terminate the pregnancy.[56] Throughout this period, the Bureau exhibited no interest in including abortion under the umbrella of the "any other immoral purpose" clause.

Ethel's story carefully articulated her blamelessness, and as she recounted her experiences to the Bureau agents she probably emphasized the aspects of her tribulations that made her the most sympathetic: the fact that she was promised marriage, the fact that she was forced to work, the fact that she could not retain her wages (Buster confiscated them as if he had the right of a husband to do so), and so on—all combined to make this an outrageous case. Her story of exploitation was portrayed in this way to garner the most pity and compassion while mitigating her own culpability. But the fact that her family had a respectable reputation, and that her father acted as her champion, predisposed the Bureau to be sympathetic to her cause. Even without the aggravating circumstances of rape, theft, and abuse, this case would likely have been considered a gross violation of the Mann Act due to the reputation of Ethel's family. This case struck the special agents in Chicago and Atlanta as an especially aggravated example of seduction. The judge in the case called it "one of the most revolting and aggravated cases of this class" that he had ever seen. After Buster pleaded guilty, the judge sentenced him to serve four years in the Atlanta Penitentiary, with no possibility of parole.[57] Buster represented the exact opposite of male respectability, or the ideal of a husband. He relied on his looks to get by, and when that did not work, he relied on deceit or force, not his intellect, honor, or work ethic. Moreover, his deception extended beyond Ethel, to the rest of her family who knew that the couple was courting. Ethel mentioned in one of her interviews that though she had previously gone on dates with boys her father was "very strict."[58] When Buster proposed marriage and Ethel's parents agreed, they too were among the injured parties, and in the fallout of the disastrous affair, their reputations were also imperiled.

The reputation of the victim and her parents emerged as a key determinant of whether the Bureau would pursue seduction cases. Having a questionable reputation immediately ended investigations of seduction, a crime that conceptually and legally could only occur to someone who had a "previously

chaste character." In 1936, the Bureau initiated an investigation into the seduction of eighteen-year-old Irene Wireman by thirty-one-year-old Lawrence Howard that was prompted by a letter to J. Edgar Hoover from a concerned neighbor. The initial investigation led the investigating agent to
believe that Lawrence had promised to marry Irene as a way to seduce her.
He concluded, "Although the victim's family is obviously poor, the Victim
appears to be a refined type of girl and is fairly well educated, having had
some college training. The Victim stated that she had never had intercourse
with any man."[59] But interviews with other townsfolk of Royalton, Kentucky,
produced a counternarrative. The postmaster told the special agent that the
parents of Irene Wireman were "confirmed bootleggers and Mrs. Wireman
has been regarded for several years as being of loose morals, Irene, according
to local gossip, . . . 'ran around with anybody who came along.'" The agent
concluded, "in view of the facts developed indicating a previous bad reputation of the victim . . . U.S. Attorney Mac Swinford stated that no prosecution will be instituted."[60] The reputation of the Wireman family meant that
no serious investigation, or prosecution, into Irene's allegations would occur. The dismissal of this case reminds us that reputation was held commu-
nally among family members in early-twentieth-century America. Reputation structured community standing and an individual's position within
the status hierarchy in spite of the American core beliefs in second chances,
equality of opportunity, and individual independence.[61] Reputation and its
twin, respectability, determined who could call upon Bureau aid and utilize
the Mann Act. In the Bureau's eyes, reputation and respectability were typically racialized.

As much as the sexual reputation of the victim might determine whether
the Bureau investigated a case, so too did race determine the level of the
Bureau's engagement. The Bureau typically treated complaints from African
Americans with negligence; generally the special agent would record the
complaint and immediately shut the case with no investigation. In 1921, the
mother of fifteen-year-old African American Bizilee Roberts complained to
the Kansas City office that Girtha DeWoody Howard, a thirty-one-year-old,
married man, had transported her daughter over state lines for immoral
purposes. Girtha was also black. Girtha and Bizilee had been engaging in an
affair when Bizilee's parents decided to separate them by sending her by
train to family in Pine Bluff, Arkansas. Bizilee exited the train early, and

because Gritha had been bragging about acquiring a marriage license her mother suspected that she had met up with Girtha and traveled to Kansas City, Kansas, to get married. To investigate this case the agents took notes of the initial complaint from Bizilee's mother, and briefly interviewed Girtha Howard who contended that he had dated Bizilee with her parent's consent and that he had no idea as to her current whereabouts. What is striking about this case is that no further investigation occurred. The age difference of the individuals and the youth of the girl—a thirty-one-year-old married man and a fifteen-year-old girl—would typically raise flags and fall within the Bureau's own definition of an aggravated case. But Mann Act cases, especially seduction cases, operated according to a logic of innocence lost or stolen. According to the racialized thinking common in the early twentieth century, an African American girl like Bizilee had no innocence to lose, especially since Girtha claimed that he had been dating the daughter with the parent's consent.[62] Most of the cases of interstate immorality that feature African American subjects and victims received very little investigative attention.

Cases with African American victims were extremely rare, and rarer still were cases that were successfully investigated and resulted in a conviction, giving credence to the claim articulated in the 1910s that the White Slave Traffic Act protected only white women. But occasionally a case emerged that seemed to be the exception that proved the rule. In 1921, "a prominent white lady" in Shreveport, Louisiana, reported to the U.S. Attorney that an African American man, Jack Stephenson, had taken a fourteen-year-old African American girl named Loretta to Kansas City, where he had sexual relations with her. The woman, the employer of the girl's mother, described the girl's mother as "an old time darky, much superior to the common ordinary type," explaining the way that this "prominent white lady" articulated the value of the mother of the victim as appropriately deferential and worthy of her and the Bureau's help.[63] The special agents described Jack as "defiant and does not seem to have any fear of prosecution" and Loretta as "timid" and "afraid." According to Loretta, Jack had started pursuing her in Shreveport, promising to marry her. After leaving Shreveport, the couple had lived as "man and wife" for four weeks in Kansas City, until Loretta left because Jack became, in her own words, "so abusive to me I could not live with him."[64] Beaten and pregnant as she was, the special agents quickly sent Loretta home to her family. In consultation with the U.S. Attorney, the special agents decided that the case was aggravated enough to take to trial, especially given the girl's age, the support that the girl's family had from white society, and the fact that Jack had been married when he first started up with Loretta. Jack pleaded guilty to a violation of the Mann Act, and a judge sentenced him to serve six months in the Caddo Parish Jail in Shreveport. Given the aggravated nature of this case, this sentence seems unduly light. Yet, the fact that a Mann Act case with both an African American subject and victim developed into a prosecution is striking, though the fact that this case was initiated by a white, respectable complainant probably explains why the Bureau pursued it. The Mann Act was typically available to whites only, but sometime a white advocate could prompt the Bureau to extend protections to African American young women on an ad hoc basis.

In policing illicit heterosexuality in the 1920s, adultery constituted one of the largest categories of Mann Act investigations conducted by the Bureau. Most states had laws prohibiting adultery in 1900, though in the late nineteenth century some states, like Florida in 1874, amended their adultery statues to punish only those cases in which the accused lived in "a state of open adultery," meaning that the couple publicly flaunted their sexual misbehavior rather than keeping their affair private and in the shadows.[65] Unlike seduction cases that had clear villains (the lying seducer) and victims (the deceived, respectable young woman), which the Bureau understood in rigidly gendered terms, adultery cases disrupted gendered notions of guilt and innocence because women could easily participate in the crime of adultery, and men could be the victims of the crime of adultery. Like some of the blackmail cases of the 1910s where judges deemed women complicit in their own victimization, adultery cases upended the gendered logic of the Mann Act. Consequently, the Department of Justice and the Bureau determined that the Bureau would only investigate cases of interstate adultery that involved young children within the home. Here, the Bureau adopted the position of acting as the protector of the young children and working to ensure family reunification whenever possible. In pursuing these aims, the Bureau articulated an ideal vision of the gendered domestic economy in the early twentieth century that other American policy makers' shared.

Even with the rise of companionate marriage, policy makers and the legal order still rendered the institution of marriage as a social positive that had specific economic functions and roles: the husband as the primary provider and the wife as the dependant and care-labor provider.[66] Supplementing the family's economic functions was the persistent nineteenth-century faith in marriage's disciplining potential. One reason that seduction laws offered marriage as a path to avoid criminal prosecution was that law makers saw marriage an appropriate punishment to the promiscuous and cavalier crime of seduction.[67] Marriage imposed on men expectations of fidelity, sobriety, responsibility, wage earning, self-discipline. In exchange for adopting these traits, a husband acquired the household labor and sexual services of his wife, her "wifely labor."[68] In return, the wife received economic support for herself and her children, and her children benefited from legitimacy.[69]

When policing interstate adultery and seeking family reunification—providing order to homes in disorder—the Bureau upheld men's claims to wifely labor and championed women's claims to paternal support. The Bureau put much faith in family reunification and saw restoring an adulteress to her lawful marriage as an appropriate punishment for a woman who had stepped outside her role as wife and mother. Men, by contrast, were typically disciplined via the state, often convicted and sentenced to serve time in jail as punishment for their abandonment of their marital and paternal responsibilities. On April 3, 1929, twenty-three-year-old Anna Grant dropped her two young children (ages five and four) off at her mother's home in Champaign, Illinois, and took off with her lover, thirty-three-year-old Wesley Hatter, who was married himself and the father of five young children between the ages of three and twelve. The illicit couple set up a home in Kansas City, posing as man and wife when local police arrested them in May, at the behest of the Bureau. The couple had met at a dance and according to Anna, she "had lost . . . [her] love" of her husband, whereas Wesley admitted to having an argument with his wife that prompted him to leave her with only four dollars and run off with Anna.[70] The U.S. Attorney in the case quickly charged the couple with conspiracy to violate the Mann Act. The fact that both adulterers ignored their commitments to care for their children was highlighted throughout the investigation, albeit in different and gendered ways. The special agent investigating noted that the "husband [Wesley] should be made to realize his responsibilities, and be compelled to contribute to the support of his children."[71] Meanwhile, Anna's husband—Zane Grant—told the Bureau that he would take her back "on account of the children."[72] In the end, Wesley

Hatter pleaded guilty and was sentenced to two months in jail, while Anna Grant's case was dismissed, and she was returned to her husband.

Returning Anna Grant to her husband privatized her punishment within the confines of her marriage, whereas Wesley Hatter's punishment was necessarily public. Here we see starkly how the inequalities of men's and women's statuses within a marriage required different types of state intervention. Allowing her husband to discipline Anna restored him to the proper place as head of household, it gave him the opportunity to reclaim his manhood, and it promoted his private right to discipline his family members. In other words, it recovered his dominance of Anna, which had been challenged by her abandonment. But Wesley's wife, as a junior partner in their marriage, could not sanction him, so the state stepped in to ensure his punishment by sentencing him to serve two months in jail. The reason the Bureau pursued this case so actively was that by committing adultery these people had abandoned their proper, gendered, parental roles: providing care labor for her children for Anna Grant and financial support of his children for Wesley Hatter.

In addition to the precondition of the presence of young children, the Bureau only pursued interstate adultery cases that had white victims and subjects. One African American woman, Mrs. George Richardson, visited the Los Angeles field office to complain that her husband had run off to Seattle with a married woman. According to Mrs. Richardson, her husband had told her, "the Government paid no attention to negroes, so far as a violation of the Mann Act was concerned, and that he felt perfectly safe." When agents seemed reluctant to investigate her complaint, she told the agents that as an American citizen she "deserved all the rights and benefits thereof, regardless of color."[73] Despite her claims to protection, Bureau agents only half-heartedly investigated her allegations, and the case was closed without being resolved, confirming George Richardson's prediction that the Mann Act would not extend to African American couples.

At the heart of many Mann Act cases lay gendered understandings of the economic order of American families. Men who sought federal aid to retrieve their wives often commented that in addition to their affective motivations they desperately needed their wives home to provide the unpaid labor of childcare and household management. In September 1921, Edward Aldrich wrote to the Bureau field office in San Francisco to report that his wife, Bertha Aldrich, had been seduced away from her home in Standard, California, by his good friend Charles Lusk. Beyond the sting of betrayal, Edward focused on the loss of his wife and the impact it had on his children. "I have two little girls under eight years that needs [*sic*] a mother, as well as a boy under seven years also," he pleaded. "Now if stealing a wife and mother, taking her into another state, ain't immoral, what is it then?"[74] During the investigation, Edward frequently commented on the difficulty he was having caring for the children. At one point, he split them up among friends and family. The investigation went on for eighteen months surviving many strange twists and turns, until it was abruptly closed when Bertha Aldrich agreed to move back in with her husband and children and return to "living quietly" in San Francisco.[75] Only the return of his wife, and her unpaid labor, allowed the family to be reunited.

Respectable forms of masculinity and familial responsibility figured prominently in the case of Floyd T. Maden. Floyd, a young husband and father from Tennessee, launched an affair with fifteen-year-old Carrie Lovella Ramsey in the late summer of 1920. After the affair became public knowledge over the winter, Floyd's wife, his parents, and the Ramsey family tried to separate the illicit couple by relocating Floyd and his family to Walla Walla, Washington. Even with most of the country between them, Carrie and Floyd continued their affair through an almost daily exchange of letters. In July, Floyd sent Carrie enough money to pay for a train ticket to Washington, and as soon as she arrived the couple resumed their liaison. The affair continued for a week until the family of Floyd's wife stepped in to break up the couple by asking for the Bureau's aid in building a Mann Act case against him. Central to the Bureau's case against Floyd was that he had brought disrepute to his family and violated his responsibility to his wife by carrying on an affair with Carrie. The special agent's questioning of Floyd focused on the money he had sent Carrie and how by giving money to her he had violated his responsibility of support inherent in his marriage contract with his wife. The agent peppered him with questions: "Are you willing to support her [his wife] here?" "Are you willing to stay with your family and support them?" "Are you willing to give your wife you[r] pay check?" "You are wil[l]ing to give her [your wife] your checks?" and so on.[76] For this special agent, a husband's commitment to his marriage could be most clearly demonstrated in material ways—his willingness to adopt the male breadwinner role and adopt his financial responsibility to his family. Floyd pleaded guilty to violating the Mann Act and was sentenced to serve sixty days in jail and pay a $150 fine for his faithlessness.[77]

Cases of adultery and seduction could be tightly intertwined when a man cheated on his wife by seducing another. In these types of cases, the Bureau carefully privileged the claims of the legal wife to paternal support for her children, over any other claims. Consequently legitimate children saw their interests protected over illegitimate progeny. This preference is starkly illustrated in the melodrama of the Hartley family of Lometa, Texas. In the spring of 1927, the community of Lometa was so incensed by the perfidy of C. R. Johnson that they raised a fifty dollar reward for any party who would return Johnson to the town alive. To earn this ire, Johnson, the choir director of the local church and the husband of twenty-one-year-old Delma Johnson née Hartley, had deserted his pregnant wife and their three-year-old child, and run off with Minnie Lee Hartley, Delma's nineteen-year-old sister. The affair had begun in early 1926 while Minnie Lee was away at college, and by the autumn of 1926, she had become pregnant. Unsure of what to do, she asked C. R. for help. He told her that her options were as follows: she could go home to Lometa, but that would force him to leave her forever; she could have an abortion; or they could run away to another part of the country and live together. She chose the romantic option of running away to another part of the country. The Lometa police tracked C. R. and Minnie Lee to their hiding place on a farm outside Clovis, New Mexico. Instead of running to the other side of the country, they had merely got out of Texas—Clovis being just on the other side of Texas–New Mexico border, but over 380 miles away from Lometa. The Lometa police charged C. R. with desertion, and after he paid his fine he disappeared, prompting the Bureau to take over the investigation. Meanwhile, Delma Johnson gave birth on February 25, 1927, while her sister gave birth on April 13, 1927. Both young women were living with their mother, a widow with three other daughters living at home. The Bureau special agent investigating the case recorded, "Mrs. Hartley who appeared to be greatly upset said that she was helpless; that she didn't know what to do; that both her girls' lives had been ruined. She continued by saying, there is Mr. Johnson's wife with two small babies, none of whom he is supporting and there is my single daughter with an illegitimate child and both babies born within a couple of months of each other and of whom C. R. Johnson is the father of both."[78] Minnie Lee signed an affidavit, which affirmed that "all I desire is that Mr. Johnson take my sister and her two babies and support them as he should and I'll continue to live here with my mother."[79]

Bureau agents tracked C. R. Johnson to Bennett, Colorado, where they interviewed him extensively in July 1927 after Delma and the young children had joined him. C. R. expressed remorse for the whole affair and told the agent that "he and his wife were getting along just fine, and that he was trying to make good, and that he had learned his lesson."[80] Upon hearing that the family had been reunited, that C. R. had taken up his marital responsibilities of support and maintenance for Delma and their two children, and that he expressed an appropriate level of shame and had been disciplined, the U.S. Attorney in Fort Worth closed the case.[81] The fate of Minnie Lee and her child did not factor in the Bureau or the U.S. Attorney's consideration of this case. There is no evidence that C. R. Johnson was held financially responsible for his illegitimate child in any way that would be comparable to the amount of state pressure that was applied on him via the Bureau to re-adopt his marital responsibility of support for his two legitimate children. Minnie Lee could have sought recompense through state courts, which may explain why Johnson ultimately settled in Colorado, beyond the reach of Texas courts. Nevertheless, when protecting young children in adultery cases, the Bureau privileged legitimate children.

Bigamy appears throughout Bureau Mann Act investigations during the 1920s and early 1930s. Many cases feature elements of bigamy, as married men tried to marry young women they seduced before procuring a divorce. Bigamy cases introduced a particular gender order that mimicked the villain-victim gender orientation of seduction cases. Though presumably a woman could be a bigamist, in the interstate bigamy cases almost all of the accused bigamists were male. Typically bigamy was born out of increased mobility. Though women had become markedly more mobile in the early twentieth century, men still took to the road with greater frequency, and while doing so found greater opportunities to commit bigamy.[82]

The Bureau's bigamy cases almost always featured elements of seduction. On May 15, 1924, twenty-two-year-old Rena Lindstrom had Benjamin F. Thomas arrested in Denver, Colorado, after she complained that he had rudely seduced her by promising marriage. She told the special agents that she had first met Benjamin in San Jose, California, where he was working as a traveling piano salesman. At the time, she was working as a stenographer for Underwood Typewriter Co., and the two started a correspondence, exchanging love letters. By March, the couple was engaged to be married. Once he settled in Phoenix, Arizona, she joined him, believing they would be married promptly. But after she arrived, he told her that there was not enough business in Phoenix to be "settled," and he talked her into joining him on a road trip through Arizona and New Mexico. On April 22, he abandoned her in Albuquerque with all the bills and only five dollars. He had told her that he was under suspicion of violating the Mann Act and that he needed to go to Los Angeles to avoid suspicion and that he would wire her money to join him. The telegram never came. The investigating agent in New Mexico discovered a rumor that Benjamin had not gone toward Los Angeles at all, but had taken off toward Denver with a woman named Alice Barnhill, to whom he had sold a phonograph. Apparently, Alice Barnhill was wealthy and was working to interest Benjamin in her eighteen-year-old daughter, Martha. Investigating agents in Denver interviewed Martha Barnhill who stated that she had married Benjamin Thomas in late April 1924, and they were living in a home purchased and furnished by her mother. When interviewed, Benjamin Thomas claimed not to have violated the Mann Act, but that Rena Lindstrom was "infatuated with him and followed of her own accord, using her own money to travel from Phoenix to Albuquerque." When the agent asked him if he had had sexual intercourse with Rena while on the road trip, he said, "[W]ell you know what you would do with a woman that was crazy about you after she had followed you half way across the country."[83]

Benjamin Thomas's cavalier attitude towards Rena and his quick marriage to Martha struck the agents as suspicious, causing them to aggressively delve into his life. The investigation revealed that Benjamin Thomas had stolen a $150 phonograph, $50 worth of records, and a $20 piano cover from his place of employment when he left San Jose, in addition to the $100 he had taken from Rena. Rena also told investigating agents that she thought that Benjamin had been married before, probably in Mobile, Alabama, where he was from. Following this lead, the special agents discovered Irma Ross Thomas, whom Benjamin had married in August 1919. Irma Thomas told the agents that though Benjamin was the father of her two children she had left him due to his ill treatment of her. She filed for a divorce after meeting with Bureau agents, yet it was not granted until October 1924. With these revelations, poor Martha Barnhill realized that her marriage to Benjamin Thomas amounted to bigamy. As a sexual transgression, bigamy threatened more than just a community's sensibilities. As a crime it relied on fraud and when revealed, quickly transformed a respectable wife like Martha Barnhill, who had a claim to her husband's economic support into an adulterous woman. Luckily Martha had not conceived a child with Benjamin, so she was spared the tragedy of her child being rendered a bastard by the deception. A New Mexico court found Benjamin Thomas guilty of violating the Mann Act and sentenced him to serve one year in federal prison. His denial of his first marriage and failure to adopt the husband role, his crass seduction of Rena Lindstrom, and his conquest of Martha Barnhill, which seemed to have been motivated by greed, combined to make Benjamin Thomas an ideal target for the "any other immoral purpose" provision of the Mann Act because this constituted a particularly aggravated case of bigamy.

When cases failed to meet a very narrow definition of "aggravated," assistant U.S. Attorneys often dismissed them. The tendency to dismiss cases that grew out of seduction or marital discord frustrated many individuals, including several Bureau agents. In 1929, J. Edgar Hoover asked field offices how they were handling Mann Act cases. T. C. Wilcox, the special agent in charge of the Detroit office, complained that the "U.S. Attorney's Office in this City do[es] not authorize enough complaints in these matters." He noted that the district attorney considered only cases where the age of the victim was exceedingly young, or a family was broken up and young children deserted, and any case with a connection to commercialized vice.[84] Throughout the country, agents reported a similar unwillingness on the part of U.S. Attorneys and judges to consider cases that lacked elements of prostitution or aggravation.[85] One agent in Denver attributed the unstated change in what constituted aggravation to the fact that over the course of the 1920s Mann Act cases had become "more and more unpopular." He wrote that "cases involving breach of promise, minor children, homes broken up, victims under 18 years of age . . . are not in many cases considered sufficiently 'aggravated' to warrant vigorous prosecution and stiff sentences."[86] Notably, all of the types of cases he listed fell into the category of cases to be pursued in the 1917 Department of Justice memorandum.

The cultural reevaluation of sex and marriage that had begun in the early 1910s continued apace during the period from 1920 to 1936. Hornell Hart, the author of "Changing Social Attitudes and Interests" published in 1933's impressive report of the President's Research Committee on Social Trends, noted that attitudes towards sexual relations, marriage, and divorce fluctuated violently from 1905 to 1932. Looking at attitudes published in mainstream periodicals, he concluded, "Particularly from 1923 to 1927 it was more frequently asserted than denied in these magazines that love, not marriage, was the only justification of sex relations, that sexual intercourse was a private matter in which society had no concern as long as children were avoided, that celibacy was abnormal and deleterious and the like."[87] By closely policing the line between illicit and licit sex, as defined by sex outside or inside of marriage, the Bureau remained slightly out of step with widespread cultural attitudes that articulated an acceptance of sex outside of marriage as long as it was accompanied by love.

While individual agents reflected a traditional view of immorality, the courts and U.S. Attorneys reflected the ongoing shift towards sexual liberalism. A 1931 immigration case indicated that a shift was occurring that could shape the future of interstate Mann Act investigations. In 1931 the Immigration Bureau sought to deport Ingrid Hansen after she had been discovered "living as man and wife" with her lover in a Los Angeles hotel. The Immigration Bureau justified her expulsion on the "any other immoral purpose" clause within the Immigration Acts of 1907 and 1910, a clause that shared both its phrasing and legal history with the Mann Act. Hansen appealed her deportation, and the Ninth Circuit court offered its decision in 1933. The court found that though Ingrid Hansen had been engaged in immoral activities prior to leaving the country to visit her homeland, and would probably be engaged in illicit sex after she returned to the United States, her purpose for returning to the United States did not fall under the "any other immoral purpose" exclusion because in all likelihood she was returning to her former home "to resume her employment as a domestic."[88] In other words, yes, she was an immoral woman, but her immorality was incidental to the purpose of her travel: "People not of good moral character, like others, travel from place to place and change their residence. But to say that because they indulge in illegal or immoral acts, they travel for that purpose, is to emphasize that which is incidental and ignore what is of primary significance."[89] The *Hansen* case signaled a sea change in the conceptualization of the "any other immoral purpose" clauses in immigration law and in the Mann Act.

Hansen meant that federal law was beginning to catch up with state laws in insisting that public, flagrant adultery violated the law, but quiet, secret, private adultery could be tolerated.[90] The *Hansen* case joined a legal trend in the 1930s of recasting laws that dealt with sexual immorality. During this decade, many states banned or struck from the books "heart balm" laws, as well as seduction, alienation of affection, and other related laws.[91] U.S. Attorneys aware of this trend might have included interstate immorality Mann Act cases within this category of unpopular or easily nullified cases and backed off of pursuing them.

The conflict over interstate immorality cases between U.S. Attorneys and Bureau agents stemmed from their very different understandings of the purpose of the law, and this, to a certain extent, can be attributed to the different cultures that U.S. Attorneys and agents came from. U.S. Attorneys, though appointed to their positions by the Department of Justice, came from a culture defined by the competition, conduct, and conflict of the courtroom. The vagaries of individual judges and juries shape the context within which they worked. U.S. Attorneys were loath to present cases that judges and juries would dismiss.[92] In contrast, Bureau agents, though also mostly lawyers, were highly conditioned under Hoover's watchful training to accept the basic premises of Bureau policy.[93] As one agent from this period remarked, "The motto of his [any agent's] life is 'For God, for country, and for J. Edgar Hoover.'"[94] Additionally, the conservative gender ideology embraced by Hoover and the agents encouraged them to see value in investigating and prosecuting cases of interstate immorality. U.S. Attorneys' refusal to prosecute cases of interstate immorality was a source of considerable frustration for the Bureau.

Agents responding to Hoover's request for information all noted that White Slave Traffic Act cases constituted the largest part of their case loads. Many mentioned that more than 50 percent of these investigations were initiated by individuals, "namely, wives of subjects who have been deserted or husbands of victims who have left with another individual."[95] These individuals, when informed that their cases was not going to be prosecuted, often responded in anger. One man wrote the attorney general complaining that a man had broken up his marriage. After providing the details of his wife's affair, the man wrote in frustration that his wife's lover was "violating City, State, and Federal laws and yet . . . it seems no one's duty to interfere according to the authorities to whom I have appealed."[96] Both interest and the Bureau's capacity to maintain this project of policing interstate immorality declined amid the changing cultural and economic climate of the 1930s, and by 1940 interstate immorality had been reconceived by the Bureau as a "victimless" crime. Though offices throughout the country still found themselves inundated with requests from private citizens for investigations, the Department of Justice and the Federal Bureau of Investigation adopted a policy to limit the agency's investigations into what amounted to domestic quarrels.[97]

◆ ◆ ◆

The use of the Mann Act by individuals embroiled in family tragedy reveals the extent to which marriages and family were under stress during the 1920s because of increased mobility and shifting standards and, during the 1930s, because of economic changes. As Americans in this period traveled from one locale to another, community surveillance was greatly undermined. Individuals turned to the Bureau based on their gendered understandings of domestic and heterosexual life that underscored American households. Women's labor was essential to men, and men often sought to protect their access to such unpaid labor. Conversely, men's wages were vital to women who had been abandoned with young children. Desertion often led women into dire poverty. Men and women turned to the Bureau in huge numbers seeking some sort of help in the personal tragedies that shattered their lives.

In their investigations of interstate immorality, the Bureau conceived of marriages in a way that was traditional and drew upon the legacy of coverture with American common law. The principle of coverture maintained that upon marriage a woman's legal identity ceased to exist independently and instead was absorbed in her husband's legal identity. As British jurist William Blackstone explained in 1765, "The very being or legal existence of the woman is suspended during the marriage, or at least is incorporated into that of the husband."[98] She became a *feme covert* and her civic and legal personhood was "covered" by that of her husband's. Under this principle, married women could not enter contracts, own property, hold public office, sue or be sued, or vote. Husbands had exclusive right to their wives bodies, labor, wages, and children. Women owed their primary obligations as citizens to their husbands and families first, and the state a distant second.[99] Dating back to the colonial era, laws governing coverture and family law remained remarkably untouched by the revolution in American law ushered in by American independence.[100]

The rise of a women's rights movement in the 1840s would begin challenging many of ideas and assumptions that governed coverture. One of the chief complaints registered by Elizabeth Cady Stanton in the "Declaration of Sentiments" in 1848 was that men had made married women "civilly dead."[101] Because their civic identity had been murdered though marriage, women faced a host of asymmetrical relationships within their marriages. Everything from property management to child custody benefited the male partner in marriage, frequently to women's harm, as Stanton astutely noted. With the dawning of the American feminist movement, women's rights activists attacked many elements of coverture. Throughout the second half of the nineteenth century, many states passed Married Women's Property Acts to ensure women of means some control over their own property. States further whittled away at coverture by allowing women to serve in elected positions on school boards. Most radical, though, was the passage of the Nineteenth Amendment in 1920, which gave women the right to vote. After a seventy-two-year fight for suffrage, the right to vote seemed to unravel coverture by enshrining in the Constitution the very idea of an independent civic voice for American women. Yet many of the more subtle facets of coverture lingered.[102]

The Bureau's Mann Act investigations into interstate immorality promoted some of those vestiges of coverture. By emphasizing the wifely labor that women owed their husbands, and emphasizing husbands' financial obligations to wives, the Bureau upheld one of the most foundational aspects of coverture—the gendered obligations of husband and wife. As one judge commented in a divorce case from 1922, "At common law the husband and wife are under obligations to perform certain duties. The husband to bring home the bacon, so to speak, and to furnish the home, while on the wife devolved the duty to keep said home in a habitable condition."[103] This is the very same vision of American marriages driving the Bureau's Mann Act investigations. Though American women were voting, taking jobs, joining unions, driving cars, and going to college in increasing numbers, the Bureau sought to defend traditional gender roles premised on the obligations of coverture. This meant that it closely upheld parental authority over daughters, policed married women's sexual choices, and screened men's financial obligations to young children.

The federal government confirmed and reproduced the family model with the man as breadwinner and the woman as wife/mother, but it did so with close attention to race, class, and respectability. Individuals who fell outside of agents' notions of appropriate victims could expect no help. J. Edgar Hoover's was able to reform the public image of the Bureau by molding it into a corps of soldiers fighting against the cultural changes that threatened to remake America in the era after World War I. Much of this cultural change hinged on shifting gender roles and the rise of sexual liberalism. When Hoover professionalized the Bureau he remained dedicated to a traditional gender ideology that he and his agents helped to enforce and promote.

7

Coerced Sex and Forced Prostitution

On the night of May 12, 1941, around 9:15 twenty-three-year-old Ann Acheson left the home of a girl friend to walk home in Whiting, Indiana. As she walked by a loitering car, a man popped out of the car and grabbed her purse. She gave chase, demanding the return of her property. As she approached the car, the man shoved her inside the car where two other men sat. Distraught, she demanded to be let out, but instead the men drove the car out of town, pulling over in the countryside outside of Lansing, Illinois. Each of the men took turns raping Ann. According to her statement, recounted in the Whiting chief of police's account, "After Ann found out what was going to happen to her she decided to make the men think everything was all right and that she was enjoying herself, so that they would come back [to Whiting] and she would have a chance to have them arrested."[1] The next evening Whiting police arrested John Joseph Camelli, Stanley Pondowsky, and Steve Wroblewski, and all admitted to having sex with Ann, though they argued it was consensual.

When confronted with the evidence, the U.S. Attorney balked at taking the case to trial, saying that the only evidence of rape was the victim's testimony, which was not enough because it would be countered by the testimony of the defendants. Furthermore, the fact that Ann had been picked up on the street probably gave him pause because the defense could easily try to argue that she was working as a street-walking prostitute. Her pretending to enjoy herself during the attack certainly made him hesitate to prosecute because it would add more fuel to the defense claims that the experience was consensual. In spite of the U.S. Attorney's refusal to take up the case, the Whiting police chief and Ann decided to take the case in front of the federal grand jury. When the grand jury indicted the three men, the U.S. Attorney had to take the case to trial and was surprised when a jury convicted all three men and a judge sentenced each of them to serve one year and one day in a federal prison for violating the Mann Act.

As the mother of a five-year-old child and a divorcee who was out walking alone at night, Ann Acheson differed strikingly from the traditional type of victim of sexual assault the Bureau endeavored to protect. She was older than the ideal victim (under the age of 18), she had previous sexual experience, she had no male relative advocating on her behalf, and her claims to having resisted the attack were deeply problematic. So why did this case successfully result in convictions? By 1941 the American public at large viewed the crime of rape in slightly different terms from the way they had in earlier eras. Though the character of the victim and the race of the accused perpetrator often still shaped prosecution, other considerations could influence a case's outcome.

The late 1930s were gripped with fears that perverse sex criminals roamed the country preying on youth. From 1937 to 1940, the Bureau publicized a "War on the Sex Criminal."[2] As America experienced a moral panic about deviant sexual predators, the concept of the sexual psychopath was incorporated into American criminal law and popular culture. The rise of Freudian theory in public awareness accompanied the hysteria about sexual psychopaths. As a result, "rape was reconceptualized from the perpetrator's point of view," rather than the victim's.[3] Diagnosing a rapist's mental deficiencies took prominence over the experience of the survivor of sexual assault. The sex crime panic took the issue of rape and sexual assault and publicized it in new ways that were subject to considerable distortions. The discourse surrounding the panic simultaneously embraced strangers as posing the gravest threat while perceiving rapists as merely sick, and family sexual assault as reflecting victims' oedipal desires.[4] The publicity surrounding the panic contributed to a legal realm where cases that fit the script of the rapist predator could be successfully pursued in front of juries, even when jurists had lingering doubts about the credibility of the victim.

In the context of growing awareness and fear of the sexual psychopath, the Ann Acheson case revolved around the criminal history of the defendants more than on the character and consent of the victim. John Camelli, at only twenty-two, had been indicted for rape in 1939. Stanley Pondowsky, also twenty-two, had been convicted of rape in June 1939 and had been convicted of larceny and burglary back in 1937. Twenty-three-year old Steve Wroblewski had a record that included two counts of rape dating back to 1937. Taken together, these three young men seemed to have a habit of preying on women and including sexual assault in their evening recreation. Consequently, the jury in Indiana, sensitized to the dangers posed by sexual predators, eagerly convicted them of violating the Mann Act.

Though the broad reading of the "any other immoral purpose" clause of the White Slave Traffic Act invited Bureau of Investigation inquiry into American bedrooms and American marriages, enforcement of the law also combated the very type of female sexual exploitation that Progressive Era reformers had intended—namely sexual assault and forced prostitution of young white women. As the Bureau investigated cases of seduction, adultery, and bigamy, it encountered a social world of pervasive sexual conflict, which was frequently characterized by allegations and experiences of sexual violence. Tales of coerced sex are woven throughout Mann Act investigations. To recall just a few, we have encountered Pearl Snyder who was repeatedly raped in a Tampa, Florida, brothel in 1911, thirteen-year-old Elise Ferrier who was ravished by her sister's supposed fiancé, and seduction victim Ethel Kennedy who was brutalized by the man who had promised to marry her. Yet prioritizing the patriarchal family as it did, the Bureau gave more attention to cases of sexual violence that had a male complainant. Cases with fathers or husbands who were defending their family's honor received greater consideration as the Bureau upheld male protection of female dependents over any attempt to protect "female sexual sovereignty," or the right of women to have control over their bodily integrity.[5]

The boundaries between these types of crime—seduction, abduction, rape, forced prostitution—blurred, though the Bureau considered these classes of interstate sexual violence cases to be particularly "aggravated." As the Bureau policed women's sexuality and men's respectability it confronted a world of sexual conflict marked by gendered sexual violence. The slippage between these different types of sexual conflict was considerable and complicated, given the fact that victims and their families constructed their stories of sexual coercion in ways that would increase their chances of gaining Bureau aid and prosecutorial support. Sexual assault survivors rarely gained legal redress for sexual crimes due to patriarchal assumptions that permeated courtrooms about women's consent. This made rape unique among violent crimes in that it has been fiendishly difficult to prosecute.[6]

At the center of both rape and prostitution stood the complicated issue of consent. For many anti–white slavery activists of the Progressive Era, from W. T. Stead to Clifford Roe, the attraction of white slavery narratives was that they set aside female consent—always a problematic concept in a liberal political order that conceived of women as operating under legal disability, with mitigated capacity for consent.[7] These white slavery stories connected the crimes of rape and prostitution, showing them to be if not inextricably intertwined, then at least two poles on a continuum of female sexual exploitation and vulnerability. Nineteenth-century purity discussions of prostitution framed it in a way to make women's consent a moot point due to unequal sexual relations and male sexual dominance.[8] White slavery narratives went a step further by actively denying young women the ability to consent to their own degradation by incorporating elements of fraud, deceit, abduction, and rape into tales of prostitution.[9]

The Mann Act case files are rife with sexual violence, of which rape is one manifestation. Many of the women who revealed their sexual terror to Bureau agents found that their "private trauma . . . often did not translate into a believable wrong."[10] But unlike, rape prosecutions, the Mann Act's "any other immoral purpose" clause carved out a broad space that covered a wide variety of sexual activities. Because all illicit sex fell under the purview of the Mann Act, the burden of proof in cases of sexual coercion between unmarried people was notably lower than in rape cases. In Mann Act cases, there was a diminished emphasis on consent, which in local rape cases formed the crux of prosecutions. In addition to the typical requirements that a victim have a previous chaste character, under most local laws successful prosecutions of rape typically required physical evidence of a woman's resistance to prove force and lack of consent. Because chastity and morality were presumed to be the provenance of white women, successful prosecutions were far more likely if the victim was white. Married women who accused strangers achieved more successful prosecutions. If the accused attacker was nonwhite, then again the chances of successful prosecution rose. "For a single woman, even a child, to convince a jury that she had been raped required a chaste past, a violent assault, and a valiant but unsuccessful struggle that culminated in penetrative sex but did not result in pregnancy."[11] The Mann

Act, in contrast, merely required evidence that sexual activity occurred over state lines between two unmarried people. All of the concerns over a woman's culpability in her own attack, which formed the core of rape cases, could be set aside.

Even with this diluted centrality of consent in Bureau investigations, special agents and U.S. Attorneys still fell back onto gendered habits of mind and judged a victim's consent or lack thereof as significant elements in their investigations. The term *rape* rarely appears in Mann Act case files, rather Bureau agents developed their own euphemistic understanding of coerced sex that was supported by victims' adoption of formalistic legal language.[12] In their discussions with Bureau agents, victims and their allies deployed scripts, or "strategic metaphors," that emphasized female vulnerability, terror, and resistance in an effort to gain the Bureau's support.[13] The structure of the White Slave Traffic Act and the popular narratives of white slavery, combined with the cultural fetishization of female sexual innocence assumed in both, prompted young women to emphasize their lack of consent and therefore lack of culpability in Bureau investigations. Bureau agents, and the victims in these cases, were well aware that aggravated cases required a measure of force, and so they emphasized male brutishness alongside their narratives of female passivity. Male sexual privilege and male dominance dictated many of the interactions in which victims encountered sexual violence. Within such a context, force had to be reckoned with, even if the "force" was verbal rather than physical violence. For many of the young women that populate Bureau case files, survival of the episode of real or imagined violence became the paramount concern. After freeing themselves from the particular context of male dominance and sexual violence, the victims who had familial support often sought retribution through the courts.[14]

Eva Ida Andrews enjoyed the full support of her husband, but even then the judge doubted her tale of abduction, captivity, and rape. Baird C. Andrews of Weston, West Virginia, reported to the local U.S. Attorney that his twenty-one-year-old wife had disappeared from their home and that he suspected that she was traveling with Sidney Lowe, a traveling salesman who was known as a "very 'smooth' talker."[15] While the Bureau searched for Eva Ida Andrews and Sidney Lowe in Tennessee, Pennsylvania, and New Jersey, her husband tracked the couple down to Harrisburg, Illinois. When interviewed by Bureau Agent Harold Nathan, Eva said that she met Sidney when he came to her door in Buckhannon, West Virginia, on March 24, 1921, and learned that Eva had $500 in the bank. He demanded that she withdraw the money from the bank or he would kill either her or her husband. A few days later, he accompanied her to the bank and from there they went to the train terminal and boarded a train bound for Philadelphia. They stayed in Pennsylvania until Sidney heard a rumor that Eva's husband had offered $1500 for her return. He then moved the couple to Trenton, New Jersey, then to Chicago, Illinois. When the couple reached southern Illinois, they had run out of money. Sidney suggested that Eva begin prostituting herself, but she refused, instead getting a job in a hotel. Empowered by having her own funds, she told Sidney that she was finished traveling with him, and, according to her statement to the investigating agent, "he told me before I left that he would be back for me in the Fall and that by that time he wanted me to have $500, which I could make going with men and that if I did not have it he would kill me."[16] Free of Sidney, Eva sent a letter to her husband, alerting him to her location. On the basis of her testimony, Sidney Lowe entered a guilty plea.[17] Even though he sentenced Sidney to serve one year at the federal penitentiary in Atlanta, the judge in the case announced that he questioned Eva's story of abduction, and that he was inclined to punish her as heavily as Sidney. "With women's enfranchisement," he stated, "her responsibilities have increased. Women must be protected against improper conduct by the men, and the male portion of the nation, in turn, must be given protection against the present-day vampires."[18]

Eva's story raised many questions about her complicity in the affair and whether she was a "present-day vampire." Her emphasis on Sidney's role as a traveling salesman seemed to point to well-known narratives of the danger that strangers posed. In their three months together, the judge implied, certainly there would have been opportunity to escape or send word to her husband. But instead, Eva stayed with Sidney until the couple became so broke that they had to sleep outside in a wagon as they traveled. Clearly the judge in the case had considerable questions about the veracity of Eva's story, but her husband supported her. Though his motivations for doing so are not noted in Bureau files, perhaps he believed her tale of abduction. Or perhaps, he sought revenge on Sidney Lowe for luring away his wife and knew that the best way to achieve a legal remedy was by supporting his wife through the trial, making it more likely Sidney would be convicted. Either way, the couple's marriage remained intact, and census records indicate that Eva gave birth to three children after this incident.[19] The case, however, illustrates the ways that abduction cases could overlap with adultery cases depending on how the woman's consent was configured or whether a husband chose to publicly support a wife's story of abduction over rumors of adultery.

Abduction cases were comprised of the following elements: sexual coercion, transport over a state line, and time. The inclusion of time as a factor reintroduced the problem of female consent because an adulterous woman could claim abduction to exonerate herself of guilt in a pleasure escapade. As in cases of sexual coercion, the Mann Act could be most successfully pursued when the victim had the full support of her family, generally her husband. Ultimately, the Bureau protected male interests—interests in defending family honor, ensuring paternity, and protecting exclusive sexual access to female dependents.[20] It was their presence and backing that added validity to women's claims of helplessness and resistance.

Sexual exploitation and abduction easily fell under the broad umbrella of the Mann Act. The wide latitude of the "any other immoral purpose" clause empowered Bureau agents to go after the exploitation of black women by white men. But lingering ideas of the White Slave Traffic Act being a racially exclusive law persisted, even in the face of campaigns by African American newspapers like the *Chicago Defender* and the Baltimore *Afro-American* to criticize the social acceptance of black concubinage and the sexual assault of black women in the Jim Crow South. The Bureau almost always ignored the sexual abuse of black women by white men, though when cases of exploitation fell into the Bureau's lap, it did pursue them. In June 1921, Linnie Wilson escaped her "illicit liaison" with Clarence Turner, a white man in Arkansas and found refuge with family members in Chicago. Clarence looked for ways to compel Linnie to return to him. He filed charges of grand larceny with the Pine Bluff sheriff's department, which convinced Chicago policemen to arrest her so that she could be extradited down South. Linnie and her lawyers quickly contacted federal authorities, charging that in the course of the seventeen-year relationship, Clarence Turner had taken her over state lines for immoral purposes several times.[21]

Linnie Wilson told Bureau agents a harrowing tale of rape and abuse. Clarence had abducted her from her aunt's home when she was only fifteen years old, raping her and keeping her captive in the attic of his home.[22] According to her attorney, Clarence had "unlawfully used 17 years of her life simply by reason of his force and power and also by reason of the helplessness of this colored girl to defend herself in Mississippi and Arkansas and the inability of her parents without the loss of their lives and property to give her the protection that any woman is entitled to."[23] The *Chicago Defender* closely covered the story, using it as an example of the depravity of Southern race relations that would tolerate forced concubinage of a black woman by a white man.[24] Looking at this case, the U.S. Attorney in Arkansas reported that in his state it was impossible to secure a conviction in a case "where any colored people are connected either as subject or victim."[25] The Illinois-based U.S. Attorney could not file charges against Clarence because all of the state lines crossed had been located in the South. Consequently, Linnie's case was dropped because ultimately southern federal courts couldn't conceive of a black woman as a victim of the White Slave Traffic Act. Although the case did not result in a conviction against Clarence, it probably contributed to the state of Illinois' refusal to extradite Linnie to Arkansas, providing her with a measure of leverage against the legal machinations of Clarence Turner. Linnie Wilson's lawyers clever use of the Mann Act and the public pressure cultivated by the *Defender* allowed northern justice to triumph over southern legal toleration of the sexual exploitation of a black woman.[26] However, the failure to prosecute reveals that once again the White Slave Traffic Act was available to *whites* only.

Paternal support of victims formed an essential element in successful Mann Act investigations; indeed, many parents contacted the Bureau to launch cases that featured elements of sexual coercion. In 1927, Arthur Hearn reported that J. Burley Leopard had taken Hearn's fourteen-year-old daughter, Gaither, over the South Carolina–Georgia border and assaulted her. On March 9, 1927, Gaither's friend Sadie Kuykendoll and the two men—Burley Leopard and Wade Middlebrook—came to visit her at her home to invite her to go out driving. After speaking to her father, she said that she would join them only if they took her to Cleveland, Georgia, to pick up her sister who would come back to Greenville with them. The men agreed, and Gaither's father gave permission for the day trip. Instead of going to Cleveland, however, the party went to Atlanta where the men rented two rooms at a hotel. Sadie and the men retired to one room to drink some whiskey they had acquired, and Gaither took the other room. Once in her room, Burley came in, lay down on her bed, and, in the words of the investigating agent recounting her testimony, "started hugging her, [and] she tried to push him away but he finally overcame her and forced her to have sexual intercourse with him."[27] The next morning, the party returned Gaither home, and she immediately told her father what had transpired. He took her to a doctor, who declared that he found evidence of trauma and revealed that she had been infected with gonorrhea. Incensed, her father immediately went to the police to file charges against Burley Leopard.

Not only was Arthur Hearn furious that his daughter had suffered at the hands of Burley Leopard, he also seemed indignant that he had consented to the road trip that led to her victimization. He pushed the police to investigate, and when they balked and local community pressure mounted for him to drop the charges, he turned to the Bureau for aid. Sadie Kuykendoll's husband and Burley's lawyer repeatedly had visited Arthur trying to convince him to withdraw the charges. Sadie claimed that Gaither had invented the entire scenario. Elie Kuykendoll, Sadie's husband, told the agent that the whole matter would be better if it were "hushed up" and that if it went to trial it would be "three to one," meaning that Sadie Kuykendoll, Wade Middlebrook, and Burley Leopard would call Gaither Hearn a liar in open court. The Bureau agent and the U.S. Attorney agreed with Arthur Hearn that a violation of the Mann Act had occurred, and that at minimum Burley Leopard had had intercourse with the fourteen-year-old, which regardless of whether or not consensual still violated the provisions of the law. A grand jury agreed, and after it returned an indictment in July 1927, both Wade Middlebrook and Burley Leopard pleaded guilty, and the court fined each four hundred dollars.

The Mann Act's lessened burden of proof—compared to laws governing sexual violence like attempted rape, assault with attempt to rape, carnal knowledge, and rape—meant that if could offer the families of victims and law enforcement a legal alternative to difficult rape prosecutions under local laws. The assault on Gaither Hearn caused considerable controversy in the community of Greenville, South Carolina. If this case had gone to trial under local laws, it would have probably not have resulted in convictions, given the fact that the accused were white men who had allies willing to cast doubt on Gaither's character. Deploying the Mann Act bypassed this entire scenario by putting the case into a different jurisdiction and by strategically using the "any other immoral purpose" section of the law. But the ability to sidestep local laws, community doubt, and questions of consent could go only so far due to the fact that the federal judge that convicted Wade Middlebrook and Burley Leopard was still a local resident and was reluctant to send the men to jail on the testimony of a fourteen-year-old girl, choosing instead to impose a fine.

One of the foundational characteristics of patriarchy is that each man has sexual access to his wife and he controls his dependents' sexual choices and other men's sexual access to his dependents.[28] In addition to the character of the victim, the single most important factor as to whether the Bureau would investigate cases of sexual assault was whether or not the victim had the support of her father and/or husband. This has prompted some to suggest that Anglo-American courts conceived of rape as a property crime against male heads of households. Yet it would be too simple to see rape as merely a property crime; it was also a physical crime of assault, as well as a moral crime of degradation.[29] The instrumental presence of fathers and husbands who sought federal intervention in their daughters' experiences of sexual coercion should be seen as male heads of household offering character witnesses for the daughters, while possibly seeking retribution and protecting their own reputations and the reputations of their family. The Bureau pursued cases of sexual violence when invited by male heads of households or other male community authorities, like local police.

Like rape prosecutions, Mann Act violations could be undermined if fathers failed to support their daughters and if families sought justice outside of the legal system. Take the case of the rape of Lillie Belle Martin in 1936. In late April, Lillie Belle visited the sheriff of Bentonville, Arkansas, to report that Waltman Harris had sexually assaulted her on the night of April 28, 1936. Her friend Esther Presley had begged Lillie Belle to accompany her on a double date with Waltman and Bert Brown. The group first went to a café and then took a drive out in the country. Bert, who was driving the car, pulled over and requested that Waltman and Lillie Belle go get some water for the group from a well. While she was getting the water, Waltman attacked Lillie Belle, raping her twice. She told Sheriff Austin that she tore his shirt off, and she showed the sheriff the bruises and scratches on her body. He became more convinced of Lillie Belle's credibility when she took him to the scene of the attack where he found much evidence of a violent struggle.

The abundance of physical evidence—on her body, the site of attack, and in the woods, the location of the attack—convinced Austin. He wanted to seek rape charges against Waltman, but worried that local measures would fail because the year earlier he had tried to charge Waltman in a different sexual assault, but had been unable to move forward because Waltman "was protected by his family and all the neighbors in his community at Hiwasse, Arkansas."[30] The sheriff, noting that the double date had begun in Arkansas, while the rape had occurred on the Missouri side of the border, decided to turn the case over to the Bureau, hoping that the feds would succeed where he might not.

The Bureau agent who took over the case quickly ran into the problem that Lillie Belle's father opposed any legal action against Waltman Harris. Lillie Belle told Special Agent Lacour that "her father was very fond of Waltman Harris and had always pressed her to encourage his company and that in some degree her father had always looked forward to her marrying Harris but that she did not care for him at all and had never felt comfortable in his company."[31] He also learned that her father had accepted one hundred dollars and possibly some cattle from the Harris family in exchange for his silence. The U.S. Attorney noted that even if "all the facts developed could be proved true" he could not prosecute because Lillie Belle Martin's family accepted payment for Waltman Harris's wrongdoing.[32] Cases in which families accepted financial restitution resembled prostitution too closely to be taken to court because the family of the victim had monetized the victim's chastity/sexuality. This posed problems in Mann Act investigations, a law that was most firmly an antiprostitution measure, because in this moment of exchange the aggrieved party, the father of the victim, became the pimp, and the liability switched from the rapist to the father—from Waltman Harris to Charles Martin in this case.

The Mann Act's focus on transportation, crossing boundaries, and illicit sex meant that the vast majority of cases investigated that dealt with noncommercial sex focused on illicit sex between individuals who were not related by blood. Yet familial coerced sex has been documented as one of the most common forms of sexual coercion. Indeed, it seems that incest was "both pervasive and invisible" until the women's liberation movement "pulled incest out of the closet" in the early 1970s.[33] The child-saving activism of the late nineteenth century and early twentieth century had focused on the problem of familial violence, but interest in child victims within the home faded in the 1920s. However, young women still experienced the trauma of familial illicit sex, placing them in a hopeless double bind. Both gender and domestic expectations articulated roles for girls that emphasized their chastity and obedience to male familial authority. A male family member's sexual coercion placed young women in impossible situations, unable to maintain both chastity and obedience.[34] The Bureau treated them like other cases of illicit extramarital sex, most often diminishing the horror of incest while relying on the typical inquisitions of a young woman's character and assumptions about female sexual duplicity.

Questions of consent figured prominently in the case of Thelma Beargeon and her uncle, Mayo Scurlock. In October 1931, Thelma's mother Emily Beargeon, contacted authorities to tell them that her brother, Mayo Scurlock, had taken her sixteen-year-old daughter from Entiat, across the Columbia River and placed her in a brothel in Seattle. Police arrested Scurlock, but in a dramatic turn of events he escaped police custody. Local officials turned to the Bureau for aid in apprehending him and Thelma after they discovered that in all likelihood the couple had headed south to Portland, and possibly on to California, crossing multiple state borders in their journeys. For the next four years, agents followed every lead, chasing the couple through Oregon and California, and returning to Entiat regularly to interview Thelma's family and friends. One such friend reported in July 1933 that she believed that Thelma must have been "hypnotized or scared into leaving home."[35] Yet in an interview six months later, the same neighbor gleefully divulged that Thelma had told her daughter that Mayo had been "intimate" with Thelma for some time before they left Entiat.[36] The Bureau collected every piece of gossip circulating about Mayo and Thelma. In September 1935, Thelma's younger sister received a strange letter that her mother believed to be from Mayo. Bureau agents tracked him down to San Francisco where the San Francisco–based U.S. Attorney was already prosecuting him, under the alias Edwin Lester, for violating the Mann Act by transporting Thelma across the Oregon-California border for the purposes of prostitution. The San Francisco jury convicted Mayo and sentenced him to serve three years at McNeil Island.

By the time Mayo had been convicted, Thelma had been living with him for four years and practicing prostitution for the entire time. Initially, Mayo encouraged her to hustle to supplement gaps in their income, but as time progressed he stopped working and starting living exclusively off her earnings. Thelma worked on the streets, in cafes, or disreputable hotels. Of her history with Mayo, Thelma said, "I will first state that Mayo Scurlock is a blood uncle of mine, being the brother of my mother. I was seven years old at the time that I first had sexual intercourse with Mayo Scurlock, and from that time until I was sixteen old we had immoral relations off and on with no degree of regularity since he was not there all of the time. During the last part of September 1931 I thought that I was in the family way and . . . I decided to leave home. He helped me decide to go with him, and we both agreed that that would be best."[37] In recounting her experiences to the Bureau, Thelma adopted a tone of distance that seemed to passively accept all responsibility or complicity in the relationship. The only motivating factor for Thelma was her shame. When she became pregnant, it was fear of exposure that drove her from her home. Thelma stayed silent about the outcome of her pregnancy, although it is clear that it never came to term, as she was practicing prostitution regularly by the spring of 1932. Similarly, when the interviewing agent asked Thelma why she never tried to contact her parents for help, she replied that she "didn't want to let her family know what kind of life she had led."[38] Though Thelma told agents that she was done with Mayo, she never seemed to hold him accountable for her poverty, her entry into prostitution, and her estrangement from her family.

Thelma may have left home for other reasons than an impending pregnancy. Special Agent F. C. Dowart asked her if she had been aware that just prior to when they left Entiat in 1931, her eight-year-old sister Pansy told their mother that Mayo had raped her. Thelma admitted that she was aware of the incident. Victims of incest who had younger sisters often tried to protect their sisters, resist their abuser, and negotiate the family dynamic. Perhaps Mayo's attack on Pansy, who was close to the same age Thelma had been when Mayo first assaulted her, prompted Thelma to plan to get Mayo away from Pansy. The claim of pregnancy could even have been a ruse, though there is no evidence in either direction. Though the Bureau noted Thelma and Pansy's allegations of child sexual abuse, this feature of the case did not account for the successful prosecution and three-year sentence of Mayo Scurlock. Rather, as a commercial prostitution case, albeit one that seemed more egregious due to the familial relationship between Mayo and

Thelma, this case sat on firm antiprostitution Mann Act foundations. Newspaper coverage of the case never mentioned that Scurlock had trafficked a young woman to whom he was related.[39] When considering illicit sex, coerced sex, and female sexual exploitation, the Bureau shared the same reluctance to consider familial rape that characterized other law enforcement entities and officials. Mann Act enforcement focused on the idea that strangers posed the gravest threat to young women, and in ignoring incest the Bureau upheld the principle of men's right of sexual access to their dependents and girls within their family sphere.[40] Scurlock's depravity was not articulated in terms of incest, and the abuse of his nieces was not considered; rather the case was framed as a run-of-the-mill interstate prostitution case.

Commercial prostitution cases constituted the most consistent category of Mann Act investigations from 1910 to 1941. There had never been any doubt within the Bureau nor in public discussions of the law that Congress had intended it to be an antiprostitution measure. J. Edgar Hoover declared in 1938 that the Mann Act "was designed to prevent panders and procurers from carrying on interstate traffic in women for immoral purposes, and by doing so prevent the nation-wide operations of vice rings." Yet most of the commercial prostitution cases were against petty criminals and pimps rather than organized networks of sex traffickers.[41] Mann Act commercial prostitution cases featured low-level petty criminals and sex workers who lived in a flexible world of vice. The Bureau built a successful case against Harry Berg in 1921 when he picked up two sex workers off the street in Atlanta and offered them work in Miami where he ran a taxi business. He thought that he and the young women could easily make more than two hundred dollars a week by joining forces.[42] Another case fell apart when the trafficked "victim," sex worker Vera Andrews, withdrew her willingness to testify. She had reported to the Bureau that her husband of two years had been living off of her proceeds from prostitution and that he had abandoned her and their child so that he could continue his pandering with another woman.[43] And Josephine Merchant's mother contacted the Bureau's office in Denver to report that her fifteen-year-old daughter had been transported to Rawlins, Wyoming, by Oliver Augustine and Lee Hasson, where the men hoped to open a sporting house that would offer gambling and prostitution to its customers. Oliver and Lee pleaded guilty to violating the Mann Act, but Josephine Merchant ran away from her mother's home and went to work in a brothel in Casper, Wyoming.[44] These cases illustrate the shifting, mobile, and informal world of low-level vice targeted by the Bureau. Cases from the cosmopolitan worlds and vice centers of New York City, Atlantic City, Chicago, Miami, and San Francisco rarely appear in the Bureau's enforcement of the Mann Act. Rather the more visibly public level of street walking and hotel-based prostitution attracted the Bureau's attention.

These cases of commercial prostitution show how much prostitution in the United States had changed after World War I. No longer did public brothel prostitution dominate the sexual market places. The closing of red-light districts throughout the country meant that the form, site, and nature of prostitution shifted, even as sexual entertainment proliferated and new opportunities for sex work such as taxi dancing, hostessing, nude modeling, and burlesque emerged. During the 1920s, women who sold sex could be found on the streets plying their trade to passersby. Illicit call houses with a madam and one or two sex workers who lived in the apartment replaced brothels. Seedy hotels remained common sites of prostitution. Because many cities had criminalized prostitution during the war, police arrests depleted the bank accounts of sex workers and typically drove them into the arms of intermediaries, like madams, pimps, and gangsters, who promised to cover court costs. Some cities managed to retain their brothels, though technically these places operated outside the letter of the law, yet typically under the close watch of the law. These cities, like El Paso, Virginia City, Cheyenne, Oklahoma City, Portland, Seattle and others, still had plenty of recognized brothels that operated in the shadow of the law.[45]

While policing interstate commercial prostitution, the Bureau encountered cases that closely resembled the narratives of white slavery that had dominated popular culture in the 1910s. The U.S. Attorney in St. Paul, Minnesota, reported to the Bureau that he was prosecuting a forgery case against a man, Jay Gossett, whom he suspected of having violated the White Slave Traffic Act. Investigation revealed that Jay had transported twenty-year-old Nellie Haynes from South Dakota to Minnesota. Nellie told Bureau Agent Werner Hanni that she had left home in July 1921 for the first time to attend Brookings College where she hoped to earn her teachers' certificate. A few weeks after moving into the dormitory, Nellie attended a street carnival where she met Jay who was selling tickets to the merry-go-round. He began flirting with her and eventually talked her into letting him walk her home and set up a date for the next evening. On that date, the couple toured Nellie's campus, visited the carnival, and walked along the railroad tracks. Later that evening, Jay told her that he wanted her to leave Brookings with him, demanded that she go pack a suitcase, and showed her a gun that he carried, threatening that he would torment her if she caused any trouble for him. Fearing him, she packed her belongings and decided to meet him at the train station where he had promised to return her great-grandmother's wristwatch, which he had taken to gain her compliance. At the train station, he refused to return her watch and instead bought tickets to Minneapolis where he installed them in the St. James Hotel. She told Special Agent Hanni that at the hotel Jay raped her, saying "he was rough with her and fought her and threw her against the walls and finally succeeded in getting her down on the bed where he forced intercourse with her."[46] She complained of pain in one of her arms, and the next day she fainted. Gossett told her that she would need to get a job so she could pay for her own medical care. Threats like this coupled with growing hunger caused her to take a job as a waitress. Meanwhile Jay stole her wages and pawned her watch, her camera, and her clothes. One night in July 27, 1921, while Jay and a friend went out for an evening's entertainment, Nellie packed up her stuff and left, renting a room in a boarding house. She told her story to the landlady of the rooming house, who advised her to go to the police. The police held her until her parents arrived and immediately arrested Jay Gossett who was charged with forgery for passing bad checks in Brookings and Minneapolis–St. Paul.

Further investigation revealed that Jay Gossett intended to coerce Nellie into prostitution. Nellie noted that though Jay hadn't yet forced her to practice prostitution, he frequently mentioned it as an opportunity for making easy money. After his arrest, the police matron warned Nellie that Jay had a venereal disease infection, and a doctor visit revealed that she had contracted gonorrhea. Jay told a friend that he didn't know what he was going to do with Nellie, "except that he would have used her until she would leave him and as long as he had her clothes to sell to get some money; that as soon as this resource would have been exhausted, Gossett would have send [sic] her on the street to commercialize herself; . . . and there is no girl good enough that he wouldn't ruin her health and reputation."[47]

Nellie's experiences featured elements common to traditional white slavery stories—the setting: hetero-social, commercial amusement sites like carnivals that straddled the line between respectability and sexual license; the protagonist: an innocent girl away from the protection of her family for the first time as she pursued education to enter the job market; the antagonist: a stranger who traveled from town to town, spending money, engaging in fraud, and coercing sex out of virtuous girls.[48] Here she found a handsome stranger that pays her special attention, yet his attentions are not pure, and he revealed himself to be a villain intent on roughly taking his pleasure from her, thoroughly ruining her, and then, in time, turning her into a public prostitute. But what compelled the Bureau's interest in the case was the unwavering support that Nellie's parents offered her; they continually asserted that Nellie had a great reputation as a morally clean girl. Her instructors and friends at Brookings College confirmed her reputation as a girl with a good character. The investigating agent was so outraged by Gossett's behavior that he signed off his first report with the following statement: "Gossett should be prosecuted for this violation, he having taken this girl away from her studies, her home, diseased her internally as well as externally and ruined her life and reputation."[49] Notice that the agent established Nellie Haynes's life and her reputation as equivalencies; without a good reputation a girl's life was effectively ruined. The U.S. Attorney did not share Agent Hanni's fervor for prosecuting Gossett, deciding to dismiss the case because Jay Gossett was already serving time in federal prison due to the forgery conviction. Nellie Haynes' life did not end with her assault, though her education did as she withdrew from school. By November 1921, just a few months after her ordeal, she married her hometown sweetheart. Perhaps she married quickly following this incident in an attempt to revive her reputation, which became even more marred when some local newspapers published details of her abduction.[50] Cases like this one seemed to have been pulled directly from the white slave tracts of the 1910s, with sensationalized tales of promised love, deceitful villains, and sexual exploitation.

Structured to cover all types of illicit interstate sex as it was, the Mann Act did not need to distinguish between forced prostitution or voluntary prostitution. Bureau agents did, however, classify forced prostitution as especially "aggravated" and often worked with U.S. Attorneys to ensure that those convicted in these cases faced tougher sentences. Cases of forced prostitution generated the most energy and in many ways spoke to the very concerns that had prompted the passage of the Mann Act. Inevitably, the agents' focus was on the impending economic violence and exploitation these women would experience, rather than the corporeal violence they had experienced. When forced prostitution appeared in Mann Act cases, tales of seduction and initiation into street walking loomed large, as in the case of Nellie Haynes.

Age, though not sexual innocence, featured prominently in the forced prostitution case of seventeen-year-old Marie Kincaid. Marie had been working as a waitress at the Idlewood Restaurant in Edwardsville, Illinois, when she met Jack Landers, a customer. One night, in April 1932, Jack asked Marie what she was going to do for work now that the Idlewood would be closing. Marie replied that she did not know. Jack then offered her a job as a waitress at his restaurant in Oklahoma City. He mentioned that he and his "wife" Sue Belle were heading directly back to Oklahoma and that they would be happy to provide transportation for Marie. During the three-day trip from Edwardsville, through Springfield, Missouri, and Tulsa, Oklahoma, to Oklahoma City, Marie recounted that at each place "Jack forced me to have intercourse sexually with him." She recalled, "When we got to Springfield, Mo., Jack then told me he didn't have a restaurant and that he had told me that to get me to leave because he wanted me to go into a house of prostitution or a whore house at Oklahoma City." Once they arrived in Oklahoma City, Marie managed to escape, and she hitchhiked her way back to Edwardsville, a trip of over 500 miles. Jack Landers followed her, tracking her down to the Idlewood where local police arrested him. Marie ended her statement to the Bureau with the following declaration, "I have never hustled and have only had sexual intercourse twice in my life before this trip. Jack tried to make a date with me at Edwardsville, Illinois, but I refused him . . . I never did this [have sex] willingly. Jack forced me and I was afraid to leave. I left as soon as I could and dared to."[51]

The Bureau took Marie's claims of forced prostitution and sexual coercion very seriously, in spite of her acknowledgement that she had no claim to chastity prior to meeting Jack Landers. Such an admission in the 1910s and even 1920s would have instantly halted a Mann Act investigation, but by the 1930s the lack of previous chastity, though still important, did not automatically preclude Bureau action. Indeed the fraudulent offer of a job, the exploitation of a young woman through the lure of employment in the context of the Depression had greater salience than her previous sexual experience. The Bureau investigation focused on the false job offer—"the promise of securing her legitimate employment in Oklahoma City"[52]—rather than her sexual history because Marie was able to provide character witnesses who attested to her respectability and morality. Marie's resistance to prostitution and her flight from Landers contributed to her credibility and proved her lack of consent to Landers' sexual assault. A judge sentenced Jack Landers to serve two years in Leavenworth after he pled guilty to violating the White Slave Traffic Act.

Fears about the rise of crime and prostitution amidst the Depression shaped prostitution cases during the 1930s, transforming what would have been common commercial prostitution cases in the 1920s into forced prostitution cases in the 1930s. On January 24, 1933, Washington Metropolitan Police arrested twenty-year-old Homer Shropshire for violating the White Slave Traffic Act. Homer was a pimp who ran girls in both Roanoke, Virginia, and Washington, DC. His relationship with the young women in his "stable" was typical of the pimp-prostitute relationship. He used a combination of romance, flattery, seduction, and physical violence to keep control of the women. At the time of his arrest, Homer was living off of the proceeds of two prostitutes—seventeen-year-old Dorothy Pollard and twenty-one-year-old Louise Parker. Both women told very similar stories about their association with Homer. Both had been raised by single fathers, their mothers having died while the girls were children. Each met Homer, who courted them, promised them marriage, and taught them the ins and outs of working as a prostitute on the street. He taught them how to lease an apartment, how to pick up clients, which men to take back to the apartment, and which men to decline. As they started in the trade, Homer coached them and earned his living off their work. As each girl became more competent, he moved them from Virginia to Washington, DC, where they could make more money. Throughout his entire association with both Dorothy and Louise, Homer maintained the illusion of a deep romantic attachment to each young woman—writing love notes, promising marriage, and so on. At the time of his arrest, police discovered a pile of correspondence that Homer had kept with numerous other women. After the grand jury indicted Homer, a jury convicted him of violating the Mann Act, and he was sentenced to serve four years in prison. The Bureau noted that though Homer came from a stable family he had been considered "extremely incorrigible" as a teenager. Indeed, his arrest record showed that he had regularly been in trouble with the law since 1927, when he was fourteen years old, for disorderly conduct, larceny, and various other petty crimes.[53]

The case of Homer Shropshire was typical of cases against pimps during the 1930s. What is remarkable about the case is what the Bureau saw in it. J. Edgar Hoover tagged the Shropshire case as an "Interesting Case," a designation that Hoover had created in 1927 to provide the press with useful information about the Bureau's activities. The Interesting Case Program became the public relations division for the Bureau. Easily accessible summaries of cases were composed and filed away, ready for the moment when they might be needed.[54] The fact that someone in the Bureau saw in the Shropshire case something special enough to be designated an "interesting case" is puzzling, until you consider the context of the Great Depression and fears about its relationship to both the rise in crime and the dissolving of traditional lines of authority, obligation, and respectability—all couched within a gendered context.

Observers, court professionals, and social hygiene activists all reported that the economic devastation of the Depression had dramatically swelled the ranks of prostitutes, driving down prices. One social hygiene investigator who interviewed brothel operators and managers in Portland in 1932 noted that though the Depression had driven down the prices for particular sex acts, "most of the operators and inmates interviewed stated that they 'were doing well,' considering the times."[55] Prices for various sex acts had plummeted. A New York City taxi driver declared in 1928 that a customer couldn't purchase "anything" in the city for ten dollars, and that fifteen dollars was the going rate for a "lay." But three years later, the average price for both oral and vaginal sex was five dollars in the city.[56] Virginia Murray of the New York Travelers Aid Society argued in 1932 that the tight labor market had caused many women to "more easily drift into prostitution than normal times."[57] Prostitutes interviewed by undercover investigators confirmed Murray's contention. "There are lots of girls who are out of work and are hustling," said twenty-six-year-old prostitute Margie Morris, "You can't tell an amateur from a professional."[58] Even with social workers more readily adopting an economic analysis of prostitution, many still relied on explaining young women's entry into sex work via family deviancy and maladjustment or female vulnerability to male villainy.[59] Amid such worries, the case of Homer Shropshire luring young women into prostitution only compounded a growing social problem. It was bad enough that women were drifting into sex work of their own accord, without the added problem of men like Homer, recruiting young women into the trade. Bureau investigators in the case of Homer Shropshire emphasized male villainy over female culpability.

The Bureau's narrative of perverted manhood, which undergirded the case of Homer Shropshire, resonated in the context of the Great Depression, which in itself was a source of crisis for American manhood. Unemployment damaged men's self-worth as many men could no longer live up to the ideal of the male breadwinner citizen. Employment was configured as the path to respectability and closely aligned with the values of vigor, virility, and independence. Male unemployment led to the degradation of men who assumed female responsibilities within the home as their wives benefited from gender segregation in the labor market and left home to earn the family's wages.[60] Filled with anxiety about the impact of the Depression on men's self-respect, examples of perverted masculinity, like bums, slackers, degenerates, and pimps—like Homer Shropshire—stood in stark contrast to the ideals of respectable citizen workers. Here pimps lazed about, living off of the immoral earnings of women's labor.

Fears that the Depression was contributing to a rise in crime, as newspapers like the *New York Times* speculated, meant that for the Bureau Homer Shropshire's pimping, which seemed so routine, represented a model of criminal masculinity that had been empowered by the rise of gangsterism in the 1920s and that needed to be confronted.[61] Social worker Virginia Murray worried that "young men, many of whom had previously been vicariously employed, have begun to travel about, too, and in many cases have migrated to larger cities where, without friends or resources, they may easily become associated with exploiters of women, prostitutes, and gangsters, and may soon learn the same practices."[62] Homer claimed that it was his work bootlegging alcohol that led him into pimping because selling whiskey necessitated dealing "with a lower class of individuals."[63] Homer's slide from a boy with respectable origins to a youthful bootlegging pimp represented all of

the dangers of youth crime for the Bureau, and for J. Edgar Hoover in particular. In a 1934 speech before the Attorney General's Conference on Crime,
Hoover reminded the audience that the era's most notorious gangsters such
as Pretty Boy Floyd and John Dillinger's "beginning[s] were quite lowly—
petty thieves, bootleggers, hangers-on of crime."[64] In other words, they shared
their origins with petty pimps like Homer Shropshire. Within the Shropshire
case, the Bureau's focus remained on Homer, not Dorothy Pollard or Louise
Parker. The women in the case were construed as incidental, important only
to the extent that their testimony would help to convict Homer. Male petty
deviance took precedence over the sexual exploitation of motherless girls,
who in the Bureau's treatment, probably should have known better than to get
caught up in his schemes.

◆ ◆ ◆

The Bureau used the Mann Act and its prohibition against crossing state
boundaries for the purposes of prostitution, debauchery, or "any other immoral purpose" to fight female sexual exploitation. Though the broad reading that the Supreme Court gave to the "any other immoral purpose" clause
opened the door to the sexual surveillance of American bedrooms, the same
clause offered the Bureau the ability to intervene in cases of coerced sex,
abduction, and forced prostitution, exactly as law makers and reformers had
intended. The broad scope of the Mann Act offered the Bureau its first mandate to investigate sex crimes and the exploitation of young women. The
flexibility of the law meant that as long as a state boundary had been
crossed, federal jurisdiction, with its lightened burden of proof, could su-
persede local jurisdictions that often relied on rape laws that were structured in a way to disadvantage victims and protect men, especially white
men. Consequently the Bureau's activities investigating these aggravated
cases sheds light onto the Bureau as a law enforcement agency, rather than
as a politically-motivated intelligence agency. But this was a protection offered only to white women. Women of color rarely appeared in cases designated as aggravated, and when they did, their cases never moved beyond
superficial investigation into prosecution—which implicitly condoned their
sexual exploitation.

   The aggravated cases of coerced sex and forced prostitution pursued by
the Bureau demonstrate the slippage between the wide variety of cases en-

compassed by the "any other immoral purpose" clause of the White Slave Traffic Act. Cases of seduction shared characteristics with abduction cases and white slavery cases. Mann Act files were inundated with hints, whispers, claims, and declarations of sexual coercion and force. Even typical cases of commercial prostitution featured narratives punctuated by male violence. Though the Mann Act offered the Bureau a more flexible tool for addressing sex violence, the Bureau still contended with female consent—whether deceived, compromised, or obliterated—in all Mann Act cases. In some ways, the differing positions and weight given to female consent is what distinguished seduction from rape and from forced prostitution. Seduction cases presumed female consent but contextualized it in a fraudulent promise of marriage. Abduction cases mitigated any consent offered by implying both coercion and the imperatives of survival once the victim was in a dependent state, but only if it was a true abduction and not a pleasure cruise. Rape in the 1920s and 1930s assumed no consent and the exercise of force, and it often required a demonstrable degree of physical resistance. In forced prostitution cases—termed white slavery in the 1910s, though referred to in more oblique ways in the 1920s and early 1930s as the term *white slavery* fell out of popular use—like seduction cases, consent was again set aside. Instead of the fraudulent promise of marriage that mitigated the importance of a woman's consent in seduction cases, it was the purpose of her defilement—public prostitution—that established the crime of white slavery.

When investigating cases of female sexual exploitation, the Bureau still relied on its traditional understandings of family and paternalistic lines of authority within families. For the Bureau, support of the male heads of household was instrumental to determining whether the agency would launch an investigation and whether U.S. Attorneys would prosecute. The Bureau investigated only when the right person invited it—a father, a husband, or a male local law enforcement authority. When the Bureau considered aggravated cases of sexual exploitation, it almost always conceived of prosecuting these crimes as defending the family (and concomitantly upholding men's rights to control the sexuality of their dependents) rather than upholding an idea of female sexual sovereignty. For young women, and they did all seem to be young, who enjoyed the support of their male relatives, the Mann Act could form another statutory tool in attempts to gain justice. Yet these women only benefited when their interests coincided with the bureaucratic imperatives of the Bureau. With its broad understanding of interstate immorality, Mann Act cases skirted the focus on female consent that sexual assault cases seemed to require. But even so, gendered understandings of sex, romance, seduction, and prostitution shaped these investigations.

8

The FBI's Assault on Sex Trafficking

When the U.S. Congress handed the Federal Bureau of Investigation (FBI) a mandate to fight white slavery implicit in the White Slave Traffic Act, the Bureau actively tracked down, investigated, and helped prosecute those that profited from sexual commerce in its pursuit of sex traffickers. Yet the changing social and sexual climate ushered in by World War I, and continuing during the 1920s and early 1930s, had shifted the focus of the Bureau from policing prostitution to policing illicit sexual behavior more broadly. But in the late 1930s, the FBI shifted its Mann Act priorities again: it de-emphasized the policing of Americans' private sexuality and returned its focus to the vexing problem of organized sex trafficking. The highly publicized War on Crime put the issue of white slavery back on the FBI's public agenda. J. Edgar Hoover declared that while every other type of crime was on the decline, white slavery was on the rise.[1] To tackle the problem of sex trafficking, the FBI launched an investigation into organized, interstate vice in Connecticut, which one newspaper declared was the "opening gun in a country-wide drive against organized prostitution."[2] The Connecticut investigation focused on a loose ring of illegal brothels operating throughout Connecticut, with ties to brothels in New York and Massachusetts, and tendrils reaching out to Rhode Island and Long Island.

Though the FBI's attention turned again towards the challenges posed by sex trafficking, the contours of commercialized sex in the late 1930s differed greatly from 1910s-era prostitution in cities and towns across America. Conceptions of female sexuality had dramatically changed as well, and the idea that a woman could not consent to prostitution, which had been central to Progressive-Era narratives of white slavery, had been discarded. The FBI's five-month investigation into sex trafficking in Connecticut and surrounding areas illuminates the opaque world of 1930s organized prostitution. With the exception of high-profile scandals like the Seabury Investigation and the Luciano racketeering trial, prostitution failed to raised public concern as a human rights issue as it had in the period before World War I, though organizations like the American Social Hygiene Association continued their crusade against prostitution. Some considered the questions of international sex trafficking in international arenas like the League of Nations, but for the most part American popular media remained silent on the topic. The FBI's investigation of sex trafficking circuits in the tristate area, however, altered the relative silence surrounding prostitution and shed light onto the day-to-day world of professional prostitution in 1936.

Even as the FBI unraveled the complex and petty world of Connecticut prostitution, the agency packaged its discoveries for media consumption, carefully articulating its own narrative of sex trafficking. The FBI conceived of sex trafficking as a challenge to law and order and in doing so discarded earlier reliance on the notion of protecting female innocence that had been so central to white slavery narratives. Instead, the FBI sought to alert the public to the dangers of trafficking, most notably the problems of third-party profiteers with connections to organized crime and exposure of the public to venereal disease. By focusing on the public health dangers of prostitution, the FBI continued its defense of traditional marriages, seeking to ensure that careless husbands would not introduce venereal diseases to the marital bed. Yet, even with the shift in ideas about the dangers of prostitution away from narratives of deceived innocence, the FBI still fell into old habits of trying to paint the sex workers within the circuit as women without agency—exploited in their degradation.

Hoover waged the War on Crime, starting in 1933, to combat three types of crimes that seemed to be on the rise—kidnapping, bank robbing, and racketeering.[3] The melodrama of the War on Crime and the Bureau's fight against the exploits of bandits like Baby Face Nelson and John Dillinger celebrate the 1930s as the *true* birth of the FBI, perhaps confusing the Bureau's 1935 renaming of the Bureau of Investigation into the Federal Bureau of Investigation as being more significant than it was.[4] In response to the War on Crime, Congress expanded the authority of the FBI in 1934 when it allowed special agents to carry firearms and arrest criminals. Furthermore Congress increased the jurisdiction of the FBI greatly when it passed a fugitive felon law and a federal bank robbery law, among others.[5] Congress doubled the budget of the FBI and provided for the hiring of two hundred more special agents, or G-Men as they were known in the vernacular.[6] As the relationship between increases in appropriations and jurisdiction on the one hand, and publicity of FBI actions, on the other, became more evident, Hoover sought to keep his G-Men in the public eye, thus reversing its nonpublic role maintained during the 1920s.[7]

The 1930s saw a rise in concern about prostitution for several reasons—most tied to the rise in organized crime and graft associated with prohibition and concerns about the growth of prostitution amid the worsening economic climate of the Great Depression.[8] The 1930 Seabury investigation of police graft and corruption in New York City revealed that police used prostitution charges to extort women of their savings, whether or not the women worked as professional prostitutes.[9] Outrage over such obvious and heavy-handed corruption seized the city. Notorious New York City madam Polly Adler commented, "Perhaps if they [the police] had confined themselves to shaking down people like me, who were violating the law, public indignation would not have risen to such a pitch."[10] Newspapers and magazines throughout the country eagerly reported on the Seabury investigation.

As the prohibition era came to a close in 1933, organized crime lords in New York City eagerly looked elsewhere to replace their lost liquor proceeds and their eyes, or at least the eyes of reigning gangsters like Dutch Schultz and Lucky Luciano, fell on the active call house trade in New York City. Luciano offered madams "protection" in exchange for a cut of the madam's profits. If a madam declined the offer, she frequently saw her home invaded and wrecked, and she and her girls might be subjected to violent attacks. By late 1935, Luciano and his associates had informal ties to many of the clandestine brothels in the city—two hundred houses and one thousand prostitutes.[11] The protection Luciano offered was primarily legal. Of the three thousand prostitutes arraigned in the city's Women's Court in 1935, only 175 of them worked in brothels protected by Luciano, and none of these women served any time in jail.[12] Luciano's activities came to the attention of New York prosecutor Thomas E. Dewey who launched an intensive and well-publicized investigation into Luciano's vice racket, ultimately securing a thirty-to-fifty-year sentence for compulsory prostitution. The investigation and conviction of Luciano earned Dewey accolades in the press.[13] More pertinent to the FBI was that Dewey's prosecution generated headlines and news stories that displaced the FBI as the nation's premier crime-fighting force. As a result, in the winter of 1935–1936 Hoover directed his east coast offices to look into the vice racket and find Mann Act violations. Hoover even claimed to be working with Dewey, a fact Dewey refuted.[14] In 1936 and 1937, Hoover personally led vice raids in Connecticut, Atlantic City, and Baltimore.[15] Newspapers and magazines quoted Hoover as saying that while every type of major crime had decreased in 1935, "white slavery had increased by 15 per cent."[16] Hoover's attention to vice reintroduced the language of white slavery and raised the Mann Act back into public prominence. Indeed, from the end of Prohibition in 1932 to the mid-1940s, the Mann Act routinely came in second place in federal convictions.[17]

The 1920s and 1930s saw a reconsideration of the nature of sex trafficking as antivice activists considered how to fight prostitution and venereal disease in the interwar climate of sexual liberation. Debates about prostitution and white slavery quietly occurred in international venues such as in the halls of the Palais des Nations in Geneva as the League of Nations incorporated existing anti–white slavery conventions into its international governance. The League restated its members' commitment to the principles enshrined in the anti–white slavery conventions of 1904 and 1910. In 1919, the League's Covenant declared that the League would hold "general supervision over the execution of all agreements with regard to the traffic in women and children."[18] By 1919, the term *white slavery* had fallen out of use, as reformers who focused on the international movements of prostitutes after World War I preferred to use the language of trafficking.[19] Accompanying this shift in terminology was an associated shift in the definition of the trafficking of women. In its extensive 1927 study of sex trafficking among Europe, North Africa, and the Americas, the League defined international trafficking as "the direct or indirect procuration and transportation for gain to a foreign country of women and girls for the sexual gratification of one or more other persons."[20] Wishing to discard the debate about innocent victims versus voluntary prostitutes that had permeated conversations about white slavery, the League's report cast every prostitute who crossed international borders as a victim of trafficking regardless of her consent, because prostitution, it argued, was so exploitative that consent became meaningless. "Technically she may have not been brought to this condition by force or fraud," the 1927 report declared. "[B]ut actually she is deceived at every step."[21] International activism in the 1930s continued this trend of setting aside the challenging issue of women's volition with the adoption of the Convention on the Suppression of Traffic in Women of Full Age in 1933, which expanded international protections against trafficking to women of all ages. All of these international conventions were intended to ban the international migration of prostitutes by setting aside any consideration of their own consent in sex work.[22] Essentially the trend within the League was to treat all women, regardless of age, as children unable to consent to sex work as a legitimate form of labor.

Changing conceptions of prostitution and white slavery in the United States mirrored those on the international front. These shifts in the legal understanding of migration and prostitution were closely intertwined because American reformers from the American Social Hygiene Association (ASHA) lent their expertise to the League throughout the 1920s and 1930s in spite of the fact that the United States was not a member of the League of Nations. ASHA president William Snow directed the League's 1927 study, and ASHA's Bascom Johnson and his associates actually conducted the multicountry investigation. During the war, Johnson had been key to the military's Commission on Training Camp Activities' conflation of promiscuity and prostitution, and after the war he continued his antiprostitution activities within the arena of legal reform. Writing in 1920, Johnson claimed that "the sexual conduct of the individual becomes a matter of public concern and, therefore, of legal regulation, only when it seriously affects the sanction of monogamous marriage, or the integrity of the family or the public health."[23] Here, monogamous marriage, a healthy family, and a healthy citizenry were mutually constitutive. He saw prostitution and promiscuity as a social menace, and he particularly emphasized the dangers posed by third-party profiteers of prostitution—madams, pimps, bell boys, taxi drivers, hotel operators and so on. Through the legal reform activism of ASHA, forty-four states had passed white–slave or compulsory prostitution laws that banned intrastate transportation for the purposes of prostitution.[24] The definition of prostitution embraced by Johnson, ASHA, and American antivice reformers included "the giving or receiving of the body, for hire, or the giving or receiving of the body for indiscriminate sexual intercourse *without hire*,"[25] thereby fully collapsing the promiscuous girl and the professional prostitute. Here, again, the issue of women's consent was swept aside, and from a public health perspective infection with venereal disease was seen as proof of criminal danger to the wider community and a threat to healthy marriages.

The FBI started embracing a broader definition of white slavery when the Supreme Court offered its approval for such an approach in the 1917 *Caminetti* decision. Though the FBI consistently prosecuted those who transported prostitutes over state lines, it did not focus on organized sex trafficking, as defined by the League of Nations and Bascom Johnson, until the launch of its campaign against white slave rackets in 1936. Hoover defined "rackets" as "any enterprise or undertaking looking toward the obtaining of a valuable consideration or privileges in an illegitimate or unethical manner."[26] Third-party profiteering off prostitution nicely fit his conception of racketeering, and, more to the point, interstate sex trafficking placed such activities directly under the jurisdiction of the FBI and the White Slave Traffic Act. Hoover argued that "the traffic in white slavery has become one of the major rackets of criminals since they were driven out of liquor by repeal of prohibition."[27]

The Connecticut vice dragnet was the first of several intensive investigations into organized vice rings throughout the country conducted by the FBI in 1936 and 1937. The five-month investigation began when Connecticut state police raided the Bethany Inn looking for a fugitive. While searching the premises, an officer discovered a trap door that concealed access to a basement level. Within the basement he found two sisters, Julia and Mildred Lenczyk, who had been hiding during the raid. The sisters had been working as prostitutes in New York City, and their pimp had brought them to Connecticut where they could earn more money. Due to Connecticut's anemic laws against prostitution—typically a mere fine of twenty-five dollars—the lieutenant leading the raid contacted the Bureau, hoping that the FBI would be able to build a more substantial Mann Act case against the owners of the Bethany Inn.[28]

Special Agent Leon G. Turrou, who led the investigation in Connecticut, uncovered a loose network of illegal brothels and call houses that exchanged tips, workers, and gossip. Most of these venues were based in Connecticut—in towns like New Haven, West Haven, Norwich, Waterbury, Norwalk, Bethany, New London, Mansfield, Southington and Wallingford—though the network extended into New York, Massachusetts, and Rhode Island. The women employed as prostitutes in these venues worked the circuit, stopping at each location for a one-week booking, before moving to another site. But most significantly, most of the women working on the circuit came to Connecticut from out of state, most typically from New York City, but also from Pennsylvania and New Jersey. Initially, Turrou intended to quietly investigate the Bethany Inn, gathering intelligence about the wider network of trafficking, and then the FBI would lead a "grand finale when the Agents could raid about a dozen houses in Connecticut and make one grand sweep of the entire situation."[29] But after the first arrests, the word of alarm spread through the vice community forcing the FBI to accelerate its time table and arrest all the players they could before every brothel and call house closed up and the prostitutes scattered. Without containing the sex workers and low-level madams, any hope of building successful Mann Act cases would have evaporated. Even with the more rapid timetable, FBI special agents swooped into Connecticut towns and detained scores of individuals connected to the racket. Very quickly the prosecuting assistant–U.S. Attorney, George Cohen, offered reduced sentences to brothel owners who pleaded guilty and who were willing to share their knowledge of the inner workings of the vice racket. Turrou used the information one person handed over to build a case against another, who would then be offered a similar deal, and so on—a process that FBI Assistant Director E. A. Tamm derisively called "horse trading" with the defendants.[30] By mid-November, thirty-nine individuals had been convicted: fourteen women, all brothel madams, between the ages of twenty-four and fifty-three; and twenty-five men, most Italian, all non-Anglo, between the ages of nineteen and forty-four, on the testimony of eighteen prostitutes held in custody as material witnesses.[31] Notably, thirty-eight of these people pleaded guilty, and only one chose to go to trial.

When the FBI compiled the "Interesting Cases" file for the Connecticut investigation, the agency attempted to focus on building a narrative that emphasized the hierarchical organization of the vice racket—one dominated by kingpins, supported by "strong-arm squads"—that brutally exploited women. This vision of the case resonated with popular understandings of organized crime, but it overstated the level of coordination among the various players. This approach also made the Connecticut vice case a story of male criminality by erasing the participation of women in vice markets; an enduring irony considering it was the very commodification of women that made this particular vice racket so profitable. Statements gathered by the FBI in the course of their investigation reveal that the Connecticut vice ring was not nearly as organized as the FBI suggested. Rather, there existed a loose confederacy of pimps and brothel operators who shared friendships, jealousies, gossip, and resources, but who also viciously competed. Rather than organized vertically in a strict hierarchy, they were organized horizontally with little pre-planning or order. To uncover the characteristics of sex work in the 1930s and describe the contours of this racket, it makes most sense to describe the experiences of a few select prostitutes who navigated the circuit. This approach has the advantage of centering these women's experiences and focusing attention on their working conditions and the choices they faced within the underground world of prostitution. The experiences of Claire Corso, Jean O'Day, and Jacqueline Whitehurst offer a window into the structure, organization, and workings of the Connecticut vice circuit.

Claire Corso was twenty-two years old when the FBI arrested her in August 1936. She told Special Agent Turrou that she had been born in Bridgeport, Connecticut, and had been working a regular job when, at the age of nineteen, her boyfriend impregnated her, causing her to lose her job and the boyfriend as well. With no resources to fall upon she began working as a prostitute in the brothel of Stella De Mayo in Waterbury. One night in early 1935, low-level gangsters Enrico Bentozzi and "Waterbury Joe," also known as Giuseppe Tarantola, invaded and threatened to take over Stella's house. Armed with knives and guns, they demanded protection money, or they would take all of the prostitutes there and place them in other houses. In the heat of the fracas, Claire slipped out the back and for several months avoided working in brothels, preferring to risk the inconsistent conditions of street prostitution in New Haven. By March of 1935, she had met Joe Dest, also known as Joseph DeStadio, a pimp in the Waterbury area. Joe Dest had connections with numerous brothel owners in the region, and through her relationship with Joe, Claire was able to work in many of the main venues of the vice racket. Typically, she, like the other women on the circuit, worked at each location for a week, thereby ensuring that the clientele would frequently see fresh faces. Sometimes Joe booked Claire, and other times she booked herself. At each place she worked, she was entitled to one half of the money earned from her labor. But inevitably other charges were subtracted from her portion—charges for doctor exams, room and board, and the booking fee. Women in Claire's position, where her "bookie" was also her lover, would typically turn over the entirety of their profits to their pimp-boyfriends. After her arrest, Claire eagerly cooperated with FBI agents because she thought it was the best way to protect Joe. According to Turrou, she spilled the details on her activities because "she believed the whole truth in this connection would reveal the fact that Joe Dest was not a 'big shot' in the prostitution racket, but was merely a 'sucker,' violating the law, not so much for his own personal gain, but on the other hand, doing favors for a gang of 'pimps' and procurers from New Jersey, who were posing as his friends."[32] Claire sought to protect Joe in any way she could, perceiving him as her boyfriend first, and pimp, second. Yet, even with her aid, the judge in the case, Judge Carroll C. Hincks, sentenced Joe Dest to serve four years in a federal penitentiary for trafficking Claire and three other women between New York, Connecticut, and Massachusetts.

The brothels that Joe booked Claire to work varied in terms of earning potential, clientele, and prestige. Most had two to three girls working at any given moment. Josie Bambini's small house in West Haven did not provide enough earnings to make it worthwhile for Claire to work there so she cut her week's booking short, preferring to visit her family in Brooklyn, who remained ignorant of her source of employment. Other places, like Margaret Collin's New Haven house catered "exclusively to a high-class clientele, such as students of Yale University, professors of that University, and other 're-spectable' persons."[33] In contrast, Claire quit after three days into a week-long booking at Nick Radano's New Garden Inn on Long Island, "because Nick insisted that I drink while I was prostituting myself there."[34] Nick Radano's requirement that the working prostitutes consume alcohol was probably a ploy to increase his liquor profits as he reasoned that customers would purchase drinks for the girls. Mike Taverner, a co-owner of the Bethany Inn, had told sex worker Mildred Lenczyk "to get the men drunk as I could and to get all the money from them that I could."[35]

The houses also varied in terms of the services offered.[36] The sex tasks offered drove the profitability of the prostitution ring, and they constituted the primary labor of the women. All of the houses in the ring offered heterosexual, penile-vaginal intercourse for between two and four dollars an encounter. Yet, as one investigator of vice conditions in Portland, Oregon, discovered in

1932, almost all working prostitutes had to offer both vaginal sex and oral sex (to "French" in the euphemism of the day) to stay competitive. When inquiring about the availability of a new girl, a madam he interviewed proclaimed, "I'll find out if she frenches, because if she isn't [sic] I don't want her. You've got to be that in this town; that's all they (customers) want." She went on to suggest that the girls who earned the most in the business were "three-ways."[37] Three-way girls offered the widest array of services. One twenty-two-year-old prostitute declared to an undercover vice investigator in New York City, "I am a three-way girl." When asked what that meant, she responded, "The natural way, and up the rectum, and French."[38] Conditions in Connecticut were moving towards the conditions found in Portland and New York City. In early 1935, madam Susie DeNicola, also known as Mary Testa, reported to Dr. A. C. Swenson that most of her customers had migrated to houses in Hudson and Newburgh, New York, because the girls in those houses were "two-way" girls, whereas all of the "houses in Waterbury and vicinity were 'one-way' houses." As a result she had decided to open a two-way house and was looking into "obtaining 'two-way' girls to work from her houses in Newark, N.J., and Philadelphia, Pa."[39] Customer demand for a broader range of sexual offerings prompted Susie DeNicola to import sex worker talent from out of state. This proved to be a smart business move because her new two-way house, the Greystone Inn, became so popular that according to FBI Special Agent in Charge Rhea Whitley, "as many as fifteen to twenty men would often be found waiting their turns to patronize the various perverted charms of these girls."[40] By 1936, many of the houses in the ring specialized in offering a wider variety of sex act to customers, as sex worker Jean O'Day discovered.

Twenty-eight-year-old Jean O'Day was trying to avoid the G-Men's raids of the Connecticut brothels she had been working at when the FBI arrested her on September 2, 1936, at the Pine-Tree Inn in Smithtown, Long Island. Once the FBI had transferred her back to Connecticut, she revealed she had been born in Toledo, Ohio, and had first started hustling in 1932 in Canton, Ohio, from which she moved to Chicago where she "played the streets and hotels."[41] While there a friend told her that there was more money to be made on the East Coast than in the Windy City, so she worked her way east, making it to New York City by Christmas of 1935.[42]

It was word-of-mouth that prompted Jean to go east, and it would be word-of-mouth advice that brought her into the orbit of the Connecticut vice ring. While in New York, Jean met another prostitute who gave her Becky Schwartz's contact information in West Haven, Connecticut. Jean wrote to Becky asking for a week's booking, and Becky scheduled her to work in the first week of 1936. While working in Becky Schwartz's house, Jean met Claire Corso's pimp-boyfriend Joe Dest, who offered to become Jean's bookie. Joe Dest would book Jean into various Connecticut and Massachusetts brothels, helping to sustain her schedule for a booking fee, in this case, ten percent of her earnings for the brothel. So if Jean earned two hundred dollars in a week, then the brothel madam took one hundred dollars, Joe Dest would get twenty dollars, and typically the brothel madam would also charge Jean room and board and doctor's licenses fees of around twenty dollars; in this example Jean's take home pay would be sixty dollars. As Turrou commented, "A girl's daily earnings sometimes ran into fabulous money in an efficiently operated house, but there were usually too many reaching hands for her ever to become prosperous."[43] But the advantage of entering into a relationship with a bookie was consistent access to customers and some protection against arrest. If the police raided a house, typically the bookie would provide bail money. Joe booked Jean to work in many of the same brothels where he had placed his girlfriend, but he also looked to place her in brothels in New Jersey and elsewhere. He contacted Joe Ferrera, a well-known, well-connected bookie in Hoboken. Ferrera's exclusive business was placing women in brothels throughout the tristate area. Ferrera told FBI agents that between 1934 until he was arrested in September of 1936 he had filled over one thousand bookings of sex workers. Like Dest, Ferrera charged 10 percent for each booking, and he made a name for himself by cultivating "a waiting list of prostitutes who had all of the peculiar qualifications demanded by operators of the houses of prostitution."[44] Dest contacted Ferrera to add Jean O'Day to Ferrera's list and, he, in turn, booked her to work at the infamous North Colony Tea Room in Wallingford, Connecticut, a brothel run by "Louie" and "Lena" Pasquini. Ferrera told Jean that the North Colony Tea Room was "a good place to work as girls made plenty of money there."[45] It was rumored that girls could make as much as four hundred dollars a week because the house was known as a three-way house that saw a large volume of customers. According to a former customer of the Pasquini's North Colony Tea Room, the tea room typically had three girls working, "one who is said to be there permanently because of her unusual charm and ability to enact what is known as 'around the world' which gives men a choice of normal sexual relation, 'sucking' or sodomy," and two others booked by Ferrera.[46] Among sex workers like Jean O'Day, it was known as "Siberia" because though the profits could be high, they were only high "owing to the unusually large number of patrons the girls were required to accommodate, and the long hours necessitated thereby."[47] On average, the workers in the North Colony Tea Room served around three hundred customers a week, usually working sixteen hours a day.[48] Joe Ferrera estimated that the Tea Room took in $2,500 a month, and the FBI considered it to be "undoubtedly the most profitable house of ill fame in the State of Connecticut."[49]

As the exclusive bookie for the Tea Room, Ferrera scheduled Jean to work for two weeks in August 1936. The first week she earned two hundred dollars as her take home, but Lena Pasquini cancelled her second week because customers complained that "I wouldn't French," and Lena noted that Jean wasn't making as much as other girls typically did.[50] So Jean turned to Ferrera, who by the end of the summer had replaced Joe Dest as her principal bookie. Aware of the FBI's crusade against organized prostitution, Ferrera attempted to schedule Jean away from the "heat" in Connecticut and sent her to Long Island, where Bureau agents discovered her working.

Casual conversations with co-workers and acquaintances drove many of Jean O'Day's decisions. She favored her independence, but as relative stranger to the region, she saw the advantages of entering into a professional relationship with a bookie. After she had exhausted the contacts of her first bookie, she traded him in for another who was much more entrenched and better connected. Joe Ferrera could easily book Jean in all the houses where Joe Dest had access, plus many more in New York, Massachusetts, and Pennsylvania. At twenty-eight, Jean O'Day was older than many of the other women working the Connecticut circuit, and she remained very closed-mouthed about any circumstances that led her into prostitution at the relatively older age of twenty-four. Instead, she revealed only as much as the special agents demanded and gave no additional details.

Like Jean O'Day, twenty-four year old Jacqueline Whitehurst preferred to work independently, relying on a bookie only when it suited her needs. In May 1935, Jackie was working in a brothel in Hudson, New York, when she met Joe Saledonis, a co-owner of the Bethany Inn, and at the time an investor in the Mountain Inn in Southington, Connecticut. He persuaded her to come to Connecticut to work for several weeks. She traveled by herself to Southington where she earned fifty dollars. The next week Saledonis charged her twelve dollars for a booking at Becky Schwartz's house in West Haven, where again she earned around fifty dollars.[51] But after 1934, Jackie rejected the paid bookie system, preferring to set all of her dates by establishing relationships directly with brothel madams. She told FBI agents she set up her own arrangements with Rose Martini who invited her to work at her Venice Restaurant in New London for a week in May when Jackie took home around one hundred dollars. Similarly, when she heard that Ethel Franco (also known as Ethel Bekris) ran a place called Ethel's Spaghetti Restaurant where a girl could earn easy cash, Jackie contacted Ethel directly for a booking. She was working on her third day there when the FBI and state police raided the "restaurant" and arrested her. But in those three days, Jackie had seen twenty-six customers and earned a total of fifty-four dollars, twenty-seven of which was hers to keep.[52] By setting up her own appointments Jackie protected her bottom line.

Overall, the sex workers who maintained their own booking schedules seemed to retain the highest percentage of their earnings. But a bookie could be key to access to new customers and new opportunities to make money. Yet with a bookie, a sex worker's control over the conditions of her labor could be compromised. Mike Taverner was a co-owner of the Bethany Inn, but he also placed girls in several nearby brothels. A week after her first booking at the Bethany Inn, Mildred Lenczyk, was on vacation because menstruation kept her from working. Mike found himself short a girl over a busy weekend, so he turned to Mildred, forcing her to pack cotton up her vagina and go to work, servicing thirty men in two days.[53] More difficult for Mildred was the fact that she was entrenched in a relationship with her pimp-boyfriend "Waterbury Joe" Abbott (Giuseppe Tarantola)—who supported Mike's insistence that she work in spite of having her period. Without a doubt, the women in the circuit who were most vulnerable to economic and labor exploitation and physical violence were those whose bookies were also their romantic partners. Turrou noted that almost without fail "the pimp[-boyfriend] takes the girl's share of her earnings and he buys her such clothing and articles as he thinks she needs" while pocketing the rest for his own profit.[54] And though the FBI claimed that prostitutes were "severely beaten if they attempted to break away from members of the rings,"[55] the only women who faced regular threats to their safety were those with pimp-boyfriends.

Hoover and the FBI carefully managed the publicity of the drive against sex traffickers in Connecticut. Special Agent in Charge Rhea Whitley argued for holding arrested traffickers over the weekend so that the "story could be broken for the benefit of the Monday-morning papers."[56] And throughout the investigation, the FBI circulated carefully prepared press releases to major newspapers. Hoover denied that the FBI was engaged in any particular campaign against sex trafficking. "'Drive?' Mr. Hoover repeated in an interview. 'No, this is not a drive. In fact, I don't like that word in law enforcement. It seems to imply a tacit admission of previous laxity.'"[57] Yet clearly Hoover saw the potential of a coordinated campaign against vice for keeping the FBI in the public eye as the nation's premier crime-fighting organization.

Within the press coverage of the sex trafficking cases, the newspapers and the FBI re-embraced the term *white slavery*. Embracing the terminology of white slavery offered the FBI a language of moral authority and implied the existence and exploitation of tortured white slaves, even if these white slaves were voluntary prostitutes who chose to traffic themselves. The language of white slavery and lingering notions of innocence helped the FBI to publicize itself as attacking organized crime while side-stepping any issues of the culpability of the sex workers themselves. When investigating organized sex trafficking, the FBI drew upon both its own institutional traditions and the wider cultural legacy of the white slavery narratives of the 1910s, yet it did so in the extraordinarily different social context of the late 1930s. Enforcement of the Mann Act in this case continued its defense of the male right to purchase sex, criminalized sex workers' behavior under the guise of protection, sought to protect traditional marriages from external threats, articulated sex trafficking as an immigrant problem, relied on deportation as a further punishment for traffickers, and attempted to assert that the victims in this case were innocents.

Suggesting that the victims in this case were innocent young women adrift whom the FBI had rescued proved to be an especially difficult challenge. Initial reports of the vice cleanup circulated well-know tropes of young country girls caught up in vice. One magazine reported, "The best estimates are that 55 per cent of the girls are from the country, or small towns, and 45 per cent from the city. A prolific source is found in the districts where there are large groups of semiilliterate, foreign-born or first generations of eastern and southern European peoples. Many of these are recruited from steel and industrial towns in Pennsylvania, Ohio, Indiana and other States."[58] And throughout the newspaper coverage, if the prostitutes were mentioned at all, their supposed youth was emphasized. At one press conference, Special Agent in Charge Rhea Whitley announced, "Young girls, many still in their teens, were rounded up in Massachusetts, New York, New Jersey and Pennsylvania and brought to West Haven, where they were told the rules of the white slave ring."[59] This much-repeated claim suggested that their supposed youth made them vulnerable for exploitation and innocent of their participation within sex work. But it was also patently false. Of the fifteen women initially held as material witnesses, the average age was twenty-four years old, with only one woman under the age of eighteen. Additionally, as we saw in the cases of Claire Corso, Jean O'Day, and Jacqueline Whitehurst, all of the prostitutes had been engaged in sex work for many years, and most chose to come to Connecticut for the opportunities to make money that it offered. This narrative of innocence via youth did not reflect the realities within this case, and the attempts to resurrect the old tropes of white slavery narratives fell flat.

By 1936 the idea of the innocent, defrauded white slave had been thoroughly dismissed within popular media. Journalist and Hoover confidant Courtney Ryley Cooper declared that "the white slave as a cringing, innocent, wholly reluctant young thing, fighting for her virtue, willing to die for her honor, a pawn for the lecherous assaults of passion-mad men—I am not using the reformers' language—all that simply does not and cannot exist."[60] The women in the Connecticut vice ring were described as "nonchalant" voluntary prostitutes who had been in the life for some time.[61] One newspaper noted some of the problems with the FBI's enforcement of the Mann Act that collapsed promiscuous girls and prostitutes into the same category. "The Mann Act is tinged with the rather unworldly theory that every prostitute is a 'slave' and that, if she crosses a State line to claim a job at her unpleasant calling, she is necessarily a 'victim' of 'white slavers' and the process was 'compulsorily.' Yet, it's pretty difficult to prove that a girl from a milltown who comes to a city brothel didn't know perfectly well what it was all about and wasn't to some extent a willing conniver at her own shame."[62] If public understandings of the Mann Act were about protecting innocent young women, and the prostitutes in the Connecticut vice case couldn't be innocent, because their deliberate participation within vice rendered their exploitation meaningless, then who and what was the FBI protecting? To justify its crackdown on vice within Connecticut, the FBI and Assistant U.S. Attorney George Cohen emphasized the public health dangers of the brothels.

As the FBI drew on its institutional imperative to sustain traditional marriages, the innocent women that the FBI sought to protect were the invisible wives and future wives of the customers who contracted venereal diseases. In 1935, Connecticut became the first state to require brides and grooms to undergo a premarital venereal disease test to protect both prospective partners and any potential children from contracting diseases. The "premarital examination law," as it was called, required a blood test rather than the affidavit of good health that most Progressive-Era premarital health laws mandated. Contraction of syphilis or gonorrhea could limit a young man's potential to become a legitimate husband. More troubling was the likely possibility that the married customers of the brothels might infect their wives. Successful treatment of syphilis was still extremely difficult in the 1930s. In 1909, German scientist Paul Ehrlich had discovered that the arsenic compound Salvarsan attacked the organism that caused syphilis, but treatment was painful, toxic, and could last as long as two years. It wouldn't be until doctors at the U.S. Public Health Service applied penicillin to syphilis and gonorrhea in 1943 that an effective treatment for both diseases would be developed.[63] "If the true story of divorce could ever be learned," wrote Courtney Ryley Cooper in his book about the FBI and vice, "this disease would be found a basic factor in the breaking up of innumerable homes. It had brought sterility by the tens of thousands of cases. It has shortened the lives of countless women; and filled hospitals through its infection of the Fallopian tubes."[64] Cracking down on organized sex trafficking and the semipublic brothels they supplied would protect American marriages, both potential and existing, while contributing to the state of Connecticut's public health objectives of increasing oversight of its venereal disease–carrying population.

All of the women working the Connecticut prostitution circuit underwent medical examinations at the beginning of each of their bookings by a trusted doctor of the madam. Though prostitution was illegal in Connecticut and therefore unregulated, house madams adopted a system of self-regulation to attract customers and assure them that the available girls were "clean."

Each Monday the doctors would exam the women, usually merely conducting a vaginal smear rather than a blood test and issue a certificate of clean health. Special Agent Turrou noted that the prostitutes "carried these doctor's certificates in the pockets of their negligees and exhibited them to men whom they took to their rooms to entertain."[65] Yet, customers of the houses still contracted syphilis and gonorrhea from the sex workers. One man bitterly reported to the FBI that "two months ago my young brother visited there [the North Colony Tea Room] in a moment of weakness and as a result of it he is now under a doctor's care."[66] The FBI repeatedly noted the threat these houses posed to the public health of the community, and it saw the fraudulent medical exams as one of the greater criminal aspects of the case. It noted that "a number of persons who patronized DeNicola's establishment in Connecticut have complained to the State and local police that they have had become afflicted with venereal diseases after having intercourse with prostitutes in houses operated by him."[67] In contrast, some of the girls working the circuit preferred working in Connecticut due to what they perceived to be the lower rates of venereal disease infection among the customers when compared to places like New York City and Hoboken. One girl from New Jersey told a doctor during her exam that "it was like a vacation coming to Connecticut where she could have clean men to patronize her charms."[68]

Self-regulation did not seem to stop the spread of venereal diseases when it ran head up against pressures to make money. Seventeen-year-old Marie Collins was visibly infected with syphilis when arrested in August 1936. She had been brought from New York, where she had been hustling for two years, to Connecticut to work in the Bethany Inn by Mike Taverner, who also booked her for a week in July to work in Becky Schwartz's house.[69] On July 6, the Monday she was to begin working at Becky's, Dr. A. C. Swenson examined her and found that she had a visibly inflamed ulcer in her vagina, which Marie claimed was a result of a scratch from her fingernail. According to Marie, she overheard Dr. Swenson tell Becky that she was "O.K." to work. That week Marie serviced around eighty men, experiencing what the FBI termed "considerable pain"; certainly, the pain must have been unbearable. While the FBI held Marie Collins as a material witness, their doctors found her to be suffering from fully developed syphilis.[70] The specter that Collins had spread syphilis to eighty men in one week because a doctor had given her a false clean bill of health haunted the FBI. Indeed, the majority of the sex workers held as material witnesses did prove to be infected with venereal disease, as did many of the defendants.[71] The U.S. Attorney's office and the FBI considered charging the seven doctors they identified as co-conspirators in the case, but in the end, after they gained the cooperation of the doctors, the agency dropped all threats of criminal charges.

For the FBI, the danger of the brothels that thrived within the vice ring was the way they endangered American families by providing a site for the spread of venereal disease. Attempts at self-regulation struck the FBI as especially fraudulent, especially considering the way that the women displayed a doctor's certificate to customers. The *Hartford Courant* declared that the worst aspect of the vice ring was that "Practically all the victims of these white slavers were diseased," and "the extent to which they spread venereal diseases can only be surmised."[72] "I sincerely hope," U.S. Attorney George Cohen said, "the disclosures in this case will arouse the public to a realization of the amount of disease that is being spread in these houses."[73] Casting the crack down on sex trafficking as a public health initiative functioned to set aside any consideration of the sex workers' agency and culpability, while at the same time configuring the victims of the vice racket to be male customers and innocent wives and wives-to-be.

One of the most striking aspects of the FBI's investigation into sex trafficking in Connecticut is the utter invisibility of the male clientele of the many brothels and call houses in the ring. Throughout the investigative case file, there is no discussion of customers, whose money, after all, made the entire racket profitable. When FBI agents and local police raided Josie Bambini's West Haven brothel, newspaper reporters related that as the raid unfolded several customers arrived at the house, unaware of the situation they were walking into: "Frightened into a bad state of jitters, they were released when agents became satisfied they were merely customers of the house of ill-fame."[74] Not once did the FBI interview a customer, and any customers' voices within the files came from customers' self-reporting by sending in tips or complaints about having contracted a venereal disease. Even within discussions of the public health dangers that these sex workers posed to customers, the FBI was careful to use gender-neutral language—using euphemisms like "a number of persons" instead of the less awkward "men."[75] Through the silence surrounding customers, the newspaper reportage, public relations releases, and the investigative file read like a defense of men's sex privilege. In the postwar period, the right of men to purchase sex freely was only challenged by a few. In 1920 Bascom Johnson argued that the sexually promiscuous woman posed the greatest public health risk, but she was closely followed by the "male who most frequently consorts with promiscuous women." In order to defend marriage, the sanctity of family and public health, Johnson declared, "that the definition of prostitution would have to be enlarged to include all males whose payment makes prostitution possible."[76] Similarly, in the 1920s New York City's Committee of Fourteen waged an ultimately failed campaign to criminalize the purchase of sex in New York. These efforts were radical and singular in their suggestion to criminalize the purchasing of sex by men.[77]

More commonly, in the late 1930s, calls rang out from a variety of sources for the legalization and regulation of prostitution. One reporter, who closely covered the Connecticut vice investigation and had interviewed the prostitutes, police officers, and the U.S. Attorney, concluded that the results of the FBI's raid had been "negligible." He argued that "instead of curbing vice, efforts to suppress it have fostered its growth in more devious and subtle ways."[78] Writing in late November, about two weeks after the last of the defendants had been sentenced, he noted that Waterbury and New Haven were again wide open and that prostitution was flourishing. Only by licensing and state regulation could the challenges of police corruption and public health be solved, he suggested.[79] Special Agent Turrou came to the same conclusion, arguing, "The legalization and federal control of prostitution is the only reasonable and intelligent course."[80]

As the FBI built its case against the traffickers it relied on using the full power of the Department of Justice and the federal government to achieve its aims. As a reporter for the *New Haven Journal-Courier* noted, the FBI aimed "a three-barrel weapon at those connected with the ring—deportation, income tax evasion and prison terms for violation of the Mann act."[81] Building Mann Act cases depended upon securing the testimony of the sex workers as well as confederates within the vice racket. Cohen relied on "horse trading" with the defendants to gain their cooperation. When first interviewed, Mike Taverner, the owner of the Bethany Inn, said that "he wasn't going to involve any more people in this mess. He said that if the government would deal leniently with him and give him a light sentence, and not institute deportation proceedings against him, he being an alien, he would then reveal the desired information, . . . [but] until then, he said, he would rather not furnish any more information."[82] Within days, Taverner became a government witness after he pleaded guilty and was sentenced to serve seven years for trafficking six women, which could have brought a maximum sentence of thirty years in prison. Cohen supplemented Mann Act charges with conspiracy charges as well. Through negotiation with the defendants, Cohen avoided costly trials and secured thirty-eight guilty pleas.

Gaining the cooperation of the sex workers formed a more formidable challenge. For three and one-half months, the FBI and local police incarcerated each of the eighteen sex workers held in the case as material witnesses. Even as the FBI took away their freedom, agents had to retain their cooperation because the testimony of these witnesses formed the keystone to the entire investigation. Courtney Ryley Cooper, journalist and all-around public relations guru for the FBI, noted that "when Special Agents of the Federal Bureau of Investigation . . . attempt to dig into syndicate white slavery, they find themselves confronted by stubborn and recalcitrant witnesses whose volubility has been thoroughly devitalized by the realization that if they talk they will become material witnesses against gangland."[83] The FBI agents tried to be extra friendly with the girls in efforts to gain their confidences and provide for their comfort. This was especially necessary after the women conducted a two-day hunger strike to protest the poor quality of the food in the prison. In response to their coordinated action, the U.S. Attorney's office secured a special appropriation to pay for better food.[84] Ultimately, the women that the FBI was "protecting" all experienced a long period of incarceration. They were paid between $33 and $39 in compensation for their testimony, which one newspaper mocked as a paltry sum compared to their weekly earnings in prostitution. Though offered medical care while held in jail, they were not offered any social services to aid them upon their release. After their release, most of the women likely returned to commercial prostitution in the vibrant world of New York City.[85]

As in the white slavery cases of the 1910s, deportation formed a powerful tool to use against the Connecticut traffickers, though the threat of deportation was more easily deployed against traffickers and madams rather than sex workers because the bookies and madams were more likely to be foreign born due to their older ages. Nineteen of the thirty-nine defendants had been born outside of the United States. Most of the prostitutes were under the age of twenty-five, meaning they had been born since 1914, when immigration to the United States from Europe dropped dramatically due to the outbreak of war in Europe. Most of the defendants, in contrast, were born between 1890 and 1910, and many had migrated to the United States with their parents as children. When they became caught up in the Mann Act investigation, these foreign-born defendants became vulnerable to deportation because the 1907 and 1910 immigration acts made profiting off prostitution a deportable offense. Deportation had consistently remained a tool used against prostitutes and people who profited from prostitution and accounted for just over 4 percent of deportation cases from 1927 to 1936.[86] Cohen told newspaper reporters that deportation "is more dreaded by aliens than heavy fines or long jail sentences and should be employed as an effective weapon against the vice racket."[87] As a result, the FBI provided the Immigration Bureau with all of the statements it collected from foreign-born defendants for use in deportation proceedings that would be launched against them immediately after they served their prison terms.[88] Even those foreign-born defendants who had become naturalized citizens, like Arturo "Louie" Pasquini, who had received his naturalization papers in 1935, faced deportation because according to the FBI any naturalization would have been based on fraudulent statements about sources of income.[89] The *New Haven Journal-Courier* applauded the strategy of following up Mann Act convictions with deportations, editorializing, "Deportation is a device by which the dross can be drained off the melting pot."[90] From 1907 through the 1930s, U.S. sex trafficking policy consistently used expulsion as a way to maintain the moral borders of the country.

Cohen worried that even with Mann Act convictions, jail time, and deportations, some of the brothel owners would continue to live off the earnings of prostitution. "I don't want any of these people facing deportation," he stated, "to leave this country with any money which they received from this shameful business."[91] As a result he gathered financial information on the most profitable houses and turned the material over to the Treasury Department so it could ensure that Uncle Sam was paid his money via taxation. When the FBI agents raided Arturo and Lena Pasquini's North Colony Tea Room it found $6,637 hidden throughout the house. Most of the money was in single dollar bills, and agents found it "in no less than forty different places—in coat sleeves, in secret drawers, in trunks, and under the rug."[92]

After the Pasquinis admitted to paying no income tax, Cohen asked the Department of Treasury to assess their wealth. All of the Pasquini's property, their cash, bank accounts, and real estate, became tied up in government liens, and the judge in the case sentenced each one to serve time in prison. In addition, Lena and Arturo had to pay an astronomical fine of $33,000 each. The couple was "rendered penniless" when the Immigration Bureau launched deportation proceedings against Arturo.[93] The FBI utilized the full force of the federal government against the defendants in the Connecticut vice case, relying on criminal convictions for Mann Act and conspiracy violations, deportation for those foreign-born defendants, and Treasury Department investigations for those who failed to file income taxes.

Yet, in resurrecting white slavery by conducting a nationwide drive against vice rackets that had spread far beyond Connecticut in late 1936 and into 1937, the FBI still relied on notions of exploitation. But the only exploitation that the FBI could grasp onto was the abuse these women faced from their pimps, but the women who faced the most difficult circumstances were those whose pimps were also their boyfriends. The pimp-boyfriends who pretended to be husbands—living as man and wife, taking their wife's earnings and her wifely labor, and disciplining her behavior—exhibited the injustice identified by the FBI. This exploitation existed within a normative, heterosexual, romantic context that mimicked normative, heterosexual, romantic relationships in the broader culture. These fictive marriages seemed to corrupt actual marriages to such an extent that all marriages between pimps and prostitutes were suspect to the FBI. The FBI seemed conflicted about how to theorize these relationships, which existed at the intersection between heterosexual romance and commercialized sexuality. How could they be legitimate marriages if the basic principal of monogamy that underwrote the marriage contract didn't exist due to the woman's participation in sex work? Speaking of the relationship between Joe Dest and Claire Corso, the FBI noted that Joe "continued to live with this young woman without marrying her."[94] Repeatedly Joe was castigated for "living as man and wife" with Claire without being man and wife. Yet the FBI denounced Albert Raymondi, who was married to his prostitute wife, as "one of the most vicious subjects in the business" because he "prostituted . . . his own wife."[95] Here Joe Dest had been condemned for acting as a husband—having complete sexual access to Claire and taking her earnings—without being a husband. Albert

Raymondi, in contrast, was condemned for not being a *proper* husband because by making his wife sexually available to other men he violated the assumptions of monogamy and exclusivity inherent in modern marriages.

Things became even more confusing for the FBI when some of the defendants insisted on marrying their prostitute-girlfriends before they started serving their prison terms. Joe Dest married Claire Corso, but the FBI argued that "it is believed that the reason he decided to marry Claire Corso was because he intends to have her continue practicing prostitution while he is incarcerated, and to aid him financially while he is serving his term in prison."[96] Similarly, James Ceglia and Constance Rossi married on November 12 in the U.S. Marshall's office before he was sent to prison. A newspaper reporter wryly commented, "It was the second time since the present white slave trials began that wedding bells have rung in the marshal's office with a slightly off-key note."[97] The *New Haven Journal-Courier* claimed that these weddings were "tainted" by the participants' connection to prostitution.[98] Like Marcus Braun's castigation of marriages between foreign-born prostitutes and their pimps in 1909, the FBI in 1936 understood marriage as an institution that required female fidelity and a male head of household who had exclusive sexual access to his wife. Pimps seemed to violate every facet of the sexual contract that formed the foundations of patriarchal marriages. By making their wives publicly available for cash, they undermined their own claims to paternity and their own roles as bread winners.

◆ ◆ ◆

The FBI's investigation into sex trafficking in Connecticut reveals that loosely organized circuits of sex work offered opportunities to female sex workers who were willing to offer the sexual services that clients demanded. But to gain access to the network of underground houses prostitutes often availed themselves of the services of a bookie who earned his living by taking a portion of her profits. Indeed, brothel madams and the doctors who examined the sex workers also handsomely profited from the labor of the women who worked on this lively circuit. Customers, always a phantom presence in the FBI's investigation of vice, benefited from a wider variety of sexual services offered and the low prices that these call houses charged, even if they exposed themselves to sexual transmitted diseases by patronizing these hidden brothels.

As it reintroduced the term *white slavery*, the FBI initially attempted to resurrect the narrative of innocence that underwrote earlier white slavery narratives by emphasizing the exploitation of the sex workers and their supposed youth. But this discourse did not resonate because it was demonstrably false on the one hand, and the sexual climate of the 1930s, with its articulations of women's sexual agency, cast this narrative as hopelessly old fashioned and naïve on the other. As one newspaper reporter declared, "'White Slaves,' that is, are enslaved as much by themselves and their own poverty and neurosis as they are by the madams, panders, and cadets."[99] So, to bypass these arguments, the FBI opted to emphasize the public health dangers that sex trafficking posed, drawing on its institutional legacy of protecting existing and future marriages.

The FBI explained its interest in investigating the Connecticut vice racket in terms of combating organized criminality, confronting a risk to public health, and ensuring the end of the exploitation of prostitutes by pimps, even if those prostitutes labored of their own choice. It imposed the full weight of the federal government in its drive against vice, relying on the Immigration and Naturalization Bureau to deport those foreign-born profiteers from sex work and on the Treasury Department to confiscate the wages of sin. The FBI's disregard of women's agency in choosing sex work fell in line with international and national reconceptions of white slavery as sex trafficking, a paradigm shift that dismissed women's consent to sex work from all discussions of migratory vice. Ultimately, the alignment of international norms, through the League of Nation's 1933 Convention on the Suppression of Traffic in Women of Full Age, and the FBI's broad enforcement of the White Slave Traffic Act against organized vice rackets, functioned to criminalize migrating prostitutes while still protecting the rights of men to purchase sex.

Conclusion

Can the Country's Moral Borders Be Policed?

As white slavery burst into the public consciousness in the early twentieth century, providing plotlines for best-selling movies and books, fuel for the imaginations of readers in the Progressive Era, and an issue to rally around for antivice activists, the administrative agencies tasked with policing white slavery—the Immigration Bureau and the Bureau of Investigation— conceived of white slavery as a problem of prostitution, both foreign and domestic. As a result of this formulation, enforcement of the Mann Act empowered the young Bureau of Investigation to police the movement of morally suspicious women across state borders at the same time that the Immigration Bureau increased its vigilance against immigrant women at the national borders. The project to halt sexual commerce led to a significant increase in the federal government's policing powers. Yet this growth was not merely an example of bureaucratic top-down growth. As early as 1911, private individuals were seeking the Bureau's assistance in solving the sexual crises their families faced. During the 1910s, when lawyers and judges debated the constitutionality of the Mann Act, the Department of Justice focused its attentions on cases of commercial prostitution or cases that resembled kidnapping or coerced seduction. They did not challenge, however, most of the exploitative aspects of prostitution nor the right of men to purchase sex. After 1917, when the Supreme Court offered the broadest possible reading of the "any other immoral purpose" clause of the statute, the Bureau had clear jurisdiction to pursue a larger variety of cases.

Not until the 1920s would the Bureau quietly, yet busily, take up Mann Act cases characterized by their lack of a commercial element and the presence of sexual misadventures. The thousands of cases investigated during this decade reflected and shored up the Bureau's interest in policing respectable domesticity, often by monitoring and disciplining the movement of women and girls. The Bureau policed men's respectability and criminality as well, especially when it utilized the Mann Act to prosecute sexual predators who preyed on vulnerable women. The War on Crime configured the White Slave Traffic Act as a tool available for use against the low-level gangsters of the vice racket, which operated loosely organized sex trafficking rings, like the one discovered in Connecticut in 1936. Significantly, within this investigation the women's choice to engage in sex work was inconsequential because the Bureau had chosen to disregard women's volition in Mann Act investigations. The Act had been passed by Congress to protect young white girls from the dangers posed to them by a variety of sources—the venal madam, the duplicitous pimp, the brothel, the city that housed the brothel, nonwhite men—yet by looking at the enforcement of the law we see that the statute was primarily used to uphold domesticity and the patriarchal family, and to quarantine vice conditions. Both of these goals were achieved by expanding state policing powers to include the policing of inappropriate sexuality and the bodies that deviated from respectability.

Enforcement of the Mann Act in the early twentieth century reminds us that despite the distance between the brothel and the home the discursive, legal, and physical ties were many. That a law designed to police prostitution also policed domesticity should not come as a surprise, given the centrality of women to both institutions, and the embodiment of male sexual privilege in both spaces. The nexus of policing sex, under the mandate of "any other immoral purpose," centered on the sexual body of the woman. But as FBI agents policed the bodies of women they also determined appropriate male relationships to women's bodies. The claims of fathers and husbands to women's reproductive labor were upheld, and men were expected to bear the responsibility of their paternal obligations. The mandate within the Mann Act permitted the federal government to police an entirely new set of behaviors—a new governable space of sexuality—while also providing a framework and justification for the expansion of the Bureau into a truly national law enforcement agency.[1]

Yet within this mandate the tension of whether the Bureau should protect women or police them was ever present. Enforcement of the Mann Act was a protective mission when the Bureau sought to fight the sexual exploitation of young white women by pimps, seducers, and sexual predators. But this

protection was racialized—available to whites only. Age constituted yet another border of protection, as the Bureau was preoccupied with protecting
only young women. Enforcement was also protective when the Bureau defended the traditional family from a range of dangers like adultery, bigamy,
and venereal disease. But women who violated gendered norms of morality
by embracing the opportunities of sex work, defying parental authority by
running away, or choosing to engage in nonconjugal sex saw their behavior
policed and typically punished. Ultimately, the enforcement of the Mann
Act in the early twentieth century offers a cautionary tale about the lingering effects of coverture. Most importantly, laws intended to police sex trafficking rarely benefit those who have been trafficked; instead these laws
mark women as bodies to be policed.

A recent Mann Act case reveals that a nexus of immigration, sex work,
and policing of masculine respectability is still present in contemporary
investigations—the same nexus that characterized early twentieth-century
investigations. In December 2007 the Western New York Human Trafficking
Task Force and Alliance (HTTFA)—a coalition between the FBI, U.S. Border
Patrol, the Erie County and Niagara County Sheriff's Offices, U.S. Immigration and Customs Enforcement, and victim services nonprofit organizations
such as the International Institute of Buffalo—cracked down on massage parlors suspected of selling sexual services.[2] The raids of four parlors resulted in
the arrest of the owners (Hong Kong native Che Ngan Tsui and his wife Len
Wah Chong), the detention of nine "victims," and juicy gossip. Several local
politicians had been instrumental in ensuring the proper zoning for the businesses and important officials like judges, immigration officers, and police
captains were among the clubs' customers.[3] The raids led to Len Wah Chong,
a forty-three-year-old Malaysian immigrant, pleading guilty of sex trafficking. She admitted to recruiting and harboring eleven women to work as prostitutes in her four massage parlors between August 2004 and October 2007.[4]
In exchange for her cooperation with the HTTFA, Chong received a lightened
sentence of only five to six years in prison. She was also required to forfeit her
properties, and pay a $350,000 restitution fee to be divided among the vic-
tims.[5] Chong's cooperation yielded four sensational Mann Act convictions of
leading men within the communities of western New York.

Chong revealed that her client list included a retired New York State Supreme Court Justice, a former prosecutor/supreme court clerk, a retired police

captain, and several sheriff's deputies. These men had, from 2001 to 2006, hired prostitutes from Chong and taken the women over state lines to regional and national conventions of their fraternal order—the Royal Order of Jesters. The Jesters is an all-male, invitation-only fraternal organization with 191 chapters and 23,000 members that celebrates the pursuit of merriment and mirth. To ensure enough merriment, the retired judge, Ronald H. Tills, not only hired one of Chong's employees, but he also engaged the services of a woman whom he had a few years earlier sent to jail for prostitution. At a convention in Ashland, Kentucky, Tills supplied the women with a hotel room, on the door of which, he posted a sign that read: "$70/hour." For his role in violating the Mann Act, in May 2009 a federal judge sentenced the 74-year old Tills, to serve eighteen months in prison and pay a $25,000 fine. The conviction of the judge was the most sensational in the Jesters case.[6]

The fact that all of the men under investigation in the Jester case had ties to the criminal justice system certainly influenced the zeal with which the U.S. Attorney's office pursued convictions. According to the U.S. Department of State, the most troubling government practice concerning human trafficking is the complicity of law enforcement officials in trafficking offenses.[7] Members of the criminal justice community in Erie and Niagara Counties expressed shock at the charges against these men.[8] In addition to the troubling abuse of their positions that these men seemed to have engaged in when hiring prostitutes, their deviation from respectable (sober) masculinity led to special condemnation. The judge in Tills's case declared, "It's not a matter to be taken lightly. . . . It involved the dehumanization of victims of human trafficking. . . . What you did was a disgrace to you, an insult to your wife and a disgrace to your profession."[9]

The women at the center of the Len Wah Chong and Jesters cases quickly disappeared from journalists' stories. Newspaper accounts reported that the nine women were ethnic Chinese, most likely from Hong Kong, a city with a thriving sex industry.[10] The U.S. Attorney leading the task force, Terrance P. Flynn, characterized the women in terms that were reminiscent of the rhetoric of early-twentieth-century white slavery reformers. "These are extremely vulnerable women," he proclaimed. "Did they come to America looking for a better life? Yes. But does anyone come to this country with aspirations to sell their bodies in a massage parlor every day to pay off debts? I would say no."[11] Throughout the initial media coverage and subsequent stories about the case, the women's voices remained mute.

Sex-worker activist and spokesperson for COYOTE (Call Off Your Old Tired Ethics) Carol Leigh expressed skepticism that the women in New York were actually sex slaves, arguing: "I think there is a moral panic surrounding prostitution and immigration. The government tends to take the position that anyone who comes here from another country to become a prostitutes is a sex slave, and from my experience [talking with San Francisco massage parlor prostitutes], that is absolutely not true."[12] Leigh may be correct in that it is likely that the nine women detained in the raid had been sex workers prior to their arrival in western New York. It is also likely that these women were well aware of the type of work that they would be expected to perform. Len Wah Chong recruited the women through friends and newspaper advertisements in New York City.[13] A friend of Chong rejected law enforcement officials' characterization of the women as sex slaves, noting that the women were free to leave the clubs and frequently traveled to New York City on the weekends.[14] Yet, from the perspective of the U.S. legal system, their consent was meaningless. The U.S. State Department adopts its definition of trafficking from the 2000 United Nations Protocol to Prevent, Suppress, and Punish Trafficking in Persons (Palermo Protocol) and the Trafficking Victims Protection Act of 2000 (TVPA), and asserts that *trafficking* refers to "the act of recruiting, harboring, transporting, providing, or obtaining a person for compelled labor of commercial sex acts through the use of force, fraud, or coercion."[15] Luis CdeBaca, the Ambassador-at-Large to Monitor and Combat Trafficking in Persons, reported that current U.S. trafficking policy no longer requires movement and mobility—crossing political boundaries—to establish criminal behavior.[16] By focusing on the activity of third-party profiteers from the sex trade and constituting their engagement in "force, fraud, or coercion," prosecution can move forward without becoming mired in discussions centered around the consent of the trafficking victim in acts of prostitution. Her will is side-stepped.

Due to the fact that the women were illegal immigrants and vulnerable to coercion, combined with the fact that some were in debt relationships with Chong, the U.S. Attorney judged them to be victims of trafficking.[17] According to the Palermo Protocol that helps guide U.S. trafficking policy, an individual's initial consent to practice prostitution is not "legally determinative."

If after their consent has been granted they are held through debt, coercion, and psychological manipulation, then the Palermo Protocol and the U.S. Government defines them as victims of trafficking regardless of their choice in the matter.[18] Additionally, U.S. policy does not treat prostitution as "a valid form of employment."[19] U.S. Attorney Flynn pointed to the women's vulnerability after Chong's conviction, stating: "It's seedy to think that she so quickly forgot what it meant to be an immigrant woman coming into this country— not having a skill, not having legal status. . . . You would think as a woman she would be sensitive to the concerns of these women coming here. . . . Obviously they're disadvantaged. They're in a world that they're not a citizen, maybe in a man's world, since it's the men who are paying for the services."[20]

The women's lack of citizenship status meant that they remained vulnerable even after they had been "rescued." According to a researcher who interviewed victims discovered through antitrafficking raids in New York, trauma and detention of women are the most common results from such raids.[21] Under the TVPA, victims of trafficking, like the women in the Chong case, can apply for legal residency and welfare benefits in the United States. The TVPA is intended to prevent instances of trafficking, protect victims, and prosecute traffickers. But the TVPA's definition of "victim" is predicated on that victim's cooperation with law enforcement officials and willingness to enable prosecution. Protection is tied to prosecution. Even with cooperation, getting a T Visa, the type created for victims of trafficking, is an "exceedingly cumbersome" process mired with bureaucratic obstacles. Most troubling is the fact that government funds that aid nonprofit groups working with victims are barred from being spent on attorneys' fees, including immigration attorneys who are necessary for applying for the visa. Consequently, applying for a T Visa is often low in the priorities of victim services purveyors.[22] Immigration and Customs Enforcement is authorized to issue 5,000 T Visas a year, in 2010, only 304 were issued, indicating the difficulty in getting one.[23] Some sources report that 50 percent of applicants are rejected. More problematically, victims are not eligible for a T Visa if they have a history of prostitution in the ten years prior to their application.[24] Given that most women who are trafficked for sex have sold sex prior to migrating, this requirement functions to exclude the vast majority of these women from a wide variety of social services connected to the T Visa. Although it is unclear what happened to the nine women at the center of the initial raid, it is likely that at least one of them cooperated with law enforcement to such a degree that she was able to apply for a T Visa (one Chinese-speaking woman testified in the Tills case). In a fate that is remarkably similar to those of immigrant prostitutes found in brothels in 1910s, the others were probably deported.

Since the 2000 issuing of the Palermo Protocol, international sex trafficking has again captured the interest, imagination, and organizing zeal of numerous activists throughout the globe. Like the white slavery narratives, current media representations of trafficking highlight the ignorance and innocence of migrant women while also emphasizing the role deceit plays in recruiting sex workers. In contemporary accounts, even the trafficked sex worker who seemingly has no innocence to lose is "rendered innocent by the ritual invocation of her poverty and desperation."[25] According to scholar and activist Jo Doezema, current policy makers are interested in "preventing 'innocent' women from becoming prostitutes, and keeping 'dirty' foreign prostitutes from infecting the nation."[26] She castigates policy makers for erasing the will of sex workers who might choose to migrate to take advantage of economic opportunities. Doezema, a former sex worker and an important theorist of transnational sex work, argues that current discourses that mirror earlier discourses of white slavery result in policies that overlook the myriad ways that voluntary sex workers are exploited; instead, adopting a labor rights perspective, she suggests the sex workers need to have the policy protections offered to other workers.[27]

Within the United States, antitrafficking measures continue to be bound with issues of how to distinguish innocent victims from hardened criminals, and sex work is framed as an illegal and clandestine enterprise for sex workers while the role of customers is ignored, and deportation is resorted to as a tool to fight sex trafficking. As women continue to migrate independently, and recent data has closely monitored the feminization of global migration, anxieties about lost domesticity and exploited sexuality abound. The centrality of women's reproductive labor to understandings of what women can, should, and should not do, means that the underlying logic of most policy towards sex trafficking is extremely gendered, and seeks to conserve traditional domestic arrangements. Yet the language of trafficking, like the language of white slavery, does not treat the issue of prostitution as equally gendered for men and women alike. Throughout accounts of trafficking and prostitution, the male customers are invisible, protected by public policy and law enforcement. In the Chong case, the men prosecuted were those who seemingly took advantage of their positions as key actors in the local criminal justice system, and it was this violation of respectability and public trust that drove much the U.S. Attorney's action against them. The numerous male customers of the massage parlor remained hidden from all accounts of the case and from any legal ramifications. Their very invisibility normalizes the idea of male sexual demand for prostitution, the idea that there is a male sex right.[28] Even in the Jesters case, the judge was castigated not so much for being a long-time customer of a brothel, but rather for disgracing his wife and the judicial bench he had once occupied.

The Palermo Protocol, the TVPA, and the Mann Act are no longer the only statutory weapons available to combat sex trafficking. As of 2013, 48 states and the District of Columbia had passed anti–sex trafficking laws.[29] Many of these laws function to recriminalize prostitution by increasing penalties for existing crimes or creating new crimes. They produce a disproportionate impact on women in the sex trade.[30] For example, California's Prop 35 passed with overwhelming support in the autumn of 2012. The law severely increases the punishment for sex trafficking and promises to criminalize trafficking by focusing, again, only on a movement of "victims." Among survivor networks, victims' advocacy groups, and sex worker rights activists, the measure is seen as a way to further criminalize the lives of sex workers.[31] Whether a measure like Prop 35 will function to limit trafficking by targeting traffickers—or will end up empowering local law enforcement to more closely police sex workers—remains to be seen. Laws like this one are part of a larger trend to further criminalize sex work as part of the antitrafficking moral crusade.[32]

Recently, the tendency within antitrafficking legislation has been to increase the resources of law enforcement as a strategy for combating trafficking.[33] The Department of Justice had made over $80 million available to assist states in their antitrafficking efforts. Most of this money, however, had been devoted to training law enforcement.[34] Sadly, there has not been a complementary trend of increasing resources for social services for sex workers and trafficking survivors. Most survivors are in dire need of shelters and counseling, especially if they are under the age of eighteen. Though the William Wilberforce Trafficking Victims Protection Reauthorization Act of 2008 provided millions of dollars for victim services, the provisions to provide grants for shelters for minors was never funded. A 2007 study found that only four facilities existed in the country to serve this population, and they had only 45 beds available between them.[35] Consequently, most young victims are returned to the homes they fled or held in juvenile detention centers.

As law enforcement becomes more robust, the largely nonprofit sector that seeks to meet the needs of trafficked women has been neglected. When the state of Texas passed one of the first state-level antitrafficking laws in 2003, it established an account for up to $10 million in grant funding to provide support to nongovernmental organizations for providing victim services. But the account was never funded, and the state of Texas has since adopted the position that Texas taxpayers shouldn't pay for the human care of trafficking victims; rather it has been suggested that any services provided should be funded by restitutions paid by convicted offenders.[36] Even when Texas accepted a federal grant from the Department of Justice, most monies available have been directed towards law enforcement training. The case in Texas is not atypical. Trafficked persons are frequently held in detention facilities, shelters, or rescue homes, which can be quite repressive. The prioritization of law enforcement over victim services functions to treat victims as suspect and criminal.[37] Consequently, women in trafficking cases are typically abandoned after the prosecution of their cases, and many find themselves in the same situation that led to their entry into sex work.[38] U.S. trafficking policy is currently antiprostitution, and antiprostitution in practice means antiprostitute, implicating as it does all sex work.[39] Policy that configures all sex workers as trafficking victims provides no aid to them and criminalizes their livelihood, leading to the tragic irony that the women who are being "rescued" end up further exploited by the very policies intended to "save" them. This irony has long roots, as the Bureau's enforcement of the Mann Act reveals.

The mandate of the Mann Act's "any other immoral purpose" clause produced the FBI's legal authority to police Americans' sexual behavior. The gender conservatism of the Bureau in the early twentieth century shaped who was perceived as a "victim" worth saving and who was seen by special agents as a deviant in need of policing. This meant that enforcement of the Mann Act could not be separated from the culture of the institution that administered it.[40] The Bureau's enforcement of the Mann Act reveals the potential of the space between the letter of the law and the implementation of law. According to J. Edgar Hoover, from 1921 to 1936, the FBI investigated around 47,500 Mann Act cases.[41] Yet during the same period of time, U.S. Attorneys achieved only 6,335 convictions, because the vast majority of cases did not move forward to prosecution.[42] Mann Act investigations before World War II can be divided into two categories: those destined for prosecution by U.S. Attorneys, and those not. While some overlap existed between these categories, the fact that only a small percentage of the tens of thousands of cases investigated by the Bureau ever advanced to U.S. Attorneys' offices speaks volumes about how the law was enforced and the growth of the criminal justice state. For those cases that made up the second category, the Bureau used its investigative powers to informally discipline a wide range of sexual behaviors. The "shadow of the law"—threats of potential legal action—became a powerful facet of FBI growth and action.[43] Plus, the Bureau's preference for yielding prosecutorial authority to local authorities fortified and strengthened local law enforcement, along the lines of the Bureau's prerogatives. Enforcement of the Mann Act expanded the activities of the FBI by extending its jurisdiction to police sexuality, which ultimately contributed to its nationwide presence.

Note on Sources

Though this investigation into white slavery, the Bureau of Investigation, and the enforcement of the White Slave Traffic Act utilizes a wide variety of sources, it is primarily based on governmental sources—records of the Immigration Bureau, the Bureau of Investigation (BOI), and Federal Bureau of Investigation (FBI)—housed at the National Archives. The most important records are BOI and FBI Mann Act investigative files. These records provide rich details of the BOI/FBI investigations, often including affidavits and testimony of the parties involved in the cases. These case files have an interesting and revealing institutional history. When Congress established the National Archives (NARA) in 1934, Hoover refused to turn over any FBI documents to the new agency. But by the early 1940s, the FBI was overwhelmed as old files consumed more and more office space. As a result, Hoover ordered his Records Management Division to review the bureau's closed Mann Act files from the years 1912 to 1919. The division advised Hoover that the files did not have any current value, but did contain "considerable information of a very personal nature and potentially damaging to the character of the person" whom had been under investigation.[1] The FBI proposed destroying the records, but NARA opposed the plan due to the records' potential historical value. Hoover hesitated to hand over the documents because the records would place the FBI in "an embarrassing position without even the defense of an indictment or authorized complaint."[2] At a stalemate, the records remained with the FBI until, in 1950, FBI Assistant Director Louis Nichols proposed a compromise solution: microfilming all of the BOI records from 1908 to 1922 and destroying the originals.[3] As a result, the Mann Act cases between 1910 and 1920, are mixed in with other BOI investigations on these rolls of microfilm.[4] Mann Act cases from 1920 to 1941 were organized under their own subject number (31) and have been turned over to NARA; however, a good portion of them remain classified.[5]

This study is based on nearly one thousand individual case files, originating from between 1910 and 1941. Initially I sought to build a sample of cases that would be broad enough to substantiate my arguments. The cases from between 1910 and 1920 were gathered by scouring every other reel of microfilm and collecting every

Mann Act case I encountered. Once Mann Act cases had their own classification system, in 1920, finding these cases became much easier as I collected cases originating every three years—1921, 1924, 1927, 1930, 1933, 1936, 1939—though many investigations spanned multiple years. Of course, as my research became more focused, I occasionally looked for cases that originated in other years.

The typical Mann Act case followed a tortuous path. The file would originate from the field office where the complaint had been lodged, usually by a family member, U.S. Attorney, or police officer (occasionally a nosey neighbor or representative of a philanthropic organization would initiate investigations). The case identified a "victim," the woman alleged to be trafficked over a state line, and a "subject," the person, usually, but not always, male, who was alleged to have taken the woman over the state line (or travelled anywhere within the territories or Washington, DC). The special agent would send a copy of the first report to Washington, DC, and possibly another copy to a different field office whose aid might be required. As the case developed, several field offices would submit reports to the originating office and Washington, DC. The files could include many meaningless memos noting each action investigators took; these actions could include everything from staking out a post office to inquiring about the subject at a saloon, to interviewing former employers or neighbors of the subjects and victims. If the case seemed to be a clear-cut Mann Act violation, the special agents investigating would check with their local U.S. Attorneys to inquire about the likelihood of them taking the case to court. Typically a case could be tried in one of two places—where it had originated or where the violators had been discovered. Individual U.S. Attorneys and judges showed a marked preference for avoiding Mann Act cases (or conversely, supporting them). The special agents threw the case to the region where it would have the most success. Frequently, at this point the case would be dismissed, informally by the special agent or U.S. Attorney, or more formally by a judge, but if the case was not dismissed, then it went before a grand jury which would return an indictment, and from there, lawyers prepared for trial. The investigative case files can range from one-page reports of a complaint to hundreds of pages, spanning several boxes. Most of the time, the special agent filing an individual report wrote the report in his own prose, paraphrasing the words of those whom he had interviewed, although occasionally verbatim transcripts of interviews were included.

When using the evocative BOI/FBI investigative case files, the quasi-legal process that produced the investigations emerges as especially important. Legal sources must be contextualized within the closed systems that produce them in order to be legible.[6] Bureaucratic cultures take precedent over the narratives offered by the subjects or victims under investigation, because the bureaucratic cultures produced their narratives. Reading within and against the archival grain, in this case within the records of agencies like the BOI/FBI, reveals vivid relationships between personal lives and bureaucratic regimes.

Notes

Introduction

1. James G. Findlay, Oct 6, 1920, 31-327-0, Case 31-327, Box 14, Record Group 65, Records of the Federal Bureau of Investigation—Bureau Headquarters Case Files, Classification 31, National Archives, College Park, MD [hereafter referred to as FBI White Slave Files].

2. James G. Findlay, Nov 9, 1921, 31-327-3, Case 31-327, Box 14, FBI White Slave Files; James G. Findlay, Apr 6, 1923, 31-327-19, Case 31-327, Box 14, FBI White Slave Files.

3. Roy Lubove, "The Progressives and the Prostitute," *The Historian* 24, no. 3 (May 1962): 308–330; Egal Feldman, "Prostitution, the Alien Woman and the Progressive Imagination, 1910–1915," *American Quarterly* 19, no. 2 (Summer 1967): 192–206; Robert E. Riegel, "Changing American Attitudes Toward Prostitution (1800–1920),"*Journal of the History of Ideas* 29, no. 3 (Jul–Sep 1968): 437–452; John C. Burnham, "The Progressive Era Revolution in American Attitudes Toward Sex," *Journal of American History* 59, no. 4 (Mar 1973): 885–908; Mark Thomas Connelly, *The Response to Prostitution in the Progressive Era* (Chapel Hill: University of North Carolina, 1980); Ruth Rosen, *The Lost Sisterhood: Prostitution in America, 1900–1918* (Baltimore: Johns Hopkins Press, 1982); Anne M. Butler, *Daughters of Joy, Sisters of Misery: Prostitutes in the American West, 1865–1890* (Urbana: University of Illinois Press, 1985); Barbara Meil Hobson, *Uneasy Virtue: The Politics of Prostitution and the American Reform Tradition* (New York: Basic Books, 1987); Timothy J Gilfoyle, *City of Eros: New York City Prostitution and the Commercialization of Sex, 1790–1920* (New York: W.W. Norton, 1992); Benson Tong, *Unsubmissive Women: Chinese Prostitutes in Nineteenth-Century San Francisco* (Norman: University of Oklahoma Press, 1994); Sharon E. Wood, *The Freedom of the Streets: Work, Citizenship, and Sexuality in a Gilded Age City* (Durham: University of North Carolina Press, 2005); and Elizabeth Alice Clement, *Love for Sale: Courting, Treating, and Prostitution in New York City, 1900–1945* (Chapel Hill: University of North Carolina Press, 2006).

4. Rosen, *The Lost Sisterhood,* 14.

5. E. J. Geehan, Nov 3, 1921, 31-327-1, Case 31-327, Box 14, FBI White Slave Files.

6. Tim Weiner, *Enemies: A History of the Bureau* (New York: Random House, 2012), xv; Rhodri Jeffreys-Jones, *The Bureau: A History* (New Haven: Yale University Press, 2007); Richard Gid Powers, *Broken: The Troubled Past and Uncertain Future of the Bureau* (New York: Free Press, 2004), 27; Athan G. Theoharis, *The Bureau & American Democracy* (Lawrence: University of Kansas Press, 2004); and Max Lowenthal, *The Federal Bureau of Investigation* (New York: William Sloane Associates, Inc., 1950).

7. "Approximate Amount of Time Spent by the Bureau of Investigation, Department of Justice, in Investigating Average Cases Involving Certain Violations of Federal Statutes," File "Bureau of Investigation," *Records of the Wickersham Commission on Law Enforcement, Part 2: Research Reports and General Subject Files,* Consulting Ed. Samuel Walker (Bethesda, MD: University Publications, 1999), reel 3, page 2.

1. The American Myth of White Slavery

1. Kate C. Bushnell, "Working in Northern Wisconsin," *W.C.T.U. State Work* (Madison, WI) 3, no. 7 (Nov 1, 1888), 7.

2. Bushnell, "Working in Northern Wisconsin," 3.

3. Kate C. Bushnell, "The Wisconsin Lumber Dens," *The Philanthropist* 3, no. 12 (Dec 1888): 3.

4. Marion Horan, "Trafficking in Danger: Working-Class Women and Narratives of Sexual Danger in English and United States Anti-Prostitution Campaigns, 1875–1914" (PhD diss., State University of New York, Binghamton, 2006), 142–162; Amy R. Lagler, " 'For God's Sake Do Something:' White-Slavery Narratives and Moral Panic in Turn-of-the-Century American Cities" (PhD diss., Michigan State University, 2000), 58–60.

5. Bushnell, "The Wisconsin Lumber Dens," 1–3; Horan, "Trafficking in Danger," 172, 169, 186.

6. Timothy J. Gilfoyle, *City of Eros: New York, Prostitution, and the Commercialization of Sex, 1790–1920* (New York: W.W. Norton & Co., 1992), 20. Ruth Rosen speculates that prostitution in the United States hit its peak between 1850 and 1900. Ruth Rosen, *The Lost Sisterhood: Prostitution in America, 1900–1918* (Baltimore: Johns Hopkins Press, 1982), 3.

7. Gilfoyle, *City of Eros,* 57, 59; Alecia P. Long, *The Great Southern Babylon: Sex, Race, and Respectability in New Orleans, 1865–1920* (Baton Rouge: Louisiana State University Press, 2004), 104–109; Emily Epstein Landau, *Spectacular Wickedness: Sex, Race, and Memory in Storyville, New Orleans* (Baton Rouge: Louisiana State University Press, 2013); Anne M. Butler, *Daughters of Joy, Sisters of Mis-*

ery: Prostitutes in the American West, 1865–90 (Urbana: University of Illinois Press, 1985); Jacqueline Baker Barnhart, *The Fair but Frail: Prostitution in San Francisco, 1849–1900* (Reno: University of Nevada Press, 1986).

8. Rosen, *The Lost Sisterhood*, 4, 7; John C. Burnham, "Medical Inspection of Prostitution in America in the Nineteenth Century: The St. Louis Experiment and Its Sequel," *Bulletin of the History of Medicine* 45, no. 3 (May/Jun 1971): 203–218, 205–206; Ann R. Gabbert, "Prostitution and Moral Reform in the Borderlands: El Paso, 1890–1920," *Journal of the History of Sexuality* 12, no. 4 (Oct 2003): 575–604; Gilfoyle, *City of Eros*, 34; Mara L. Keire, *For Business and Pleasure: Red-Light Districts and the Regulation of Vice in the United States, 1890–1930* (Baltimore: Johns Hopkins Press, 2010), 10. Property owners profited to such a degree from renting to brothel owners that they themselves became targets of social reformers seeking to eradicate red-light districts. See Peter C. Hennigan, "Property War: Prostitution, Red-Light Districts, and the Transformation of Public Nuisance Law in the Progressive Era," *Yale Journal of Law and the Humanities* 16, no. 123 (2004): 123–198. For the overlapping of racially and morally segregated districts, see Kevin J. Mumford, *Interzones: Black/White Sex Districts in Chicago and New York in the Early Twentieth Century* (New York: Columbia University Press, 1997); Chad Heap, *Slumming: Sexual and Racial Encounters in American Nightlife, 1885–1940* (Chicago: University of Chicago Press, 2009); and Ivan Light, "The Ethnic Vice Industry, 1880–1944," *American Sociological Review* 42, no. 3 (Jun 1977): 464–479, 469.

9. Donna J. Guy, *Sex and Danger in Buenos Aires: Prostitution, Family, and Nation in Argentina* (Lincoln: University of Nebraska Press, 1991), 38 and 47; Laurie Bernstein, *Sonia's Daughters: Prostitutes and Their Regulation in Imperial Russia* (Berkeley: University of California Press, 1996), 20; Alain Corbin, *Women for Hire: Prostitution and Sexuality in France after 1850,* trans. Alan Sheridan (Harvard University Press, 1990), 4; Edward J. Bristow, *Prostitution and Prejudice: The Jewish Fight against White Slavery, 1870–1939* (New York: Schocken Books, 1982), 30.

10. Eileen J. Findlay, "Decency and Democracy: The Politics of Prostitution in Ponce, Puerto Rico, 1890–1900," *Feminist Studies* 23, no. 3 (Autumn 1997): 471–499; Nell Damon Galles, "Prostitutes, Fornicators, and Feebleminded Sex-Perverts: Social Control and the Progressive Era Woman" (PhD diss., University of New Mexico, 2005), 41–42. St. Augustine is quoted in William Sanger, *The History of Prostitution* (New York: Arno Press, 1972 [1858]), 91.

11. For information on the Ladies National Association and their campaign to repeal Britain's Contagious Disease Acts, see Judith R. Walkowitz, *Prostitution and Victorian Society: Women, Class, and the State* (Cambridge: Cambridge University Press, 1980), 90–136.

12. Stephanie Limoncelli, "The Politics of Humanitarianism: States, Reformers, and the International Movement to Combat the Traffic in Women, 1875–1960"

(PhD diss. University of California at Los Angeles, 2006), 68, 70; Josephine E. Butler, "The Moral Reclaimability of Prostitutes" (May 1870), in *Josephine Butler and the Prostitution Campaigns: Diseases of the Body Politic,* vol. 1, ed. Ingrid Sharp, 121–127 (London: Routledge, 2003), 121, 124–125.

13. Judith R. Walkowitz, "The Politics of Prostitution," *Signs* 6, no. 1 (Autumn 1980): 123–135, 130–131.

14. W. T. Stead, "The Maiden Tribute to Modern Babylon" (6 July–10 July 1885), in *Josephine Butler and the Prostitution Campaigns: Diseases of the Body Politic,* vol. 4, ed. Jane Jordan, 115–234 (London: Routledge, 2003), 119; quoted in Judith R. Walkowitz, *City of Dreadful Delight: Narratives of Sexual Danger in Late-Victorian London* (Chicago: University of Chicago Press, 1992), 82.

15. Stephanie A. Limoncelli, *The Politics of Trafficking: The First International Movement to Combat the Sexual Exploitation of Women* (Stanford: Stanford University Press, 2010), 56–57.

16. Quoted in Bristow, *Prostitution and Prejudice,* 35.

17. David Roediger, *The Wages of Whiteness: Race and the Making of the American Working-Class* (New York: Verso, 1999), 65–93; Gunther Peck, "Feminizing White Slavery in the United States: Marcus Braun and the Transnational Traffic in White Bodies, 1890–1910," in *Workers Across the Americas: The Transnational Turn in Labor History,* ed. Leon Fink, 221–244 (New York: Oxford University Press, 2011), 222.

18. Quoted in Bristow, *Prostitution and Prejudice,* 36.

19. Alfred S. Dyer, "The European Slave Trade in English Girls" (1880), in *Josephine Butler and the Prostitution Campaigns: Diseases of the Body Politic,* vol. 4, ed. Jane Jordan (London: Routledge, 2003), 27.

20. Deborah Gray White, *Ar'n't I a Woman: Female Slaves in the Plantation South* (New York: Norton, 1985); and Stephanie M. H. Camp, *Closer to Freedom: Enslaved Women and Everyday Resistance in the Plantation South* (Chapel Hill: University of North Carolina Press, 2004); Donna J. Guy, " 'White Slavery,' Citizenship, and Nationality in Argentina," in *White Slavery and Mothers Alive and Dead* (Lincoln: University of Nebraska Press, 2000), 73; Joel Quirk, *The Anti-Slavery Project: From the Slave Trade to Human Trafficking* (Philadelphia: University of Pennsylvania Press, 2012), 23–53; Seymour Drescher, *Abolition: A History of Slavery and Antislavery* (New York: Cambridge University Press, 2009).

21. Ronald Takaki, *Strangers from a Different Shore: A History of Asian Americans* (Boston: Little, Brown, and Company, 1989), 79.

22. George Anthony Peffer, *If They Don't Bring Their Women Here: Chinese Female Immigration before Exclusion* (Chicago: University of Illinois Press, 1999), 102; Stuart Creighton Miller, *Unwelcome Immigrant: American Image of the Chinese, 1785–1882* (Chicago: University of Chicago Press, 1969), 67 and 79; Lucie Cheng Hirata, "Free, Indentured, Enslaved: Chinese Prostitutes in Nineteenth-

Century America," *Signs* 5, no. 1 (Autumn 1979): 3–29, 24; and George Anthony Peffer, "Forgotten Families: The Development of the Chinese American Community in San Francisco, 1860–1880," in *Remapping Asian American History*, ed. Sucheng Chan, 49–67 (Walnut Creek, CA: Alta Mira Press, 2003).

23. Quoted in Lagler " 'For God's Sake Do Something'," 35.

24. Eric Foner, *Reconstruction: America's Unfinished Revolution, 1863–1877* (New York: Harper Collins, 1992); Carole Pateman, *The Sexual Contract* (Stanford: Stanford University Press, 1988); and, Amy Dru Stanley, *From Bondage to Contract: Wage Labor, Marriage, and the Market in the Age of Slave Emancipation* (New York: Cambridge University Press, 1998).

25. Quoted in Miller, *Unwelcome Immigrant*, 153.

26. Special Committee on Chinese Immigration, *Chinese Immigration. The Social, Moral, and Political Effect of Chinese Immigration. Policy and Means of Exclusion* (Sacramento: State Printing Office, 1877), 20; Erika Lee, *At America's Gates: Chinese Immigration During the Exclusion Era, 1882–1943* (Chapel Hill: University of North Carolina Press, 2003), 30; George Anthony Peffer, "Forbidden Families: Emigration Experiences of Chinese Women under the Page Law, 1875–1882," *Journal of American Ethnic History* 6, no. 1 (1986): 28–46, 28–29.

27. Lagler, " 'For God's Sake Do Something'," 42–43; Peggy Pascoe, *Relations of Rescue: The Search for Female Moral Authority in the American West, 1874–1939* (New York: Oxford University Press, 1990), 13–16, 95. For white Progressive-Era antislavery activism among the Chinese community in New York City, see Mary Ting Yi Lui, "Saving Young Girls from Chinatown: White Slavery and Woman Suffrage, 1910–1920," *Journal of the History of Sexuality* 18, no. 3 (Sep 2009): 393–417.

28. "Chinese Slavery," *San Francisco Chronicle*, Apr 17, 1892, 1.

29. Pascoe, *Relations of Rescue*, 13–16, 95; Lagler, " 'For God's Sake Do Something'," 42–43; "Chinese Slave Girl is Freed at Marysville," *San Francisco Chronicle*, Feb 13, 1921, D7.

30. Horan, "Trafficking in Danger," 5; Lagler, " 'For God's Sake Do Something,'" 51; David J. Pivar, *Purity Crusade: Sexual Morality and Social Control, 1868–1900* (Westport, CT: Greenwood Press, 1973), 67–68; Blanche Glassman Hersh, *The Slavery of Sex: Feminist-Abolitionists in America* (Urbana: University of Illinois Press, 1978), 170; for an example of English abolitionists' visits to the United States, see "Rapport de Secrétaire de Bureau International sur son voyage en Amérique," *La Traite Des Blanches* 19 (May 1907), 3–4.

31. Charlton Edholm, *Traffic in Girls and Work of Rescue Mission* (Chicago: Charlton Edholm, 1899), 15–14.

32. Peck, "Feminizing White Slavery," 224.

33. For more on debt peonage, see Pete Daniel, *The Shadow of Slavery: Peonage in the South, 1901–1969* (Urbana: University of Illinois Press, 1972); Gerald

Davis Jaynes, *Branches without Roots: Genesis of the Black Working Class in the American South, 1862–1882* (New York: Oxford University Press, 1986); and Douglas A. Blackmon, *Slavery by Another Name: The Re-Enslavement of Black Americans from the Civil War to World War II* (New York: Doubleday, 2008).

34. Some historians, however, like Emily Landau, have suggested "the success of Jim Crow depended upon remembering, revising, and repressing knowledge about antebellum slavery in order to form new cultural memories that better served the ideological imperatives of white supremacy." Emily Landau, "Black Girls, White Slaves, Octoroon Prostitutes: Sex, Race, and Memory in Turn-of-the-Century New Orleans," presented at the Organization of American Historians' Annual Meeting, Washington, DC, March 2010.

35. Jean Fagin Yellin, *Women & Sisters: The Antislavery Feminists in American Culture* (New Haven: Yale University Press, 1989), 9–26.

36. *The Philanthropist* 1, no. 1 (Jan 1886), 8; Evelyn Brooks Higginbotham, "African-American Women's History and the Metalanguage of Race," *Signs* 17, no. 2 (Winter 1992): 251–274, 262–266; Jennifer Morgan, *Laboring Women: Reproduction and Gender in New World Slavery* (Philadelphia: University of Pennsylvania Press, 2004). For more on the late-nineteenth century development of a "national amnesia, historical revisionism, and the racialization of patriotism," see Cecilia Elizabeth O'Leary, *To Die For: The Paradox of American Patriotism* (Princeton: Princeton, University Press, 1999), 130–135, 133; David W. Blight, *Race and Reunion: The Civil War in American Memory* (Cambridge: Harvard University Press, 2001).

37. Gaines M. Foster, *Moral Reconstruction: Christian Lobbyists and the Federal Legislation of Morality, 1865–1920* (Chapel Hill: University of North Carolina, 2002), 35–39; Pivar, *Purity Crusade*, 63, 85; "The London International Congress," *The Philanthropist* 1, no. 7 (Jul 1886): 5; and Ruth Bordin, *Women and Temperance: The Quest for Power and Liberty* (Philadelphia: Temple University Press, 1981), 111.

38. Kristin Luker, "Sex, Social Hygiene, and the State: The Double-Edged Sword of Social Reform," *Theory and Society* 27, no. 5 (Oct 1998): 606–607.

39. Quoted in Barbara Leslie Epstein, *The Politics of Domesticity: Women, Evangelism, and Temperance in Nineteenth-Century America* (Middletown, CT: Wesleyan University Press, 1981), 126.

40. Luker, "Sex, Social Hygiene, and the State," 608; Pivar, *Purity Crusade*, 100, 114.

41. Pivar, *Purity Crusade*, 104–107, 173–174; Mary E. Odem, *Delinquent Daughters: Protecting and Policing Adolescent Female Sexuality in the United States, 1885–1920* (Chapel Hill: University of North Carolina Press, 1995), 8–37.

42. Lagler, "'For God's Sake Do Something,'" 55; Guy, "'White Slavery,'" 77; "The International Traffic in Girls," *The Philanthropist* 2, no. 5 (May 1887): 2.

43. Bushnell, "Working in Northern Wisconsin," 3.

44. "Foreign Regulation and American Womanhood," *The Philanthropist* 3, no. 11 (Nov 1888): 4.

45. For an example of the threat posed by European regulation, see "The International Federation Conference," *The Philanthropist* 9, no. 8 (Aug 1894): 2.

46. James R. Grossman, *Land of Hope: Chicago, Black Southerners, and the Great Migration* (Chicago: University of Chicago Press, 1989); Alferdteen Harrison, ed., *Black Exodus: The Great Migration from the American South* (Jackson: University of Mississippi Press, 1991).

47. "Robt. Spriggs Convicted," *St. Louis Palladium*, Mar 24, 1906, 2; "New Vice Phase Startles," *Chicago Daily Tribune*, Mar 10, 1906, 4; Lagler, "'For God's Sake Do Something,'" 159.

48. Clifford G. Roe, *The Great War on White Slavery* (Chicago: Roe and Steadwell, 1911), 30.

49. George Kibbe Turner, "The Daughters of the Poor: A Plain Story of the Development of New York City as a Leading Center of the White Slave Trade of the World, under Tammany Hall," *McClure's Magazine* 34 (Nov 1909): 45–61.

50. Ernest A. Bell, *Fighting the Traffic in Young Girls, or, War on the White Slave Trade* (Chicago: Southern Bible House, 1910), 260.

51. Nancy F. Cott, "Marriage and Women's Citizenship in the United States, 1830–1935," *American Historical Review* 103 (Dec 1998): 1440–73.

52. Bushnell, "The Wisconsin Lumber Dens," 2.

53. Rosen, *The Lost Sisterhood*, 10; "New American Responsibilities and Dangers," *The Philanthropist* 14, no. 1 (Jan 1899): 13–14; "State Regulation of Vice in Ohio," *The Shield* 4, no. 48 (Aug 1901): 61; and "American Regulation," *The Philanthropist* 18, no. 4 (Jan 1904): 1–2.

54. "The United States," *The Shield* 8, no. 82 (Apr 1905): 38.

55. Quoted in Kristin L. Hoganson, *Fighting for American Manhood: How Gender Politics Provoked the Spanish-American and Philippine-American Wars* (New Haven: Yale University Press, 1998), 188.

56. Quoted in ibid., 190.

57. Laura Briggs, "Familiar Territory: Prostitution, Empires, and the Question of U.S. Imperialism in Puerto Rico, 1849–1916," in *Families of a New World: Gender Politics and State Development in a Global Context*, ed. Lynne Haney and Lisa Pollard, 40–63 (New York: Routledge, 2003), 50.

58. Paul A. Kramer, "The Darkness Enters the Home: The Politics of Prostitution during the Philippine-American War," in *Haunted by Empire: Geographies of Intimacy in North American History*, ed. Ann Laura Stoler, 366–404 (Durham: Duke University Press, 2008), 366.

59. Philippa Levine, *Prostitution, Race, and Politics: Policing Venereal Disease in the British Empire* (New York: Routledge, 2003); and Philip Howell, *Geographies*

of Regulation: Policing Prostitution in Nineteenth-Century Britain and the Empire (Cambridge: Cambridge University Press, 2009); for an example of outrage see, H. H. Van Meter, *The Truth about the Philippines from Official Records and Authentic Sources* (Chicago: The Liberty League, 1900), 82–85; Kramer, "The Darkness," 367, 370. For more on American prostitutes working in Far East brothels, see Eileen Scully, "Prostitution as Privilege: The 'American Girl' of Treaty Port Shanghai, 1860–1937," *International History Review* 20, no. 4 (Dec 1998): 855–883; and Eileen P. Scully, "Taking the Low Road to Sino-American Relations: 'Open Door' Expansionists and Two China Markets," *Journal of American History* 82, no. 1 (Jun 1995): 62–93.

60. Quoted in Kramer, "The Darkness," 382–383.

61. "Regulation in Honolulu," *The Shield* 4, no. 48 (August 1901), 60–61; Kramer, "The Darkness," 384, 387.

62. Kramer, "The Darkness," 391–392, 395; "Gov. Roosevelt on Regulation," *The Philanthropist* 15, no. 2 (July 1900): 8; Maurice Gregory, "Visit to the United States," *The Shield* 4, no. 41 (Dec 1901): 82–83; José Flores Ramos, "Virgins, Whores, and Martyrs: Prostitution in the Colony, 1898–1919," in *Puerto Rican Women's History: New Perspectives*, ed. Félix V. Matos Rodríguez and Linda C. Delgado, 83–104 (Armonk, NY: M.E. Sharpe, 1998), 86.

63. Shah notes "the entanglement of race in modern science, governance, and morality reveals a paradox at the core of modernity itself. Modernity, on the one hand, promotes ideas of universality and, on the other hand, obsessively objectifies difference." Nayah Shah, *Contagious Divides: Epidemics and Race in San Francisco's Chinatown* (Berkeley: University of California Press, 2001), 5–7, quote on 5; Miller, *The Unwelcome Immigrant*, 157; Matthew Frye Jacobson, *Whiteness of a Different Color: European Immigrants and the Alchemy of Race* (Cambridge: Harvard University Press, 1999).

64. Quoted in Miller, *The Unwelcome Immigrant*, 159.

65. Quoted in Hoganson, *Fighting for American Manhood*, 189.

66. Quoted in ibid., 190.

67. Quoted in ibid.

68. "Legalizing Social Vice in the Philippines," *The Philanthropist* 15, no. 3 (Oct 1900): 4.

69. "Social Injustice in the Philippines," *The Philanthropist* 18, no. 3 (Oct 1903): 6–7.

2. A National White Slavery Squad

1. Committee on Interstate and Foreign Commerce, "Memorandum in re White-Slave Trade" Dec. 17, 1909 (Washington, DC: Government Printing Office, 1909), 10.

2. Pamela Haag, *Consent: Sexual Rights and the Transformation of American Liberalism* (Ithaca: Cornell University Press, 1999), 66 and 69; Hugh Heclo, *Modern Social Politics in Britain and Sweden: From Relief to Income Maintenance* (New Haven: Yale University Press, 1974), 305.

3. "To Send Home French Women," *Warren (PA) Evening Mirror,* June 22, 1908, 1.

4. "Amazing Facts about the White Slave Traffic," *Savannah Tribune,* May 15, 1909, 6; Ernest A. Bell, *Fighting the Traffic in Young Girls, or, War on the White Slave Trade* (Chicago: Southern Bible House, 1910), 76, 260; "Roosevelt Stands by the Paris Agreement," *Oakland Tribune,* Jun 20, 1908, 1; "White Slave Test Cases," *Daily Free Press* (Carbondale, IL), Jun 24, 1908, 1, "Etats-Unis," *La Traite des Blanches* Apr 1909, 23, 4–5; "Federal Officers Raid Chicago Levee," *Waterloo (IA) Times-Tribune* (IA), Jun 28, 1908, 9; "Landis Upholds White Slave Law," *Chicago Tribune,* Jul 10, 1908, 14; "Sellers of Girls Indicted," *Chicago Tribune,* Jul 24, 1910; and, "Agreement between the United States and Other Powers for the Repression of the Trade in White Women," Treaty Series, no. 496 (Washington, DC: Government Printing Office, 1908). The Dufours surname appears variously as "Dufor," "Dafour," and "Dufors."

5. Martha Gardner, *The Qualities of a Citizen: Women, Immigration, and Citizenship, 1870–1865* (Princeton: Princeton University Press, 2009), 89–95; Nancy Fraser and Linda Gordon, "A Genealogy of 'Dependency': Tracing a Keyword of the U.S. Welfare State," in *Justice Interruptus: Critical Reflections on the "Postsocialist" Condition,* ed. Nancy Fraser, 121–150, (New York: Routledge, 1997); Darrell Hevenor Smith and H. Guy Herring, *The Bureau of Immigration: Its History, Activities, and Organization* (Baltimore: Johns Hopkins Press, 1924), 2–5; and Deirdre M. Moloney, *National Insecurities: Immigrants and U.S. Deportation Policy since 1882* (Chapel Hill: University of North Carolina, 2012), 13.

6. Immigration Bureau, *Annual Report of the Commissioner-General of Immigration to the Secretary of Commerce and Labor for the Fiscal Year ended June 30, 1907* (Washington, DC: Government Printing Office, 1907), 62.

7. Adam McKeown, "Migration Control and the Globalization of Borders: China and the United States, 1898–1911," in *Interactions: Transregional Perspectives on World History,* ed. Jerry Bentley, Renate Bridenthal, and Anand Yang, 109–135 (Honolulu: University of Hawaii Press, 2005), 114.

8. Prescott F. Hall, "The Recent History of Immigration and Immigration Restriction," *Journal of Political Economy* (Oct 1913), in "Hearings before the Committee on Immigration and Naturalization," House of Representatives, 63rd Cong., H.R. 6060 (Washington, DC: Government Printing Office, 1913), 20.

9. Victor Safford, *Immigration Problems: Personal Experiences of an Official* (New York: Dodd, Mead, and Co., 1925), 88.

10. "Arrest and Deportation of Prostitutes and Procurers of Prostitutes," Department of Commerce and Labor Circular No. 156, Sep 26, 1907, *Records of the Immigration and Naturalization Service, Series A: Subject Correspondence Files, Part 5: Prostitution and "White Slavery"*, ed. Alan Kraut (Bethesda, MD: University Publications of America, 1997), [hereafter *INS.A.5.PWS*], roll 1.

11. Moloney, *National Insecurities*, 60, 66; "This Government Begins Crusade Against White Slave Traffic Between Europe and U.S.," *Logansport (IN) Reporter*, Oct 22, 1907, 4; Oscar S. Strauss to O. Edward Janney, Dec 17, 1907, case file 51777/30, *INS.A.5.PWS*, roll 1.

12. *Annual Report of the Commissioner General of Immigration for the Fiscal Year ended June 30, 1909* (Washington, DC: Government Printing Office, 1909), 84; "Report of the Commissioner General of Immigration," in *Reports of the Department of Commerce and Labor, 1910* (Washington, DC: Government Printing Office, 1911), 236; Braun to Commissioner General, Sep 16, 1908, case file 52484/1, *INS.A.5.PWS*, roll 3.

13. "World Fair Notes," *Oshkosh (WI) Daily Northwestern* (Oshkosh, WI), May 26, 1893, 1.

14. "Immigration Post Abroad," *New York Times*, Mar 22, 1903; "Congress Gets Report on Braun's Arrest," *New York Times*, Feb 9, 1906; Theodore Roosevelt, *The Letters of Theodore Roosevelt*, vol. 3, ed. Elting E. Morison (Cambridge: Harvard University Press, 1951), 254–255; "Will Hunt the 'Reds,'" *The Mansfield (OH) News*, May 2, 1903; Gunther Peck, "Feminizing White Slavery in the United States: Marcus Braun and the Transnational Traffic in White Bodies, 1890–1910," in *Workers Across the Americas: The Transnational Turn in Labor History*, ed. Leon Fink, 221–244 (New York: Oxford University Press, 2011), 227.

15. Marcus Braun, *Immigration Abuses: Glimpses of Hungary and Hungarians* (New York: Pearson Advertising Co., 1906), 116; Francesco Cordasco and Thomas M. Pitkin, *The White Slave Trade and the Immigrants: A Chapter in American Social History* (Detroit: Blaine Ethridge Books, 1981), 25.

16. Helen Bullis to Frank Sargent, Oct 8, 1907, case file 51652/41-B, *INS.A.5.PWS*, roll 1; "Expenses incurred by Inspector Frank L. Garbarino," Nov 2, 1907, case file, 51661/46-B, *INS.A.5.PWS*, roll 1. The sum $38.50 is comparable to approximately $845.40 today. For more on undercover methods see Jennifer Fronc, *New York Undercover: Private Surveillance in the Progressive Era* (Chicago: University of Chicago Press, 2009).

17. Marcus Braun to Frank Sargent, Aug 1, 1908, case file 52484/1, *INS.A.5.PWS*, roll 3.

18. Ann Gabbert reports that the city finances of El Paso, TX were so dependent upon the tax the city police imposed on prostitutes, that the city was financially incapable of outlawing prostitution until the 1930s. Ann R. Gabbert, "Pros-

titution and Moral Reform in the Borderlands: El Paso, 1890–1920," *Journal of the History of Sexuality* 12, no. 4 (Oct 2003): 575–604.

19. Marcus Braun to Commissioner General, "Braun U.S. White Slavery Report," Sep 29, 1908, case file 52484/1-A, *INS.A.5.PWS*, roll 3, pages 4 and 23–24 [hereafter referred to as "Braun U.S. White Slavery Report"]; Kei Tanaka, "Japanese Picture Marriage and the Image of Immigrant Women in Early Twentieth-Century California," *Japanese Journal of American Studies* no. 15 (2004): 115–138.

20. "Braun U.S. White Slavery Report," 3.

21. Ibid., 17.

22. Ibid., 7.

23. Canada was a popular entry point for those seeking to evade U.S. immigration laws. See Erika Lee, *At America's Gates: Chinese Immigration During the Exclusion Era, 1882–1943* (Chapel Hill: University of North Carolina Press, 2003), chapter 5; William H. Siener, "Through the Back Door: Evading the Chinese Exclusion Act along the Niagara Frontier, 1900 to 1924," *Journal of American Ethnic History* 27, no. 4 (summer 2008): 34–70; "Braun U.S. White Slavery Report," 2–4, 7–8, and 23–24.

24. For information on women's citizenship see Gardner, *Qualities of a Citizen;* Candice Lewis Bredbenner, *A Nationality of Her Own: Women, Marriage, and the Law of Citizenship* (Berkeley: University of California Press, 1998); Nancy F. Cott, "Marriage and Women's Citizenship in the United States, 1830–1935," *American Historical Review* 103 (Dec 1998): 1440–73, 1456; and Nayan Shah, *Stranger Intimacy: Contesting Race, Sexuality, and the Law in the North American West* (Berkeley: University of California Press, 2011), 4.

25. "Braun U.S. White Slavery Report," 8.

26. Ibid., 9–11; "White Slave Trade," *Galveston (TX) Daily News*, Nov 17, 1907, 9; see, Jessica R. Pliley, "The Petticoat Inspectors: Women Boarding Inspectors and the Gendered Exercise of Federal Authority," *Journal of the Gilded Age and Progressive Era* 12, no. 1 (Jan 2013): 95–126.

27. "Braun U.S. White Slavery Report," 13.

28. Deirdra Moloney, *National Insecurities,* 28–50.

29. "Braun U.S. White Slavery Report," 26.

30. Ibid., 31.

31. Andrew Tedesco, "Enclosure F," in "Braun U.S. White Slavery Report," 7, 15.

32. Ibid., 10; Braun to Commissioner General (Daniel Keefe), Oct 2, 1909, case file 52484/1-G, *INS.A.5.PWS*, roll 3, [hereafter "Braun European White Slavery Report"].

33. "Memo for the Acting Commissioner General [F. H. Larned]," Oct 19, 1908, case file 52484/1-A, *INS.A.5.PWS*, roll 3; "Braun U.S. White Slavery Report," 5, 23, and 29.

34. "Letter to Inspector," Mar 10, 1909, case file 52484/3, *INS.A.5.PWS,* roll 4.

35. Ibid.

36. Commissioner George Billings to Commissioner-General Frank Larned, Jun 29, 1909, case file 52484/11, *INS.A.5.PWS,* roll 4; "Col. Billings Says 'White Slave' Traffic is Dead," *Lowell (MA) Sun,* Mar 18, 1909, 26.

37. James Dunn (?) to Commissioner General Frank Larned, Oct 20, 1909, case file 54284/12, *INS.A.5.PWS,* roll 5; F. H. Larned to Daniel J. Leonard (Immigrant Inspector in Boston), June 24, 1909, case file 52484/11, *INS.A.5.PWS,* roll 4; "Confidential Circular," Mar 19, 1909, case file 52484/3, *INS.A.5.PWS,* roll 4.

38. Alfred Hampton to Commissioner General Frank Larned, Mar 25, 1909, case file 52484/16, *INS.A.5.PWS,* roll 5.

39. Frank R. Stone to Commissioner General Daniel Keefe, May 13, 1909; Frank R. Stone to Commissioner General Daniel Keefe, May 15, 1909; Frank R. Stone to Commissioner General Daniel Keefe, Jun 7, 1909; Frank R. Stone to Commissioner General Daniel Keefe, May 21, 1909; Frank R. Stone to Commissioner General Daniel Keefe, May 29, 1909; Frank R. Stone to Commissioner General Daniel Keefe, June 25, 1909, case file 52484/8, *INS.A.5.PWS,* roll 4.

40. Case file 52484/8, *INS.A.5.PWS,* roll 4; David Lehrhaupt to Commissioner General Frank Larned, Jun 25, 1909, and Sep 2, 1909, case file 54284/25A, *INS.A.5.PWS,* roll 5.

41. Daniel J. Keefe to the Secretary of Commerce and Labor, Jan 12, 1910, case file 52483/1-B, *INS.A.5.PWS,* roll 2; Keller v. United States, 213 U.S. 138 (1909); William H. Taft, "Message from the President of the United States transmitting, with accompanying letters in response to Senate Resolution No. 86, of December 7, 1909, Information Concerning the Repression of the Trade in White Women," Senate, 61st Cong., 2nd Sess., Doc. No. 214 (Washington, DC: Government Printing Office, 1909), 4; and Frederick K. Grittner, *White Slavery: Myth, Ideology, and American Law* (New York: Garland Publishing ,Inc., 1990), 85–86.

42. William H. Taft, "Message from the President of the United States transmitting, in further response to Senate Resolution No. 86, of December 7, 1909, Information Concerning the Repression of the Trade in White Women," Senate, 61st Cong., 2nd Sess., Doc. No. 214, Part 2 (Washington, DC: Government Printing Office, 1910), 13.

43. Ibid., 14.

44. Daniel J Keefe to Marcus Braun, Feb 11, 1909, case file 52484/1-D, *INS.A.5.PWS,* roll 3; F. H. Larned to Marcus Braun, Jul 8, 1909, case file 52484/1-D, *INS.A.5.PWS,* roll 3.

45. Quote in Marcus Braun to Commissioner General of Immigration, Jun 23, 1909, case file 52484/1-D, *INS.A.5.PWS,* roll 3; Marcus Braun to Commissioner General of Immigration, Jan 25, 1909, case file 52484/1-C, *INS.A.5.PWS,* roll 3; "White Slavers Facing Despair," *Chicago Daily Tribune,* Jan 15, 1909, 11;

"Amazing Facts about the White Slave Traffic," *Savannah Tribune*, May 15, 1909, 6; Marcus Braun to the Secretary of Labor and Commerce Charles Nagel, Sep 16, 1909, case file 52484/1-F.

46. Marcus Braun to Henry White, American Ambassador to France, July 27, 1909, case file 52484/1-E; Marcus Braun to the Secretary of Labor and Commerce Charles Nagel, Sep 16, 1909, case file 52484/1-F; S. Pichon to Henry White, July 7, 1909, case file 52484/1-E, *INS.A.5.PWS*, roll 3.

47. Marcus Braun to Daniel J. Keefe, Oct 6, 1909, case file 52484/1-H, *INS.A.5.PWS*, roll 4; "Braun European White Slavery Report," 13, 28, 39; "Memorandum for the Assistant Secretary," Oct 12, 1909, case file 52484/1-H, *INS.A.5.PWS*, roll 4.

48. "Braun European White Slavery Report," 9.

49. Ibid., 10–11, 39.

50. Ibid., 41–42.

51. Ibid., 33–34. A kopeck is 1/100 of a ruble.

52. George J. Kneeland, *Commercialized Prostitution in New York City* (New York: The Century Co., 1913), 126–127.

53. "Braun European White Slavery Report," 12, 14, 18, 40–41. William Hogarth famously depicted the assumed narrative of a prostitute's downward path towards disease, poverty, and death in his 1732 engravings, "The Harlot's Progress."

54. Adam McKeown, "Ritualization of Regulation: The Enforcement of Chinese Exclusion in the United States in the United States and China," *American Historical Review* 108, no. 2 (Apr 2003), 377–403, 385, 390, 394.

55. Daniel J. Keefe, in William H. Taft, "Message from the President," Part 2, 8.

56. Pliley, "The Petticoat Inspectors," 110.

57. "Braun European White Slavery Report," 1; "Memorandum for the Assistant Secretary," Oct 12, 1909, case file 52484/1-H, *INS.A.5.PWS*, roll 4.

58. Aristide Zolberg, *A Nation by Design: Immigrant Policy and the Fashioning of America* (Cambridge: Harvard University Press, 2006), 264–267; "Braun European White Slavery Report," 44; Eithne Luibhéid, *Entry Denied: Controlling Sexuality at the Border* (Minneapolis: University of Minnesota Press, 2002), 9; Allan Brandt, *No Magic Bullet: A Social History of Venereal Disease in the United States since 1880* (New York: Oxford University Press, 1985), 147–154. The United States declined to join the 1910 and 1921 international agreements to fight the trafficking of women and children. Stephanie A. Limoncelli, *The Politics of Trafficking: The First International Movement to Combat the Sexual Exploitation of Women* (Stanford: Stanford University Press, 2010), 10.

59. Katherine Benton-Cohen, "The Rude Birth of Immigration Reform," *Wilson Quarterly* 34, no. 3 (Summer 2010): 16–22, 18–191; Robert F. Zeidel, *Immigrants,*

Progressives, and Exclusion Politics: The Dillingham Commission, 1900–1927 (DeKalb: Northern Illinois University Press, 2004), 38–50. The firm restrictionists included Senator Henry Cabot Lodge (R-MA) and Representative John L. Burnett (D-AL). The one avowed antirestrictionist was Representative William S. Bennet (R-NY). The moderate restrictionists included Senator William P. Dillingham (R-VT), Representative Benjamin Howell (R-NJ), Charles P. Neill, Jeremiah Jenks, William Wheeler, and the three senators who interchangeably occupied the ninth spot on the commission: Asbury Latimer (D-SC), Anselm J. McLaurin (D-MS), and Leroy Percy (D-MS).

60. The Dillingham Commission's investigators into white slavery visited New York City, Chicago, San Francisco, Seattle, Portland, Salt Lake City, Ogden, UT, Butte, MT, Denver, Buffalo, Boston, and New Orleans. Its report on white slavery is largely dominated by first Chicago, and then Seattle.

61. Thetus W. Sims (D-TN) in United States House, *Congressional Record* 45 (Jan 19, 1910), 811; Pamela Haag, *Consent: Sexual Rights and the Transformation of American Liberalism* (Ithaca: Cornell University Press, 1999), 66.

62. United States Immigration Commission (1907–1910), "Importation and Harboring of Women for Immoral Purposes," *Reports of the Immigration Commission* (final) (Washington, DC: Government Printing Office, 1911), 65, 74, 83, and 86.

63. Edward J. Bristow, *Prostitution and Prejudice: The Jewish Fight against White Slavery, 1870–1939* (New York, Schocken Books, 1982), 165–70, quote on 168.

64. Desmond King, *Making Americans: Immigration, Race, and the Origins of the Diverse Democracy* (Cambridge: Harvard University Press, 2000), 62.

65. George Kibbe Turner, "The City of Chicago: A Study of the Great Immoralities," *McClure's Magazine* 28 (April 1907): 575–592, 581; George Kibbe Turner, "The Daughters of the Poor: A Plain Story of the Development of New York City as a Leading Center of the White Slave Trade of the World, under Tammany Hall," *McClure's Magazine* 34 (November 1909): 45–61, 47; Bristow, *Prostitution and Prejudice*, 161.

66. Val Johnson, "'The Moral Aspect of Complex Problems': New York City Electoral Campaigns against Vice and the Incorporation of Immigrants, 1890–1901," *Journal of American Ethnic History* 25, no. 2/3 (2006): 74–106, quotation on 77; Mark Thomas Connelly, *The Response to Prostitution in the Progressive Era* (Chapel Hill: University of North Carolina Press, 1980), 61–62; Hasia R. Diner, *The Jews of the United States, 1654 to 2000* (Berkeley: University of California Press, 2004, 171; and Francesco Cordasco and Thomas Monroe Pitkin, *The White Slave Trade and the Immigrants: A Chapter in American Social History* (Detroit: Blaine Ethridge Books, 1981), 12.

67. Donna Guy, *Sex and Danger in Buenos Aires: Prostitution, Family, and Nation in Argentina* (Lincoln: University of Nebraska Press, 1991); Bristow, *Prostitu-*

tion and Prejudice, 165–70; and Charles Van Onselen, *The Fox and the Flies: The World of Joseph Silver, Racketeer and Psychopath* (London: Jonathan Cape, 2007).

68. Quoted in Bristow, *Prostitution and Prejudice,* 235. For more on Jewish women's activism against white slavery, see Linda Gordon Kuzmack, *Women's Cause: The Jewish Women's Movement in England and the United States, 1881–1933* (Columbus: Ohio State University Press, 1990); Faith Rogow, *Gone to Another Meeting: The National Council of Jewish Women, 1893–1993* (Tuscaloosa: University of Alabama Press, 1993), 136–138; and Marion A. Kaplan, *The Jewish Feminist Movement in Germany: The Campaigns of the Jüdischer Frauenbund, 1904–1938* (Westport, CT: Greenwood Press, 1979), 108–113.

69. Quoted in Cordasco and Pitkin, *The White Slave Trade,* 30.

70. United States House, *Congressional Record* 45 (Jan 14, 1910), 932.

71. United States Immigration Commission (1907–1910), "Importation and Harboring of Women for Immoral Purposes," 83.

72. Cordasco and Pitkin, *The White Slave Trade,* 32.

73. For example, see "Congress Receives White Slave Report," *New York Times,* Dec 11, 1909, 4; "White Slavery Crimes Probed by Commission," *Los Angeles Herald,* Dec 11, 1909, 1; "More Rigid Inspection to Break Up 'White Slave' Traffic," *Fort Worth Star-Telegram,* Dec 10, 1909, 1; "White Slave Trade Report Gives Out Facts Regarding Practices," *Grand Forks (ND) Daily Herald,* Dec 11, 1909, 1; "The White Slave Trade," *Savannah Tribune,* Dec 11, 1909, 3.

74. "World Vice Ring the Acme of Evil," *Chicago Daily Tribune,* Dec 11, 1909, 6.

75. Michael J. Lacey and Mary O. Furner, eds., "Social Investigation, Social Knowledge, and the State: An Introduction," in *The State and Social Investigation in Britain and the United States,* 3–62 (Cambridge: Cambridge University Press, 1993), 4.

76. Ormsby McHarg, in Taft, "Message from the President," Part 1, 4.

77. Daniel J. Keefe, in Taft "Message from the President," Part 2, 4.

78. Ibid., 12.

79. Quoted in Brian Donovan, *White Slave Crusades: Race, Gender, and Anti-Vice Activism, 1887–1917* (Urbana-Champaign: University of Illinois Press, 2006), 170, fn 19.

80. Quoted in Bristow, *Prostitution and Prejudice,* 158.

81. Jane Addams, *A New Conscience and an Ancient Evil* (New York: Arno Press, 1972 [1912]), 58.

82. Emma Goldman, "The Traffic in Women," in *Anarchism and Other Essays* (New York: Mother Earth Publishing Association, 1910).

83. Maude E. Miner, *Slavery of Prostitution: A Plea for Emancipation* (New York: MacMillan, 1916), 30.

84. Grace Abbott, *The Immigrant and the Community* (New York: Century Co., 1917), 74.

85. Ibid., 76.

86. Ibid.

87. O. Edward Janney, *The White Slave Traffic in America* (New York: National Vigilance Committee, 1911), 22.

3. Endangered Daughters

1. George Kibbe Turner, "The Daughters of the Poor: A Plain Story of the Development of New York City as a Leading Center of the White Slave Trade of the World, under Tammany Hall," *McClure's Magazine* 34 (Nov 1909): 45–61, 46.

2. "Rally to Crush White Slave Sin," *Chicago Daily Tribune*, Nov 21, 1907, 3.

3. "Two Girls Lured to Ohio," *Chicago Daily Tribune*, Jun 21, 1907, 3.

4. Harold M. Meyer and Richard C. Wade, *Chicago: Growth of a Metropolis* (Chicago: University of Chicago Press, 1969), 230.

5. Robert G. Spinney, *City of Big Shoulders: A History of Chicago* (Dekalb: Northern Illinois Press, 2000), 68, 123; William Cronen, *Nature's Metropolis: Chicago and the Great West* (New York: W.W. Norton & Co., 1991).

6. "Appalling Discoveries by Government Agents Show Chicago to Be Greatest White Slave Market in America," *Chicago Daily Tribune*, Jul 26, 1908, F4.

7. "Asks Aid in Saving Girls," *Chicago Daily Tribune*, Jul 13, 1908, 3.

8. Clifford G. Roe, *The Great War on White Slavery* (Chicago: Roe and Steadwell, 1911), 39–40; "Arrest Man as a Pander," *Chicago Daily Tribune*, Jan 10, 1910, 3; George Kibbe Turner, "The City of Chicago: A Study in the Great Immoralities," *McClure's Magazine* 28 (Apr 1907): 575–592, 581.

9. Roe, *The Great War,* 33; Josephine Conger-Kaneko, "The Traffic in Girl Slaves," *The Progressive Woman* 4, no. 38 (Jul 1910): 4–5.

10. Roe, *The Great War,* 41.

11. Kathy Peiss, *Cheap Amusements: Working Women and Leisure in Turn-of-the-Century New York* (Philadelphia: Temple University Press, 1986); Nan Entad, *Ladies of Labor, Girls of Adventure: Working Women, Popular Culture, and Labor Politics at the Turn of the Twentieth Century* (New York: Columbia University Press, 1999); Brian Donovan, *White Slave Crusades: Race, Gender, and Anti-Vice Activism, 1887–1917* (Urbana: University of Illinois Press, 2006); Frederick K. Grittner, *White Slavery: Myth Ideology and American Law* (New York: Garland Publishing, Inc., 1990); David J. Langum, *Crossing over the Line: Legislating Morality and the Mann Act* (Chicago: University of Chicago Press, 1994); Timothy J. Gilfoyle, *City of Eros: New York, Prostitution, and the Commercialization of Sex, 1790–1920* (New York: W.W. Norton & Co., 1992; Mark Thomas Connelly, *The Response to Prostitution in the Progressive Era* (Chapel Hill: University of North Carolina Press, 1980); and Ruth Rosen, *The Lost Sisterhood: Prostitution in America, 1900–1918* (Baltimore: Johns Hopkins Press, 1982).

12. Jeremiah Jenks quoted in Roe, *The Great War,* 329.

13. Janet Eileen MicKish, "Legal Control of Socio-Sexual Relationships: Creation of The Mann White Slave Traffic Act of 1910," (PhD diss., Southern Illinois University at Carbondale, 1980), 148–149.

14. Maude E. Miner, *The Slavery of Prostitution: A Plea for Emancipation* (New York: MacMillan, 1916), 93.

15. "Child 'White Slaves' Talk," *Chicago Daily Tribune,* Jul 30, 1909, 3.

16. Turner, "The City of Chicago," 582.

17. "New Law Inspires White Slave Raid," *Chicago Daily Tribune,* Jul 26, 1909, 3; "Child 'White Slaves' Talk," *Chicago Daily Tribune,* Jul 30, 1909, 3; "Guilty, Says Jury: White Slave Case," *Chicago Daily Tribune,* Aug 5, 1909, 3; and Conger-Kaneko, "The Traffic in Girl Slaves," 4–5. Pandering is essentially pimping.

18. Miner, *Slavery of Prostitution,* 97.

19. "Girls Tell of Dangers of Great City," *Oakland Tribune,* Jan 18, 1908, 7.

20. "Stagestruck Girls Accuse Two Men in Conspiracy Case," *Chicago Daily Tribune,* May 2, 1908, 2. For more press coverage of the case, see "Held as Enticer of Girls," *Chicago Daily Tribune,* Feb 5, 1908, 5; "Prison Looms Up for All 'Slavers,'" *Chicago Daily Tribune,* May 22, 1908, 7; and "Young Girls Make Charges Against Theatrical Agent," *Chicago Daily Tribune,* Jan 7, 1908, 3.

21. Turner, "The City of Chicago," 577, 581; Herbert Asbury, *Gem of the Prairie: An Informal History of the Chicago Underworld* (New York: Knopf, 1940), 272.

22. Herbert Asbury, *The Barbary Coast: An Informal World of the San Francisco Underworld* (New York: Knopf, 1933), 105.

23. Chicago Vice Commission, *The Social Evil in Chicago: A Study of Existing Conditions with Recommendations by the Vice Commission of Chicago* (Chicago: Gunthorp-Warren Printing Co., 1911), 194.

24. "Girls Tell of Dangers of Great City," *Oakland Tribune,* Jan 18, 1908, 7.

25. Asbury, *Gem of the Prairie,* 270.

26. Karen Abbott, *Sin in the Second City: Madams, Ministers, Playboys, and the Battle for America's Soul* (New York: Random House, 2007), 155–156.

27. Jack C. D. Salle, "A History of the Mann Act to 1915" (master's thesis, Tennessee Technological University, 1969), 34–35; "Edwin W. Sims, US District Attorney," *Chicago Daily Tribune,* Aug 2, 1908, D3; William Stiles Bennett, United States House, *Congressional Record* 45 (Jan 25, 1910), 967.

28. Edwin Sims, "Menace of the White Slave Trade," in Ernest A. Bell, *Fighting the Traffic in Young Girls, or, War on the White Slave Trade* (Chicago: Southern Bible House, 1910), 70–71.

29. Herbert F. Margulies, "James R. Mann: The Illinois Years," *Illinois Historical Journal* 90, no. 3 (Autumn 1997): 191–210.

30. William Howard Taft, "Message to the Two Houses of Congress at the Second Session of the Sixty-First Congress," Dec 7, 1909, in *Presidential Addresses*

and State Papers (From March 4, 1909 to March 4, 1910), Vol. 1 (New York: Doubleday, Page & Co., 1910), 486; White Slave Traffic Act, ch. 395, 36 Stat. 825–27 (1910); Langum, *Crossing over the Line,* 40; Grittner, *White Slavery,* 87.

31. Committee on Interstate and Foreign Commerce, "Memorandum in re White-Slave Trade" Dec 17, 1909 (Washington, DC: Government Printing Office, 1909), 9.

32. Gaines M. Foster, *Moral Reconstruction: Christian Lobbyists and the Federal Legislation of Morality, 1865–1920* (Chapel Hill: University of North Carolina, 2002), 120.

33. Committee on Interstate and Foreign Commerce, "Memorandum in re White-Slave Trade," 4.

34. Quoted in Foster, *Moral Reconstruction,* 127.

35. Committee on Interstate and Foreign Commerce, "Memorandum in re White-Slave Trade," 4.

36. Ibid., 9–10.

37. Ibid., 4.

38. Ibid., 10.

39. Rosen, *The Lost Sisterhood,* 113.

40. Ibid., 133.

41. Committee on Interstate and Foreign Commerce, "Memorandum in re White-Slave Trade," 10, emphasis mine.

42. For more on African American women who worked in America's brothels, see Cynthia M. Blair, *I've Got to Make My Livin': Black Women's Sex Work in Turn-of-the-Century Chicago* (Chicago: University of Chicago Press, 2010), 50–85; Kevin J. Mumford, *Interzones: Black/White Sex Districts in Chicago and New York in the Early Twentieth Century* (New York: Columbia University Press, 1997), 93–120; and, Alecia P. Long, *The Great Southern Babylon: Sex, Race, and Respectability in New Orleans, 1865–1920* (Baton Rouge: Louisiana State University Press, 2004), 191–203.

43. "Speech of Hon. Charles L. Bartlett of GA," Jan 26, 1910, Appendix to the Congressional Record, *Congressional Record* 45, 12; Foster, *Moral Reconstruction,* 131–146.

44. Quoted in Grittner, *White Slavery,* 87; O. Edward Janney, *The White Slave Traffic in America* (New York: National Vigilance Committee, 1911), 116–117.

45. United States House, *Congressional Record* 45 (Jan 19, 1910), 810.

46. WC Adamson, William Richardson, CL Bartlett, "Views of the Minority," United States House, *Congressional Record* 45 (Jan 19, 1910), 822.

47. United States House, *Congressional Record* 45 (Jan 26, 1910), 1032.

48. Ibid., 1033.

49. United States House, *Congressional Record* 45 (Jan 19, 1910), 820.

50. United States House, *Congressional Record* 45 (Jan 26, 1910), 1033.

51. United States House, *Congressional Record* 45 (Jan 19, 1910), 818.

52. Ibid., 812.

53. Ibid., 820.

54. United States House, *Congressional Record* 45 (Jan 26, 1910), 1031.

55. United States House, *Congressional Record* 45 (Jan 11, 1910), 527.

56. United States House, *Congressional Record* 45 (Jan 19, 1910), 814.

57. Glenda Gilmore, *Gender and Jim Crow: Women and the Politics of White Supremacy in North Carolina, 1886–1920* (Chapel Hill: University of North Carolina Press, 1996).

58. United States House, *Congressional Record* 45 (Jan 19, 1910), 821.

59. Ibid.

60. Ibid., 812.

61. William Paul Dillingham, "White Slave Traffic Act of June 25, 1910: Its Passage through the Senate of the United States—with Views of the Majority and Minority of the Senate Committee on Immigration," Senate, 61st Cong., 2nd Sess., Doc. No. 214, Part 2 (Washington, DC: Government Printing Office, 1910), 20.

62. Ibid., 21.

63. Daniel J. Keefe to Secretary of Commerce and Labor Charles Nagel, Jan 12, 1910, case file 52483/1-B, *Records of the Immigration and Naturalization Service, Series A: Subject Correspondence Files, Part 5: Prostitution and "White Slavery"*, ed. Alan Kraut (Bethesda, MD: University Publications of America, 1997), [hereafter *INS.A.5.PWS*], roll 2; William H. Taft, "Message from the President of the United States transmitting, in further response to Senate Resolution No. 86, of December 7, 1909, Information Concerning the Repression of the Trade in White Women," Senate, 61st Cong., 2nd Sess., Doc. No. 214, Part 2 (Washington, DC: Government Printing Office, 1910), 12; Martha Gardner, *The Qualities of a Citizen: Women, Immigration, and Citizenship, 1870–1865* (Princeton: Princeton University Press, 2009), 78–86; Hans P. Vought, *The Bully Pulpit and the Melting Pot: American Presidents and the Immigrant, 1897–1933* (Macon, GA: Mercer University Press, 2004), 79. The Mann Act applied to the interior of the District of Columbia, the territories, and colonial possessions including the Panama Canal Zone, as well as the crossing of district, territorial, and state lines. Committee on Interstate and Foreign Commerce, "White Slave Traffic," House of Representatives, 61st Cong., 2nd Sess., Report No. 47 (Washington, DC: Government Printing Office, 1910), 2.

64. Sanford J. Ungar, *FBI* (Boston: Little, Brown and Company, 1975), 39; Richard Gid Powers, *Broken: The Troubled Past and Uncertain Future of the FBI* (New York: Free Press, 2004), 39, 51–52; Rhodri Jeffreys-Jones, *The FBI: A History* (New Haven: Yale University Press, 2007), 39–40.

65. Powers, *Broken*, 54.

66. *Annual Report of the Attorney General of the United States for the Year Ended June 30, 1910* (Washington, DC: Government Printing Office, 1910), 25–26. See case 696, Roll 118, RG 65, Federal Bureau of Investigation, Investigative Case Files of the Bureau, 1908–1922, M1085, National Archives, College Park, MD [hereafter cited as BOI Microfilm Records].

67. "Wanted Help," *Atlanta Journal,* Sep 6, 1911, 13.

68. L. J. Baley, "U.S. vs. L. Athanasaw, Violation White Slave Traffic Act," Oct 26, 1911, 2807-6, page 4, Case 2807, Roll 136, BOI Microfilm Records.

69. Louis Athanasaw and Mitchell Sampson, "Plaintiffs in Error v. U.S.," *227 U.S. 326 (1913). Transcript of the Record,* Mar 21, 1912, 23.

70. L. J. Baley, "U.S. vs. L. Athanasaw, Violation White Slave Traffic Act," Oct 26, 1911, 2807-6, page 4, Case 2807, Roll 136, BOI Microfilm Records.

71. Daughton, "U.S. vs. L. Athanasaw, White Slave Traffic Act," Oct 31, 1911, 2807-7, page 5, Case 2807, Roll 136, BOI Microfilm Records.

72. L. J. Baley, "U.S. vs. L. Athanasaw, Violation White Slave Traffic Act," Oct 26, 1911, 2807-6, page 7, Case 2807, Roll 136, BOI Microfilm Records.

73. L. J. Baley, "U.S. vs. L. Athanasaw, et al., Violation White Slave Traffic Act," Feb 20, 1912, 2807-17, and L. J. Baley, "U.S. vs. L. Athanasaw, et al., Violation White Slave Traffic Act," Feb 21, 1912, 2807-18, Case 2807, Roll 136, BOI Microfilm Records. Athanasaw appealed the sentence, his lawyers alleging that the Mann Act was unconstitutional and that the prosecuting attorneys had failed to prove the purpose of debauchery in the minds of the defendants. His case made it to the Supreme Court, which affirmed the conviction and the legality of the Mann Act. See Athanasaw v. U S, *227 U.S. 326 (1913). Transcript of the Record,* Mar 21, 1912, 12.

74. L. J. Baley, "U.S. vs. Marian Lawrence et al., Violation White Slave Traffic Act," Oct 26, 1911, 2878-1, pages 1–2, Case 2878, Roll 136, BOI Microfilm Records.

75. L. J. Baley, "U.S. vs. Marian Lawrence, et al., Violation White Slave Traffic Act," Oct 26 and 27, 1911, 2878-1, page 2, Case 2878, Roll 136, BOI Microfilm Records.

76. L. J. Baley, "U.S. vs. Marian Lawrence, et al., Violation White Slave Traffic Act," Oct 27, 1911, 2878-1, Case 2878, Roll 136, BOI Microfilm Records.

77. L. J. Baley, "U.S. vs. Marian Lawrence, et al., Violation White Slave Traffic Act," Mar 9, 1912, Case 2878, Roll 136, BOI Microfilm Records.

78. L. J. Baley, "U.S. vs. Marian Lawrence, et al., Violation White Slave Traffic Act," Mar 4, 1912, 2878-11, Case 2878, Roll 136, BOI Microfilm Records.

79. L. J. Baley, "U.S. vs. Marian Lawrence, et al., Violation White Slave Traffic Act," Feb 13, 1912, 2878-1, Case 2878, Roll 136, BOI Microfilm Records. Pearl Snyder almost failed to make it to the trial. She had been staying with Agnes Couch, presumably in Atlanta, GA.

80. "Fined as 'White Slaver,'" *Atlanta Constitution,* Mar 13, 1912, 15.

81. Attorney General George W. Wickersham to Honorable J. R. Knowland (R-CA), Mar 20, 1912, RG 60, General Records of the Department of Justice, Formerly Classified Subject Correspondence, 1919–45. Class 31 Mann Act, Box 2620, National Archives, College Park, MD.

82. See Athanasaw v. U S, *227 U.S. 326 (1913). Transcript of the Record,* Mar 21, 1912.

83. Elizabeth Lang makes this point in her work on the Mann Act, although, as my work reveals, she overstates the degree to which the BOI focused on commercial cases. See Elizabeth Grace Lang, "White-Slave Traffic Act in the Early Years of Enforcement" (master's thesis, University of Virginia, 2004), 25.

84. United States House, *Congressional Record* 45 (Jan 19, 1910), 818; "New Law Indictment," *Waterloo Reporter,* Sep 4, 1910, 9; *Annual Report of the Attorney General of the United States for the Year 1912* (Washington, DC: Government Printing Office, 1912), 78. In 1912, most female prisoners were held at the Kansas State penitentiary in Lansing, Kansas, but room was quickly running out.

85. Connelly, *The Response to Prostitution,* 118; Donovan, *White Slave Crusades;* Mumford, *Interzones,* 3–18.

86. "The Laws on the 'White Slave' Traffic Should Protect the Women of All Races," *Broad Axe* (Chicago, IL), Nov 9, 1912, 2.

87. "We Are Pleased to Note," *Cleveland Gazette,* Nov 23, 1912, 2.

88. Howard B. Woolston, *Prostitution in the United States,* vol. 1, *Prior to the Entrance of the United States into the World War* (New York: The Century Company, 1921), 87.

4. Creating a Moral Quarantine

1. James L. Bruff, "White Slave Investigations, Mobile, Alabama," May 26, 1911, page 13, Case 1908, Roll 131, RG 65, Federal Bureau of Investigation, Investigative Case Files of the Bureau, 1908–1922, M1085, National Archives, College Park, MD [hereafter cited as BOI Microfilm Records].William Armbrecht as U.S. Attorney, Year: *1910;* Census Place: *Mobile Ward 8, Mobile, Alabama;* Roll: *T624_27;* Page: *7B;* Enumeration District: *0107;* Image: *931;* FHL microfilm: *1374040.* Ancestry.com accessed Oct 8, 2012.

2. Illinois, General Assembly, Senate Vice Committee, "Report for the Senate Vice Committee: Created under the Authority of the Senate of the Forty-Ninth General Assembly" (Chicago, 1916), 353; "Memorandum for the Attorney General, showing Status of Work Performed by Special Agents under the Supervision of the Chief of the Bureau of Investigation," June 25, 1910, Record Group 65, Records of the Bureau of Investigation, Administrative Reports on Cases, 1908–1911, Box 10, Entry 22, Volume 29, 44–47, National Archives, College Park, MD; Stanley

W. Finch, "The United States Government in the Fight Against the White Slave Traffic," *The Light* 16, no. 89 (Jan 1913): 16–22, see 18.

3. "Birthday Record," *The Centralia (WA) Daily Chronicle-Examiner,* Jul 20, 1915, 6; "S. W. Finch, Dies; an FBI Organizer," *Washington Post,* Nov 22, 1951, B2; "Stanley W. Finch a Candidate," *New York Times,* Aug 25, 1892, 8; "50,000 Make 'Easy Living' in White Slave Traffic," *Fort Wayne Journal-Gazette,* Sep 15, 1912, 33; Ancestry.com. *1910 United States Federal Census* [database on-line]. Provo, UT, USA: Ancestry.com Operations Inc, 2006, accessed Oct 9, 2012.

4. "Uncle Sam's New Secret Service," *Anaconda (MT) Standard,* Oct 9, 1910, 32.

5. Illinois, General Assembly, "Report for the Senate Vice Committee," 355.

6. Ibid., 354.

7. "50,000 Make 'Easy Living' in White Slave Traffic."

8. "New Legislation Urged to Block Traffic in Girls," *Cedar Rapids Evening Gazette,* May 8, 1912, 12.

9. "United States in New War on White Slavery," *Fort Wayne Journal-Gazette,* Apr 27, 1913, 43; Stanley W. Finch, "The White Slave Traffic," Senate Doc. 62nd Congress, 3rd Session, Document No. 982 (Washington, DC: Government Printing Office, 1912), 7.

10. "50,000 Make 'Easy Living' in White Slave Traffic"; "All Girls in Peril; Men Fighting Vice," *Cedar Rapids Republican,* Feb 22, 1913, 5.

11. Miroslava Chávez-García, *States of Delinquency: Race and Science in the Making of California's Juvenile Justice System* (Berkeley: University of California Press, 2012), 57.

12. Finch, "The White Slave Traffic," 3.

13. Attorney General George W. Wickersham to Honorable J. R. Knowland (R-CA), Mar 20, 1912, Box 2620, RG 60 General Records of the Department of Justice, Formerly Classified Subject Correspondence, 1919–45. Class 31 Mann Act, Box 2620, National Archives, College Park, MD [hereafter cited as DOJ Mann Act Records]; U.S. Congress, House, Committee on Appropriations, *Hearings before Subcommittee of House Committee on Appropriations in charge of Sundry Civil Appropriations Bill for 1913: Part II* (Washington, DC: Government Printing Office, 1912), 1490; James Bronson Reynolds, "The Association's Department of Legislation and Law Enforcement," *Vigilance* 25, no. 5 (May 1912): 6–7; "Funds Inadequate to Fight White Slavery," *The Light* 15, no. 84 (Mar 1912): 13–15; "The Work of the United States Department of Justice," *Vigilance* 25, no. 4 (Apr 1912): 13–17; and *Hearings before Subcommittee of House Committee on Appropriations in charge of Sundry Civil Appropriations Bill for 1914* (Washington, DC: Government Printing Office, 1913), 868.

14. *Sundry Civil Appropriation Bill for 1914,* 872, 878, 880; "What the United States Government is Doing," *Vigilance* 24, no. 11 (Dec 1911): 15–16; and "General

White Slave Traffic Conditions" (Washington, DC), Case 3065, Roll 139, BOI Microfilm Records.

15. Howard B. Woolston, *Prostitution in the United States,* vol. 1, *Prior to the Entrance of the United States into the World War* (New York: The Century Company, 1921), 38; Stanley W. Finch to Clifford G. Roe, May 21, 1912, Box 2620, DOJ Mann Act Records; *Sundry Civil Appropriation Bill for 1914,* 880; "50,000 Make 'Easy Living' in White Slave Traffic."

16. Stanley W. Finch to Clifford G. Roe, May 21, 1912, Box 2620, DOJ Mann Act Records.

17. Ibid.

18. *Sundry Civil Appropriation Bill for 1914,* 876.

19. William Elsey Connelly and Ellis Morton Coulter, *History of Kentucky* (Chicago: American Historical Society, 1922), 4:144; William Luxon Wallace, 'IIL, RU 830, Alumni Records Office, Yale University, Records of the Alumni from the Classes of 1701–1978, box 969, Manuscripts and Archives, Yale University Library, New Haven, CT; Michael Grossberg, "Institutionalizing Masculinity: The Law as a Masculine Profession," in *Meanings for Manhood: Constructions of Masculinity in Victorian America,* ed. Mark C. Carnes and Clyde Griffen (Chicago: University of Chicago Press, 1990): 133–151. The emphasis on restraint, moderation, and order is taken from George L. Mosse, "Nationalism and Respectability: Normal and Abnormal Sexuality in the Nineteenth Century," *Journal of Contemporary History* 17, no. 2, Sexuality in History (Apr 1982): 221–246, 232.

20. John Tosh, "Hegemonic Masculinity and the History of Gender," in *Masculinities in Politics and War: Gendering Modern History,* ed. Stefan Dudink, Karen Hagemann, and John Tosh, 41–58 (Manchester: Manchester University Press, 2004), 42; Kevin P. Murphy, "Citizens Made and Remade: Sexual Scandal, Manhood, and Self-Government Reform in the Progressive-Era United States," in *Representing Masculinity: Male Citizenship in Modern Western Culture,* ed. Stefan Dudink, Karen Hagemann, and Anna Clark, 193–212 (New York: Palgrave Macmillan, 2007), 194–195. For more on ideals of masculinity and citizenship during the Progressive Era, see Kevin P. Murphy, *Political Manhood: Red Bloods, Mollycoddles, & the Politics of Progressive Era Reform* (New York: Columbia University Press, 2008); Thomas Winter, *Making Men, Making Class: The YMCA and Workingmen, 1877–1920* (Chicago: University of Chicago Press, 2002); and Michael S. Kimmel, *Manhood in America: A Cultural History* (New York: The Free Press, 1996), 101–112.

21. L. F. Englesby, "General Investigation White Slave Traffic," Oct 14, 1913, Case 4349, Roll 149, BOI Microfilm Records.

22. L. F. Englesby, "General Investigation White Slave Traffic," Oct 20, 1913, Case 4349, Roll 149, BOI Microfilm Records; L. F. Englesby, "General Investigation White Slave Traffic," Oct 21, 1913, Case 4349, Roll 149, BOI Microfilm Records.

23. Athan G. Theoharis, "A Brief History of the FBI's Role and Powers," in *The FBI: A Comprehensive Reference Guide,* ed. Athan G. Theoharis (Phoenix: The Oryx Press, 1999), 4–5.

24. Kimberley Johnson, "The 'First New Federalism' and the Development of the Administrative State, 1883–1929," in *The Oxford Handbook of American Bureaucracy,* ed. Robert F. Durant, 52–75 (New York: Oxford University Press, 2011), 53–54; *Sundry Civil Appropriation Bill for 1914,* 862 and 880.

25. "White Slavery Resorts Forced to Make Report," *Lima Daily News,* Jan 1, 1914, 3; *Sundry Civil Appropriation Bill for 1914,* 880–881.

26. Woolston, *Prostitution in the United States,* 38, 50, 93–94.

27. Jill Harsin, *Policing Prostitution in Nineteenth-Century Paris* (Princeton: Princeton University Press, 1985), 361–362; Alfred W. McCoy, "Covert Netherworld: The Impact of American Empire on U.S. State Formation and Global Surveillance," Wilbur Lucius Cross Lecture, Oct. 11, 2012, Yale University.

28. Both Grgurevich and Garbarino had been lead white slave investigators during the Immigration Bureau's dragnet. See Exhibit C in "Message from the President of the United States transmitting, in further response to Senate Resolution No. 86, of December 7, 1909, Information Concerning the Repression of the Trade in White Women," Senate, 61st Cong., 2nd Sess., Doc. No. 214, Part 2 (Washington, DC: Government Printing Office, 1910), 25.

29. Betjamin, "General Investigations, White Slave Conditions," Dec 12, 1911, Case 3065, Roll 139, BOI Microfilm Records.

30. L. E. Ross, "U.S. vs. Feliciano Ramos—White Slave Case," Aug 31, 1911, Roll 131, BOI Microfilm Records.

31. Frank Garbarino, "White Slave Investigations, San Francisco, CA," Oct 2, 1910, Case 1184, Roll 123, BOI Microfilm Records.

32. Torrie Hester, "Deportation: The Origins of an International and National Power" (PhD diss., University of Oregon, 2008), 109. The number of prostitutes deported each year after 1910 peaked in 1913 with 294. See Bureau of Immigration, *Annual Report of the Commissioner General of Immigration to the Secretary of Labor for the fiscal year ended June 30, 1913* (Washington, DC: Government Printing Office, 1914), 110–113; Mae Ngai, *Impossible Subjects: Illegal Aliens and the Making of Modern America* (Princeton: Princeton University Press, 2004), 57; Erika Lee, *At America's Gates: Chinese Immigration During the Exclusion Era, 1882–1943* (Chapel Hill: University of North Carolina Press, 2003).

33. John J. Grgurevich, "General Investigation White Slave Traffic Conditions," Jul 19, 1913, Case 4596, Roll 148, BOI Microfilm Records.

34. T. S. Marshall, "In re Bernard Jackson, Alleged Violation of the White Slave Traffic Act," Apr 22, 1912, Case 3065, Roll 139, BOI Microfilm Records.

35. Marlene D. Beckman, "The White Slave Traffic Act: Historical Impact of a Federal Crime Policy on Women," in *Criminal Justice Politics and Women: The*

Aftermath of Legally Mandated Change, ed. Claudine Scheber and Clarice Feinman, 85–101 (New York: Haworth Press, 1985), 86.

36. L. E. Ross, "U.S. vs. Leona Reed—White Slave Case," Dec 17, 1911, 3095-3, Case 3095, Roll 140, BOI Microfilm Records.

37. L. E. Ross, "U.S. vs. White Slave Traffic," Jan 5, 1912, Case 1916, Roll 131, BOI Microfilm Records; women made up 62 of the 529 defendants involved in prosecutions of the Mann Act. Of the 39 of these 62 cases that had gone to trial, 38 were found guilty. "List of Prosecutions Instituted under the White Slave Traffic Act of June 25, 1910, Showing Pending Cases and Cases Disposed of Prior to October 31, 1912," *Annual Report of the Attorney General for the year of 1912,* 442–451. In the 1910s, men had a much better chance of facing a jury of one's peers than women. Although a few states allowed women to sit in a jury box in 1910s, it was not until 1975 that the Supreme Court required courtrooms throughout the country to be open to women.

38. George W. Wickersham, "Department Circular No. 297 to U.S. Attorneys," May 13, 1912, RG 60, General Records of the Department of Justice, Administrative Orders, Circulars and Memoranda, 1856–1968, Box 2, National Archives, College Park, MD.

39. J. R. Darling, "Re Closing of Houses in Milwaukee. White Slave Traffic," Jun 14, 1912, Case 1454, Roll 126, BOI Microfilm Records; Charles DeWoody to Stanley Finch, June 22, 1912, Case 1454, Roll 126, BOI Microfilm Records.

40. "Editorial: The Justice of a Nation," *Vigilance* 26, no. 1 (Jan 1913): 1–2, italics in original.

41. Ruth C. Engs, *The Progressive Era's Health Reform Movement* (Westport, CT: Praeger, 2003), 12; James F. Gardner, Jr., "Microbes and Morality: The Social Hygiene Crusade in New York City, 1892–1917" (PhD diss., Indiana University, 1974), 13; and David J. Pivar, *Purity and Hygiene: Women, Prostitution, and the "American Plan"* (Westport, CT: Greenwood Press, 2002), 123–132.

42. Kristin Luker, "Sex, Social Hygiene, and the State: The Double-Edged Sword of Social Reform," *Theory and Society* 27, no. 5 (Oct 1998): 601–634.

43. Peter C. Hennigan, "Property War: Prostitution, Red-Light Districts, and the Transformation of Public Nuisance Law in the Progressive Era," *Yale Journal of Law and the Humanities* 16, no. 123 (2004): 123–198.

44. *Hearings before Subcommittee of House Committee on Appropriations in Charge of Sundry Civil Appropriation Bill for 1915* (Washington, DC: Government Printing Office, 1914), 1156.

45. John Allen Noakes, "Enforcing Domestic Tranquility: State Building and the Origin of the (Federal) Bureau of Investigation, 1908–1920" (PhD diss., University of Pennsylvania, 1993), 143.

46. Illinois, General Assembly, "Report for the Senate Vice Committee," 354.

47. James S. Pula, "Bruce Bielaski and the Origin of the FBI," *Polish American Studies* 68, no. 1 (Spring 2011): 43–57, 45–46; "Bielaski A Fighter, But Quiet About It," *New York Times,* Jun 30, 1922, 3; "Bruce Bielaski, Justice Aide, Dies," *New York Times,* Feb 20, 1964, 29.

48. "Kaiser's Spies Beaten at Their Own Game," *Akron Register-Tribune,* Jan 31, 1918, 7.

49. "World's Purity Congress at Kansas City," *Survey* 33, no. 9 (Nov 28, 1914): 221.

50. "'Too Much Eugenics'," *Washington Post,* Nov 6, 1914, 4.

51. Division Superintendent DeWoody, Jan 31, 1911, "Case 1596, 1," Volume 45, Box 15, Bureau Administrative Reports on Cases, Record Group 65, Records of the Bureau of Investigation, National Archives, College Park, MD; Attorney General George W. Wickersham to Honorable J. R. Knowland (R-CA), Mar 20, 1912, "Statement Showing Typical Individual Instances of Violations of White Slave Law," page 11, Box 2620, DOJ Mann Act Records.

52. "Judge Laments Fact that Law is So Easy," *Logansport (OH) Pharos,* Mar 20, 1911, 3.

53. *Annual Report of the Attorney General of the United States for the year 1911* (Washington, DC: Government Printing Office, 1911), 25.

54. C. B. Weakley, Aug 25, 1916, Case 9512, Roll 191, BOI Microfilm Records.

55. Leon Bone, Aug 5, 1916, Case 9819, roll 192, BOI Microfilm Records.

56. Simmons and Ross, "Investigation of Alleged Violation of White Slave Traffic Act by L. H. Tempest," Sep 2, 1911, Case 2521, Roll 134, BOI Microfilm Records.

57. L. E. Ross, Sep 4, 1911, Case 2521, Roll 134, BOI Microfilm Records.

58. Charles De Woody to Stanley W. Finch, Jan 24, 1912, Case 2758, Roll 136, BOI Microfilm Records.

59. Henry J. Dannenbaum to George Wickersham, Jul 29, 1911, Box 2620, DOJ Mann Act Records.

60. William Harr to U.S. Attorney in Jackson, MS, Feb 10, 1913, Box 2620, DOJ Mann Act Records.

61. Case 2671, Roll 136, BOI Microfilm Records; Peggy Pascoe, *What Comes Naturally: Miscegenation Law and the Making of Race in America* (New York: Oxford University Press, 2009).

62. Leon Bone, "In re. Ku Wu—White Slave Case," Apr 14, 1912, 3819-1, and Apr 22, 1912, 3819-5, Case 3819, Roll 144, BOI Microfilm Records.

63. Lamarioux, "In re. Investigation of White Slave case of Violet Hall," Oct 28, 1911, 2876-1, page 2, Case 2876, Roll 136, BOI Microfilm Records.

64. J. G. Tucker, "Investigation in re. Daisy Fenton, White Slave Matter," Dec 8, 1911, Case 3055, Roll 139, BOI Microfilm Records.

65. Gail Bederman, *Manliness and Civilization: A Cultural History of Gender and Race in the United States, 1880–1917* (Chicago: University of Chicago Press,

1995), 2. For more on Johnson, see Randy Roberts, *Papa Jack and the Era of White Hopes* (New York: The Free Press, 1983); Geoffrey C. Ward, *Unforgivable Blackness: The Rise and Fall of Jack Johnson* (New York: Vintage Books, 2006); Al-Tony Gilmore, *Bad Nigger! The National Impact of Jack Johnson* (Port Washington, NY: Kennikat Press, 1975); Graeme Kent, *The Great White Hopes: The Quest to Defeat Jack Johnson* (Stroud, UK: Sutton, 2005); and Theresa Runstedtler, *Jack Johnson, Rebel Sojourner: Boxing in the Shadow of the Global Color Line* (Berkeley: University of California Press, 2012).

66. Gilmore, *Bad Nigger!*, 95–105; Kevin J. Mumford, *Interzones: Black/White Sex Districts in Chicago and New York in the Early Twentieth Century* (New York: Columbia University Press, 1997), 4.

67. African nationalist Marcus Garvey would face the same treatment by the Bureau when in 1920 he traveled abroad with his secretary and later wife, Amy Jacques. See Ula Yvette Taylor, *The Veiled Garvey: The Life and Times of Amy Jacques Garvey* (Chapel Hill: University of North Carolina Press, 2002), 34–36; for more on the Cable Act see Martha Gardner, *The Qualities of a Citizen: Women, Immigration, and Citizenship, 1870–1865* (Princeton: Princeton University Press, 2009), 146; William Harr to U.S. Attorney in Jackson, MS, Feb 10, 1913, Box 2620, DOJ Mann Act Records.

68. Quoted in Gilmore, *Bad Nigger!*, 119.

69. Joanne Meyerowitz, "Transnational Sex and U.S. History," *American Historical Review* 114, no. 5 (Dec 2009): 1273–1286, quotation on 1280.

70. The U.S. military has a strong tradition of regulating prostitution from the Civil War forward. See Marilyn E. Hegarty, *Victory Girls, Khaki-Wackies, and Patriotutes: The Regulation of Female Sexuality during World War II* (New York: New York University Press, 2008); Cynthia Enloe, *Bananas, Beaches, and Bases: Making Feminist Sense of International Politics* (London: Pandora, 1989), 85–87; Ji-Yeon Yuh, *Beyond the Shadow of Camptown: Korean Military Brides in America* (New York: New York University Press, 2002), 10–11; and Laura Briggs, "Familiar Territory: Prostitution, Empires, and the Question of U.S. Imperialism in Puerto Rico, 1849–1916," in *Families of a New World: Gender Politics and State Development in a Global Context,* ed. Lynne Haney and Lisa Pollard, 40–63 (New York: Routledge, 2003).

71. Guy D. Goff, "New Interpretation of the White Slave Traffic Act," *The Light* 17, no. 99 (Sep–Oct 1914): 29–31, quote on 30.

72. *Sundry Civil Appropriation Bill for 1914,* 888.

73. Tony G. Poveda, "Controversies and Issues," in *The FBI: A Comprehensive Reference Guide,* ed. Athan G. Theoharis, 101–142 (Phoenix: Oryx Press, 1999), 104; Noakes, "Enforcing Domestic Tranquility," 114, 116, 143; Richard Gid Powers, *Broken: The Troubled Past and Uncertain Future of the FBI* (New York: Free Press, 2004), 75.

5. Defining Immoral Purposes

1. William Snow, "History of Prostitution in the United States," vol. 2, unpublished manuscript, 2, SW 116:1 and 166:2, Staff Mss, Bascom Johnson, American Social Health Association, RG SW045, Social Welfare History Archives, University of Minnesota, Minneapolis, MN.

2. John D'Emilio and Estelle B. Freedman, *Intimate Matters: A History of Sexuality in America* (New York: Harper and Row, Publishers, 1988), 234.

3. Robert L. Anderson, *The Diggs-Caminetti Case, 1913–1917: For Any Other Immoral Purpose,* vol. I (Lewiston, NY: Edwin Mellen Press, 1990), 14 and 29.

4. Ibid., 44–50.

5. Ibid., 41.

6. Ibid., 119.

7. Of the 334 stories about white slavery and the Mann Act published in 1913 by the *Atlanta Constitution, Ogden Examiner, Bakersfield Californian,* and *Picqua (OH) Leader-Democrat,* 119 (35 percent) of them covered the Diggs-Caminetti trial, and most of them appeared on the front page of newspapers.

8. United States House, *Congressional Record* 50 (Aug 1, 1913), 3004–3005.

9. Joseph Giovinco, "The Diggs-Caminetti Case," *Manuscripts* 48, no. 1 (Summer 1996): 207–211.

10. United States House, *Congressional Record* 50 (Aug 1, 1913), 3006.

11. David J. Langum, *Crossing over the Line: Legislating Morality and the Mann Act* (Chicago: University of Chicago Press, 1994), 110. Langum offers a detailed and engaging account of the Caminetti case.

12. Anderson, *The Diggs-Caminetti Case,* 15.

13. "The Mann Act," *Ogden (UT) Examiner,* Feb 26, 1914, 4.

14. "Sharks and Minnows," *Atlanta Constitution,* Sep 6, 1913, 4.

15. "A New Ruling in White Slave Case," *Burlington (IA) Hawk-Eye,* Sep 23, 1913, 1.

16. Ibid.

17. "The Chaotic Mann Law," *Atlanta Constitution,* Sep 25, 1913, 4.

18. *Hearings before Subcommittee of House Committee on Appropriations in charge of Sundry Civil Appropriation Bill for 1915* (Washington, DC: Government Printing Office, 1914), 1156.

19. Bureau Chief A. Bruce Bielaski affirmed the policy of pursuing vice cases, abduction cases, and rejecting cases of interstate immorality (cases involving unmarried consenting adults travelling from one state to another). *Sundry Civil Appropriation Bill for 1915,* 1157–1158.

20. Blackburn Esterline, "Memorandum, Special Examiner to the Attorney General to the Attorney General," Oct 21, 1913, 145825–258 ½, page 34, Box 2620, RG 60, General Records of the Department of Justice, Formerly Classified Subject

Correspondence, 1919–45. Class 31 Mann Act, Box 2620, National Archives, College Park, MD [hereafter cited as DOJ Mann Act Records].

21. Wilbur F. Crafts to James C. McReynolds, Jan 3, 1914, Box 2620, DOJ Mann Act Records.

22. James C. McReynolds to Wilbur F. Crafts, Jan 6, 1914, Box 2620, DOJ Mann Act Records. The *Atlanta Constitution*, in an editorial, wrote: "Unless the department of justice has been more active than it has led the public to believe, the enforcement of the act has thus far been confined to a few sensational cases, such as the one now on trial, not to mention the unspeakable 'Jack' Johnson case." As the previous chapter shows, the Bureau had been quite active in enforcing the Mann Act, but it did so under a cloak of secrecy. "Sharks and Minnows," *Atlanta Constitution*, Sep 6, 1913, 4.

23. *Caminetti v. United States*, 242 U.S. 485–486 (1917). Curiously, Justice Holmes was silent in his fears that the Mann Act provided a tool for blackmailers. The *Caminetti* decision was written by William R. Day, with Justices Holmes, Van Devanter, Pitney, and Brandeis concurring. The dissent was penned by Justice Joseph McKenna, with the concurrence of Chief Justice White and Justice Clarke.

24. *Caminetti v. United States*, 242 U.S. 502 (1917). "Gives Wider Scope to White Slave Law," *New York Times*, Jan 16, 1917, 1.

25. "Found Him Guilty; Johnson to Prison," *Burlington (IA) Hawk-Eye*, Apr 15, 1913, 9.

26. Guy D. Goff, "New Interpretation of the White Slave Traffic Act," *The Light* 17, no. 99 (Sep–Oct 1914): 29–31, quote on 30.

27. *U.S. v. Holte*, 236 U.S. 140 (1915), 1; "Woman Accused under Mann Act," *Syracuse Herald*, Jul 18, 1914, 23.

28. Goff, "New Interpretation of the White Slave Traffic Act," 29.

29. *U.S. v. Holte*, 236 U.S. 140 (1915), 6.

30. "Uncle Sam, Blackmailer," *New York Times*, Jul 27, 1914, 6.

31. "Extends White Slave Act," *New York Times*, Feb 2, 1915; "Conspiracy to Violate the White Slave Act," *The Virginia Law Register* 1, no 5 (Sep 1915): 392. For an astute analysis of this case, see Pamela Haag, *Consent: Sexual Rights and the Transformation of American Liberalism* (Ithaca, NY: Cornell University Press, 1999), 67–68.

32. Langum, *Crossing over the Line*, 83.

33. George C. Calmes, "In re: Mrs. Ritter, et al., Alleged Attempt to Blackmail in connection with the White Slave Traffic Act & Impersonating U.S. Officer," Aug 20, 1915, page 2, Case 8752, Roll 186, RG 65, Federal Bureau of Investigation, Investigative Case Files of the Bureau, 1908–1922, M1085, National Archives, College Park, MD [hereafter cited as BOI Microfilm Records].

34. Calmes, "In re: Mrs. Ritter," Aug 20, 1915, Case 8752, Roll 186, BOI Microfilm Records.

35. Ibid.

36. Albert G. Ingram to Lewis J. Baley, Sep 1, 1915, Case 8752, Roll 186, BOI Microfilm Records.

37. Ibid.

38. J. William Thurmond to Lewis J. Baley, Sep 17, 1915, Case 8752, Roll 186, BOI Microfilm Records.

39. Lewis Baley to A. Bruce Bielaski, Sep 3, 1915, Case 8752, Roll 186, BOI Microfilm Records.

40. Hinton G. Clabaugh to A. Bruce Bielaski, Dec 13, 1916, pages 5–6, Case 9689, Roll 191, BOI Microfilm Records.

41. Ibid., 5.

42. "Aim to end Blackmail," *Washington Post,* Sep 20, 1916, 2.

43. Knox wrote about his experience prosecuting blackmail cases in his autobiography, John C. Knox, *A Judge Comes of Age* (New York: Charles Scribner's Sons, 1940), 63–75.

44. "Held in $50,000 Bail in Slave Extortion," *New York Times,* Jan 15, 1916, 6.

45. "Blackmailer to Prison," (Baltimore) *Sun,* Sep 27, 1916, 2; "Blackmail Case Ready for Trial," *New York Tribune,* Sep 23, 1916, 3.

46. "Government Aid to Blackmailers," *New York Times,* Jan 14, 1916, quoted in Angus McLaren, *Sexual Blackmail: A Modern History* (Cambridge: Harvard University Press, 2002), 88.

47. "The Blackmail Act," *New York Times,* Sep 20, 1916, 8.

48. "Government Aid to Blackmailers," *New York Times,* Jan 14, 1916, 8.

49. William J. Burns, "Blackmailing Now the Big American Crime," *New York Times,* Jul 23, 1916, SM9.

50. See McLaren, *Sexual Blackmail,* 86–92; Langum, *Crossing over the Line,* 77–97.

51. "Gang Uses Women in Blackmail Plots," *New York Times,* Apr 28, 1916, 22; William J. Burns, "Blackmailing Now the Big American Crime," *New York Times,* Jul 23, 1916, SM9.

52. Langum, *Crossing over the Line,* 87.

53. Claude R. Porter to Attorney General Thomas Gregory, Jan 31, 1917, Box 2621, DOJ Mann Act Records.

54. See David J. Pivar, *Purity and Hygiene: Women, Prostitution, and the "American Plan"* (Westport, CT: Greenwood Press, 2002), 130; Kristin Luker, "Sex, Social Hygiene, and the State: The Double-Edged Sword of Social Reform," *Theory and Society* 27, no. 5 (Oct 1998): 601–634, 614. Emphasis mine.

55. M.J. Exner, "Prostitution in its Relations to the Army on the Mexican Border," *Social Hygiene* 3, no. 2 (Apr 1917): 205–220, 206 and 208.

56. Allan Brandt, *No Magic Bullet: A Social History of Venereal Disease in the United States since 1880* (New York: Oxford University Press, 1985), 53. For a bio-

power analysis of the history of public health along the U.S.-Mexican border, see Alexandra Minna Stern, "Buildings, Boundaries, and Blood: Medicalization and Nation-Building on the U.S.-Mexico Border, 1910–1930," *The Hispanic American Historical Review* 79, no. 1 (Feb 1999): 41–81; Exner, "Prostitution in its Relations to the Army on the Mexican Border," 206 and 208. Fosdick had strong associations to John D. Rockefeller, Jr.'s Bureau of Social Hygiene (BSH). In 1914 he published *European Police Systems,* a comprehensive study of policing in Europe that the BSH published as the companion piece to Abraham Flexner's *Prostitution in Europe.* Mark Thomas Connelly, *The Response to Prostitution in the Progressive Era* (Chapel Hill: University of North Carolina, 1980), 137–138; Nancy K. Bristow, *Making Men Moral: Social Engineering During the Great War* (New York: New York University Press, 1996), 5.

57. Raymond B. Fosdick, "Report on the Mexican Conditions, Confidential Report, August 10, 1916," quoted in Penn Borden, *Civilian Indoctrination of the Military: World War I and Future Implications for the Military-Industrial Complex* (New York: Greenwood Press, 1989), 102.

58. Brandt, *No Magic Bullet,* 54.

59. Quoted in Borden, *Civilian Indoctrination of the Military,* 104.

60. Quoted in Connelly, *The Response to Prostitution,* 138.

61. Snow, "History of Prostitution," 3; Connelly, *The Response to Prostitution,* 241.

62. Snow, "History of Prostitution," 38, 124; Brandt, *No Magic Bullet,* 77. It was rumored that the Austrian Army had lost one and one-half million men, or 67 divisions, due to venereal disease infections. In the summer of 1917, the British forces had hospitalized the equivalent of two of their infantry divisions (23,000 men) due to infections. The French Army had reported over one million cases of syphilis and gonorrhea between 1914 and the summer of 1917. Bristow, *Making Men Moral,* 11; Edward M. Coffman, *The War to End All Wars: The America Military Experience in World War I* (New York: Oxford University Press, 1968), 80.

63. Coffman, *The War to End All Wars,* 80.

64. The phrase "invisible armor" comes from a speech Secretary Newton gave in October 1917 as the first American troops departed for Europe. Quoted in Connelly, *The Response to Prostitution,* 146.

65. Snow, "History of Prostitution," 31.

66. Luker, "Sex, Social Hygiene, and the State," 611.

67. Bristow, *Making Men Moral,* 34.

68. Luther H. Gulick, *Morals and Morale* (New York: Associated Press, 1919), 127.

69. Snow, "History of Prostitution," 222.

70. John H. Biddle, Bulletin No 1. War Department, Jan 17, 1918, FF34 Jackson Family, William S., Department of Justice, Bureau of Investigation, 1917–1918,

Jackson Family Papers, WH1017, Box 14, Western History Collection, The Denver Public Library, Denver, CO.

71. Quoted in Thomas C. Mackey, *Red Lights Out: A Legal History of Prostitution, Disorderly Houses, and Vice Districts, 1870–1917* (New York: Garland Publishing, 1987), 373.

72. Ibid., 378.

73. Quoted in Brandt, *No Magic Bullet,* 75; Bristow, *Making Men Moral,* 104–105.

74. Coffman, *The War to End All Wars,* 80.

75. Maude E. Miner, "Girls and Khaki: Some Practical Measures for the Protection of Young Women in Time of War," *Survey* (Dec 1, 1917), 236–240, 236.

76. Quoted in Ronald Schaffer, *America in the Great War: A Managed Society* (New York: Oxford University Press, 1991), 103.

77. Quoted in Bristow, *Making Men Moral,* 113.

78. Quoted in Brandt, *No Magic Bullet,* 76.

79. Quoted in ibid., 85.

80. Snow, "History of Prostitution," 52.

81. Charles B. Braun to Robert L. Barnes, Jan 11, 1915, Box 1, Folder: "USA" 1915–16 A–G, RG 21, Western District of Texas, "Records of Special Agent Charles B. Braun," National Archives, Southwest Region, Fort Worth, TX [hereafter referred to as "Braun Files"].

82. Charles B. Braun to Robert L. Barnes, June 3, 1915, Box 1, Folder: "USA" 1915–16 A–G, Braun Files.

83. Charles B. Braun to Robert L. Barnes, June 26, 1915, Box 1, Folder: "USA" 1915–16 A–G, Braun Files.

84. A. Bruce Bielaski to All Special Agents and Local White Slave Officers, Jan 7, 1916, Box 1, Folder: "USA" 1915–16 A–G, Braun Files; SAC Breniman to Charles Braun, telegram, Feb 3, 1917, Box 2, Folder: "US" 1916–17 A–B, Braun Files.

85. Robert L Barnes to Charles B Braun, Aug 4, 1917, Box 2, Folder: "USA" June–Dec 1917 A–F, Braun Files.

86. Charles B. Braun to A. Bruce Bielaski, Mar 20, 1918, Box 2, Folder: "Department of Justice Letters" A–M, Braun Files.

87. Snow, "History of Prostitution," 108–109.

88. Emerson Hough, *The Web: A Revelation of Patriotism, The Story of the American Protective League, How 250,000 American Business Men Became Detectives to Help Win the War* (Chicago: The Reilly & Lee Co., 1919), 12.

89. Charles B. Braun to Tom S. Henderson, Jr., Jun 13, 1917, Box 2, Folder: "USA," Jun–Dec 1917 A–F, Braun Files; A. M. Briggs to Charles B. Braun, Jun 6, 1917, Box 2, Folder: "USA," Jun–Dec 1917 A–F, Braun Files. For more on the APL, see Joan M. Jensen, *The Price of Vigilance* (New York: Rand McNally & C0., 1968); William H. Thomas, Jr., *Unsafe for Democracy: World War I and the US. Depart-*

ment of Justice's Covert Campaign to Suppress Dissent (Madison: University of Wisconsin Press, 2008), 37; and Christopher Capozzola, Uncle Sam Wants You: World War I and the Making of the Modern American Citizen (New York: Oxford University Press, 2008), 42–45, 132–135.

90. Garna L. Christian, "The Ordeal and the Prize: The 24th Infantry and Camp MacArthur," Military Affairs 50, no. 2 (Apr 1986): 65–70, 66; Charles Braun, "In re.: Maggie Foster (col)," Dec 24, 1917, Box 2, Folder: "Department of Justice Letters" A–M, Braun Files; Linda Kerber, No Constitutional Right to Be Ladies: Women and the Obligations of Citizenship (New York: Hill and Wang, 1999), 47–80.

91. Charles B. Braun, "In re. Women, Camp MacArthur," Texas, Feb 4, 1918, Box 3, Folder: "US 1918," Braun Files; Guy D. Goff referred to the Mann Act as a moral quarantine in "New Interpretation of the White Slave Traffic Act," The Light 17, no. 99 (Sep–Oct 1914): 29–31, quote on 30.

92. Statement of Mrs. Mattie Edwards, "In re. Hotel Raleigh," Dec. 14, 1917, Box 3, Folder: "U.S." 1918, Braun Files.

93. For a description of the "quarantine and cure" policy, see T. W. Gregory, "Circular No. 812," Apr 3, 1918, FF34 Department of Justice, Jackson Family Papers, WH 1017, Box 14, Western History Collection, Denver Public Library, Denver, Co. Brandt, No Magic Bullet, 85; and Christopher Cappozzola, "The Only Badge Needed Is Your Patriotic Fervor: Vigilance, Coercion, and the Law in World War I America," Journal of American History 88, no. 4 (Mar 2002): 1354–1382, citation on 1373. For more on the widespread use of vagrancy laws to police women's sexuality during World War I, see Courtney Q. Shah, "'Against Their Own Weakness': Policing Sexuality and Women in San Antonio, Texas, during World War I," Journal of the History of Sexuality 19, no. 3 (Sep 2010): 458–482; David J. Pivar, "Cleansing the Nation: The War on Prostitution, 1917–21," Prologue: The Journal of the National Archives 12, no. 1 (Spring 1980): 29–40, 32.

94. Quoted in Brandt, No Magic Bullet, 85.

95. Alan Johnson, Jr., "Report on Augusta, Georgia," Nov 17, 1917 quoted in Bristow, Making Men Moral, 131.

96. Raymond B. Fosdick, Chronicle of a Generation: An Autobiography (New York: Harper, 1958), 147–148.

97. Bushnell despised the ASHA and what she saw as its neo-regulationist goals. She called it a "bastard 'social hygiene' mongrel" and believed that ASHA president William Snow was "determined to fasten his nefarious system [of regulation] upon the entire civilized world. He may have the power to do it, for he has his hand (so to speak) in the pocket of the son of the richest man, almost, in the world, the pocket of John D. Rockefeller, Jr." See K. Bushnell to Alison Neilans, Aug 2, 1918, and K. Bushnell to Alison Neilans, Apr 24, 1919, 3AMS/D/51/01, Letters and Reports of Mrs. Katharine Bushnell, folder 2 of 2, Records of the Association

for Moral and Social Hygiene, Box 122, Women's Library, London Metropolitan University, London, UK [hereafter referred to as the AMSH Records].

98. Quoted in Brandt, *No Magic Bullet,* 86.

99. Katherine Bushnell to Alison Neilans, Dec 25, 1917, 3AMS/D/51/01, Letters and Reports of Mrs. Katharine Bushnell, folder 1 of 2, AMSH Records.

100. Alison Neilans, [n.d., probably 1918 or 1919], 3AMS/D/51/01, Letters and Reports of Mrs. Katharine Bushnell, folder 2 of 2, AMSH Records.

101. "Circular of Warning to Women Arrested by Morals Squad," 3AMS/D/51/01, Letters and Reports of Mrs. Katharine Bushnell, folder 2 of 2, AMSH Records.

102. Katherine Bushnell to Alison Neilans, Aug 16, 1917, 3AMS/D/51/01, Letters and Reports of Mrs. Katharine Bushnell, folder 2 of 2, AMSH Records; Alison Neilans to K. Bushnell, Dec 19, 1919, 3AMS/D/51/01, Letters and Reports of Mrs. Katharine Bushnell, folder 2 of 2, AMSH Records; Alison Neilans to Millicent Fawcett, Mar 5, 1920, 7MGF/A/1/208, Millicent Fawcett Papers, Box 2, Women's Library, London Metropolitan University, London, UK.

6. Policing Seduction and Adultery

1. Criminal cases of forced sex could be rendered moot if the assailant married the victim. Additionally, no conception of marital rape existed prior to the mid-twentieth century. Ariela R. Dubler, "Immoral Purposes: Marriage and the Genus of Illicit Sex," *Yale Law Journal* 115 (2006): 756–812, see 777.

2. Cases of incest and interracial sex legally stood far outside the perimeter of legal marriage and thus were marked as indelibly illicit. These cases will be addressed in the next chapter.

3. J. Edgar Hoover, quoted in "White Slave Traffic Gains: Hoover Asks Public Aid in Drive to Wipe Out Violations," *Boston Evening Recorder,* Aug 17, 1936; and the fact that 50 percent of the cases were initiated by private individuals came from Special Agent in Charge to J. Edgar Hoover, Feb 28, 1929, 31-03-11, File 31-03, Box 1, Record Group 65, Records of the Federal Bureau of Investigation— Bureau Headquarters Case Files, Classification 31, National Archives, College Park, MD [hereafter referred to as FBI White Slave Files]; in 1930, Hoover would claim that 70 percent of the Mann Act violations were initiated by citizens' complaints, "Sources of Complaints Received by the Bureau of Investigation, Department of Justice, Concerning Federal Law Violations," File "Bureau of Investigation," *Records of the Wickersham Commission on Law Enforcement, Part 2: Research Reports and General Subject Files,* Consulting Ed. Samuel Walker (Bethesda, MD: University Publications, 1999), reel 3, page 2 [hereafter referred to as the Wickersham Files].

4. David J. Langum, *Crossing over the Line: Legislating Morality and the Mann Act* (Chicago: University of Chicago Press, 1994), 150, 168.

5. Dubler, "Immoral Purposes," 763.

6. The literature on the history of marriage as an institution and legal status is vast. For discussions of the gendered obligations and benefits of marriage, see Melissa Murray, "Marriage as Punishment," *Columbia Law Review* 100, no. 2 (2011): 101–168; Christina Simmons, *Making Marriage Modern: Women's Sexuality from the Progressive Era to World War II* (New York: Oxford University Press, 2009), 71; Nancy Cott, *Public Vows: A History of Marriage and the Nation* (Cambridge: Harvard University Press, 2000), 168–169; Hendrik Hartog, *Man and Wife in America: A History* (Cambridge: Harvard University Press, 2000); and, Reva Siegel, "The Modernization of Marital Status Law: Adjudicating Wives' Rights to Earnings, 1860–1930," *Georgetown Law Journal* 82 (Sep 1994), 2127–2212.

7. Margot Canaday, *The Straight State: Sexuality and Citizenship in Twentieth-Century America* (Princeton: Princeton University Press, 2009).

8. George Chauncey, *Gay New York: Gender, Urban Culture, and the Making of the Gay Male World, 1890–1940* (New York: Basic Books, 1994).

9. Throughout his life J. Edgar Hoover would deny having played a meaningful role in the Palmer Raids, claiming to have been a lowly clerk at the time. Recent research has revealed that Hoover was the bureaucratic mastermind behind the raids—he made Attorney General A. Mitchell Palmer and Immigration Commissioner General Anthony Caminetti's antiradical, anti-immigrant dreams a reality. In the Palmer Raids, three characteristics that would define much of Hoover's forty-eight-year-long career were apparent—rampant anticommunism, bureaucratic/organizational genius, and political policing. For an engaging look at Hoover's role in the Palmer Raids see Kenneth D. Ackerman, *Young J. Edgar: Hoover, the Red Scare, and the Assault on Civil Liberties* (New York: Carroll & Graf Publishers, 2007); on the Harding Administration scandals and the DOJ and Bureau's involvement, see Laton McCartney, *The Teapot Dome Scandal: How Big Oil Bought the Harding Administration and Tried to Steal the Country* (New York: Random House, 2008); Athan G. Theoharis, *The Bureau & American Democracy* (Lawrence: University of Kansas, 2004); Gene Caesar, *Incredible Detective: The Biography of William J. Burns* (Englewood Cliffs, NJ: Prentice-Hall, Inc., 1968); and Alpheus Thomas Mason, *Harlan Fiske Stone: Pillar of the Law* (New York: Viking Press, 1956).

10. At the time, the competing federal police forces included the Treasury Department's Secret Service (protecting the president, currency, the flag, and prohibition), Federal Marshals, the IRS, the Coast Guard, and Military Intelligence. The Bureau did not have jurisdiction over "violations of the counterfeiting, narcotic, customs and smuggling, immigration, and postal laws." J. Edgar Hoover, *Some Legal Aspects of Interstate Crime* (Washington, DC: Government Printing Office, 1938), 7.

11. Theoharis, *The Bureau,* 33–34, 173. Hoover reduced the number of agents from 441 in 1924 to 383 in 1932. However, the number of agents would again rise in 1935 to over five hundred.

12. The training school was initially located in New York, but was soon moved to Washington, DC, where it remained until the Quantico facility was opened in 1972.

13. Max Lowenthal, *The Federal Bureau of Investigation* (New York: William Sloane Associates, Inc., 1950), 377.

14. Lawrence Rosen, "The Uniform Crime Report: The Role of Social Science," *Social Science History* 19, no. 2 (Summer 1995): 215–238.

15. Melvin Purvis, *American Agent* (Garden City, NY: Doubleday, Doran & Co., Inc., 1936), 36.

16. Prohibition cases fell under the jurisdiction of the Prohibition Bureau of the Treasury Department and were often investigated by the Coast Guard. Technically the Bureau had no authority in these cases, although it did work informally with Prohibition Agents. Theoharis, *The Bureau,* 36; Homer Cummings and Carl McFarland, *Federal Justice: Chapters in the History of Justice and the Federal Executive* (New York: The MacMillan Co., 1937), 474.

17. Tim Weiner, *Enemies: A History of the Bureau* (New York: Random House, 2012), xv; Rhodri Jeffreys-Jones, *The Bureau: A History* (New Haven: Yale University Press, 2007); Richard Gid Powers, *Broken: The Troubled Past and Uncertain Future of the Bureau* (New York: Free Press, 2004), 27; Theoharis, *The Bureau & American Democracy*; and Max Lowenthal, *The Federal Bureau of Investigation* (New York: William Sloane Associates, Inc., 1950).

18. "Approximate Amount of Time Spent by the Bureau of Investigation, Department of Justice, in Investigating Average Cases Involving Certain Violations of Federal Statutes," File "Bureau of Investigation," reel 3, page 2, Wickersham Files.

19. "Sources of Complaints Received by the Bureau of Investigation, Department of Justice, Concerning Federal Law Violations," File "Bureau of Investigation," reel 3, page 2, Wickersham Files.

20. Athan G. Theoharis, "Political Policing in the United States: The Evolution of the Bureau, 1917–1956," in *The Policing of Politics in the Twentieth Century,* ed. Mark Mazower, 191–211 (Providence, RI: Berghahn Books, 1997), 194–195.

21. Athan Theoharis, *J. Edgar Hoover, Sex, and Crime: An Historical Antidote* (Chicago: Ivan R. Dee, 1995), 61. Hoover's concern about personal sexual morality might strike some readers as interesting or hypocritical, given the wide-spread popular cultural representations of Hoover as a transvestite. Rumors of Hoover's cross-dressing first emerged in Anthony Summers's salacious biography, which asserts that Hoover was homosexual and enjoyed cross-dressing, and the Italian-

American mafia had photographic proof of such activities and thus blackmailed Hoover to keep the Bureau from seriously investigating the mafia. Most Hoover biographers summarily reject this thesis as both unconfirmed and probably untrue. It is highly unlikely that Hoover cross-dressed, although there is some uncertainty about his sexual orientation. Hoover never married, and he spent most of his time with his Assistant Director Clyde Tolson. For a systematic refutation of Summers's allegations, see Theoharis, *J. Edgar Hoover, Sex, and Crime,* 21–56. For the source of the rumor, see Anthony Summers, *Official and Confidential: The Secret Life of J. Edgar Hoover* (New York: Putman's Sons, 1993), 254.

22. Department of Justice Circular No. 647, Jan 26, 1917, RG 60, General Records of the Department of Justice, Miscellaneous Records, 1865–1968, Box 3, Circulars, 1916–1917, Administrative Orders, Circulars and Memoranda, 1856–1968, National Archives, College Park, MD.

23. Special Agent in Charge to J. Edgar Hoover, Mar 22, 1929, 31-03-25; Special Agent in Charge to J. Edgar Hoover, 19 Apr 1929, 31-03-28; File 31-03, Box 1, FBI White Slave Files.

24. For works on the rise of modern sexuality and its effect on courtship and marriage, see Julian B. Carter, *The Heart of Whiteness: Normal Sexuality and Race in America, 1880–1940* (Durham: Duke University Press, 2007); Pippa Holloway, *Sexuality, Politics, and Social Control in Virginia, 1920–1945* (Chapel Hill: University of North Carolina, 2006); Pamela Haag, *Consent: Sexual Rights and the Transformation of American Liberalism* (Ithaca, NY: Cornell University Press, 1999); Sharon R. Ullman, *Sex Seen: The Emergence of Modern Sexuality in America* (Berkeley: University of California Press, 1997); Mary E. Odem, *Delinquent Daughters: Protecting and Policing Adolescent Female Sexuality in the United States, 1885–1920* (Chapel Hill: University of North Carolina Press, 1995); Beth Bailey, *From Front Porch to Back Seat: Courtship in Twentieth-Century America* (Baltimore: John Hopkins University Press, 1988); Kathy Peiss, *Cheap Amusements: Working Women and Leisure in Turn-of-the-Century New York* (Philadelphia: Temple University Press, 1986); and Pamela Fass, *The Damned and the Beautiful: American Youth in the 1920s* (New York: Oxford University Press, 1977).

25. John D'Emilio and Estelle B. Freedman, *Intimate Matters: A History of Sexuality in America* (New York: Harper and Row, Publishers, 1988), 241.

26. Bailey, *From Front Porch to Back Seat.*

27. D'Emilio and Freedman, *Intimate Matters,* 224, 267; Lynn Dumenil, *The Modern Temper: American Culture and Society in the 1920s* (New York: Hill and Wang, 1995), 134; Pamela S. Haag, "In Search of 'the Real Thing': Ideologies of Love, Modern Romance, and Women's Sexual Subjectivity in the United States, 1920–1940," in *American Sexual Politics: Sex, Gender, and Race since the Civil War,* ed. John C. Fout and Maura Shaw Tantillo, 161–192 (Chicago: University of

Chicago Press, 1993), 166; Michael E. Parrish, *Anxious Decades: American Prosperity and Depression, 1920–1941* (New York: W.W. Norton & Co., 1992), 157; and Simmons, *Making Marriage Modern,* chapter 3.

28. Elaine Tyler May, *Great Expectations: Marriage and Divorce in Post-Victorian America* (Chicago: University of Chicago Press, 1980), 2.

29. Ibid., 88, 90.

30. Ibid., 79.

31. Kathleen Drowne and Patrick Huber, *The 1920s* (Westport, CT: Greenwood Press, 2004), 109.

32. Quoted in Robert S. Lynd and Helen Merrell Lynd, *Middletown: A Study of Contemporary American Culture* (New York: Harcourt, Brace and Co., 1929), 114.

33. Quoted in Virginia Scharff, *Taking the Wheel: Women and the Coming of the Motor Age* (New York: the Free Press, 1991), 138.

34. Drowne and Huber, *The 1920s,* 249.

35. Parrish, *Anxious Decades,* 39. In 1915 there were fewer than 2.5 million cars registered, by 1920 there were more than 9 million, by 1925, almost 20 million, and by 1930, over 26.5 million. Frederick L. Allen, *The Big Change: American Transforms Itself, 1900–1950* (New York: Harper & Brothers Publishers, 1952), 124.

36. Allen, *The Big Change,* 123.

37. Lynds, *Middletown,* 137.

38. Courtney Ryley Cooper, *Designs in Scarlet* (Boston: Little, Brown and Co., 1939), 20 and 22.

39. Purvis, *American Agent,* 216.

40. W. W. Spain, Oct 19, 1921, 31-36-1, page 1, Case 31-36, Box 2, FBI White Slave Files.

41. Odem, *Delinquent Daughters,* 38–62.

42. H. W. Humble, "Seduction as a Crime," *Columbia Law Review* 21 (1921): 144–154, 144.

43. Murray, "Marriage as Punishment," 119.

44. Lawrence M. Friedman, "Name Robbers: Privacy, Blackmail, and Assorted Matters in Legal History," *Hofstra Law Review* 30, no. 4 (Summer 2002): 1093–1132, 1095.

45. Friedman, "Name Robbers," 1099.

46. Stephen Robertson, "Making Right a Girl's Ruin: Working-Class Legal Cultures and Forced Marriage in New York City, 1890–1950," *Journal of American Studies,* 36, no. 2 (2002): 199–230, 205–206.

47. Robertson, "Making Right a Girl's Ruin," 206.

48. Robert Peterson, Dec 17, 1927, 31-20636-3, Case 31-20636, Box 63, FBI White Slave Files.

49. Murray, "Marriage as Punishment"; Case 31-27930, Roll 113A, Box 9, FBI White Slave Microfilm Files, Record Group 65, Records of the Federal Bureau of Investigation—FBI Headquarters Case Files, Classification 31, National Archives, College Park, MD [hereafter referred to as FBI White Slave Microfilm Files].

50. Application No. 250029, Oct 19, 1929, *Cuyahoga County Marriage Records, 1810–1973* , Vol. 157–158, page 506; Application No. 18557, Jul 11, 1934, *Cuyahoga County Marriage Records, 1810–1973* Vol. 171–172, page 112, Ancestry .com, accessed Jan 26, 2013.

51. Robertson, "Making Right a Girl's Ruin," 205–206.

52. A. C. Sullivan, Apr 22, 1927, 31-18111-3, page 2, Case 31-18111, Box 59, FBI White Slave Files.

53. "Ethel Margaret Kennedy Affidavit, Apr 30, 1927," page 2, in Albert J. Law, May 3, 1927, 31-18111-4, Case 31-18111, Box 59, FBI White Slave Files.

54. A. C. Sullivan, Apr 22, 1927, 31-18111-3, page 4, Case 31-18111, Box 59, FBI White Slave Files.

55. Ibid., 1.

56. Leslie Reagan, *When Abortion Was a Crime: Women, Medicine, and the Law in the United States, 1867–1973* (Berkeley: University of California Press, 1997), 64–66.

57. R. H. Vetterli, Dec 16, 1927, 31-18111-21, page 2, Case 31-18111, Box 59, FBI White Slave Files.

58. "Ethel Margaret Kennedy Affidavit, Apr 30, 1927," page 1, in Albert J. Law, May 3, 1927, 31-18111-4, Case 31-18111, Box 59, FBI White Slave Files.

59. W. F. Whitely, Jun 3, 1936, 31-43298-3, Case 31-43298, Box 95, FBI White Slave Files.

60. D. R. Morley, Dec 29, 1936, 31-43298-6, Case 31-43298, Box 95, FBI White Slave Files.

61. Friedman, "Name Robbers," 1095–1099.

62. Cheryl Hicks, " 'Bright and Good Looking Colored Girls': Black Women's Sexuality and 'Harmful Intimacy' in Early-Twentieth-Century New York," *Journal of the History of Sexuality* 18, no. 3 (Sep 2009): 418–456, 419.

63. Historian Leon Litwack has argued that the use of the phrase "old time darky" by white Southerners was used in contrast to the New Negroes who, because they had never been enslaved, did not understand that their freedom was significantly curtailed. Leon Litwack, *Trouble in Mind: Black Southerners in the Age of Jim Crow* (New York: Knopf, 1998), 214; Agent J. L. Webb, Jul 9, 1921, 31-2719-1, Case 31-385, Box 16, FBI White Slave Files.

64. J. R. Burger, Jul 15, 1921, 31-2719-3, page 2, Case 31-385, Box 16, FBI White Slave Files.

65. Lawrence M. Friedman, *Crime and Punishment in American History* (New York: Basic Books, 1993), 322; and Friedman, "Name Robbers," 1102.

66. Cott, *Public Vows,* 157. Also see, Alice Kessler-Harris, *In Pursuit of Equity: Women, Men, and the Quest for Economic Citizenship in 20th-Century America* (New York: Oxford University Press, 2001), 19–63; and Robert Self, *All in the Family: The Realignment of American Democracy since the 1960s* (New York: Hill and Wang, 2012), 18.

67. Murray, "Marriage as Punishment," 122, fn 106.

68. Reva Siegel, "The Modernization of Marital Status Laws: Adjudicating Wives' Rights to Earnings, 1860–1930," *Georgetown Law Journal* 82 (Sep 1994): 2139.

69. Michael Willrich, "Home Slackers: Men, the State, and Welfare in Modern America," *Journal of American History* 87, no. 2 (Sep 2000): 460–489.

70. J. D. Glass, May 20, 1929, 31-26661-1, Case 31-26661, Roll 107A, Box 9, FBI White Slave Microfilm Files.

71. W. W. Wright, Jun 5, 1929, 31-26661-2, page 2, Case 31-26661, Roll 107A, Box 9, FBI White Slave Microfilm Files.

72. George Costello, Jun 29, 1929, 31-26661-3, Case 31-26661, Roll 107A, Box 9, FBI White Slave Microfilm Files.

73. George G. Grotewohl, Nov 9, 1921, 31-404-1, page 2, Case 31-404, Box 17, FBI White Slave Files.

74. E. M. Blanford, Sep 27, 1921, 31-3337-1, page 3, Case 31-100, Box 5, FBI White Slave Files.

75. H. W. Hess, Jan 30, 1923, 31-100-4, Case 31-100, Box 5, FBI White Slave Files.

76. B. F. McCurdy, Sep 2, 1921, 31-3170-1, page 5, Case 31-51, Box 3, FBI White Slave Files.

77. B. F. McCurdy, Oct 17, 1921, 31-51-1, Case 31-51, Box 3, FBI White Slave Files.

78. E. B. Hubley, May 31, 1927, 31-18793-1, page 5, Case 31-18793, Box 60, FBI White Slave Files.

79. Ibid., 4.

80. H. J. Sticken, Jul 7, 1927, 31-18793-6, page 3, Case 31-18793, Box 60, FBI White Slave Files.

81. Fred S. Dunn, Case 31-18793, 31-18793-7, Box 60, FBI White Slave Files.

82. Friedman, *Crime and Punishment in America,* 199.

83. L. J. Barkhausen, May 17, 1924, 31-8884-2, page 2, Case 31-8884, Box 39, FBI White Slave Files.

84. T. C. Wilcox to J. Edgar Hoover, Feb 27, 1929, 31-03-9x, File 31-03, Box 1, FBI White Slave Files.

85. Only two field offices noted that they never faced any hesitancy from the U.S. Attorneys' offices—Salt Lake City and Oklahoma City.

86. S. J. McAfee to T. C. to J. Edgar Hoover, Mar 4, 1929, 31-03-16, File 31-03, Box 1, FBI White Slave Files.

87. Hornell Hart, "Changing Social Attitudes and Interests," in President's Research Committee on Social Trends, *Recent Social Trends in the United States* (New York: McGraw-Hill Book Co., Inc., 1933), 418.

88. *Hansen v. Haff*, 65 F.2d 94 (9th Cir. 1933) rev'd, 291 U.S. 559 (1934): 559–566, 562. I am indebted to Ariela Dubler's essay "Immoral Purposes," for alerting me to the presence of this case.

89. *Hansen v. Haff*.

90. Dubler, "Immoral Purposes," 799.

91. Friedman, "Name Robbers," 1120.

92. There is a strong judicial tradition opposing the Mann Act's constitutionality that goes back to the very birth of the law. Again and again, judges wrote briefs opposing the reach of the law into the personal realm. Additionally, most law journals came out opposing the law. See the dissent in *Caminetti v. United States*, 242 U.S. 470, 37 S. Ct. 192 (1917); "Criminal Conspiracy to Violate the Mann Act," *Columbia Law* Review 15, no. 4 (Apr 1915): 337–340; R.W.A., "The Scope of the Mann Act," *Michigan Law Review* 15, no. 5 (Mar 1917): 425–426; "The Scope of the White Slave Traffic Act," *Virginia Law Review*, 4, no. 8 (May 1917): 653–660; "Interstate Immorality: The Mann Act and the Supreme Court," *Yale Law Journal* 56, no. 4 (Apr 1947): 718–730; and William Seagle, "The Twilight of the Mann Act," *American Bar Association Journal* 55 (Jul 1969): 641–647.

93. Purvis, *American Agent*, 49.

94. Summers, *Official and Confidential*, 47.

95. Special Agent in Charge to J. Edgar Hoover, Feb 28, 1929, 31-03-11, File 31-03, Box 1, FBI White Slave Files.

96. Harry Larner to Attorney General Stone, Jul 23, 1924, 31-0-170, RG 60, General Records of the Department of Justice, Formerly Classified Subject Correspondence, 1910–1945, Class 31 Mann Act, Box 2621, Sec. 36, National Archives, College Park, MD.

97. "Memorandum of the Director [Clyde Tolson]," May 4, 1940, File 31-HQ-00, Box 1, Section 1, FBI White Slave Files.

98. Blackstone's *Commentaries* can be found at http://avalon.law.yale.edu /18th_century/blackstone_bk1ch15.asp, accessed Dec 27, 2013.

99. Linda Kerber, *No Constitutional Right to Be Ladies: Women and the Obligations of Citizenship* (New York: Hill and Wang, 1998), 11.

100. Kerber, *No Constitutional Right to Be Ladies*, 13–15; Christine Stansell, *The Feminist Promise: 1792 to the Present* (New York: The Modern Library, 2010), 12.

101. "Declaration of Sentiments," can be found at http://ecssba.rutgers.edu /docs/seneca.html, accessed Dec 27, 2013.

102. These include restrictions on women's jury service and military service.

103. Quoted in Siegel, "The Modernization of Marital Status Law," 2127.

7. Coerced Sex and Forced Prostitution

1. Allan O. Hunter, Jul 28, 1941, 31-62042-2, page 3, Case 31-62042, Reel 304A, FBI White Slave Microfilm Files, Record Group 65, Records of the Federal Bureau of Investigation—FBI Headquarters Case Files, Classification 31, National Archives, College Park, MD.

2. Estelle B. Freedman, "'Uncontrolled Desires': The Response to the Sexual Psychopath, 1920–1960," in *Passion and Power: Sexuality in History,* ed. Kathy Peiss and Christina Simmons, 199–225 (Philadelphia: Temple University Press, 1989), 205–206.

3. Patricia L. N. Donat and John D'Emilio, "A Feminist Redefinition of Rape and Sexual Assault: Historical Foundations and Change," *Journal of Social Issues* 48, no. 1 (1992): 9–22, 11.

4. Linda Gordon, "The Politics of Child Sex Abuse: Notes from American History," *Feminist Review* 28 (Spring 1988): 56–64, 59–60; Rachel Devlin, *Relative Intimacy: Fathers, Adolescent Daughters, and Postwar American Culture* (Chapel Hill: University of North Carolina Press, 2005).

5. Estelle B. Freedman, *Redefining Rape: Sexual Violence in the Era of Suffrage and Segregation* (Cambridge, MA: Harvard University Press, 2013), 6.

6. Susan Brownmiller, *Against Our Will: Men, Women, and Rape* (New York: Fawcett Columbine [1976] 1993); Roy Porter, "Rape—Does It Have a Historical Meaning?," in *Rape,* ed. Sylvana Tomaselli and Roy Porter, 216–236 (Oxford: Basil Blackford, 1986); Anna Clark, *Women's Silences, Men's Violence: Sexual Assault in England, 1770–1845* (London: Pandora, 1987); Karen Dubinsky, *Improper Advances: Rape and Heterosexual Conflict in Ontario, 1880–1929* (Chicago: University of Chicago Press, 1993); Kim Stevenson, "Unequivocal Victims: The Historical Roots of the Mystification of the Female Complainant in Rape Cases," *Feminist Legal Studies* 8 (2000): 343–366; Diane Miller Sommerville, *Rape and Race in the Nineteenth-Century South* (Chapel Hill: University of North Carolina Press, 2004); Lisa Linquist Dorr, *White Women, Rape, and the Power of Race in Virginia, 1900–1960* (Chapel Hill: University of North Carolina Press, 2004); Sharon Block, *Rape and Sexual Power in Early America* (Chapel Hill: University of North Carolina, 2006); Stephen Robertson, "Shifting the Scene of the Crime: Sodomy and the American History of Sexual Violence," *Journal of the History of Sexuality* 19, no. 2 (May 2010): 223–242; and Estelle B. Freedman, "'Crimes Which Startle and Horrify': Gender, Age, and the Racialization of Sexual Violence in White American Newspapers, 1870–1900," *Journal of the History of Sexuality* 20, no. 3 (Sep 2011): 465–497.

7. Melvin I. Urofsky, *Louis D. Brandeis: A Life* (New York: Pantheon Books, 2009), 210.

8. Ellen Carol DuBois and Linda Gordon, "Seeking Ecstasy on the Battlefield: Danger and Pleasure in Nineteenth-century Feminist Sexual Thought," in

Pleasure and Danger: Exploring Female Sexuality, ed. Carole Vance, 31–49 (London: Pandora Press, 1989), 33.

9. Pamela Haag, *Consent: Sexual Rights and the Transformation of American Liberalism* (Ithaca: Cornell University Press, 1999), 63–74.

10. Block, *Rape and Sexual Power,* 1.

11. Freedman, *Redefining Rape,* 21, 26, quote on 27.

12. Dubinsky, *Improper Advances,* 17.

13. For more on "strategic metaphors," see Arlene J. Díaz, *Female Citizens, Patriarchs, and the Law in Venezuela, 1786–1904* (Lincoln: University of Nebraska Press, 2004), 15; Eileen J. Findlay, "Courtroom Tales of Sex and Honor: *Rapto* and Rape in Late-Nineteenth Century Puerto Rico," in *Honor, Status, and Law in Modern Latin America,* ed. Sueann Caulfield, Sarah C. Chambers, and Lara Putnam, 201–222 (Durham, NC: Duke University Press, 2005), 203.

14. Block, *Rape and Sexual Power,* 4, 86.

15. John C. Rider, Jun 7, 1921, 31-2428-1, Case 421, Box 17, Record Group 65, Records of the Federal Bureau of Investigation—FBI Headquarters Case Files, Classification 31, National Archives, College Park, MD [hereafter referred to as FBI White Slave Files].

16. Harold Nathan, Jul 15, 1921, 31-2428-4, Case 421, Box 17, FBI White Slave Files.

17. Joseph E. P. Dunn, Oct 8, 1921, 31-2428-10, Case 421, Box 17, FBI White Slave Files.

18. "Judge Reprimands Woman in the Case," *Cumberland Evening Times,* Sep 24, 1921, 16.

19. Ancestry.com, accessed April 16, 2013.

20. Freedman, *Redefining Rape,* 22.

21. For more on the African American community's campaigns against black women's sexual exploitation by white men, see Danielle L. McGuire, *At the Dark End of the Street: Black Women, Rape, and Resistance—A New History of the Civil Rights Movement from Rosa Parks to the Rise of Black Power* (New York: Knopf, 2010), 28–30. For examples of African American newspapers condemning the concubinage of black women by white men, see "Families Ready to Leave Savannah after Gun Attack," *Chicago Defender* Sep 15, 1923, 3; Nettie George Speedy, "Slave Girl Free," *Chicago Defender* Oct 6, 1923, 1; "Isn't It Strange," *Chicago Defender* Nov 7, 1925, 22; "Social Equality," *Afro-American* Jul 20, 1929, 6; "Looses Sweetheart, Sends the Sheriff to Get Her," *Chicago Defender,* Jun 25, 1921, 1; Case 31-28, Box 2, FBI White Slave Files.

22. "Affidavit of Lizzie Wilson," Jun 22, 1921, Case 31-28, Box 2, FBI White Slave Files.

23. Richard E. Westbrooks to Judge Charles F. Clyne, Jun 21, 1921, Case 31-28, Box 2, FBI White Slave Files.

24. See "Girl's Story Bares Horror of Concubine Life in South," *Chicago Defender,* Jul 23, 1921, 3; Darlene Clark Hine, "Rape and Inner Lives of Black Women in the Middle West: Preliminary Thoughts on the Culture of Dissemblance," *Signs* 14, no. 4 (Summer 1989): 912–920, citation on 914.

25. L. J. Darkheusen, Oct 17, 1921, 31-28-1, Case 31-28, Box 2, FBI White Slave Files.

26. The use of extradition to recover black concubines fleeing to the North was also a feature of the case of Marie Armstead. See, Nettie George Speedy, "Slave Girl Free," *Chicago Defender* Oct 6, 1923, 1.

27. William H. Poling, Mar 25, 1927, 31-18240-1, page 2, Case 31-18240, Box 59, FBI White Slave Files.

28. Porter, "Rape," 221 and 235; Block, *Rape and Sexual Power,* 11.

29. Stevenson, "Unequivocal Victims," 351.

30. J. P. Lacour, Jul 29, 1936, 31-44495-1, page 2, Case 31-44495, Box 111, FBI White Slave Files.

31. Ibid., 4.

32. Ibid., 5. Karen Dubinsky's research into rape prosecutions in Ontario revealed the following: "The practice of negotiating, for money or sometimes for goods such as livestock or even farmland, was widespread and occurred in cases of voluntary and involuntary sexual crime." Dubinsky, *Improper Advances,* 22.

33. Block, *Rape and Sexual Power,* 1; Gordon, "The Politics of Child Sexual Abuse," 56.

34. Linda Gordon, *Heroes of Their Own Lives: The Politics and History of Family Violence, 1880–1960* (New York: Viking, 1988), 204–205.

35. H. A. King, Jul 31, 1933, 31-36369-10, page 2, Case 31-36369, Box 73, FBI White Slave Files.

36. R. C. Eberstein, Jan 8, 1934, 31-36369-15, Case 31-36369, Box 73, FBI White Slave Files.

37. F. C. Dorwart, Sep 12, 1935, 31-36369-38, page 2, Case 31-36369, Box 73, FBI White Slave Files.

38. Ibid., 5.

39. Gordon, *Heroes of Their Own Lives,* 236; *Oregonian Daily,* Mar 5, 1934, in F. C. Dorwart, Sep 12, 1935, 31-36369-39, page 5, Case 31-36369, Box 73, FBI White Slave Files.

40. Freedman, *Redefining Rape,* 158–161.

41. J. Edgar Hoover, *Some Legal Aspects of Interstate Crime* (Washington, DC: Government Printing Office, 1938), 11. Just perusing my sample of cases, I find that in 1924, noncommercial illicit immorality cases (including cases characterized by sexual violence) comprise 73.6 % of my cases, whereas commercial prostitution cases constituted 26.3%; in 1927, noncommercial illicit immorality, 81.6%, commercial prostitution, 18.3%; in 1932, noncommercial illicit immorality,

61.5%, commercial prostitution, 38.4%. It should be noted that my sampling was random, yet targeted and as a result may not represent fully quantifiable evidence.

42. Leon E Bone, Oct 22, 1921, 31-106-1, Case 31-106, Box 5, FBI White Slave Files.

43. T. B. White, Nov 1, 1921, 31-321-1, Case 31-321, Box 14, FBI White Slave Files.

44. Fred I. Keepers, Nov 23, 1921, 31-434-3, Case 31-434, Box 18, FBI White Slave Files.

45. Elizabeth Alice Clement, *Love for Sale: Courting, Treating, and Prostitution in New York City, 1900–1945* (Chapel Hill: University of North Carolina Press, 2006), 177–178, 198; Ann R. Gabbert, "Prostitution and Moral Reform in the Borderlands: El Paso, 1890–1920," *Journal of the History of Sexuality* 12, no. 4 (Oct 2003): 575–604; George Williams III, *The Red-Light Ladies of Virginia City, Nevada* (Riverside, CA: Tree by the River Publishing, 1984); "Portland, OR, Dec 4–5, 1932," H9-H10, Prostitution, 1932–1941, MSS 1541, Oregon Social Hygiene Association, Oregon Historical Society Research Library, Portland, OR.

46. Werner Hanni, Aug 14, 1921, 31-2959-2, page 4, Case 163, Box 8, FBI White Slave Files.

47. Ibid., 13.

48. Joanne Meyerowitz, *Women Adrift: Independent Wage Earners in Chicago, 1880–1930* (Chicago: University of Chicago Press, 1988), 102–103.

49. Werner Hanni, Aug 14, 1921, 31-2959-2, page 16, Case 163, Box 8, FBI White Slave Files.

50. Gerald P. Murphy, Oct 19, 1921, 31-163-20, page 4, Case 163, Box 8, FBI White Slave Files.

51. C. N. Ottosen, Apr 27, 1932, 31-35530-1, pages 2–3, Case 31-35330, Box 71, FBI White Slave Files.

52. F. F. Yearsley, Jul 9, 1932, 31-35530-13, page 1, Case 31-35330, Box 71, FBI White Slave Files.

53. "I.C. #31-37099 Homer B. Shropshire," Jul 11, 1933, RG 65, Records of the Federal Bureau of Investigation—Interesting Case Write-Ups, Box 14, National Archives, College Park, MD; J. B. Little, "Parole Report," Apr 15, 1933, 21-37099-13, page 2, Case 31-37099, Box 74, FBI White Slave Files.

54. Gerald K. Haines and David A. Langbart, *Unlocking the Files of the FBI: A Guide to Its Records and Classification System* (Wilmington, DE: Scholarly Resources, Inc., 1993), 258–259.

55. Quoted in "Portland, OR, Dec 4–5, 1932," 3; Clement, *Love for Sale,* 206–207.

56. See reports from Oct 2, 1928, Box 35, 1927–1930, Folder: Go-Betweens; and May 9, 1931 and Sep 30, 1931, Box 35, Folder: 1931 House of Prostitution,

Committee of Fourteen Records, New York Public Library, Manuscripts and Archives Division, New York City, NY.

57. Virginia Murray, "The Relation of Prostitution to Economic Conditions," *Journal of Social Hygiene* 18, no. 6 (June 1932): 314–321, 315.

58. Jan 22, 1932, Box 35, Folder: 1932, Committee of Fourteen Records, New York Public Library, Manuscripts and Archives Division, New York City, NY.

59. Clement, *Love for Sale*, 193–211; Lara Campbell, *Respectable Citizens: Gender, Family, and Unemployment in Ontario's Great Depression* (Toronto: University of Toronto Press, 2009), 46–49; Jamie Schmidt Wagman, "Women Reformers Respond during the Depression: Battling St. Louis's Disease and Immorality," *Journal of Urban History* 35, no. 5 (Jul 2009): 698–717.

60. Campbell, *Respectable Citizens*, 59–60; Margaret Hobbs, "Rethinking Antifeminism in the 1930s: Gender Crisis or Workplaces Justice? A Response to Alice Kessler-Harris," *Gender & History* 5, no. 1 (Spring 1993): 4–15, 7; Margot Canaday, *The Straight State: Sexuality and Citizenship in Twentieth-Century America* (Princeton: Princeton University Press, 2009), 96; Alice Kessler-Harris, *Out to Work: A History of Wage-Earning Women in the United States* (New York: Oxford University Press, 1982), 254–55, 260.

61. "Crime Wave Starting," *New York Times*, Feb 11, 1930, 8.

62. Murray, "The Relation of Prostitution to Economic Conditions," 316–317.

63. John B. Little, Feb 1, 1933, 31-37099-4, page 5, Case 31-37099, Box 74, FBI White Slave Files.

64. J. Edgar Hoover, "Detection and Apprehension," Speech delivered before the Attorney General's Conference on Crime, Washington, DC, Dec 11, 1934, page 3, RG 60, General Records of the Department of Justice, Records of the Special Executive Assistant to the Attorney General, 1933–40, Box 12, National Archives, College Park, MD.

8. The FBI's Assault on Sex Trafficking

1. "G-Men Launch Drive Against White Slavery," *Mansfield (OH) News Journal*, Aug 21, 1936, 19.

2. "Hoover Opens War on Vice Over U.S.," *Washington Post*, Aug 23, 1936, M12.

3. Athan G. Theoharis and John Stuart Cox, *The Boss: J. Edgar Hoover and the Great American Inquisition* (Philadelphia: Temple University Press), 123.

4. For examples of this approach, see Sanford J. Ungar, *FBI* (New York: Little Brown and Co., 1975); Ronald Kessler, *The Bureau: The Secret History of the FBI* (New York: St. Martin's Press, 2002); and Theoharis and Cox, *The Boss*.

5. Theoharis and Cox, *The Boss*, 129.

6. Ibid., 130.

7. Ibid., 138.

8. Elizabeth Clement argues that Prohibition led to a bifurcation of the sex industry—legal dance halls, movie houses, and burlesque theaters that only served soda on the one hand, and speakeasies patronized by prostitutes and madams operating outside the law on the other. But both sides of the New York City sex industry saw repeated crack downs during the 1930s. See Elizabeth Alice Clement, *Love for Sale: Courting, Treating, and Prostitution in New York City, 1900–1945* (Chapel Hill: University of North Carolina Press, 2006), 178–211; and Andrea Friedman, "'The Habitats of Sex-Crazed Perverts': Campaigns Against Burlesque in Depression-Era New York City," *Journal of the History of Sexuality* 7, no. 2 (Oct 1996): 203–238.

9. Clement, *Love for Sale*, 193–194.

10. Polly Adler, *A House Is Not a Home* (New York: Rinehart & Company, Inc., 1950), 176.

11. "Bawdy Business," *Time*, May 25, 1936, 15; Clement, *Love for Sale*, 205.

12. John M. Murtagh and Sara Harris, *Cast the First Stone* (New York: McGraw-Hill Book Company, Inc., 1957), 242; Charles Winick, "Organized Crime and Commercial Sex," in *Handbook of Organized Crime in the United States*, ed. Robert J. Kelly, Ko-Lin Chin, and Rufus Schatzberg, 289–310 (Westport, CT: Greenwood Press, 1994), 295; Robert J. Kelly, *Encyclopedia of Organized Crime in the United States: From Capone's Chicago to the New Urban Underworld* (Westport, CT: Greenwood Press, 2000), 198–202; Martin A. Gosch, *The Last Testament of Lucky Luciano* (Boston: Little, Brown, and Co., 1975), 191–193.

13. Mary M. Stolberg, *Fighting Organized Crime: Politics, Justice, and the Legacy of Thomas E. Dewey* (Boston: Northeastern University, 1995).

14. "J. E. Hoover's Men Working on Vice," *New York Sun*, Feb 8, 1936.

15. Frederick K. Grittner, *White Slavery: Myth, Ideology, and American Law* (New York: Garland Publishing, Inc., 1990), 148; David J. Langum, *Crossing over the Line: Legislating Morality and the Mann Act* (Chicago: University of Chicago Press), 1994), 170.

16. "'G Men' Center upon White Slavers," *Literary Digest* 122, Aug 29, 1936: 26–27.

17. Langun, *Crossing over the Line*, 168.

18. See Article 23 (c) of the League's Covenant. League of Nations, *Records of the International Conference on the Traffic in Women and Children* (Geneva: League of Nations Publications, 1921), 9–10.

19. By 1910, feminists active in the international anti-white slavery movement began arguing for a change in terminology because they feared the term *white slave* could be perceived as too exclusive and was not at all accurate to what the movement was attempting to do, that is, protect all women regardless of race.

Now certainly some anti–white slavery activists operating on the international level were interested only in white women (usually their national compatriots), but by the mid 1910s those most active in transnational groups shied away from discussing prostitution in this type of racialized way. By 1921, the phrase the *traffic in women and children* emerged as preferable to *white slavery*, in that it was seen as more precise and it nicely hedged issues related to force/choice dichotomy. For more on feminists in the international white slavery movement, see Jessica Pliley, "Claims to Protection: The Rise and Fall of Feminist Abolitionism in the League of Nations' Committee on the Traffic in Women and Children, 1919–1937," *Journal of Women's History* (Winter 2010): 90–113.

20. League of Nation, *Report of the Special Body of Experts on Traffic in Women and Children, Part One* (Geneva: League of Nations Publications, 1927), 9.

21. League of Nations, *Report of the Special Body of Experts,* 19.

22. Pliley, "Claims to Protection;" Barbara Metzger, "Towards an International Human Rights Regime during the Inter-War Years: The League of Nations' Combat of Traffic in Women and Children," in *Beyond Sovereignty: Britain, Empire and Transnationalism, c. 1880–1950,* Kevin Grant, Philippa Levine, and Frank Trentmann, eds, 54–79 (New York: Palgrave MacMillan, 2007), 74; and Stephanie A. Limoncelli, *The Politics of Trafficking: The First International Movement to Combat the Sexual Exploitation of Women* (Stanford: Stanford University Press, 2010), 82.

23. Bascom Johnson, "Law Enforcement Against Prostitution from the Point of view of the Public Official," Publication No. 297 (New York City: American Social Hygiene Association, Inc., 1920), 428.

24. Johnson, "Law Enforcement," 431.

25. Kristin Luker, "Sex, Social Hygiene, and the State: The Double-Edged Sword of Social Reform," *Theory and Society* 27, no. 5 (Oct 1998): 601–634, 614. Emphasis mine.

26. "What is a 'Racket,' A 'Racketeer,' and 'Racketeering?'" *The Federal Juror* (January 1936), located in RG 65, Records of the Federal Bureau of Investigation, Director's Office Records and Memorabilia, J. Edgar Hoover's Scrapbooks, 1913–1972, Box 17, National Archives, College Park, MD.

27. "G Man Vice Drive to Hit All Rackets," *Miami Tribune,* Feb 9, 1936.

28. L. G. Turrou, Aug 8, 1936, 31-42685-22 , Sec 1, pages 4–5, 31-42685, Sec 1, Box 88, Record Group 65, Records of the Federal Bureau of Investigation—FBI Headquarters Case Files, Classification 31, National Archives, College Park, MD [hereafter referred to as CT Vice Case].

29. E. A. Tamm, "Memorandum for the Director," Aug 28, 1936, 31-42685-59, Sec 3, CT Vice Case.

30. E. A. Tamm, "Memorandum for the Director," Nov 12, 1936, 31-42685-247, Sec 12, CT Vice Case.

31. "I.C. #31-42685 The Connecticut White Slave Ring," 38–56, RG 65, Records of the Federal Bureau of Investigation—Interesting Case Write-Ups, Box 14, National Archives, College Park, MD.

32. L. G. Turrou, Sep 9, 1936, 31-42685-95, Sec 3, page 22, CT Vice Case.

33. L. G. Turrou, Sep 15, 1936, 31-42685-111, Sec 4, page 14, CT Vice Case.

34. L. G. Turrou, Sep 9, 1936, 31-42685-95, Sec 3, page 18, CT Vice Case.

35. L. G. Turrou, Aug 8, 1936, 31-42685-22, Sec 1, page 15–17, CT Vice Case.

36. Heather Lee Miller, "Trick Identities: The Nexus of Work and Sex," *Journal of Women's History* 15, no. 4 (Winter 2004): 145–152, citation on 146–147.

37. "Portland, OR, Dec 4–5, 1932," H-12, page 7, Prostitution, 1932–1941, MSS 1541, Oregon Social Hygiene Association, Oregon Historical Society Research Library, Portland, OR. For more on the terminology of sex acts, see Jonathon Green, *Slang Down the Ages: The Historical Development of Slang* (London: Kyle Cathie Limited, 1993), 249, 285–286.

38. February 7, 1929 Report, Committee of Fourteen Records, Box 36, 1927–1929, Folder: 49 St.–57th St., New York Public Library, Manuscripts and Archives Division, New York City, NY.

39. L. G. Turrou, Sep 30, 1936, 31-42685-139, Sec 5, page 13, CT Vice Case.

40. R. Whitley to Hoover, Feb 13, 1937, 31-42685-295, Sec 14, page 2, CT Vice Case.

41. L. G. Turrou, Sep 22, 1936, 31-42685-125, Sec 5, page 10, CT Vice Case.

42. Throughout FBI files of prostitution-oriented Mann Act investigations from 1935 to 1938 is the repeated claim that New York City and surrounding areas were a much more profitable sex market than Chicago and Pittsburgh.

43. Leon G. Turrou, *Where My Shadow Falls: Two Decades of Crime Detection* (New York: Doubleday & Company, Inc., 1949), 137.

44. "I.C. #31-42685 The Connecticut White Slave Ring," 27.

45. L. G. Turrou, Sep 22, 1936, 31-42685-125, Sec 5, page 12, CT Vice Case.

46. A Yankee Descendant to J. Edgar Hoover, Aug 12, 1936, 31-42685-3?, Sec 2, CT Vice Case.

47. L. G. Turrou, "Parole Report of Adeline Pasquini," Nov 10, 1936, 31-42685-231, Sec 11, page 2, CT Vice Case.

48. Turrou, *Where My Shadow* Falls, 139.

49. L. G. Turrou, Sep 22, 1936, 31-42685-125, Sec 5, page 20, CT Vice Case; R. Whitley to Hoover, Feb 13, 1937, 31-42685-295, Sec 14, page 4, CT Vice Case.

50. L. G. Turrou, Sep 22, 1936, 31-42685-125, Sec 5, page 12, CT Vice Case.

51. L. G. Turrou, Sep 1, 1936, 31-42685-85, Sec 3, page 18, CT Vice Case.

52. L. G. Turrou, Aug 26, 1936, 31-42685-51, Sec 2, page 35–37, CT Vice Case.

53. L. G. Turrou, "Parole Report of Migel Taverner," Nov 18, 1936, 31-42685-258, Sec 12, CT Vice Case.

54. "I.C. #31-42685 The Connecticut White Slave Ring," 4.

55. L. G. Turrou, "Summary Report for the US Attorney," Oct 12, 1936, 31-42685-163, Sec 6, page 4, CT Vice Case.

56. E. A. Tamm, "Memorandum for the Director," Aug 21, 1936, 31-42685-39, Sec 1, CT Vice Case.

57. "G-Men Seek to Break Up Vice Racket," *Hartford Courant*, Oct 26, 1936, 4.

58. "'G Men' Center Upon White Slavers," *Literary Digest* 122 (Aug 29, 1936), 26.

59. "3 Arrested Here in Conn. Vice Ring," *New York Post*, Aug 22, 1936.

60. Courtney Ryley Cooper, *Here's to Crime* (New York: Little, Brown and Co., 1937), 241–242.

61. "Vice Witnesses Steady, Despite Cross Firing," *New Haven Journal-Courier*, Oct 21, 1936, 1, 2.

62. "'White Slavers' Beware: Here Come the G-Men!" *New York Sunday Mirror*, Sep 27, 1936.

63. Allan M. Brandt, "AIDS in Historical Perspective: Four Lessons from the History of Sexually Transmitted Diseases," *American Journal of Public Health* 78, no. 4 (1988): 367–371; J. K. Shafer, "Premarital Health Examination Legislation: History and Analysis," *Public Health Reports* 69, no. 5 (May 1954), 487–493, 488.

64. Courtney Ryley Cooper, *Designs in Scarlet* (Boston: Little, Brown and Co., 1939), 104.

65. L. G. Turrou, Aug 26, 1936, 31-42685-56, Sec 2, page 110, CT Vice Case.

66. A Yankee Descendant to J. Edgar Hoover, Aug 12, 1936, 31-42685-3, Sec 1, CT Vice Case.

67. L. G. Turrou, "Memorandum for the Special Agent in Charge," Sep 8, 1936, 31-42685-87, Sec 3, page 1, CT Vice Case.

68. L. G. Turrou, Sep 30, 1936, 31-42685-139, Sec 5, page 13, CT Vice Case.

69. L. G. Turrou, Aug 17, 1936, 31-42685-30, Sec 2, page 12, CT Vice Case.

70. L. G. Turrou, Aug 26, 1936, 31-42685-56, Sec 2, page 110, CT Vice Case.

71. L. G. Turrou, Sep 30, 1936, 31-42685-139, Sec 5, pages 5–6, CT Vice Case.

72. "A Vice Ring Broken Up," *Hartford Courant*, Nov 14, 1936, 12.

73. "Chief Vice Booker Gets Four Years," *Hartford Courant*, Nov 18, 1936, 6.

74. "U.S. Holds Four in Vice Raids," *New Haven Evening Register*, Aug 18, 1936, 2.

75. L. G. Turrou, Sep 8, 1936, 31-42685-87, Sec 3, page 1, CT Vice Case.

76. Johnson, "Law Enforcement," 428–429.

77. Thomas C. Mackey, *Pursuing Johns: Criminal Law Reform, Defending Character, and New York City's Committee of Fourteen, 1920–1930* (Columbus: Ohio State University Press, 2005).

78. "Sex Salons Thrive Despite Cleanup," (Bridgeport, CT) *Sunday Herald*, Nov 21, 1936.

79. Alden R. Whitman, "Sex Salons Thrive Despite Cleanup: Regulation Instead of Suppression Suggested," (Bridgeport, CT) *Sunday Herald*, Nov 21, 1936.

80. Turrou, *Where My Shadow Falls,* 142.

81. "Vice Syndicate Witness Taken in Drive Here," *New Haven Journal-Courier,* Sep 3, 1936, 2.

82. L. G. Turrou, Aug 26, 1936, 31-42685-56, page 9, 31-42685, Sec 2, CT Vice Case.

83. Cooper, *Here's To Crime,* 250.

84. R. Whitley to Hoover, Feb 13, 1937, 31-42685-295, Sec 14, pages 9–10, CT Vice Case.

85. "12 Witnesses in Vice Expose Get Freedom," *New Haven Evening Register,* Nov 13, 1936, 1, 2.

86. "Immoral Classes Deported During the Fiscal Years 1927 to 1936," RG 102, Records of the Children's Bureau, Central File, 1937–1940, Box 784, National Archives, College Park, MD.

87. "Cohen Urges Wide Support in Vice Drive," *New Haven Evening Register,* Sep 1, 1936, 1, 2.

88. R. Whitely to Byron H. Ulh, Mar 10, 1937, 31-42685-295X, Sec 14, CT Vice Case.

89. L. G. Turrou, "Parole Report of Arturo Pasquini," Nov 9, 1936, 31-42685-227, Sec 11, CT Vice Case.

90. "Deporting Criminals," *New Haven Journal-Courier,* Nov 3, 1936, 6.

91. "Man, Wife, Fined $66,000 for Vice," *New Haven Evening Register,* Nov 2, 1936, 2.

92. R. Whitley to Hoover, Feb 13, 1937, 31-42685-295, Sec 14, page 4, CT Vice Case.

93. Ibid.

94. "I.C. #31-42685 The Connecticut White Slave Ring," 17.

95. E. A. Tamm, "Memorandum for the Director," Nov 12, 1936, 31-42685-248, Sec 12, CT Vice Case.

96. L. G. Turrou, "Parole Report of Joseph DeStadio," Nov 23, 1936, 31-42685-272, Sec 11, page 3, CT Vice Case.

97. "Prisoner In New Haven Takes Bride Before Starting Three-Year Term," *Hartford Courant,* Nov 13, 1936, 3.

98. "Mann Act Marriage," *New Haven Journal Courier,* Nov 16, 1936.

99. "'White Slavers' Beware: Here Come the G-Men!," *New York Sunday Mirror,* Sep 27, 1936.

Conclusion

1. Nikolas Rose and Mariana Valverde, "Governed by Law?" *Social & Legal Studies* 7, no. 4 (Dec 1998): 541–551, 549.

2. The Western New York Human Trafficking Task Force is one of thirty-eight taskforces nationwide that is funded in part by the Department of Justice.

Department of State, *Trafficking in Persons Report,* 10th ed., June 2010 (Washington DC: Government Printing Office, 2010), accessed June 16, 2010, http://www.state.gov/g/tip/rls/tiprpt/2010/, 339–340.

3. Denise Jewell Gee, "Political Aid for Massage Parlor Operators Revealed: Couple Who Won Support for Ventures Now Face Charges of Importing Women for Prostitution," *Buffalo (NY) News,* Dec 14 2007, A1.

4. United States Attorney Terrance P. Flynn, "Chong Admits to Human Trafficking" [Press Release of the United States Attorney's Office, Western District of New York] Apr 17, 2008.

5. Dan Herbeck, "Massage Parlor Owner's Prostitution Role Nets Prison," *Buffalo (NY) News,* Nov 20, 2008, B1.

6. As of June 2010, the other convictions in the Jesters case include Erie County Sheriff's Deputy Michael Lesinki (charges brought), retired police captain John Trobridge (two years probation), and former prosecutor and law clerk Michael R. Stebick (four months home confinement and $5,000 fine). For more on the Jesters case, see Dan Herbeck, "Ex-Judge Target in Interstate Sex Case," *Buffalo (NY) News,* Mar 9, 2008, A1; Dan Herbeck, "Ex-Lockport Officer to Plead in Sex Case," *Buffalo (NY) News,* Mar 15, 2008, A1; Dan Herbeck, "Ex-Officer Admits to Facilitating Prostitution," *Buffalo (NY) News,* Mar 21, 2008, D1; Dan Herbeck, "Woman Jailed by Tills Joined Him on Trip," *Buffalo (NY) News,* Apr 6, 2008, A1; Dan Herbeck, "Deputies Eyed in Jesters Investigation," *Buffalo (NY) News,* May 24, 2008, D1; Dan Herbeck, "Plea Deal Expected for Lawyer in Vice Case," *Buffalo (NY) News,* Aug 2, 2008, D1; Tom Buckham, "Lawyer in Jesters Case Pleads Guilty to Transporting Prostitutes Illegally," *Buffalo News (NY),* Aug 8, 2008, D5; Dan Herbeck, "Tills Admits Recruiting Prostitutes," *Buffalo (NY) News,* Sep 5, 2008, A1; Dan Herbeck, "Contrite Retired Cop Avoids Prison in Jesters Case," *Buffalo (NY) News,* May 7, 2009; Carolyn Thompson, "Ex-NY Judge Gets Prison for Recruiting Prostitutes," *Associated Press,* Aug 7, 2009; Phil Fairbanks and Dan Herbeck, "Ex-Justice Tills Given Prison Term in Sex Case," *Buffalo (NY) News,* Aug 8, 2008, B1; and "Ex-Deputy Charged in Jesters Case," *Buffalo (NY) News,* Jun 9, 2010, B10.

7. Department of State, *Trafficking in Persons Report,* 31.

8. Dan Herbeck, "Ex-Lockport Officer to Plead in Sex Case," *Buffalo (NY) News,* Mar 15, 2008, A1.

9. Dan Herbeck, "Contrite Retired Cop Avoids Prison in Jesters Case," *Buffalo (NY) News,* May 7, 2009, B3.

10. Aaron Besecker and Dan Herbeck, "Making a Case Against Exploitation: Agents Say Women in Massage Parlor Busts Were Forced into Prostitution to Repay Debts," *Buffalo (NY) News,* Jan 19, 2008, A1. For more on the Honk Kong sex industry, see Zi Teng, "Chinese Migrant Sex Workers in Hong Kong," *Research for Sex Work* 9 (June 2006): 29–32.

11. Aaron Besecker and Dan Herbeck, "Making a Case Against Exploitation: Agents say Women in Massage Parlor Busts Were Forced into Prostitution to Repay Debts," *Buffalo (NY) News*, Jan 19, 2008, A1.

12. Ibid. Margo St. James, an activist and co-founder of COYOTE (Call Off Your Old Tired Ethics), has argued that prostitution needs to be treated as any other freely chosen type of economically rewarding labor. Judith Lorber, *Paradoxes of Gender* (New Haven: Yale University Press, 1994), 67. The sex worker position within feminists' debates about prostitution has rightly been described as a neoliberal position that first and foremost posits the sex worker as an individual capable of making rational economic decisions that embody her own free choice and agency. This rhetoric obscures the patriarchal and global capitalistic structure within which sex work gains its monetary value. For a great radical feminist critique of this approach, see Sheila Jeffries, *The Industrial Vagina: The Political Economy of the Global Sex Trade* (New York: Routledge, 2009): 15–37.

13. Aaron Besecker, "Recruiter of Prostitutes Takes Plea; Malaysian Woman Agrees to Aid in Probe of Human Trafficking," *Buffalo (NY) News*, Apr 18, 2008, D1.

14. Besecker and Herbeck, "Making a Case Against Exploitation."

15. Department of State, *Trafficking in Persons Report*, 33.

16. Luis CdeBaca, "Opening Remarks": "Abolition Past and Present: Scholars, Activists, and the Challenge of Contemporary Slavery," Gilder Lehman's 14th Annual International Conference, Yale University, New Haven, CT, November 8, 2012.

17. Two of the victims owed the owners $25,000 and $8,000. Ibid.

18. Department of State, *Trafficking in Persons Report*, 9.

19. Ibid., 8. This is according to the William Wilberforce Trafficking Victims Protection Reauthorization Act of 2008.

20. Aaron Besecker, "Recruiter of Prostitutes Takes Plea: Malaysian Woman Agrees to Aid in Probe of Human Trafficking," *Buffalo (NY) News*, Apr 18, 2008, D1.

21. Melissa Ditmore, "Kicking Down the Door: The Effects of Anti-Trafficking Raids in the USA," *Research For Sex Work* 11 (Jul 2009): 10–11, 11.

22. Phone interview with Amy Fleischauer of the International Institute of Buffalo, June 17, 2010. For those interested in American action against trafficking should be aware of Freedom Network.

23. Jennifer A. L. Sheldon-Sherman, "The Missing 'P': Prosecution, Prevention, Protection, and Partnership in the Trafficking Victims Protection Act," *Penn State Law Review* 117 (2012): 443–617, 462; Helga Konrad, "Trafficking in Human Beings: A Comparative Account of Legal Provisions in Belgium, Italy, the Netherlands, Sweden, and the United States," in *Trafficking and Women's Rights*, ed. Christien L. van den Anker and Jeroen Doomernik, 118–137 (New York: Palgrave Macmillan, 2006), 131–132.

24. Sheldon-Sherman, "The Missing 'P,' " 466.

25. Jo Doezema, "Loose Women or Lost Women? The Re-emergence of the Myth of White Slavery in Contemporary Discourses of Trafficking in Women," *Gender Issues* (Winter 2004): 23–50, 34.

26. Doezema, "Loose Women or Lost Women?," 37.

27. Jo Doezema, "Forced to Choose: Beyond the Voluntary v. Forced Prostitution Dichotomy," in *Global Sex Workers: Rights, Resistance, and Redefinition*, ed. Kamala Kempadoo and Jo Doezema, 29–50 (New York: Routledge, 1998), 46–47. For an account of Doezema's experiences as a sex worker in Amsterdam, see Wendy Chapkis, *Live Sex Acts: Women Performing Erotic Labor* (New York: Routledge, 1997), 117–122.

28. Carol Pateman, *The Sexual Contract* (Stanford: Stanford University Press, 1988), 14.

29. Polaris Project, "2013 State Ratings on Human Trafficking Laws," http://www.polarisproject.org/what-we-do/policy-advocacy/national-policy/state-ratings-on-human-trafficking-laws, accessed April 29, 2014.

30. Christie Thompson, "Escorted to Jail," *Chicago Reporter,* Nov 1, 2012, http://www.chicagoreporter.com/escorted-jail#.Uzsti8cceAc, accessed November 7, 2012.

31. "Trafficking from the Top Down: Why Prop 35 Passed and Why It Matters," PostWhoreAmerica Blog, http://postwhoreamerica.com/trafficking-from-the-top-down-why-prop-35-passed-and-what-it-means/, accessed November 7, 2012; "Vote No on Prop 35," http://againstthecaseact.com/, accessed November 7, 2012; Victoria Kim, "Anti-Sex Trafficking Proposition 35 Is Surprisingly Controversial," *Los Angeles Times,* October 30, 2012, http://www.latimes.com/news/local/la-me-prop35-20121031,0,4262985.story, accessed November 7, 2012.

32. Ronald Weitzer, "The Movement to Criminalize Sex Work in the United States," *Journal of Law and Society* 37, no. 1 (March 2010): 61–84.

33. Kevin Bales and Ron Soodalter, "Supply and Demand," in *The Slave Next Door: Human Trafficking and Slavery in America Today* (Berkeley: University of California Press, 2009), 78–116.

34. Amy Ferrell, "Environmental and Institutional Influences on Police Agency Responses to Human Trafficking," *Police Quarterly* 20, no. 10 (2013): 1–27, 3; Sheldon-Sherman, "The Missing 'P,' " 467.

35. Kimberly Kotrla, "Domestic Minor Sex Trafficking in the United States," *Social Work* 55, no. 2 (April 2010) 181–187, 184.

36. Office of the Attorney General of Texas, *Texas Human Trafficking Prevention Task Force Report to the Texas Legislature,* (Jan 2011), 38.

37. Carole Vance, "States of Contradiction: Twelve Ways to Do Nothing about Trafficking While Pretending to," *Social Research* 78, no. 3 (Fall 2011): 933–948, 936.

38. Cathy Zimmerman, Mazeda Hossain, and Charlotte Watts, "Human Trafficking and Health: A Conceptual Model to Inform Policy, Intervention, and Research," *Social Science & Medicine* 73 (2011): 327–335, 330–331.

39. Ronald Weitzer, "Sex Trafficking and the Sex Industry: The Need for Evidence-Based Theory and Legislation," *Journal of Criminal Law and Criminology* 101, no. 4 (Fall 2011): 1337–1369, 1344.

40. Jane Scoular, "What's Law Got to Do With It? How and Why Law Matters in the Regulation of Sex Work," *Journal of Law and Society* 37, no. 1 (Mar 2010): 12–39, 26.

41. J. Edgar Hoover quoted in "White Slave Traffic Gains: Hoover Asks Public Aid in Drive to Wipe Out Violations," *Boston Evening Recorder*, Aug 17, 1936.

42. David J. Langum, *Crossing Over the Line: Legislating Morality and the Mann Act* (Chicago: University of Chicago Press, 1994), 150, 168. From what I have been able to figure out, the 6335 number includes plea bargains and courtroom convictions. These are the cases that involved some type of punishment: a fine, a sentence, or both. The FBI touted its efficiency at the time in filling jail cells or taking in proceeds. And from this perspective, the agency would not have distinguished between a guilty plea and a guilty conviction.

43. Rose and Valverde, "Governed By Law?," 550.

Note on Sources

1. Quoted in Athan Theoharis, *J. Edgar Hoover, Sex, and Crime: An Historical Anecdote* (Chicago: Ivan R. Dee, 1995), 67.

2. Ibid.

3. Ibid.

4. Athan Theoharis, *The FBI: An Annotated Bibliography and Research Guide* (New York: Garland Publishing, Inc., 1994), 4–5.

5. I have not been able to discern why so many of the Mann Act cases from 1920–1941 are still classified; all evidence points to their continual classification being a result of an administrative error by archivists at NARA.

6. Stephen Robertson, "What's Law Got to Do With It? Legal Records and Sexual Histories," *Journal of the History of Sexuality*, 14, no. 1/2 (Jan/Apr 2005): 161–185, 163.

Acknowledgments

This book would not have been possible without the fabulous faculty and graduate students in the history department at the Ohio State University. Donna J. Guy, Birgitte Søland, Judy Tzu-Chun Wu, Paula Baker, Kevin Boyle, William R. Childs, Warren Van Tine, David Stebenne, Alison Efford, Ryan Irwin, Kate Epstein, Lincoln Nemetz-Carlson, Robert Bennett, and Nicole Jackson were all instrumental in shaping my time there. The initial research for this project was funded by OSU's Presidential Fellowship, the Genevieve Brown Gist Award that funds research into women's history, several College of Humanities summer research awards, and a Coca-Cola Critical Difference for Women Grant. Additionally, a P.E.O. Scholar Award from the P.E.O. Sisterhood allowed me to travel more widely for my research.

But my entire experience at OSU was shaped by the tutelage of one woman—Susan M. Hartmann. She has provided an excellent example of how to be a scholar, mentor, colleague, and friend with a delicate balance of grace and tenacity. One of the fabulous aspects of being a Susan Hartmann student is that you become embedded in a community. I am particularly grateful for the support of Stephanie Gilmore, Pippa Holloway, Susan Freeman, Marilyn E. Hegarty, Lindsey Patterson, Meredith Clark-Wiltz, Caryn Neumann, Jane Berger, and Leila J. Rupp. Engagement with this community continues to sustain my feminist politics, strengthen my scholarly resolve, and feed my spirit.

My work has taken me to new places, new encounters and new friendships. My colleagues at Texas State University–San Marcos have been unwavering in their support. I would like to thank Mary Brennan, Kenneth Margerison, Jesús F. de la Teja, Peter Siegenthaler, Jeff Helgeson, Ronald Angelo Johnson, José Carlos de la Puente, Margaret Menninger, Elizabeth Bishop, John McKiernan-González, Nancy Berlage, and Emily Hanks. Dwight Watson has proved himself to be a great mentor, conversationalist, and friend. Texas State also provided material support for this project with a Research Enhancement Program Grant and a Library Research Grant. Others scattered around the world deserve my gratitude. They include Emily Epstein Landau, Philippa Levine, Stephen Legg, Robert Kramm, Harald Fischer-Tiné,

Heike Paul, and Katharina Gerund. David Correll, Sarah Ferretti, Meg and Jo-
hannes Koch, and Carolyn Bandel all provided me with couches to sleep on, din-
ners to savor, and delightful conversation to enjoy.

   In 2012, I had the pleasure of being the first year-long fellow in modern-day
slavery and human trafficking at the Gilder Lehman Center for the Study of Slavery, Resistance, and Abolition, which is part of The Whitney and Betty MacMillan Center for International and Area Studies at Yale University. As nearly everyone who encounters him is undoubtedly aware, David Blight is extraordinarily
generous. He ensured that my time in New Haven was welcoming and fruitful,
and I had the pleasure of taking advantage of the joyful conviviality fostered by
the Gilder Lehrman Center. David Spatz and Melissa McGrath were especially
helpful and supportive. Rachel Purvis, Debby Applegate, Beverly Gage, Crystal
Feimster, and Edward Rugemer shared their time and insights with me. My time
at Yale was enhanced by the Gilder Lehrman Center's hosting of its annual conference on the theme of "Abolition Past and Present: Scholars, Activists, and the
Challenge of Contemporary Slavery," which brought me into continually rewarding contact with Joel Quirk, Louise Shelley, Claude D'Estree, and Anna Mae
Duane. I had the additional pleasure of being adopted by the ISS Brady-Colloquium
of Grand Strategy and International History while at Yale. Amanda Behm, Adam
Tooze, Jenifer Van Vleck, and Sarah Kovner welcomed my perspective and stimulated my own work. Additional thanks go to Christina Bain and Timothy McCar-
thy, who welcomed my participation in the Working Group on Modern Slavery
and Trafficking at the Carr Center for Human Rights Policy in Harvard's Kennedy School.

   I would be remiss if I didn't express my gratitude to the various archives I utilized in researching *Policing Sexuality*. First, a word of appreciation goes to Stephen Underhill at the National Archives in College Park who not only shared my
love of researching the FBI, but also allowed me into the hallowed stacks of the
archives. I am also thankful for the staff at Women's Library in London, the Social
Welfare History Archives at the University of Minnesota, the Rockefeller Archive
Center, the New York Public Library, the Oregon Historical Society, the Library of
Congress, and the Western History Collection at the Denver Public Library. Finally, a special word of thanks goes to Brian Distelberg and Joyce Seltzer at Harvard University Press, who have both made the process of publishing my first
book as clear and easy as can be.

   Lastly, this project has shaped my life for many years, and consequently it had
shaped the lives of those closest to me. If a book takes on a life of its own, then in
this case Audra R. Jennings would be this book's midwife. Her friendship has
continuously supported me, while her perceptive eye greatly improved my work.
By coincidence, she hosted me when I first visited Ohio State and she remains my
intellectual sister. Of course, my parents endlessly supported this project; thank

you, Gary and Mary Beth Pliley, and Angela Pierce for your endless faith. Sadly, my mother, who was my greatest cheerleader, did not live to see the book in print. But I know she too would have been full of joy. Then there is Donovan Pierce. This book is as much his as it is mine. Thank you for your patience, your conversations, your wit, and your delight.

Index